THE HOLIDAY WHICH? GUIDE TO
WEEKEND BREAKS

Edited by Ingrid Morgan

Published by Consumers' Association
and Hodder & Stoughton

Which? Books are commissioned and researched by The Association
for Consumer Research and published by Consumers' Association,
2 Marylebone Road, London NW1 4DX and Hodder & Stoughton,
47 Bedford Square, London WC1B 3DP

First edition 1988, reprinted 1989
Copyright © 1988 and June 1989 Consumers' Association Limited

British Library Cataloguing in Publication Data

The Holiday Which? guide to weekend breaks
    1. Great Britain – Visitors guides
    I. Morgan, Ingrid
    914.1'04858

    ISBN 0-340-38164-7

Designed by Paul Saunders
Cover illustration by John Crawford Fraser
Maps by David Perrott Cartographics
Typeset by Marlin Graphics Ltd
Printed and bound in Great Britain by
BPCC Hazell Books Ltd
Member of BPCC Ltd
Aylesbury, Bucks, England

Acknowledgements to:
Val Campbell
Frances Roxburgh

THE HOLIDAY WHICH?
GUIDE TO WEEKEND BREAKS

Contents

Introduction 6
Holiday Which?
Weekend Break Awards 11

Choosing an area 12
Seasonal reasoning 14

CITIES
Bath 18
Cambridge 29
Canterbury 37
Durham 43
Edinburgh 48
Glasgow 58

Lincoln 64
London 70
Norwich 100
Oxford 106
Stratford 116
York 122

GENTLE COUNTRYSIDE
The Cotswolds 132
The Scottish Borders 149
The Stour Valley 161

The Thames Valley 170
Upland Dorset 180
The Welsh Marches 189

NATIONAL PARKS
Dartmoor 200
Exmoor 210
The Lake District 220
The North York Moors 239

The Peak District 250
Snowdonia 260
The Yorkshire Dales 274

SCENIC COASTS
The Argyll Coast 286
The Cornish Coast 297
The Northumbrian
Coast 310

The Pembrokeshire
Coast 317
The South Coast 325

MORE INFORMATION
Tourist Boards 352
Hotel groups and tour
operators 352
Special interest
weekends 358

Alternative
accommodation 364
Index 367
Weather statistics 376
Maps 378

Introduction

Second honeymoon? Somewhere to take the children or somewhere to get away from them? A rest cure or a breath of fresh air? Blow away the cobwebs if you live in the city or see the bright lights if home is remote and rural. The weekend is a British phenomenon, and never have short breaks been more popular. Even the doctors tell us that a fortnight's holiday and plenty of short breaks are better for you than a continental-style month off.

In this book we describe a selection of Britain's most interesting cities and attractive country areas. Wherever you live, there will be somewhere within comfortable driving distance for a long weekend. We have aimed to strike a balance between civilised cities, seaside areas (including some traditional resorts), countryside for gentle touring and the more rugged landscape of the national parks. For each area we summarise the scenery and attractions, picking out the nicest villages, valleys, beaches and so on, and suggest places to visit – the best historic houses and gardens; railways, country and theme parks, zoos and other places for family outings; museums for rainy days; and walks for good ones.

Of course, the main component of a short break for many people is the place where you stay. Do you simply seek a roof over your head and a hearty breakfast before you set off walking? Or would you prefer to stay put and be pampered, despite the damage to your wallet? In each chapter we've included descriptions and details of a special selection of places to stay. They're a cross section, ranging from luxurious or simple country house hotels to town guesthouses, jolly local pubs and family-run farmhouses to restaurants with bedrooms – all the best of their kind in the area, and offering value for money (although some are inevitably an expensive treat).

At the end of the book there are chapters on activity and special interest breaks around the country; how to go about finding alternative accommodation – such as self-catering cottages; and details of tour operators who offer inclusive package arrangements, and hotel companies who offer special break deals. There are also maps of the areas and cities covered in the book, showing places to visit and sights; on the area maps we mark the locations of our recommended hotels.

How to use this guide

What are your priorities? Scenery? Peace and quiet? Lots to see and do? Creature comforts? Sandy beaches? Our table on page 12 should help you decide which areas might suit you. On page 14 the section on 'Seasonal Reasoning' could narrow down the choice; it is intended only as a guide – if you want to visit the Argyll coast in December or try to find a hotel in Cornwall for a weekend in August, we are not trying to stop you. In each area and city chapter, too, you'll find a 'When to go' section, with details of local events and festivals; it doubles as a 'when not to go' section.

Each of our areas appears in green on the maps at the back of the book. In the chapters, we give an introductory description and then a shortlist of places to visit and a guide to things to see and do; we aim to give you a flavour and point you in the right direction, rather than overwhelm you with detail. We've sorted the sights and things to do under various headings: 'Historic houses and gardens', 'Museums', 'Railways' and so on; places especially geared to children are listed under 'Family outings'. We've used the abbreviations (NT) and (NTS) to denote which properties belong to the National Trust, or the National Trust for Scotland; members enjoy free admission. Opening dates we quote are inclusive: 'May to Oct' means that a sight is open from the beginning of May to the end of October.

For each region we suggest several circular walks of varying lengths and difficulties, taken from our sister publication, the *Holiday Which? Good Walks Guide*, which is available from bookshops or from Consumers' Association, Castlemead, Gascoyne Way, Hertford SG14 1LH. The Guide covers 200 walks throughout Britain.

The sections on 'Where to stay' give general advice on the type of accommodation available in the area, with suggested bases, plus our specific recommendations.

Finally, each chapter contains a list of addresses and telephone numbers for further information.

Our recommended hotels

In this book you will find a selection of places to stay, all inspected by members of the *Holiday Which?* team. In each area we have picked out the best of what's available, be it simple guesthouse, farmhouse, city-centre town house, or luxury country-house hotel. Most of our recommended places have something special about them: many are privately owned and managed, and very individual; the atmosphere may be particularly warm and welcoming, and occasionally even eccentric; and several are run on house-party lines, with guests helping themselves to drinks in the sitting room and eating at a communal table. All have been chosen because we think that a stay there would be a part of the weekend 'treat' that a short break should be.

It follows that most of our recommendations are not necessarily the sort of places that a business traveller would choose to stay at, and many fall short when it comes to facilities such as 24-hour service and shoe cleaning, trouser presses and conference rooms. It is perhaps a little sad to find, however, that a colour television is now almost a standard item in hotel (and guesthouse) bedrooms throughout the country; we have nevertheless managed to find a few hotels where one's bed does not face the inevitable box.

Very few purpose-built modern chain hotels have found their way into this book; this does not mean that they do not offer weekend breaks, or that their facilities are inadequate – quite the contrary, sometimes. On page 351, in our chapter on hotel groups and tour operators, we give details of deals and packages available in this sort of hotel; many, particularly those designed to fill city-centre business hotels at the weekend, are very good value, and there are enticing offers for families too. Of course chain, city-centre, and even business hotels need not be dull; nor do tour operators offer only such hotels. As we describe in that chapter, everything is possible on a package, and it is well worth looking through a few of the brochures we list. In London, where hotel prices are sky high, it is particularly worth booking a special deal through a hotel group or tour operator: some packages are cheaper than booking direct with the hotel itself. In that chapter, we've quoted the lowest package price we could find against relevant hotels.

'Special interest' weekend breaks are becoming increasingly popular, and an enormous number of hotels offer opportunities to learn a skill, take up a new sport, or simply sit back and listen to an expert. In this book you'll find possibilities for a weekend painting course in a working farmhouse in Constable country (see the chapter on the Stour Valley), wine tasting and vineyard visiting in Kent (see Canterbury), trout or salmon fishing (North York Moors), or ballooning (Bath) – to name but a few. If you have a particular interest in mind, or like the idea and want to know more, turn to our chapter on 'Special interest weekends' on page 358.

On the next page we explain how the information in our hotel recommendations is arranged:

Bedrooms We list the main facilities or gadgets (TV, direct dial telephone); 'teamaking' means that a kettle and teabags/packets of coffee/UHT milk are provided. We do not list all the little extras that are increasingly being provided (bubble bath, shower caps, sewing kits, mineral water, fruit, biscuits, magazines, sherry). A luxury hotel with prices to match will almost always have an array of goodies in the bedroom.

Facilities Again, we list the main ones (parking, lift, hairdresser, sports and children's facilities). We do not give information on babysitting – most hotels that cater for children offer to provide someone if requested in advance, but arrangements vary widely (from the in-house chambermaid to a local agency), and none can, of course, be guaranteed to be acceptable to a child. We do, however, say where babylistening (using the bedroom telephone left off the hook) is an option.

Restrictions Dogs, children and smokers may or may not be welcome to you; all arouse considerable passion for and against. We don't enter into any arguments.

Open Dates are inclusive.

Credit/charge cards accepted We list the major cards: Access (Eurocard/Mastercard), Amex (American Express), Diners (Diners' Club), Visa (Barclaycard/Bank Americard/Carte Bleue)

Price category Our hotels fall into five price bands, denoted by £ to £££££. All prices are for bed and breakfast per person, sharing a double or twin room with bath. In some hotels, bed and breakfast terms are not available; in these cases, our price category is intended simply as a guide. Single room or occupancy rates are generally higher (anything up to about 80%).

Prices are those current as we went to press in summer 1988. Some hotels increase their prices annually, others twice a year; some offer winter reductions, others summer reductions.

£	= You can expect to pay under £20
££	= You can expect to pay between £20 and £30
£££	= You can expect to pay between £30 and £40
££££	= You can expect to pay between £40 and £55
£££££	= You can expect to pay over £55

Special rates A large number of our recommendations offer special rates for stays of two or more nights. The nature of offers varies widely: reductions for winter stays, summer stays, spring or autumn stays; reductions for weekend stays (usually, but not always, in cities); reductions for weekday stays; reduced rates for a Sunday night (in a few places, a Sunday is free if it's the third night). Prices of these 'special breaks' quoted by the hotels can be confusing: sometimes a rate per person per night, sometimes a rate per person for two nights; and sometimes a rate for two people for one night. We've converted all 'break' prices to a rate per person (sharing a double or twin room with bath) per night, so you can easily compare hotels; but bear in mind that this may not be the way the hotel quotes the price.

Weekend or short breaks are rarely referred to so simply in hotel or tour operator brochures. Instead, you'll be offered 'special breaks', 'highlife weekends', 'honeymoon and celebration specials'; 'luxury' is a word that crops up often. The short break market is competitive and expanding, and more and more goodies are being included in the deal to tempt you: champagne and flowers, a heart-shaped box of chocolates, theatre tickets, 10-course breakfasts. Depending on your wishes, any of these may be desirable; but luxurious surroundings do not necessarily go hand in hand with 'luxury' breaks. We do not refer to any titles used by hotels or operators; we simply state the nature of the break (season, number of nights and so on). We also say whether the rate includes bed and breakfast (B&B) or dinner, bed and breakfast (DB&B).

In the majority of our hotels, breakfast on a 'weekend break' is the full English (or Welsh or Scottish) variety, even if the hotel generally provides only a Continental breakfast during the week. On tour operator breaks (even if these are mid-week), breakfast is also almost always full English. It's always worth checking exactly what is included in the price; when a cooked breakfast is charged as an extra, the cost (particularly in London) can be considerable.

Most hotels charge extra for a single room; a few (particularly in London) offer 'no single room supplement' at weekends. Some tour operators offer good single rates too, again particularly at weekends. We've quoted single room or occupancy prices (in brackets) if they differ from the rate per person sharing a double or twin room.

Hotels which welcome children generally offer some reductions for children sharing a room with one or two adults. In a few cases, children occupying their own room qualify for a good reduction, too. Sometimes different reductions are offered by the same hotel (for instance, children may be free when accompanying adults on a weekend break, half price when not). The term 'free' generally applies only to accommodation – there are almost always charges for meals, including breakfast; however, a 'half-price' deal may include meals, and may actually work out better value. Some offers are more generous in terms of child age limits than others. If you intend to take a weekend break with 16 year old twins, it's obviously important to check very carefully what reductions are available. It's also worth looking at the offers made by hotel groups and tour operators (see page 352).

The Holiday Which? Weekend Break Awards

Holiday Which? inspectors travelling the length and breadth of Britain know excellence when they see it – be it in a cosy farmhouse B&B, a sophisticated country-house hotel, a city-centre guest house of character, a well-laid out farm park for children, or an exciting museum. They nominated their favourite places, and we list our special awards here.

For a fine new art gallery:
❀ **Burrell Collection, Glasgow** (*page 58*)

For an exciting way to experience history:
❀ **Jorvik Viking Centre, York** (*page 123*)

For an excellent and varied outdoor museum:
❀ **North of England Open Air Museum, Beamish** (*page 45*)

For a splendid nostalgia railway ride through fine scenery:
❀ **North York Moors line** (*page 241*)

For an interesting and novel industrial archaeological visit:
❀ **Llechwedd Slate Caverns, Blaenau Ffestiniog** (*page 262*)

For an excellent outing for children of all ages:
❀ **Cotswold Wild Life Park , Burford** (*page 135*)

For a well-run, homely farmhouse hotel-cum-art school:
🏨 **Dedham Hall, Dedham** (*page 166*)

For a charming, informal country-house hotel:
🏨 **Tyddyn Llan, Llandrillo** (*page 270*)

For a smart but relaxed country-house hotel:
🏨 **Summer Lodge, Evershot** (*page 187*)

For a luxurious and very gracious English country-house hotel:
🏨 **Buckland Manor, Buckland** (*page 141*)

For an experience of Georgian living in a town guest house:
🏨 **Six King Circus, Bath** (*page 26*)

For a gourmet treat in a sophisticated inn:
🏨 **The Royal Oak, Yattendon** (*page 178*)

CHOOSING AN AREA

Here is a chart to help you on your way. Identify your needs in the column on the left, then see which cities or areas would suit you best. You may be in for a few surprises. Of course, most areas and cities will have some possibilities for museum visiting, family outings, walking and so on: below we've indicated those which are particularly good.

Cities	Bath	Cambridge	Canterbury	Durham	Edinburgh	Glasgow	Lincoln	London	Norwich	Oxford	Stratford
Places to stay											
Very comfortable country house hotels										•	
Super comfortable city hotels	•				•	•		•			
Charming guest houses and inns											•
Budget guest houses and B&Bs											
Gastronomy	•				•	•		•		•	
Things to do											
Scenic car tours											
Rural pottering in pretty villages											
Sightseeing without a car	•	•	•	•	•		•	•	•	•	•
Good bathing											
Challenging walking											
Gentle walking in attractive scenery											
Cultural events	•	•			•	•		•		•	•
Places to visit											
Castles					•			•			
Cathedrals			•	•		•	•	•	•		
Churches and abbeys	•	•						•	•	•	
Gardens											
Historic houses	•				•			•			•
Industrial archaeology											
Museums and galleries	•	•			•	•		•	•	•	
Family Outings											
Nostalgia railways											
Zoos, farm or wildlife parks								•			
Museums suitable for children	•				•	•		•			

	York	**Gentle countryside**	The Cotswolds	The Scottish Borders	The Stour Valley	The Thames Valley	Upland Dorset	The Welsh Marches	**National Parks**	Dartmoor	Exmoor	The Lake District	The North York Moors	The Peak District	Snowdonia	The Yorkshire Dales	**Scenic Coasts**	The Argyll Coast	The Cornish Coast	The Northumbrian Coast	The Pembrokeshire Coast	The South Coast
			•		•		•			•		•		•				•				•
	•																					
			•		•	•	•	•				•				•			•			•
				•			•					•	•		•	•			•		•	•
			•		•	•						•										•
				•			•				•	•	•	•		•				•		
			•			•	•				•				•							
	•				•																•
												•		•				•	•	•	•	•
			•				•		•	•	•	•	•	•	•	•						
	•		•	•	•	•	•		•	•	•	•	•	•	•	•	•	•	•	•	•	•
	•																				•
					•		•							•				•	•	•	•
	•						•												•	•	
			•	•	•		•	•				•									
			•				•								•	•				•
	•			•		•	•					•						•			•
											•				•			•			•
	•																				•
								•	•	•	•		•							•
		•			•			•							•				•	•
	•				•				•			•								•

Seasonal reasoning

SPRING

The itch to move about again, travel a little, breathe fresh air and watch Nature doing her stuff comes over many who have struggled through a British winter. The British spring isn't often all the poets claim – but here and there, now and then, you may be lucky. Where best to take a break in March, April or May? They're erratic transitional months that can relapse into wintry temperatures, but the optimism of lengthening days and clearer skies is spring's chief advantage over autumn for between-season weather. Rainfall is more often a matter of scudding showers than settled damp; statistically at least there's more sunshine than in autumn, gaining warmth steeply between March and May.

This is the season to go and look at mountains, if only from the comfort of a car, and the **Lake District** is good for this. Its convoluted scenery can be appreciated from a network of small roads; close at hand there are daffodils round the lakes and cavorting lambs on the fellsides. The **Welsh Marches**, less mountainous, also specialise in these; and the **Pembrokeshire coast** breaks out in wild flowers by May. On the **Cornish coast** spring is often mild and early, but northern seasides are inhospitable until May – the month of rhododendrons in **Argyll**. Late spring has the advantage of sheltered sightseeing if the weather disappoints as historic buildings and other indoor retreats open up; it's worth doing homework on their dates. Gardens may be open all year, or earlier in the year than their houses. The **Peak District** and the **Scottish Borders** both combine fine countryside with a good supply of stately homes. Strolling round historic cities can be a bit bleak in spring, especially in the north, but the relative absence of crowds (except over Easter) make it a good season for looking at **York** and **Canterbury**.

SUMMER

Britain's holiday industry is booming with stay-here British tourists as well as those from abroad. In June this is seldom a problem but during July and August, in the better-known attractive places, overcrowding can spoil things just as much as bad weather. By the time the sea is warm enough for bathing in the south and south-west, resorts are heavily booked. Cornwall has traffic jams; so does the south coast where day trippers converge each weekend; and after the school term finishes it is apparent that the family seaside holiday is no lapsed tradition. In the north-west **Argyll** is quieter – except in August, month of Games and Gatherings. And in the north-east the **Northumbrian coast** is a fine place for short summer breaks: castles are open, boat trips running and this area never seems to get very crowded. Inland, don't attempt the Cotswolds in high season – nearly every congested village is on some coach tour's route – and the Thames Valley too is well-trodden. But in **Dorset**, the **Welsh Marches** and the **Scottish Borders** you can wander quietly. The top of Snowdon is eroded by tourist feet, the Lake District approaches saturation point and the edges of Dartmoor and Exmoor are inundated; but the **Yorkshire Dales** and **North York Moors** offer escape if you avoid certain areas. The heather starts to flower about the middle of August.

City visiting in summer needs planning. **Edinburgh** absorbs crowds happily – they suit it – and the summer influx is only a build-up to the frenetic Festival weeks in September. **Glasgow** too is invigorating. But York's medieval streets are choked and its exhibitions queued for, and Canterbury gets swamped by cross-Channel admirers. In June, an excellent time for most urban pottering, Oxford and Cambridge hold their examinations and close colleges to visitors. In July and August when the undergraduates have gone they have oddly differing appeal – Oxford becomes a systematic showpiece, while **Cambridge** is relatively relaxed. **Durham**, though livelier in term time, is pleasant for a low-key summer break; so are **Lincoln** and **Norwich**.

AUTUMN

As the weather improves in spring so it deteriorates in autumn, in sharp shifts between bland plateaux; a steep drop in temperature almost always comes in late October or early November, but up till then "Indian Summer" days are always possible. So unfortunately is rain, and overcast days not mellow but merely dull. The south-west stays warm longest. **Dartmoor**, **Exmoor** and the **Cornish coast** are good areas for autumn walking – though some sights and some hotels close as soon as high season is over. The north cools fast and is often cloud-shrouded, especially the north-west coast, but along the **South coast** the emptying resorts and villages are pleasant to explore. Early autumn is the time to visit the **Stour Valley** while it's still in generous leaf; or watch the changing colours of forest and bracken in the **Lake District** or **Snowdonia**, **Yorkshire** or the

Peak District (where an alternative to autumn tints is Matlock Bath's illuminations). You might meander down the **Thames Valley** while the sights are still open but the worst of the crowds have gone.

By October it's advisable to choose your area with an eye to the indoor possibilities still open, even in cities. Edinburgh rather slumps after the Festival, closing or changing temporary exhibitions. It rains more in **Glasgow**, but this matters much less in a city where your time is best spent inside art galleries and museums. Any cathedral city looks wonderful in slanting autumn sunshine and offers at least one port in a storm. **Bath** is very civilised all autumn, with concerts in the Pump Room; and **Stratford** much less congested. Best of all is **London**, between tourist tat and Christmas clutter, absorbing to explore when misty autumn days flatter its motley streets, and rich in resources if the weather is stormy.

WINTER

For all but the hardiest, a dream winter break in Britain is firmly based on warmth and comfort of the log-fire sort with good meals cooked by somebody else, and some optional forays into picturesque snowscapes. The first part is widely attainable, the second usually not. You may indeed be seriously and inconveniently snowed up in high ground from Dartmoor to Yorkshire; elsewhere, a philosophical preparation for chill, dull and downright ugly weather is the best policy. Statistics suggest that the far south-west has milder winters, but this is more often a matter of frost-free nights than balmy days; statistics are unhelpful about where the wind (or freezing gale) is likely to be blowing hardest, or where dank mists will linger all day.

Wide open spaces whether coastal or inland are no fun in bad visibility: areas with lots of local detail make more sense. The **Cotswolds** can be unexpectedly crisp and clear in January and February, and though teashops may be shut the empty villages can be examined as at no other season. Or choose a city – **Bath**, **Lincoln** or **Oxford** – where the close-packed historic charm can be appreciated ·in relatively short expeditions. If it must be a wilderness, the **Lake District** offers the best choice of accommodation combined with the best hope of finding walkable winter landscape somewhere in its varied terrain.

CITIES

Bath, Cambridge, Canterbury, Durham, Edinburgh,
Glasgow, Lincoln, London, Norwich, Oxford,
Stratford, York

Bath

- A beautiful showcase city where the pace of life is leisurely and the quality – and cost – of living is high
- Lots to see and do: museums of outstanding range and quality, enticing shops, concerts and plays – too much for one weekend visit
- Plenty of civilised and charming hotels, some excellent restaurants and tearooms galore
- Not ideal for families: expensive and with little to keep younger children amused. Historic houses are the main attractions for an excursion

Bath has a tradition of tourism and leisure which dates back to Roman times and it is still a place where people come to relax and enjoy a high standard of living, if only for a weekend. The Romans built the city on the site of the only hot springs in Britain, developing an elaborate system of baths and a sophisticated social centre. But it was the Georgians who gave the city its appearance and character and transformed Bath into the most fashionable spa in the country. In addition to the elegant crescents and parades, with their houses of honey-coloured stone, Bath still retains much of the atmosphere of that gracious age and is a city conducive to leisured strolling and candlelit dining. You can still take tea or attend concerts and recitals in the Georgian Pump Room, or stay in a converted town house designed by John Wood the Younger.

There are beautiful vistas over the steep-sided wooded Avon valley, and the city is almost surrounded by parks. When you have explored Roman and Georgian Bath, seen the Abbey and sampled Sally Lunn's teacakes (in the oldest house in Bath) there are still plenty of interesting museums and excursions.

Top sights

The Roman Baths The most impressive Roman remains in Britain, the Baths are still supplied with hot spring water at the rate of about 250,000 gallons per day. Even the non-archaeologically-minded cannot fail to be fascinated by the sophistication of this purpose-built leisure centre. Apart from the Great Bath, discovered in 1880, there are the remains of Turkish and cooling baths and fragments of a Temple to Sulis, the goddess who presided over the hot springs. In the museum are finds (including mosaics, coins and bronzes) discovered during the excavations which still continue today. [*Open all year, daily*]

Royal Crescent   The most splendid street in Bath is undoubtedly John Wood the Younger's fine, sweeping Crescent, begun in 1767. No 1 has been restored as a typical Georgian residence [*open Mar to Christmas, Tues to Sat, and pm Sun*] with lavishly furnished rooms and a kitchen museum.

Other sights

GEORGIAN BATH

In addition to Royal Crescent, there are many other streets and buildings worth seeing. **The Circus** is the triumph of Wood the Elder who also designed **Queen Square** and the **Parades**. Many other streets have some architectural importance; for curiosity value see Robert Adam's delightful **Pulteney Bridge**, lined with shops like the Ponte Vecchio in Florence.

The elegant **Assembly Rooms**, designed by John Wood the Younger in 1771, now house the Museum of Costume (see below). And the **Pump Room** with its giant Corinthian columns, its statue of Beau Nash and its two sedan chairs still evokes the atmosphere of Bath's second Golden Age. You can take tea to the strains of the Pump Room trio and there are often evening concerts and piano recitals. The **Theatre Royal** has another fine 18th-century interior and is well worth a visit.

MUSEUMS AND GALLERIES

American Museum (at Claverton Manor, 3 miles from centre)   A thoroughly well-presented American folk museum with recreations of typical 17th- to 19th-century interiors from a Puritan 'keeping room' to the elegant parlours of prosperous merchants. [*Open April to Oct, pm only, Tues to Sun and Bank Hol Mons*]

Camden Works Museum   Fascinating award-winning museum (now renamed the **Bath Industrial Heritage Centre**) which centres on a recreation of a local Victorian brass foundry and mineral-water manufactory. Also a display on the history of Bath stone with replica mine face. [*Open all year, pm only; Feb to Nov daily, Dec (not Christmas) and Jan weekends*]

Holburne Museum   A collection of fine European silver and porcelain, English paintings (Gainsborough, Reynolds, Stubbs) and 17th- and 18th-century furniture, plus a centre for the work of 20th-century artist-craftsmen. [*Open mid Feb to mid Dec; daily except Sun am, and Mons Nov to Easter*]

Museum of Costume   A large and very fine museum housed in the famous Assembly Rooms (see above). Interesting period rooms and settings and specialised collections. [*Open all year, daily*]

Victoria Art Gallery   Housed in a splendid Victorian building (the Public Library), the gallery has a permanent collection of paintings, prints, ceramics and some local history material. [*Open daily except Bank Hols*]

There are a number of more specialised museums, mostly rather small: the **Carriage Museum** (stage coaches, hansom cabs and the Royal Mail coach, housed in the old stables of the Circus), the **Geology Museum**, the **Postal Museum**, and **Herschel House**, with a small museum devoted to the musician and astronomer, William Herschel. **Sally Lunn's House** is a favourite place of pilgrimage; the oldest house in Bath (1482), it is part museum (Roman and medieval foundations, original kitchen) and part restaurant (buns made to the original, secret recipe).

CHURCHES

Bath is not really a city for churches although the late Perpendicular **Abbey**, small by cathedral standards, does have points of great beauty including the stone fan-vaulted nave.

Shopping

Most of the shops in the centre are of the sort to appeal to visitors, with a good range of boutiques, antique shops (and markets) and craft shops. Bookshops are mainly of the browsing kind, many selling locally made crafts and gifts, but there are also some serious antiquarian booksellers. The museum shops are good sources of books on Bath itself. The most appealing shopping streets are narrow lanes and pedestrian precincts such as Abbey Green, Northumberland Place (for chic boutiques) and the Corridor. Everyday supermarkets and chain shops are south of the centre.

Getting around

There are several multi-storey car parks; parking in most streets is restricted (maximum two hours). There is a bus service and bicycles can be hired but walking is probably the best way to see the city. Free walking tours of the city are arranged from April to November by the Mayor's Corps of Honorary Guides; tours last about two hours and include the main points of architectural and historical interest but no museums. There are also regular bus tours (some open-top buses, some tours combined with a guided walk), and there are one-hour boating cruises along the Avon Valley from Pulteney Bridge to Bathampton (also evening cruises in July and August). You can hire boats from Bath Boating Station, Bathwick.

Excursions

Monkton Farleigh Mine (4 miles east)   Europe's largest World War II underground ammunition depot, once top secret. Hourly guided tours of labyrinth of tunnels and chambers. [*Open all year: Easter to Oct daily, Oct to April weekends only*]

Dyrham Park (7 miles north)   A fine William and Mary house with 18th-century furnishings and a formal garden. Large park with picnic area. (NT) [*Open Apr to Oct, pm only, Sat to Wed*]

Corsham Court (10 miles north-east)   Elizabethan mansion with fine Methuen collection of Old Master paintings displayed in Georgian state rooms. Spacious gardens with arboretum. [*Open mid Jan to mid Dec, pm only, Tues to Thurs and weekends*]

Sheldon Manor (11 miles north-east)   Manor house dating from 1282, still lived-in and loved. [*Open April to Sep, pm only, Thurs, Sun and Bank Hols*]

Lacock Abbey and Village (14 miles south-east)   An unspoiled village (NT), with a 13th-century abbey converted into a house in 1540. [*Abbey open April to early Nov, pm only, closed Tues (and Good Friday)*]. The Fox Talbot Museum is of interest to amateurs of photography.

When to go

At any time of year there is plenty to see and do in Bath; one weekend's visit is barely sufficient to cover the main attractions. There are, however, two cultural festivals which could influence your planning and (in the first case) also accommodation availability. The Bath International Festival of Music and the Arts takes place from the third week of May to the end of the first week in June; concerts are held in many historic buildings in and around Bath. The Bath Georgian Festival Society organises seasons of concerts, recitals and operas in the Pump Room from

March to June and from late September to early December; many events are at weekends. Summer visitors can enjoy boat trips and more excursions but if you want to explore the city itself an off-season break could be just as rewarding. Several hotels offer reductions for midweek stays in winter.

Information

The Tourist Information Centre, Abbey Church Yard, Bath; tel: (0225) 462831.

Bath International Festival, Linley House, 1 Pierrepoint Place, Bath BA1 1JY; tel: (0225) 62231.

Telephone (0225) 461111 for details of walking tours.

The Huntingdon Centre at the Vineyards, the Paragon, Bath, is a centre for the appreciation of the history and architecture of the city. For details of their half-day programme 'Discover Georgian Bath', telephone (0225) 333895.

Where to stay

There is a very wide range of accommodation from the most elegant and luxurious town house to a variety of simple guesthouses and bed and breakfast establishments. There are also some converted country houses not far from the centre of the city.

BATH
Apsley House Hotel
Newbridge Hill, Bath BA1 3PT   *Tel: (0225) 336966*

A short drive from the centre of town, this Regency house of Bath stone has been converted to provide spacious accommodation. Bedrooms have been carefully decorated: modern brass bedsteads and reproduction furniture are set off by traditional fabrics. Bathrooms are unusually spacious with bath and shower cubicle. The lounge and dining room are, in effect, one large room divided by a screen covered in the same bold floral fabric as the curtains. Both rooms have comfortable furniture upholstered in blue or pink and look over the lawned garden at the back. Lovingly looked after by the owners, it is all spacious, airy and clean.

Bedrooms: *7 (double, twin), all with bath/shower. Direct dial telephone. TV. Hairdryer on request. Trouser press*
Facilities: *Parking*
Restrictions: *No children under 14. No dogs. Smoking discouraged in dining room*

Open: *All year*
Credit/charge cards accepted: *Access, Amex, Diners, Visa*
Price category: *££££*
Special rates: *Winter and spring, 2 or more nights DB&B £37.50-£47.50 pp per night. Children in parents' room £35*

BATH
The Francis
Queen Square, Bath BA1 2HH   *Tel: (0225) 24257*

This traditional hotel is set in the 18th-century Queen Square in the centre of Bath. The building retains many original features; the cocktail bar has fine cornicing and is elegant with Louis XV style chairs, the dining room has an elaborate plasterwork ceiling and is a pleasing room with flowers and gracious glasses. The lounge is on the way to the dining room, and consequently a little passage-like; but it too is attractive, with bold floral chintz loose covers and matching curtains. You can have a snack lunch in the dark green Roman Bar. The bedrooms are decorated to a good standard, some with floral chintzy curtains or small spriggy prints. A reasonably quiet, central, solid Trusthouse Forte hotel.

Bedrooms: *94 (single, double, twin, triple, family, suites), all with bath. Direct dial telephone, TV, teamaking*
Facilities: *Parking. Lift. Babylistening on request*
Open: *All year*
Credit/charge cards accepted: *Access, Amex, Diners, Visa*
Price category: *££££*
Special rates: *Children under 16 in parents' room free. Weekends, 2-4 nights DB&B £52 per person per night*

BATH
Number Nine
Miles Buildings, Bath BA1 2QS   *Tel: (0225) 25462*

In a traffic-free street just behind the Hole In The Wall restaurant, a small hotel in a pretty Georgian terrace. Bedrooms are mostly spacious, attractively and individually decorated combining co-ordinated traditional fabrics with lace or cotton; many beds have draped coronas, there are extra cushions, and a mixture of antique and reproduction furniture. Some may find the shower rooms a little small. Further bedrooms are in another building round the corner, decorated more simply but in similar taste. There's a first-floor sitting room where plants and books add to the homely comfort. Guests eat breakfast in the warm and welcoming dining room; on the large sideboard is an array of silver and glass as well as a drinks tray. Although there is only limited parking, and a small garden at the back, it is quiet and central.

Location: *Off George Street*
Bedrooms: *9 (double, twin) 3 in annexe, all with bath/shower. Direct dial telephone. TV, teamaking. Hairdryer on request*
Facilities: *Parking*
Restrictions: *No children under 14 (during peak season). No dogs*

Open: *All year except 2 weeks in Jan (subject to seasonal demand)*
Credit/charge cards accepted: *Access, Amex, Diners, Visa*
Price category: £££
Special rates: *Children in parents' room £5*

BATH
Paradise House
88 Holloway, Bath BA2 4PX   *Tel: (0225) 317723*

These two adjacent Georgain houses, built even before Bath became
fashionable, form a delightful B&B seven minutes' walk from the centre.
Set on a no-through road, it is quiet with lovely views over the city. The
inside is beautifully cared for and Laura Ashley fabrics have been used
extensively and with flair. Narrow stairs lead to the bedrooms which vary
in size; those at the back have the view. With stripped pine doors, some
modern and some pine furniture, they are welcoming and comfortable
and the provision of biscuits is a nice touch. The breakfast room is
separated from the sitting room by a curtained arch. Both rooms are
decorated in fresh green and white with tablecloths to match and old
photographs on the walls. The sitting room has a marble fireplace and
board games for guests' use. Outside is a glorious, surprisingly large
terraced garden, well kept with lawns, rose-covered pergolas and
herbaceous borders. This B&B is a gem of its kind. A weekend booking
for Saturday night only may not be accepted.

Bedrooms: *9 (double, twin), 7 with bath. Direct dial telephone, TV, teamaking.*
Hairdryer
Facilities: *3 garages. Croquet. Babylistening*
Restrictions: *No dogs*
Open: *End Jan to mid Dec*
Credit/charge cards accepted: *Access, Amex, Diners, Visa*
Price category: ££
Special rates: *Children in parents' room £7*

BATH
The Priory Hotel
Weston Road, Bath BA1 2XT   *Tel: (0225) 331922*

About seven minutes' drive from the town centre, this is a late Georgian
house of Bath stone built in Gothic style, with a large garden. Beautifully
furnished, decorated and situated, the high standard of comfort makes it
feel more like a private country house. The inter-connecting public
rooms, including the magnificent drawing room, are spacious and
sympathetically decorated in traditional English style with chintz fabrics
and antique furniture entirely in keeping with the grand architectural
details. Oil paintings, fresh flowers, books and magazines are plentiful.
The dining room divides into rooms of two distinct styles – one is
traditional with antique furniture, the other more modern with cane
chairs and a fine mural. The comfortable bedrooms (named after flowers)
vary in size but all are stylishly decorated with bright co-ordinated chintz
fabrics and fine antiques adding to the individuality of each room. The

well-tended garden, mostly lawn with plenty of trees, shrubs and herbaceous borders, is typically English and a delightful refuge. Smart and elegant but not overwhelmingly formal, the Priory retains the best traditions of the English country house hotel.

Bedrooms: 21 (single, double, twin), 1 with four-poster, all with bath. Direct dial telephone, TV, teamaking, hairdryer, trouser press
Facilities: Parking. Heated swimming pool. Croquet
Restrictions: No dogs
Open: All year
Credit/charge cards accepted: Access, Amex, Diners, Visa
Price category: ££££
Special rates: Nov to April, weekdays, 2 nights DB&B from £59.50 pp per night; weekends from £64.50 pp per night. Children in parents' room £20 (with breakfast)

BATH
The Royal Crescent
Royal Crescent, Bath BA1 2LS   Tel: (0225) 319090

Occupying the key position in John Wood's stunning architectural masterpiece, this hotel is justifiably famous. Accommodation is divided between the main house and the faultlessly sympathetic additions (The Dower House and The Pavilion) at the back, across the large, secluded lawned garden. The interior is splendid and stately. Bedrooms combine comfort and elegance to perfection: antique furniture is in keeping with the period, co-ordinated fabrics swag pelmets, drapes, half-testers or coronas, and generally embellish the fine rooms to the point of grandeur. Bathrooms are equally individually decorated, some with stencilling or murals. Mineral water and fresh flowers are provided in all rooms; suites also have a drinks tray and a visitors book. Guests may eat breakfast in the basement dining room of the main house which also has a choice of magnificent drawing rooms with elaborate cornicing, and Georgian portraits on the walls. The elegant panelled restaurant (candlelit at night), the bar and another drawing room are in The Dower House, providing a cleverly arranged suite of rooms. Altogether discreet and elegant, superbly situated and magnificently decorated. There are occasional special-interest weekends (antiques, ballooning).

Bedrooms: 45 (single, double, twin, suites), 10 in Dower House, 7 in Pavilion, all with bath. Direct dial telephone, TV, hairdryer. Minibar in suites and 2 Pavilion rooms
Facilities: Parking. Lift. Croquet. Heated plunge pool, 2 jacuzzis
Restrictions: No dogs
Open: All year
Credit/charge cards accepted: Access, Amex, Diners, Visa
Price category: £££££
Special rates: 2 nights B&B £64 pp per night; 2 nights DB&B £93.50 pp per night. Sunday night only, B&B £58 pp per night, DB&B £87.50 pp per night. Children in parents' room £10

BATH
Six King Circus   ⌂
Bath BA1 2EW   *Tel: (0225) 28288*

This marvellous Georgian house in the delightful Circus has been restored with the most loving care to its original glory. The large entrance hall provides the first taste of the superb original plasterwork that adorns the whole house. There is a beautiful yellow and golden breakfast room (the wallpaper was specially designed) with fine antiques including two unusual knife boxes. The elegant L-shaped drawing room has a pianoforte and a breakfront bookcase; drinks are offered to guests from a corner cupboard. Bedrooms vary only in size: all are sympathetically decorated with fine fabrics; although it has not always been possible to avoid reproduction furniture, nothing jars. The most modern touches are the provision of a hairdryer and kettle in each room but TV is available only on request. Even the space used for bathrooms does little to spoil the perfect proportions of the original architecture. It's quite expensive for bed and breakfast but an unusual opportunity to stay in one of the finest examples of Georgian architecture. *Holiday Which? Weekend Break Award.*

Bedrooms: 6 *(double, twin), all with bath. Direct dial telephone, teamaking. Hairdryer*
Facilities: *Parking. Library*
Restrictions: *No children under 14. No pets. No smoking in Breakfast Room*
Open: *All year except Jan*
Credit/charge cards accepted: *Visa*
Price category: *££££*

BATH
Somerset House
35 Bathwick Hill, Bath BA2 6LD   *Tel: (0225) 66451/63471*

A fine listed Regency house where guests are encouraged to join in as part of an extended family. Most weekends between October and May are run as 'Special Interest' events with themes such as Roman Bath, Opera or Gastronomic Weekends with wine tastings. This makes it seem like an enjoyable educational establishment run with enthusiasm by the Seymours. The hall has a talkative parrot and terriers run around. There's one very 'lived in' informal sitting room with piano and books and a first-floor drawing room with fine cornicing and bold striped paper. The basement dining room is reminiscent of an old kitchen with tiled floor, a large pine dresser and a range used as a gas log fire. Much of the food is home produced – including yoghurt and vegetables – and the wine list resembles a diary with stories of the family on their holidays. The large gently sloping garden has trees and shrubs and a model railway track. Bedrooms, named after George III's children with a portrait in each, are decorated, mostly, with Laura Ashley fabrics and a rag doll. There are electric blankets in each room but TV is available only on request. A truly idiosyncratic place with the atmosphere of an informal residential course, where guests are invited to feel at home. It's strictly no-smoking.

Bedrooms: 9 *(single, double, twin, family), all with bath. Direct dial telephone, teamaking, hairdryer*
Facilities: *Parking*
Restrictions: *No children under 10. No smoking*
Open: *All year*
Credit/charge cards accepted: *Access, Amex, Visa*
Price category: *££*
Special rates: *Nov to May, 2 nights midweek, DB&B £28.50 pp per night. Children in parents' room ⅔ of tariff*

BATH
Sydney Gardens
Sydney Road, Bath BA2 6NT   Tel: *(0225) 64818/445362*

A substantial Victorian semi-detached house, run as a no-smoking bed and breakfast hotel. In spite of the proximity of the railway line, it is remarkably quiet; there's a small private garden adjacent to Sydney Gardens park. Bedrooms are spacious, bright and cheerfully decorated, with modern pine furniture. The breakfast room is cheerful with swagged cotton curtains and straightforward furniture. Guests may eat as much as they like. The lounge is spacious and bright with a Victorian fireplace, fine cornicing and a view over the garden to the park beyond. A piano, books and magazines add to the friendly charm. A clean and jolly hotel where you have the sensation of staying with people you know. The Smithsons are obliging hosts and will probably anticipate your needs even before you ask, making it a home from home for many people.

Bedrooms: 6 *(double, twin, family), all with bath. Direct dial telephone, TV, teamaking, hairdryer*
Facilities: *Parking. Croquet*
Restrictions: *No smoking*
Open: *End Jan to end Dec, except Christmas*
Credit/charge cards accepted: *Access, Visa*
Price category: *££*
Special rates: *Children in parents' room £15. Winter midweek breaks, prices on application*

BATHFORD
Eagle House
Church Street, Bathford, Avon BA1 7RS   Tel: *(0225) 859946*

If you don't need/want to be in the centre of Bath, this charming listed Georgian house set in a quiet village will suit those in search of unpretentious comfort. It is neither luxurious nor 'interior designed' but airy and bright, and visitors will feel like paying guests in a private house. The stone flagged entrance hall leads to the octagonal panelled drawing room, overlooking the garden, which has two areas of mixed but comfortable chairs and sofas, fine cornices and a coloured marble fireplace. There is a large antique sideboard with drinks and a table with lots of magazines and local information. The large breakfast room is jolly and bright with yellow walls and orange cloths and a large oak dresser. Up the fine staircase, the bedrooms (named after trees) are comfortable and furnished with some antiques in homely style, some with chintz fabrics. The large terraced garden has many fine trees and a sandpit (the owners have children). An informal family atmosphere in which to relax.

Location: *3 miles north-east of Bath*
Bedrooms: *6 (double, twin, family), all with bath. Direct dial telephone, TV, teamaking, hairdryer. Iron on request*
Facilities: *Parking. Sandpit*
Open: *Jan to Christmas*
Credit/charge cards accepted: *None*
Price category: £
Special rates: *Mid Nov to mid Feb, 2 nights including Sunday, or 3 nights: one free theatre ticket per double room. Children in parents' room free*

Cambridge

- A university city where the gentle pace of academic life seems all-pervasive and the historic colleges provide most of the sightseeing interest
- Ideal for lazy sightseers and people without cars; the few major sights are concentrated in the centre which is compact, charming and pleasant to walk around
- Plenty of parks and green spaces; an ideal place for summer picnics and boating expeditions
- Interesting excursions, several likely to appeal to (older) children, some within easy biking distance
- We don't rate Cambridge highly for creature comforts like hotels and restaurants, but it's OK for pubs

In many ways Cambridge is hardly a city at all; it has few wide streets and no cathedral. Huge areas of green surround the city centre. Take away the colleges and, you might feel, there'd be nothing left.

The blend of college buildings and greenery is best appreciated from the Backs, a broad swathe of water meadows, pastures and neatly cultivated gardens along the River Cam. There are few obligatory sights; the major colleges, the Fitzwilliam Museum and the handful of interesting old churches are all within easy walking distance of King's Parade, the fine main thoroughfare of the city. King's College Chapel, the chief glory of Cambridge, should be admired from the Backs and, if possible, from a pew; services are held most days in termtime as well as on Sundays and the King's College Choir sings at evensong.

For all its quiet charm, Cambridge cannot be written off as a sleepy market town of tweedy students on bicycles. It is in the forefront of computer technology and medical research and has, in recent years, taken on a new prosperity. There are some smart shops and controversial modern buildings.

Top sights

Fitzwilliam Museum An important collection of paintings, sculpture, armour and other artefacts. Pictures include works by

Titian, Rembrandt, Gainsborough, Hogarth and Turner and there is a fine selection of French Impressionist paintings. Other highlights include some beautiful illuminated manuscripts, the English pottery and porcelain collection and a room full of Egyptian mummies. The upstairs rooms (pictures) are normally open only in the afternoons, the lower rooms in the mornings. [*Open all year, daily except Sun and pm Mon*]

King's College Chapel A magnificent fan-vaulted chapel, the supreme example of Perpendicular architecture in England. The stained glass windows and superb carved screen and choir stalls date from the 16th century. Rubens' *Adoration of the Magi* was presented to the college in 1961 and is now the altarpiece.

Other sights

COLLEGES AND UNIVERSITY BUILDINGS

There are some 30 colleges of which half have medieval origins. Visitors can usually enter courtyards, chapels and certain gardens; the Tourist Information Centre can provide an official list of opening times for each college and blackboards outside the porters' lodges indicate daily changes. Most colleges are closed to the public in exam time (early May to mid June) and at all times you are asked to remember that colleges are private places of study and to be reasonably quiet. Guided tours are arranged through the Tourist Information Centre. Below is a shortlist of the finest (in date order):

Clare Founded in 1326 but with a fine Baroque old court and ornate 17th-century bridge over the Cam – and lovely gardens on the Backs.

Queens' Founded by two Queens of England (Margaret of Anjou, wife of Henry VI, and Elizabeth Woodville, wife of Edward IV). It has charming courts on a domestic scale, the half-timbered President's Lodge and a gaudily decorated 15th-century dining hall.

Trinity The largest college, famous for its vast Great Court. In Wren's Library, dating from 1676, there are carvings by Grinling Gibbons and some famous books and manuscripts from the library are displayed.

Other colleges well worth seeing include **Peterhouse**, the oldest college, founded by the Bishop of Ely in 1284, although largely rebuilt in the 19th century; **Pembroke**, with a medieval gatehouse and Library and a Chapel designed by Christopher Wren (1663); **Corpus Christi** for its fine medieval Old Court; **St John's** for its Tudor gateway and the Bridge of Sighs; **Jesus** for its cloistered seclusion and the chapel with pre-Raphaelite decoration. Some are famous for their students and benefactors: **Magdalene** has a Pepys Library; at **Christ's**, where Darwin and Milton studied, Milton is said to have planted the mulberry tree in the Fellows' Garden; and one of the students at **Emmanuel**, where 21 of the Pilgrim Fathers studied, was John Harvard who gave his name to Harvard University.

There are also a few fine university (rather than college) buildings, such as the **Senate House**, a Palladian building next to King's College Chapel, and the medieval **Old Schools** building, both normally closed to the public. Many of the faculties are now housed in modern buildings on the west side of town; for a taste of controversial architecture see the **History Faculty** building on West Road, or **Robinson College**. A university institution well worth visiting is the **Botanic Garden**.

MUSEUMS AND GALLERIES
Kettles Yard   A highly personal gallery of modern paintings and sculpture collected by a former director of the Tate Gallery. [*Open all year except Christmas, pm only, Tues to Sat*]

The **Folk Museum** is a rambling 16th-century house crammed with exhibits illustrating local everyday life. The **Scott Polar Research Institute**, with memorabilia of the major Polar expeditions, is worth seeing [*open afternoons except Sun*]. There are a few other museums attached to university departments which have little appeal to non-specialists.

CHURCHES
Apart from King's College Chapel, Cambridge's churches are interesting rather than outstandingly beautiful. **St Bene't's** is the oldest, with an Anglo Saxon tower; **Great St Mary's** is the university church, with panoramic views from the tower; **The Round Church** is one of only a few Norman round churches in the country. Others, like **Great St Andrew's** and **Little St Mary's**, have intriguing memorials.

Shopping

There is a market daily except Sundays in Market Hill, and there are several pedestrian shopping malls and shopping centres (Lion Yard, Grafton Centre). The more unusual and specialist shops are in and around King's Parade and Trinity Street. Cambridge has many good bookshops, Heffers being the largest and most famous, and there are also a number of high quality clothes shops, selling well-cut country clothes.

Getting around

The relatively small size of the city makes it ideal for wandering around on foot. A car is a considerable hindrance: the two main north-south routes are closed to private cars in the middle and the one-way system is complicated. The Tourist Information Centre organises guided walking tours (about two hours) and can provide a list of shops which hire out bicycles. The city minibus service can be useful.

Punting along the Backs is great fun and the best way to enjoy the scenery; you can continue south through the rural scenery of Grantchester meadows. However it is an acquired skill and there's always the risk that you'll get separated from your pole and end up in the river; the lazy or inexpert can hire a 'chauffeurpunt'. The boatyards at Mill Lane (off Trumpington Street) and Quayside (off Magdalene Street) are open from Easter to early October.

Excursions

Grantchester (2 miles south-west)   Walk, cycle or punt through the river meadows to the villages of Grantchester, with Rupert Brooke's Vicarage, and Trumpington, where the church has a 13th-century brass.
Anglesey Abbey, Lode (6 miles north-east)   A 13th-century Augustinian foundation, later converted to a country house; fine collections of furniture and paintings. (NT) [*Open April to mid Oct, pm only, Wed to Sun (except Good Friday) and Bank Hol Mons*]
Wimpole Hall (8 miles south-west)   A vast and splendid 18th-century mansion altered and added to by several famous architects including James Gibbs and Sir John Soane. There is a landscaped park and a home farm for rare breeds of domestic animals. (NT) [*Open April to Oct, pm only, daily except Mon (unless a Bank Hol) and Fri*]
Imperial War Museum, Duxford (8 miles south)   A large collection of historic aircraft plus a chance to sit in Concorde or a high-tech simulator capsule. [*Open mid Mar to Oct, daily*]
Linton Zoo (9 miles south-east)   A zoo and wildlife breeding centre set in 10 acres of lovely gardens. Big cats to bird-eating spiders. [*Open all year, daily*]
Newmarket (14 miles east)   The racecourse and the National Museum of Horseracing. [*Open April to Nov, Tues to Sat; plus Sun pm, Mons in Aug and Bank Hols*]
Audley End (16 miles south)   Close to the market town of

Saffron Walden, a huge and richly furnished Jacobean mansion later altered by Robert Adam and with a park landscaped by Capability Brown. A miniature railway in the grounds operates in the afternoons. [*Open April to early Oct, Tues to Sun and Bank Hol Mons*]

Ely (16 miles north)   The majestic Romanesque cathedral dominates this attractive fenland town and is one of the finest in the country. The octagonal lantern tower, a masterpiece of medieval engineering, dates from the 14th century. There is a small stained glass museum, open May to Oct.

Huntingdon (16 miles north-west)   Oliver Cromwell's birthplace with a Cromwell museum in his old school. You can visit nearby Houghton Mill and Ramsey Abbey (both NT). In summer there are boat trips along the Ouse past neighbouring market towns like St Ives.

When to go

Cambridge is probably at its most beautiful in spring when the daffodils and crocuses are out on the Backs; from around Easter you can hire boats. Avoid May and early June if you want to visit the colleges as it is exam time; after exams comes 'May Week' (actually in June) with endless revelries including the intercollegiate boat races or 'Bumps' and the May Balls. In late June there is the traditional Midsummer Fair. The Cambridge Festival, lasting a fortnight from late July, features concerts, opera, plays and folk singing and dancing. At all times of year there is much more going on in term-time than during the vacations.

Autumn and winter are less appealing; you can't hire a boat after the middle of October and the National Trust properties (see 'Excursions') are shut. Cambridge can be very cold and bleak. The highlight is the Christmas Eve festival of Nine Lessons and Carols in King's College Chapel – the original of all such services and televised world wide. Tickets are obtainable by queueing and if the event does fall on a weekend you will spend most of your time doing just that.

Information

The Tourist Information Centre, Wheeler Street, Cambridge CB2 3QB; tel: (0223) 322640

The Festival Administrator, Mandela House, Regent Street, Cambridge CB2 1BY; tel: (0223) 358977

Festival Box Office, The Corn Exchange, Wheeler Street, Cambridge CB2 3QB; tel: (0223) 357851 (tickets)

The Tourist Information Centre also organises weekend breaks to coincide with the Festival.

Where to stay

For a city which attracts so much tourist interest, the range of accommodation in Cambridge is very disappointing. There are very few traditional or purpose-built hotels (except a couple two and four miles from the centre); most are in converted houses and may be without facilities such as lifts. The vast majority of the accommodation on offer is in guesthouses or bed-and-breakfast establishments, generally unexceptional.

CAMBRIDGE
Arundel House
53 Chesterton Road, Cambridge CB4 3AN   *Tel: (0223) 67701*

This Victorian terrace is well situated overlooking Jesus Green and the Cam, about five to ten minutes' walk from the centre; it has a small garden, too. Inside, public rooms are spacious and have been simply but well decorated and furnished – button-back chairs in the lounge, wood tables and armless chairs in the slightly pub-style restaurant. Bedrooms are also simply furnished, but are light and airy and do not lack gadgets – including a coin operated video (there's a 'library' of films for hire). There are a few family rooms, and a children's menu is available. This is an unexciting but good-value base.

Bedrooms: *81 (single, double, twin, family), 6 in annexe. 26 with bath, 36 with shower. Direct dial telephone, TV (with coin operated video), teamaking. Hairdryer*
Facilities: *Parking. Babylistening*
Restrictions: *No smoking in part of restaurant, or at breakfast*
Open: *All year except Christmas*
Credit/charge cards accepted: *Access, Amex, Diners, Visa*
Price category: *££*
Special rates: *Weekends (Thurs to Sun), 2 to 4 nights DB&B £29 (single £35) pp per night*

CAMBRIDGE
Centennial
63/69 Hills Road, Cambridge CB2 1PG   *Tel: (0223) 314652*

A terrace of Victorian houses, situated on a busy road near the station, about 15 minutes' walk from the centre. Bedrooms are comfortable and reasonably spacious, light and airy. There's a large modern lounge, a basement dining/breakfast room with Windsor chairs and closely packed tables, and a pub-style bar. Cooking is simple, homely and good, with Greek overtones. This is a clean and good-value base – with the added bonus of a car park.

Bedrooms: 22 *(single, double, twim, family), 17 with bath or shower. Direct dial telephone, TV, teamaking. Hairdryer on request*
Facilities: *Parking*
Restrictions: *No dogs*
Open: *Closed 10 days at Christmas*
Credit/charge cards accepted: *Access, Amex, Diners, Visa*
Price category: ££
Special rates: *Children £7 in parents' room*

CAMBRIDGE
The Garden House
Granta Place, Mill Lane, Cambridge CB2 1RT   Tel: (0223) 63421

One of the best-located hotels in Cambridge, on the riverside 5 to 10 minutes' walk from the centre, and quiet. It's a spacious and modern building, with much glass through which to enjoy the views of punts and garden. The public rooms are huge, decorated largely in a rather impersonal international style, with colour schemes of orange/rust/brown/mustard – which gives them a rather dated appearance, though they're well-kept and comfortable. The bedrooms, many with river view and/or their own balcony, are spacious, with well appointed bathrooms. This hotel is a good base if you don't seek a cosy atmosphere, but value quiet, convenience and a car park.

Bedrooms: *117 (single, double, twin, suite), all with bath and shower. Direct dial telephone, TV (with in-house video), teamaking. Hairdryer, trouser press, minibar*
Facilities: *Parking. Lifts. Babylistening*
Restrictions: *No dogs*
Credit/charge cards accepted: *Access, Amex, Diners, Visa*
Price category: £££
Special rates: *Weekends excluding Christmas, 2 nights B&B (plus an allowance of £15 per day towards dinner) £47.25 (single £62.25) pp per night; £5 pp supplement for river view. Children under 12 free when sharing parents' room on a break; otherwise children in parents' room £15*

CAMBRIDGE
May View Guest House
12 Park Parade, Cambridge CB5 8AL   Tel: (0223) 66018

A fine Victorian end-of-terrace house, in a quiet position overlooking Jesus Green. There are just six bedrooms, all attractively decorated and furnished with antiques and paintings; the largest now has a four-poster bed. There's a breakfast room (polished wood floor, grandfather clock) which looks out onto the small and pretty Italian-style sun-trap garden. This is an extremely well-cared-for and well-run bed-and-breakfast establishment, very reasonably priced.

Bedrooms: *6 (double, twin), none with bath (3 public bathrooms), one with four-poster*
Restrictions: *No dogs. No children under 7*
Credit cards accepted: *None*
Price category: £

CAMBRIDGE
Parkside Guest House
25 Parkside, Cambridge CB1 1JE   *Tel: (0223) 311212*

A small bed-and-breakfast guesthouse opposite Parker's Piece offering reasonable standards of comfort for the low price and central location. Bedrooms are clean and bright with modern pine furniture and some have spruce shower cabinets. There is a small, rather ordinary breakfast room (with one no-smoking table) and a lounge/bar in a lean-to extension at the back, overlooking the garden. Breakfast is served till 1.30pm; lunch and dinner can be arranged on request.

Bedrooms: *11 bedrooms (single, double/family and twin), 5 with shower. Direct dial telephone, TV. Hairdryer on request*
Facilities: *Parking. Babylistening*
Open: *All year*
Price category: ££
Special rates: *Children in parents' room: under 2, £2; 2 to 9, £5*

Canterbury

- Tremendous historical impact, centred on the magnificent cathedral, but thin on other sights; just enough to see over a leisurely weekend
- The centre is compact and charming but very crowded in high summer
- Small museums in historic buildings are worth visiting but are closed on Sundays when there is also restricted access to the cathedral during services
- There's a reasonable range of accommodation from cheap guesthouses to comfortable, though not outstanding, hotels

Stand on the spot where St Thomas à Becket was murdered over 800 years ago, follow the route taken by Chaucer's pilgrims to Becket's shrine; visit the tomb of Sir Thomas More: Canterbury's great appeal is that its history includes people and events most of us have heard of. It has been the headquarters of the English church since the 6th century and the present cathedral is the focus of the city both historically and visually.

Parts of Canterbury are very picturesque: there are pleasant gardens and quaint buildings lining the city walls and stretches of the River Stour, barely more than a stream. But although many buildings date from medieval times, much of the city was destroyed by war-time bombing and there has been some insensitive rebuilding.

The main street changes its name several times, from St Peter's to High Street, St George's Street and St George's Place; there are several fine half-timbered buildings. The cathedral precincts occupy nearly a quarter of the area of the city within the walls and include the historic King's School.

Top sight

The Cathedral Parts of the cathedral date from 1070, though most of what you see is more recent; architectural styles range from Norman to Perpendicular. There is much to see: the huge Gothic nave, the largest Norman crypt in England with its beautifully decorated Lady Chapel, the ceiling of Bell Harry tower, tombs (including that of the Black Prince) and spectacular stained glass.

Other sights

Hospital of St Thomas In the 12th-century undercroft of the Poor Priests' Hospital is a dormitory for poor pilgrims to Becket's shrine. In the refectory above is a beautiful 13th-century mural of Christ in Glory. [*Open all year, daily*]

Roman Mosaic A room, now underground, containing a Roman mosaic pavement, the remains of a hypocaust (an underfloor heating system) and a few other archaeological finds. [*Open all year, daily except Sun, pm only Oct to Mar*]

Quite long stretches of the **city walls** exist, though of the gates which pierced them only Westgate (see below) has withstood the demands over the years for broader roads into the city. There are good walks round the walls, through some of the pleasant green spaces such as Westgate Gardens and Dane John Gardens.

Along the river the 13th-century **Greyfriars**, the **Blackfriars Refectory** and the **Alchemist's Tower** (an 18th-century folly) are worth looking out for. **The Norman staircase** in the courtyard of King's School is splendid.

MUSEUMS AND GALLERIES

Canterbury Heritage Housed in the Poor Priests' Hospital, a lovely medieval building, this is a high tech 'time-walk' museum tracing the life of the city since Roman times. Exhibits include Roman silver spoons and the world's first passenger railway engine. [*Open all year Mon to Sat, and Sun pm in summer*]

Royal Museum and Art Gallery The Beaney Institute, a splendid piece of mock-medieval Victoriana in the High Street, contains a local history museum with collections of Roman glass and silver, some Dutch School paintings and a regimental museum. [*Open daily except Sun*]

The Canterbury Pilgrim's Way A new tourist 'experience', based on Chaucer's Canterbury Tales: visitors walk the reconstructed route of a medieval pilgrimage to the shrine of Thomas à Becket, 'witnessing' his martyrdom. [*Open all year, daily*]

Westgate A fortified gatehouse and city prison, rebuilt around 1380 and now displaying a collection of arms and armour, mainly 18th- and 19th-century. The condemned cell can be seen and there are good views from the roof. [*Closed for repair as we went to press; usually open all year, daily except Sun, pm only Oct to Mar*]

The Canterbury Centre, in the church of St Alphege, holds small exhibitions about the city.

CHURCHES

St Augustine's Abbey, just outside the city walls, is in ruins: little remains apart from the outlines of the Norman abbey church, and parts of the pre-conquest St Pancras' chapel. King Ethelbert is buried in the College. **St Dunstan's**, where Henry II dismounted to start his barefoot walk to the Cathedral in penance for the murder of Thomas à Becket, contains the head of Sir Thomas More, brought here after his execution – there is an interesting display telling the story of his life. Of Roman origin and used as a church from the 6th century, **St Martin's** is one of the oldest churches in the country. The west wall is a beautiful mixture of colours and textures. **St Mildred's** is the oldest church within the city walls, famous for its hatchments (boards displaying the arms of deceased worthies).

Shopping

The centre is a mainly pedestrianised shopping area with department stores and a small indoor shopping arcade. There are antique and gift shops and galleries down little side streets. Familiar shops like Laura Ashley and Liberty's are housed in interesting old buildings; a curiosity is the ancient King's School Shop.

Getting around

There are car parks within the city walls, reasonably near to the sights. The city can easily be explored on foot in one day. Walking tours of around 1½ hours are organised by the Canterbury Guild of Guides, starting from Longmarket. The Tourist Information Centre supplies sheets describing suggested city trails. There are river tours in summer from Blackfriars and the Weavers (a row of restored Tudor cottages).

Excursions

Chilham Castle Gardens (6 miles west) Fine grounds of a Jacobean house joining the original Norman castle keep. Jousting and falconry displays. [*Open April to mid Oct, daily*]
Bekesbourne, Howletts Zoo Park (3 miles south-east) Fifty acres of parkland with great cats, elephants, roaming herds of deer and a large breeding colony of gorillas. [*Open all year, daily*]

When to go

In summer Canterbury is teeming with cross-Channel visitors; a late spring or autumn visit is preferable. The city holds an international arts festival in September and October each year, providing three weeks of concerts, drama, dance and exhibitions. There are ceremonies to mark the death of Thomas à Becket on December 29th.

Information

The Tourist Information Centre, 13 Longmarket, Canterbury CT1 2JS; tel: (0227) 455490.

What's On in Canterbury; tel: (0227) 67744.

Canterbury Festival, 59 Ivy Lane, Canterbury CT1 1TV; tel: (0227) 452853.

Where to stay

Among the remaining black and white buildings in the centre are to be found a few hotels. There has been considerable modernisation over the years, and most retain little old world charm. A few hotels and most of the guesthouses are outside the city walls, though usually only a short walk to the centre.

CANTERBURY
Ann's
63 London Road, Canterbury CT2 8JZ   *Tel: (0227) 68767*

About ten minutes' walk from the town centre, the situation of this large Victorian house is better than it would seem from the address – the London Road is not very main, it's sufficiently leafy, and the hotel is set well back from the road. Indeed, it's a good place for a quiet stay (B&B only), and offers excellent comfort at very moderate prices. The Clements have restored the house with care, and each bedroom has been lovingly decorated in co-ordinated colourschemes; several have four-posters, and all is bright, clean and pretty. There's a small lounge with TV where guests may help themselves to sherry (pale cream), and an attractive large breakfast room with new golden pine furniture, and flowers on the tables. Liz Clements offers home-made muesli, 11 sorts of tea, and diet jams; for those who don't want English breakfast, there are yoghurts and cheeses.

Bedrooms: *19 (double, twin and family), 7 with four-poster, 12 with shower. Planned for 1989: 16, all with shower. 3 on ground floor. TV, teamaking*

Facilities: *Parking*
Restrictions: *No dogs*
Open: *All year*
Credit/charge cards accepted: *None*
Price category: £
Special rates: *Cots provided free. Winter only, double rooms let half-price for single occupancy*

CANTERBURY
The Chaucer
Ivy Lane, Canterbury CT1 1TT   *Tel: (0227) 464427*

An attractive red brick building situated just off the ring road that skirts the city walls, the Chaucer offers traditional Trusthouse Forte comfort. Public rooms (bar, lounge and restaurant) are restful and refined, bedrooms well decorated and furnished. The historic theme is emphasised in the dining room (avocado Becket, pilgrims' sole, squire's chicken) and some dishes are decidedly adventurous (Tudor trout comes stuffed with chestnut and cucumber); there's enough to please the more conservative eater, though, and a special menu for children, too. A solid, comfortable base for those who do not seek great individuality; the lack of a lift may be a consideration.

Bedrooms: *45 (single, double, twin, family), all with bath. TV, teamaking*
Facilities: *Parking. Babylistening*
Restrictions: *No smoking in part of dining room*
Open: *All year*
Credit/charge cards accepted: *Access, Amex, Diners, Visa*
Price category: £££
Special rates: *2-4 nights (must include a Sat) DB&B £40 (£47 single) pp per night. Children under 16 sharing parents' room free, 25% off adult rate in own room*

CANTERBURY
County
High Street, Canterbury CT1 2RX   *Tel: (0227) 66266*

The situation is the main feature of this hotel, right in the heart of the shopping area (pedestrianised) and old town, close to the cathedral. First licensed in the 16th century, there's still a Tudor theme in parts: the façade, beamed bar and coffee shop, and now heavy four-poster beds in the recently created 'Tudor bedrooms'. But some areas are not in keeping with this style, particularly the restaurant, an air-conditioned room which lacks natural light, and is decorated in a rather eclectic style. The upstairs residents' lounge is large and baronial in atmosphere, but rather impersonal. Bedrooms are well decorated and equipped; those called 'Georgian' have half-tester beds. Cooking is ambitious, with many dishes in a nouvelle cuisine style; vegetarians are not catered for, and "all meats are cooked pink" (unless you wish to specify otherwise); the three-course table d'hôte luncheon is good value. A traditional hotel, centrally situated.

Bedrooms: *74 (single, double, twin, suite), some with fourposter, all with bath. Direct dial telephone, TV, teamaking, hairdryer, trouser press*
Facilities: *Parking, lift. Babylistening*
Restrictions: *No dogs*
Open: *All year*
Credit/charge cards accepted: *Access, Amex, Diners, Visa*
Price category: £££
Special rates: *Nov to Mar, weekends, 2 nights B&B £26 pp per night. Extra bed in parents' room £14; cot £8. On weekend breaks, children under 4 sharing parents' room free*

CANTERBURY
Ebury
65/67 New Dover Road, Canterbury CT1 3DX   *Tel: (0227) 68433*

This large Victorian building, well set back from the road, lies outside the city walls about 10 minutes' walk from the centre. It's a family-run concern, and it shows; bedrooms are well cared for, spacious and airy, though not luxurious or particularly pretty. There's a large, light lounge, with fine fireplaces and deep sofas and armchairs; the atmosphere is sedate and rather old-fashioned. The dining room is unexciting, and cooking is plain (mainly grills). However, a definite plus is the large walled garden, and a very fine new indoor swimming pool and spa bath.

Bedrooms: *15 (single, double, twin, family), 13 with bath, 2 with shower. Direct dial telephone, TV, teamaking*
Facillities: *Parking. Indoor swimming pool, spa bath. Babylistening*
Restrictions: *Small, 'well-behaved' dogs only*
Open: *All year except Christmas Eve to mid Jan*
Credit/charge cards accepted: *Access, Visa*
Price category: ££
Special rates: *2 nights DB&B (not Suns) £25 pp per night (July to Oct £27.50). Children free in parents' room except July to Oct (£8)*

Durham

- Few, but spectacular and historic, attractions – just enough for a short weekend
- A poor selection of places to stay but we recommend two comfortable country house hotels outside the city
- Durham can be visited as a day trip from the North York Moors, the Yorkshire Dales or the Northumbrian coast

Durham is one of the most beautiful and arresting of cities, set dramatically above the River Wear in lovely wooded surroundings, dominated by the massive Norman cathedral. The historic centre of the city, built on a craggy peninsula outlined by an exaggerated loop in the river, is now virtually closed to traffic. Much of the old town, including the castle, is occupied by the university. It is fairly well-preserved with cobbled, twisting streets and tiny, rather unsavoury passages or 'vennels' between the buildings. The classic walk is from the market place up to Palace Green, a large lawn bounded by ancient buildings, through the Cathedral Close and down the length of the North and South Baileys, lined with 17th- and 18th-century houses, and on through a gate in the medieval walls to Prebends Bridge. From here is the most famous view of the cathedral. On the far side of the river, there are some pretty streets and more fine views. You can also walk right round the inner bank of the peninsula where the woods with their wild flowers (including overpowering wild garlic) are carefully managed by the Dean and Chapter.

Unless you go in really fine weather, and plan to spend hours lazing on or by the river, there is little to do once you have visited the cathedral and the castle. Shopping is limited and caters mainly for local day-to-day needs, with just a few shops for visitors. However, Durham makes a good base for visiting the Beamish North of England Open Air Museum.

Top sight

The Cathedral Durham Cathedral, unlike many cathedrals of Norman origin, is still mainly Norman in style, and is usually regarded as the finest example in Britain. Its massive simplicity makes it impressive to the eye, both inside and out. But what makes it remarkable is a feature which represents the beginning of the end of the Norman style: the rib-vaulted roof, the first to be built on this scale.

As well as the remains of St Cuthbert, the Cathedral houses the tomb of the Venerable Bede in the beautiful Galilee chapel. You can climb the central tower (the latest part of the Cathedral, built in 1465) for good views of the surrounding country. The treasury, in the undercroft, is a well-displayed collection of plate with relics associated with St Cuthbert, including the remains of his wooden coffin. The Monks' dormitory houses a large collection of carved stones from the 2nd to the 7th centuries.

Other sights

THE CASTLE
Built as a fortress to protect the Cathedral and home of the Prince Bishops, **Durham Castle** is not just an ancient monument – it has been in continuous occupation for over 900 years and is now a hall of residence for one of the university colleges. As a result times of opening are very restricted and guided tours (45 minutes) compulsory. There is quite a lot to see: the 13th-century Great Hall; the 15th-century kitchens which still produce over 300 meals a day; the 16th-century chapel; and a Norman gallery and crypt chapel dating from 1080. [*Open April 1-21 and July to Sep, daily except Sun am; Oct to June (termtime) pm only, Mon, Wed and Sat*]

MUSEUMS
Two small specialist museums have sprung from university departments. The **Museum of Archaeology**, in the Old Fulling Mill on the river bank, has a collection of local finds [*open all year, daily; pm only Nov to Mar*]. The **Museum of Oriental Art** is on the campus; exhibits include porcelain, T'ang tomb figures, Indian miniatures and a room illustrating the history of writing from Egyptian hieroglyphics to Chinese calligraphy [*open all year, except Sun am April to Oct and weekends Nov to Mar*]. There is also a military museum, the **Durham Light Infantry Museum** [*open all year, Tues to Sat plus Sun pm and Bank Hols*].

The medieval church of St-Mary-le-Bow has been converted to a heritage centre with audio visual shows, 18th-century costumes and brass rubbing. [*Open late May to late Sep, pm only*]

Getting around

Durham's historic centre must be explored on foot. The limited parking in Palace Green is reserved for local traffic and the disabled, but there is a multi-storey car park ('Cathedral Car Park') just off Market Place. Here you can also take a half-hourly courier bus up to the castle and cathedral, and another route includes the Durham Light Infantry Museum.

Rowing boats can be hired from Browns Boathouse, Elvet Bridge, from April to October.

Excursions

Durham County Council organises regular 'ride and ramble' coach tours on alternate Sundays from May to October; join at Durham bus station.

Cocken Wood Picnic Area (4 miles north) The steep banks of the River Wear, opposite the ruins of **Finchale Priory**, a 13th-century Benedictine retreat. [*Open all year, daily except Sun am*]

✿ **Beamish, North of England Open Air Museum** (12 miles north) *Holiday Which? Weekend Break Award.*

The museum is set in a large expanse of countryside, dotted with imported and restored buildings including a little village complete with Co-op, illustrating aspects of past life in the county. There is a reconstructed colliery and genuine drift mine, with an engine house and winding engine, and an atmospheric row of miners' cottages which have been authentically furnished to show the colliers' lifestyle at different periods. [*Open all year: mid Mar to mid Oct, daily except Sun am; mid Oct to mid Mar, closed Wed, Thurs and Sun pm*]

Barnard Castle, Bowes Museum (20 miles south-west)   A fine private collection of pictures, furniture, costumes etc, housed in a château-like purpose-built museum. [*Open all year except Sun mornings and Christmas week*]

When to go

The University Regatta takes place in mid June and the Miners' Gala on a Saturday in July (to be avoided unless you have come specifically to watch it). Durham Theatre Company performs plays in the Cathedral in August (Mystery plays every third year: next in 1990) and there is a Festival of 20th-century music in the castle in October. The city is more lively during termtime.

Information

The Tourist Information Centre, Market Place, Durham City DH1 3NJ; tel: 091-384 3721

'Ride and ramble' coach tours; tel: 091-386 4411

Durham Theatre Company tel: (0325) 469861

Where to stay

There are very few hotels in Durham. One option, as the city is so small, is to stay outside the city and visit Durham for the day. We recommend two country hotels not far from Barnard Castle (see 'Excursions').

DURHAM
The Royal County
Old Elvet, Durham City DH1 3JN   *Tel: 091-386 6821*

This is the best, if not the only, hotel in Durham and was once a coaching inn. It has a good, fairly central location (opposite Elvet bridge) with a car park and less noise than one might expect. The 'new ' wing – added in 1972 – contains most of the bedrooms, all fairly standard, but pleasant enough. The older bedrooms have recently been refurbished; so an older room on the back is likely to be the best bet. Public areas have been redecorated in airy colour schemes; there is a smart new Bowes Brasserie (breakfast and snack meals) and an elegant, formal restaurant. The brave attempts at original décor, however, have contributed little to the atmosphere which is very much county hotel turned chain.

Bedrooms: *120 (single, double, twin, family) all with bath. Direct dial telephones, TV, teamaking*
Facilities: *Parking, lifts. Hairdresser. Babylistening*
Restrictions: *No dogs in public areas*
Open: *All year*
Credit/charge cards accepted: *Access, Amex, Diners, Visa*
Price category: *£££*
Special rates: *Weekends, 2 nights DB&B plus Sunday lunch, £40 pp per night. Children under 14 free in parents' room*

COATHAM MUNDEVILLE
Hall Garth
Coatham Mundeville, Darlington DL1 3LU   *Tel: (0325) 313333*

About 20 minutes' drive from Durham, Hall Garth is a rambling building of 16th-century origin but with Georgian, Victorian and modern additions. It is surrounded by over 10 acres of grounds and the traditional walled garden encloses a swimming pool and tennis court. The stables have been reconstructed to provide a bar and annexe. Bedrooms are large, some with good views over the countryside. The hotel has something of the atmosphere of a minor country house but caters for a mainly business clientèle during the week; at weekends it could suit families. Dinner is charged according to the price of the main course.

Location: *3½ miles north of Darlington; ½ mile east of A1/A167 junction (sign to Brafferton)*
Bedrooms: *21 (single, double, twin and family), 10 in annexe, 5 with four-poster beds, all with bath or shower. Direct dial telephone, TV, teamaking*
Facilities: *Parking. Sauna. Swimming pool (outdoor, heated), tennis, croquet, putting. Children's playground*
Restrictions: *No smoking in dining room*
Open: *3 Jan to 21 Dec*
Credit/charge cards accepted: *Access, Amex, Diners, Visa*
Price category: *££*
Special rates: *Weekends, 2 or 3 nights DB&B £34.50 pp per night. Children under 16 free in parents' room*

HEADLAM
Headlam Hall

Headlam, near Gainford, Darlington DL2 3HA   Tel: (0325) 730238

A creeper-clad Jacobean mansion (with Georgian additions) surrounded by lovely formal gardens with lush lawns and terraces, Headlam Hall is between Darlington and Barnard Castle (7 miles from each), but feels in the middle of nowhere. Although within convenient distance of Durham (under half an hour's drive), it does offer a weekend break in itself for those seeking calm and comfort. There is a grand but welcoming hall-cum-lounge and a second sitting room of more domestic proportions. Rooms are furnished with reproduction and antique pieces. Bedrooms are large and peaceful, with names like 'peacock' and 'peach' giving a clue to colour schemes. The dining room is formal but with a relaxed atmosphere and the cooking is good.

Location: *Headlam is 2 miles north-east of Gainford*
Bedrooms: *16 bedrooms (double, twin, suites); 2 with antique four-poster beds, 14 with bath, 2 with shower. Direct dial telephones, TV*
Facilities: *Parking. Snooker. Croquet, fishing, putting, tennis. Babylistening*
Restrictions: *No dogs in bedrooms or restaurant (and by arrangement only)*
Open: *3 Jan to Christmas*
Credit/charge cards accepted: *Access, Visa*
Price category: *££*
Special rates: *Weekends, Oct to May 40% discount, June to Sept 20% discount (off B&B rates). Children free in parents' room*

Edinburgh

- An historic city of contrasts in a dramatic setting with a formidable catalogue of sights, enough for a multitude of short visits – the temptation is to try to see too much
- Non-stop cultural events during the Festival; much quieter the rest of the year
- Some attractive hotels near the centre, and all-day hospitable pubs
- You need stamina for the long slopes and abrupt steeps of the terrain; not ideal for the elderly or young children

Beautiful and stimulating, Edinburgh is so full of high viewpoints and interesting detail that it demands to be explored on foot. The clear division into Old Town and New helps you plan your time. The Old Town lies between the castle and the Palace of Holyroodhouse; immediately beyond is Edinburgh's mountainous backyard: Arthur's Seat rises over 800 feet, behind the bold line of the Salisbury Crags. The New Town, built to accommodate the overflow from medieval housing, is orderly and Anglophile, its first succession of elegant streets and squares named for Hanoverian royalty. Behind it the land slopes away, allowing glimpses of the Firth of Forth down the north-south streets of the grid pattern – and making the whole area oddly invisible in the view from Castle Rock.

In between, one-sided Princes Street with its Gardens makes one of the most attractive main thoroughfares of any city: it has the view of Castle Rock above the trees, the vista of Calton Hill to the east, the classical galleries on The Mound and the street-level Gothic spire of the Scott Monument – and you can usually hear bagpipes somewhere beyond the traffic.

Top sights

Edinburgh Castle   The city's high fortress is an agglomeration of 500 years' military building and rebuilding. It's still a barracks as well as a showplace, with tartan-trewed soldiery in evidence. Once past the 18th-century parade ground – now the car park except during the annual Tattoo – the daily tourist invasion stomps up steep cobbled approaches past towers, ramparts and gun batteries to Crown Squre, the centre of the medieval citadel. Sightseeing includes a large military museum, the modest 15th-century Palace apartments, the Scottish crown jewels and the pretty little Norman chapel of St Margaret. Lots of cannons – from old Mons Meg to the modern 'one-o'clock-gun' you set your watch by – and far-ranging views. [*Open all year, daily except Sun am Oct to Mar*]

The Palace of Holyroodhouse The Queen's official Scottish home is a Restoration palace built, round a courtyard of classical Renaissance distinction, for Charles II who never visited it. Only a roofless nave remains of the 12th-century Abbey of Holyrood; and of the royal residence begun in 1501, only the sturdy tower most famous as the scene of the murder of Rizzio, secretary of Mary Queen of Scots. Here in the Historic Apartments some of the appealing original decoration survives. Elsewhere the guided tour offers elegant staterooms, elaborate plaster ceilings, a mixed bag of Royal portraits and plenty of Royal anecdotes. [*Open all year, daily; partial closure during official visits*]

The National Gallery of Scotland Two classical buildings occupy The Mound, dividing Princes Street gardens. The one with sphinxes and Queen Victoria is the Royal Scottish Academy, housing annual exhibitions, and the less exuberant portico beyond is the National Gallery where major collections are on permanent display. European painting in chronological order – masterpieces, old favourites, some surprises; Scottish artists in a newer wing. [*Open all year, daily except Sun am*]

Other sights

THE OLD TOWN
For all the historical reasons, the city first grew in the lee of Castle Rock and along the ridge between the fortress and the Palace of Holyroodhouse. The tall narrow tenements of the medieval layout have mostly been demolished. But the **Royal Mile** and its adjacent wynds and courts, much restored, is an area of immense if rather commercialised charm. The natural (and chronological) place to start is the Castle; down Castle Hill, Lawnmarket and High Street there are close-packed old houses, small museums, historic pubs and souvenir shops. Along Canongate the attractions thin out in a slum-cleared stretch before the approach to the Palace. The attractions of the Royal Mile are, in descending order:
Outlook Tower and Camera Obscura Two floors of photographic and holographic exhibitions lead to the rooftop view and the little darkened room where all Edinburgh is projected with

magic simplicity onto a round white table. Most effective on a bright day. Fascinates even sophisticated children. [*Open all year, daily*]

Gladstone's Land   Sequence of attractive 17th-century rooms, glowingly restored, in a prosperous merchant's tenement: painted ceilings, period furniture, polish and pot pourri. (NTS) [*Open April to Oct, daily except Sun am*]

Lady Stair's House   17th-century townhouse set down a narrow close, more attractive outside than in (but free of charge); it contains Burnsiana, Stevensonia, Walter Scottery – exhibited relics of the three great writers. [*Open all year, Mon to Sat*]

Wax Museum   Pretty 1766 Assembly Rooms building now full of lurid waxworks: historic Scots, the Royal Family, children's classics and a Chamber of Horrors. [*Open all year, daily*]

Museum of Childhood   Splendid collection of toys and games, antique or (for adults) nostalgic; grouped over several floors, with model streets and costume at the top. [*Open all year, Mon to Sat*]

John Knox's House   Appealing 15th-century townhouse with one interesting painted ceiling. John Knox possibly lodged here: related exhibits, and a continuous video enactment of his theological battles with Mary Queen of Scots. [*Open all year, Mon to Sat*]

Huntly House   (see 'Museums and Galleries')

THE NEW TOWN
Across the green divide of the central gardens, the 18th-century New Town begins at Princes Street. New Edinburgh spread in ever-grander residential developments with acclaimed architectural unity, guarded today by a Conservation Committee. A drive around reveals the scale, the green spaces and the planned vistas of Britain's largest area of Georgian building; but to appreciate its detail you must walk. Charlotte Square is considered the most perfect. Attractive shops line George Street and are scattered elsewhere; and there are plenty of pubs in the narrower thoroughfares.

HISTORIC BUILDINGS AND VIEWPOINTS
The Georgian House   The north side of Charlotte Square, designed by Robert Adam, is Edinburgh's finest stretch of civic Georgian building. Number 7 has been authentically restored to give an idea of its lifestyle in 1800, above and below stairs. Visitors ring the bell and are admitted to drawing room, dining room, kitchen etc, beautifully furnished and equipped in every detail. (NTS) [*Open April to Oct, daily except Sun am; Nov, Sat pm and Sun pm*]

Walter Scott Monument   Scott in marble sits on the launching pad of this Gothic rocket, rising 200 feet from statuettes in elaborate arches to the pinnacled spire familiar in every view of Edinburgh. Inside it, 287 steps give narrow access to vertiginous viewing platforms. [*Open all year Mon to Sat*]

Calton Hill Useful knoll (355 feet) for all-round views, with assorted monuments – dramatic on the skyline from Princes Street, oddly surreal at closer quarters. Classical round mini-temple, domed Observatory, a single cannon; Nelson's tower like a stone telescope with viewing platform 143 steps up; and the National Monument, a spare portico of twelve tall columns, all that was built (before funds ran out) of a projected facsimile of the Parthenon.

MUSEUMS AND GALLERIES

Huntly House Three linked 16th-century buildings in Canongate hold Edinburgh's main local history museum. A rambling layout of colourful and often magnificent exhibits, including clocks and muskets, glass and silver, shopfronts and sedan chairs. [*Open all year, Mon to Sat*]

National Portrait Gallery and **National Museum of Antiquities** Strictly Scottish portraits, of and often by famous Scots; from Mary Stuart to Muriel Spark. In the museum (same building, shared entrance hall) important archaeology – neolithic, Roman and Christian – from Scottish sites, and ground-floor displays relating to Scottish life up to modern times. [*Open all year, except Sun mornings*]

Royal Museum of Scotland, Chambers Street Scotland's major general museum, in a very fine Victorian building: the galleries open off a huge light hall of glass and white wrought iron. The original emphasis was industrial: working models enliven the science collection. The natural history galleries include a comprehensive zoo of stuffed animals and the suspended skeleton of a Blue Whale; the permanent collection of Oriental art and ceramics is backed up by important exhibitions. Definitely something for everyone. [*Open all year, daily except Sun am*]

National Gallery of Modern Art Representative collection of 20th-century art founded in 1960 and moved in 1984 to its neo-classical premises at the western end of the New Town. International and Scottish painting indoors, sculpture in the grounds. [*Open all year, daily except Sun am*]

The **Talbot Rice Art Centre** (part of Edinburgh University, in South Bridge) houses the Torrie Collection of European painting and various exhibitions. Galleries displaying contemporary art include the **City Arts Centre** and the **Fruit Market Gallery**, facing each other in Market Street.

CHURCHES

The tallest spire in the city belongs to the **Tolbooth Kirk** on Castle Hill, built in the 1840s; Pugin designed its pinnacles and interior wood carving. The most distinctive crown spire decorates **St Giles' Cathedral**, High Street. Not properly a cathedral since Scotland abolished bishops in 1688, St Giles' is a focal point of Scottish history. Statues and relics (including the saint's) were swept away in the Reformation; added aisles and chapels have made the interior almost square. The **Tron Kirk**, founded in 1637, is named for its site of the former city weighing place. Further down the Royal Mile the 17th-century **Canongate Church** has a pretty gabled front topped with a little cross borne by a stag, a reference to the vision that inspired the foundation of Holyrood Abbey. South of the Royal Mile, **Greyfriars Kirk** has a church-yard full of illustrious graves, some protected by iron mortsafes against bodysnatchers. Nearby 'Greyfriars Bobby', who watched over his master's grave for 14 years, is commemorated with a little statue.

In the designs for the New Town, two churches were intended to close vistas, from the outer sides of Charlotte and St Andrew squares. Domed St George's is now **West Register House**, annexe of the Scottish Register Office; and **St Andrew's** with spire and portico was erected in George Street instead of its square, having lost its place to a magnificent private mansion (now the Royal Bank of Scotland).

WALKS AND VIEWS

The various photogenic views of Edinburgh from Castle Rock, Scott's Monument and Calton Hill are dwarfed by that from **Arthur's Seat**: an energetic climb to the windy summit is rewarded on a clear day by a panorama of city, sea and distant mountains. More peacefully you can stroll in the **Royal Botanic Garden**, large and lush, north of the New Town; the scented Plant Houses are a relaxing sequence of temperate and tropical, and there are exhibitions in Inverleith House. Suggested routes in the city centre are widely available in explanatory booklets, and there are many guided walks. On summer evenings you can learn about Old Town ghosts and ghouls or New Town architecture. Details from the Tourist Office and the New Town Conservation Centre (see **Information**).

Shopping

Princes Street is the Edinburgh equivalent of London's Oxford and Regent Streets, with branches of everything from Liberty's to

Littlewoods. At the eastern end of the Gardens the modern Waverley Shopping Centre is an attractive pedestrian complex with lots of greenery, fountains and café space. In the Old Town the Royal Mile is full of tartan, knitwear and souvenirs; Victoria Street is lined with boutiques and small old specialist shops; Grassmarket below is increasingly worth a wander. In the New Town George and Rose are the most concentrated shopping streets and the 'West End' around Stafford Street a useful smaller centre. Antiques are well distributed round Edinburgh: St Stephen Street, well down the slope of the New Town, makes interesting browsing. Notable bookshops (new) are in South Bridge, George Street and elsewhere; (secondhand) in Victoria Street, and Haddington Place in the 'East End'.

Getting around

Exploring by car (except for a look round the New Town) is impracticable. The car park near the bus station has constant queues and the one behind Castle Rock is inconveniently far from the sights. Walking is the best bet, with a bus ride the length of Princes Street or between Old Town and New – you need change for the exact fare. A bus tour can help you get your bearings: they leave from Waverley Bridge.

Excursions

Lauriston Castle (5 miles north-west) Tower house of the 16th century, much extended in the 19th, with croquet lawns beside the Firth of Forth. Very furnished indeed by its last Edwardian owners: full of whims and comforts, and some unusual collections. Guided tours only. [*Open April to Oct, daily except Fri; Nov to Mar, Sat pm and Sun pm*]

Dalmeny House (7 miles north-west) Gothic Revival mansion completed in 1817 for the 4th Earl of Rosebery. Inside, Rosebery and Rothschild family portraits, tapestries, porcelain and some of the finest French 18th-century furniture from the famous Mentmore collection. [*Open May to Sep, pm only, Sun to Thurs*]

Hopetoun House (10 miles west) Opulent 18th-century remodelling by the Adam family of the Hope family seat, in vast landscaped grounds. The earlier rooms (by William Bruce) much outdone in magnificence by the Adam State Apartments; notable collection of paintings, not confined to family portraits. [*Open Easter, then daily May to mid Sep*]

At **Queensferry** you can admire at close quarters the Forth

Bridge and the Forth Road Bridge; at **Cramond** there are pretty cottages, boats and a walk beside the river Almond; **Leith** has an attractively restored quayside with glimpses of the docks beyond.

When to go

The Athens of the North has a latitudinal disadvantage – what Stevenson described as one of the vilest climates under heaven. 'The weather is raw and boisterous in winter, shifty and ungenial in summer, and a downright meteorological purgatory in the spring'. In autumn, too, bright umbrellas can be the only notes of colour in a grey city. But it's worth carrying a camera for the sunny spells.

During the Edinburgh International Festival, three hectic weeks in August, every hotel is booked out. Plays, music, dance, jazz, films, the Fringe events and the Military Tattoo transform the city. Immediately afterwards there is a lull, when exhibitions close or change and culture takes a rest. But through most of the year there are plays and concerts, art shows and antiques fairs. On several evenings in May and June there are Beating the Retreat parades in the Castle Esplanade.

Information

Tourist Office/Information Centre: Waverley Market, Princes Street, Edinburgh EH1 1BQ; tel: 031-557 2727

Travel Centre (bus services and tours): Waverley Bridge, Edinburgh EH1 1BQ; tel: 031-226 5087

Edinburgh Festival Office, 21 Market Street, Edinburgh EH1 1DF; tel: 031-226 4001

Edinburgh Festival Fringe Society, 170 High Street, Edinburgh EH1 1QS; tel: 031-226 5257

Military Tattoo Office, 31-33 Waverley Bridge, Edinburgh EH1 1BQ; tel: 031-225 1188.

Where to stay

There's no shortage of central hotels in Edinburgh's attractive Georgian terraces – though they can be less than attractive inside. Those within walking distance of Princes Street are quite expensive, and prices in general go higher during the Festival.

The grand old city hotels in the middle are now mostly chain-owned, and their weekend breaks are often good value. Further out, abundant guest houses offer bed and breakfast: the Tourist Office will supply details.

EDINBURGH
Caledonian
Princes Street, EH1 2AB   *Tel: 031-225 2433*

The grand old rose-red monstrosity at the bottom end of Princes Street was built in 1903 by the Caledonian Railway Company, and today combines the splendours of its defunct railway station with a tranquil elegance inside, in spite of its noisily convenient location. Public rooms include two restaurants – the formally French 'Pompadour' and the all-day 'Gazebo' – and a friendly lounge popular for morning coffee and afternoon tea. On-going refurbishment means that some bedrooms are solidly old-fashioned – those with the dramatic view of the Castle – while others are stylishly co-ordinated; all are comfortable and beautifully kept.

Bedrooms: *238 (single, double, twin, suite) all with bath. Direct dial telephone, TV and in-house video, minibar, trouser press, hairdryer*
Facilities: *Parking (200 cars), lift*
Restrictions: *No pets*
Open: *All year*
Credit/charge cards accepted: *Access, Amex, Diners, Visa*
Price category: *£££££*
Special rates: *Weekends, 2 nights B&B with 1 dinner (in Gazebo restaurant) £40 pp per night. Children under 14 free in parents' room*

EDINBURGH
George
George Street, EH2 2PB   *Tel: 031-225 1251*

Part 18th-century, part modern block not visible from the Corinthian frontage, this is the most attractive of Edinburgh's big chain hotels. It's two minutes' walk from Princes Street, and New Town traffic noise though constant is very muted indoors. The public areas are architecturally splendid, especially in the vast Carvery restaurant – there's another, more intimate, with its own street entrance. The lounge is a columned people-watching space, and the bar features dignified dark walls and leather Chesterfields. Older bedrooms are lofty and decorative, furnished with many real antiques; a similar style looks less happy in the starker modern ones; all are comfortable and well equipped.

Bedrooms: *195 (singles, doubles, twins, suites), all with bath. Direct dial telephone, TV, teamaking, minibar. Hairdryer, trouser-press*
Facilities: *Parking for 30 cars; lift; babylistening*
Open: *All year*
Credit/charge cards accepted: *Access, Amex, Diners, Visa*
Price category: *£££££*
Special rates: *Sat and/or Sun night, B&B £35 pp per night. Children under 12 sharing parents' room free*

EDINBURGH
The Howard
32-36 Great King Street, EH3 6QH   *Tel: 031-557 3500*

In a New Town Georgian terrace five or ten minutes' walk from Princes Street and relatively quiet, this hotel is small, comfortable and much less impersonal than those of the big chains (only one other hotel is owned by the company). Public rooms include a modern lounge, a cosy basement bar and a soothingly dim-lit restaurant with some period elegance. Bedrooms are spacious on the first floor, smaller above, with pleasant colour schemes and good modern furniture – though recent renovation has been rather patchy. Not cheap, but good value for a winter break – in the summer months it fills up with appreciative Americans.

Bedrooms: *25 (singles, doubles, twin and family), all with bath and/or shower, TV, teamaking*
Facilities: *Parking; lift*
Restrictions: *No dogs in public rooms*
Open: *All year*
Credit/charge cards accepted: *Access, Amex, Diners, Visa*
Price category: *£££*
Special rates: *Winter, weekends, 2 or 3 nights DB&B, £37.50 (single £45) pp per night. Children in parents' room £10*

EDINBURGH
Mount Royal
53 Princes Street, EH2 2DG   *Tel: 031-225 7161*

If you want to be right at the centre of things, this is good value among the chain hotels: a 1930s building among the older ones on Princes Street, rising seven storeys above the shops with a wonderful view across to the Castle. The first-floor lounge, bar, café and restaurant are light and modern open-plan areas with plants and a piano, friendly and accessible to passers-by. Recent major refurbishment has reached only the top-floor bedrooms; the rest should be completed by early 1989. Meanwhile they're a little worn and sparse, but bathrooms are good, and bay windows make the most of the front view.

Bedrooms: *159 (single, double, twin, family) all except 2 with bath. Direct dial telephone, TV, teamaking. Hairdryer and trouser-press on request*
Facilities: *Lift. Babylistening on request*
Restrictions: *No pets in public areas*
Open: *All year*
Credit/charge cards accepted: *Access, Amex, Diners, Visa*
Price category: *£££*
Special rates: *Weekends, 2 nights DB&B £29.50 to £41.50 pp per night. Children under 16 free in parents' room, 75% of the adult rate in own room*

EDINBURGH
The Piries Hotel
4-8 Coates Gardens, EH12 5LB   *Tel: 031-337 1108*

Near Haymarket station and about ten minutes' walk from Princes Street, this Victorian terrace hotel combines three bow-windowed houses. Elaborate 19th-century ceiling cornices have been attractively restored, and the décor throughout of pale walls and carpets, framed prints and elegant dark furniture suits the building. Facilities include a jacuzzi, sauna and sunbed. Bedrooms are light and comfortable; there's a lounge bar, a cocktail bar, and a restaurant serving well-prepared Scottish food.

Bedrooms: *17 (single, double, twin, family), one with four-poster; 4 with bath, 5 with shower (and 4 public bathrooms). Direct dial telephone, TV, teamaking*
Facilities: *Babylistening*
Open: *All year*
Credit/charge cards accepted: *Access, Amex, Diners, Visa*
Price category: ££
Special rates: *Children in parents' room: under 3 10% of full rate, 3-12 half price*

EDINBURGH
Prestonfield House
Prestfield Road, EH16 5UT   *Tel: 031-668 3346*

Ten minutes' drive from the city centre among the green fields behind the Salisbury Crags, this historic Jacobean house caters in grand style, and frequently on a large scale. But chandeliers and rows of ancestral oils, panelling and tapestries, formal candlelit restaurants and elaborate food are only half the story. Up the stone stairs the atmosphere alters to eccentric country-house in five captivating bedrooms – here a decorative ceiling, there a nursery fender – not luxury, but great charm. You breakfast in your room, with a view. Both homely and highly professional, this restaurant-with-rooms is one of a kind, and some worn edges are forgiven.

Location: *South of city, signposted off A68*
Bedrooms: *5 (double, twin), 2 with shower (2 public bathrooms). TV, teamaking, trouser-press*
Facilities: *Parking (and helipad)*
Open: *All year*
Credit/charge cards accepted: *Access, Amex, Diners, Visa*
Price category: ££
Special rates: *Children up to 12 in parents' room charged £2 per year of age*

Glasgow

- European culture capital for 1990, Glasgow has undergone a dramatic transformation in the last ten years and makes an interesting weekend break
- First-class art galleries and museums and some splendid Victorian architecture
- Other sights are few and all are widespread in a big, busy city: you need transport
- Stylish shopping and evening attractions
- Short on charming hotels; but there are a couple of civilised exceptions which provide a welcome retreat from the city clamour

Glasgow is big, sprawling and unpicturesque. Its traffic problem has been tackled by urban motorways and expressways that dominate a lot of skyline. It has lost its medieval roots almost to the last building – the 13th- to 15th-century cathedral is stranded beyond housing development and high-rise Strathclyde University – and the centuries before its industrial-revolution prosperity are barely represented. But it has magnificent Victorian architecture: tour the City Chambers' interior to discover the sheer extravagant opulence favoured by the British Empire's second city.

Glasgow is again a teeming trade and business centre, with an atmosphere of rampant civic energy. Cranes and sky-high scaffolding fill many vistas, music and pavement artists enliven the streets, there are cheerful pubs, some excellent restaurants, concerts, theatres and the Scottish Opera. But the most compelling reason for a visit is art. Central Glasgow has splendid municipal collections, and on the south-western outskirts the Burrell, opened in 1983, ranks among the best personal collections in Europe.

Top sights

❁ **The Burrell Collection** (in Pollok Park, three miles south-west of the city centre). *Holiday Which? Weekend Break Award.*
A sympathetic modern building – glass walls, woodland back-

drop – shows off the huge and varied collection of Sir William Burrell (1861-1958). Over 8,000 items (though never all on show) span exotic countries and ancient civilisations: superb Chinese ceramics, and tapestry and stained glass from medieval Europe are major interests; French 19th century dominates painting and drawing. Treasures and setting are a wonderful combination, internationally acclaimed. [*Open all year, daily except Sun am*]
Pollok House Handsome 18th-century house and gardens across the park from The Burrell: graceful rooms, and very interesting paintings – the Spanish collection includes Goya and El Greco. [*Open all year, daily except Sun am*]

Other sights

North-east of the centre, **Glasgow Cathedral** is fine Early English Gothic, complex and satisfying to explore. Close behind it the **Necropolis** provides a green and sculpted skyline; isolated across the traffic is **Provand's Lordship**, sole modest remnant of medieval housing, now a small museum of great charm.

North-west of the centre, the **Tenement House** (NTS) is an 1890s flat, occupied from 1911 to 1965 by a tenant who never threw anything away, and preserved as she left it: decades of small-scale social history. You can also tour the **Glasgow School of Art**, a functional and fascinating building by Charles Rennie Mackintosh.

ART GALLERIES AND MUSEUMS
Hunterian Art Gallery Glasgow University's 1980 tower ele-gantly displays the definitive Whistler Collection, plus Old Masters (Rembrandt, Rubens) and portraitists (Raeburn, Reynolds, Romney). In the Mackintosh Wing is the reconstructed home of Charles Rennie Mackintosh, architect and designer, doyen of the Glasgow Style. [*Open all year, Mon to Fri and am Sat*]
Kelvingrove Art Gallery and Museum Elaborate, imposing Victorian building on the edge of Kelvingrove Park: downstairs the Scottish Natural History section (with dinosaurs) and the knights in armour have great child-appeal. Paintings in the first-floor galleries include fine Italian, Dutch, Flemish, French and British collections [*Open all year, daily except Sun am*]
The People's Palace (in Glasgow Green, by the Clyde south-east of the city centre) Sturdy, much-embellished red sandstone building where Glasgow's social history is appealingly told in tableaux, models, murals and paraphernalia. Attached is contras-tingly delicate Winter Garden of glass and white-painted iron, with lofty palms. [*Open all year, daily except Sun am*]

Shopping

Glasgow is the shopping centre for half the population of Scotland. Old-established Buchanan Street (grand), Argyle Street (comprehensive) and Sauchiehall Street (varied and cheerful) are now largely pedestrian areas. Covered shopping centres are popular and there are several enormous new complexes including Princes Square. Bookshops are plentiful but scattered; antique shops tend to gather under one roof, as at Victorian Village in West Regent Street and the Virginia Galleries, occupying an interesting former tobacco market in Virginia Street. Weekend bargain markets are Glasgow favourites – The Barras in the East End covers acres, and Candleriggs fills a huge glass-roofed hall. Tartanry and souvenirs are generally available but nowhere dominate the scene.

Getting around

You need transport to see the sights – strolling in Glasgow is chiefly for shoppers. A car is more useful here than in most big cities, in spite of merciless one-way systems and peculiarly irritating traffic lights. There's an abundance of taxis. Several bus companies compete confusingly since deregulation; some even give change. A useful fixed-fare underground line affectionately known as the Clockwork Orange circles the centre. For a panorama of Glasgow with an excellent running commentary, sit upstairs on the bus tour from St Enoch Square, every afternoon of a long summer season.

Excursions

The Hill House, Helensburgh (18 miles north-west). The best domestic achievement of Charles Rennie Mackintosh, built in 1902. [*Open all year, daily (pm only) except Christmas and New Year*]
Loch Lomond (20 miles north-west) You can drive along (but not round) Scotland's largest inland loch, mountain-enclosed and island-studded. Boat trips from Balloch.

When to go

On fine summer days Glasgow's spacious parks are an added pleasure, but most of its attractions are indoor, all-weather and year-round. There are cultural events all year too and the summer season begins strongly with the Mayfest, occupying most of the month and encompassing jazz, rock, cabaret and street events as well as drama, classical music, dance and exhibitions. Glasgow looks set to sustain the impetus – from the 1988 Garden Festival to its 1990 year as European City of Culture, and beyond.

Avoid excursions to Loch Lomond in July and August when it is very crowded.

Information

Tourist Information Centre, 35-39 St Vincent Place, Glasgow G1 2ER; tel: (041) 227 4894

Travel Information Centre, St Enoch Square, Glasgow G1 4BW; tel: (041) 226 4826

Mayfest, tel: (041) 22755

Where to stay

Really central accommodation ranges from businesslike modern blocks to shabby Victorian guesthouses, with few attractive hotels in between – but there are one or two astonishing exceptions. Better areas for moderately-priced accommodation lie west beyond Glasgow University, or south towards Pollok Park.

GLASGOW
Babbity Bowster
16-18 Blackfriars Street, G1 1PE   *Tel: 041-552 5055*

This stylish pub-with-rooms began life as a Georgian merchant's townhouse, and after many less prosperous years (as a fruit and veg warehouse, later derelict) has been rebuilt with care. The open ground floor is a friendly bar, where the daytime atmosphere of a civilised coffee-house moves towards all-out evening jollity. You can eat here, or in the wood-and-gingham restaurant above. At the top, surprisingly peaceful bedrooms are identically businesslike but pretty, in pale blue and white. It makes a relaxed and very convenient *pied à terre* from which to see the city.

Bedrooms: 6 *(twin), all with shower*
Facilities: *Parking*
Open: *All year except 25 Dec and 1 Jan*
Credit/charge cards accepted: *Access, Amex, Visa*
Price category: ££

GLASGOW
Beacons Hotel
7 Park Terrace, G3 6BY   *Tel: 041-332 9438*

Wide views over the city from this hotel in one of Glasgow's most attractive and exclusive areas, near Kelvingrove Park. It's part of a fine Victorian terrace, and many of the bedrooms are suitably spacious. They're pleasantly if unremarkably decorated and furnished, with good bathrooms. There's a cheerful breakfast room (with the view) and in complete contrast an ultra-modern black and white bar-restaurant in the basement, open to non-residents and popular. Various suites cater for business and social functions, and the hotel has a young and lively atmosphere. A comfortable off-centre base, good value at weekends.

Bedrooms: *36 (single, double, twin and family) all with bath. Direct dial telephone, TV (including satellite) and in-house video, teamaking. Hairdryer, trouser press*
Facilities: *Lift*
Open: *All year*
Credit/charge cards accepted: *Access, Amex, Diners, Visa*
Price category: *££*
Special rates: *Weekends, 1 or more nights, B&B £19.50 (single £26) pp per night. Children in parents' room £8 (£5 at weekends)*

GLASGOW
One Devonshire Gardens
1 Devonshire Gardens, G12 0UX   *Tel: 041-339 2001*

You ring the doorbell at the end of a handsome Victorian terrace in the West End of Glasgow to enter a creation of opulent chic. In the drawing room, where you drink aperitifs and coffee, sophisticated colours and heavyweight fabrics set off handsome sofas and repro antiques; in the restaurant, theatrically lit and luxurious, delicious food is served with friendly ceremony. Bedrooms are individually designed in the richly draped house style, and bathrooms are sybaritic. Everything fosters the illusion that you're the select guest of some 19th-century notable.

Bedrooms: *8 (double, twin), all with bath. Direct dial telephone, TV. Hairdryer, trouser-press*
Facilities: *Parking*
Restrictions: *Dogs by prior arrangement only*
Open: *All year*
Credit/charge cards accepted: *Access, Amex, Diners, Visa*
Price category: *££££*
Special rates: *Children in parents' room free*

GLASGOW
The White House
11-13 Cleveden Crescent, Glasgow G12 0PA   *Tel: 041 339 9375*

The White House consists of three terraced houses in a West End crescent of blonde sandstone designed by the renowned Glasgow architect, John

Burnet senior. Period proportions and features contribute to the comfort of the interior which has been thoughtfully modernised. Apart from the hall (carpeted in the owner's Ferguson tartan) and lobbies, there are no public rooms as such but suites all have fitted kitchens and sitting areas. Not that there is any obligation to self-cater; meals can be provided by room service and a courtesy car is available in the evening to ferry guests to three associated restaurants. Bedrooms are large, airy and gracious with a blend of antique and well-designed modern furniture and lighting and a variety of prints, posters and paintings. There are extra touches such as small bottles of champagne to welcome new guests and impeccable housekeeping includes fresh flower arrangements and washing up in the kitchens. Quiet, civilised, not for the gregarious.

Bedrooms: *32 suites (single, double and twin), including 6 in mews cottages, all with bath. Direct dial telephone, TV (with teletext and video). Hairdryer on request, trouser press. Kitchens*
Facilities: *Parking*
Restrictions: *No pets*
Open: *All year*
Credit/charge cards accepted: *Access, Amex, Diners, Visa*
Price category: ££££
Special rates: *Children in parents' room, £10*

LANGBANK
Gleddoch House
Langbank, Renfrewshire, PA14 6YE   *Tel: (0475 54) 711*

A well-run country hotel/club/business retreat, with a touch of country-house, half an hour's drive from the Burrell Collection or from central Glasgow. The 1920s house, built in Edwardian style for a shipping magnate, stands proud in its gardens between golf course, green fields and the Clyde estuary. Public rooms are warmly welcoming – a baronial hall/lounge with log fire and chesterfields, a clubby red and green bar lightened by its fine view over the water, an elegant restaurant in the conservatory-style extension. The Clubhouse provides another bar and restaurant, less formal but sharing the house reputation for good food. Individually attractive bedrooms named after birds combine comfortable furniture, pretty fabrics and some solid original features; attentive housekeeping runs to fruit and biscuits.

Bedrooms: *32 (single, double, twin, suites) all with bath. Direct dial telephone, TV, teamaking. Hairdryer, trouser-press*
Facilities: *Parking. Squash, sauna, indoor swimming pool, snooker. Riding, golf, fishing. Babylistening*
Restrictions: *No dogs in public rooms*
Open: *All year except Christmas and New Year*
Credit/charge cards accepted: *Access, Amex, Diners, Visa*
Price category: ££££
Special rates: *Friday to Sunday, 2 or 3 nights DB&B £45 pp per night (includes free golf). Reductions for children by arrangement*

Lincoln

- Well off the main tourist track; peaceful, even at the height of summer, and with just enough to see comfortably in a weekend
- Attractive, unspoilt medieval streets with appealing shops, tearooms and restaurants. You need to be fit to tackle Steep Hill
- Not much to see in the immediate surroundings of the city, but several fine country houses worth an afternoon's excursion
- A few comfortable hotels

Two pictures of Lincoln dominate books and pamphlets on the city. One is of the massive cathedral, the other is the view up Steep Hill, a picturesque cobbled street of medieval and Georgian houses. These two images do represent the best of what Lincoln has to offer: a superb cathedral in an impressive setting (crowning the only hill for miles) and, around it, a maze of attractive streets where traffic is restricted. This small area is 'uphill' Lincoln, and after a few hours' exploring you could be forgiven for thinking you'd seen it all. This is the time to visit one of the museums, all good of their kind.

The rest of the city, down at the bottom of the hill, is much less appealing. There is the odd pretty medieval church tucked between chain stores; here and there a fine black-and-white house disguised behind an unsightly modern shop front. There are some Roman remains and a medieval Guildhall. But the city lacks parks and open spaces; and the river Witham and Brayford Pool (an inland port built by the Romans) are something of a disappointment. More rewarding is a visit to Doddington Park or one of the other houses we list below.

Top sights

The Cathedral One of the largest in England, along with York Minster and St Paul's, with an imposing setting. It was rebuilt after the original Norman building was almost destroyed in an earthquake in 1185. The huge and intricately carved West Front is at present concealed, during restoration. Inside highlights include two superb medieval stained-glass rose windows in the transepts (the 'Dean's Eye' and the 'Bishop's Eye'), the 'crazy' vaulting and some beautifully carved 14th-century choir stalls, as well as the majestic bare nave itself. Look out, too, for the famous 'Lincoln Imp', said to have been turned to stone when he got too close to the angels above in the magnificent choir. You can climb the 335 steps of the central tower at regular set times. In the Library, designed by Sir Christopher Wren and built in 1674, one of the four original copies of the Magna Carta is sometimes exhibited. There are three guided tours of the cathedral daily.

Usher Gallery An interesting museum of the decorative and fine arts whose nucleus is the Usher collection of antique watches and clocks, portrait miniatures and English silver and porcelain. The Exley collection of ceramics and glass is particularly well-displayed. Upstairs are rooms devoted to Tennyson (with early photographs and memorabilia), to the 18th-century watercolourist Peter de Wint, and to local views by his contemporaries. [*Open all year, daily except Sun am*]

Other sights

UPHILL LINCOLN

Around the cathedral which dominates the medieval part of the city is the **Minster Yard**, with attractive old houses of different periods, including the 13th-century **Old Palace** of the bishops. Opposite the West Front of the cathedral **Exchequergate**, a massive building with a tunnel-like arch, leads into **Castle Hill**, the central square which provides a focus for the upper part of Lincoln. **Bailgate**, originally the main street of the outer bailey of the castle, is now an attractive shopping street, leading eventually to **Newport Arch**, the only Roman arch in Britain through which traffic still passes. Close to the castle is the recently discovered Roman site of **St Paul in the Bail**. And opposite Bailgate is **Steep Hill**, lined with old shops and with several timbered-framed inns, the most remarkable buildings being the **Jew's House** and adjacent **Jew's Court**, dating from the 12th century.

THE CASTLE

Lincoln Castle, built by William the Conqueror in 1068, is almost as much of a landmark as the cathedral. It has well-preserved battlements and its Norman remains include two towers, one large and almost ruined, the other small and mostly intact. The area within the walls has been developed a good deal over the centuries to include a prison (with an interesting Victorian chapel) and the present-day County Courts. [*Open all year, daily except Suns Nov to Mar*]

MUSEUMS AND GALLERIES

Museum of Lincolnshire Life A folk museum housed in rambling Victorian barracks. The re-created domestic interiors and old shops are fun for nostalgic adults and younger children. [*Open all year, daily except Sun am Oct to June*]

Towards the lower part of town just north of the river, the **City and County Museum** (mainly archaeology and natural history) is housed in part of a 13th-century friary – the earliest surviving Franciscan church in England [*open all year, daily except Sun am*]. The **National Cycle Museum** displays cycles dating from 1820 to the present day. [*Open all year, daily*]

Shopping

The most appealing shopping streets are Bailgate, Eastgate and Steep Hill, all good for antiques, books, clothes or presents. There are chain stores and supermarkets in High Street.

Getting around

Lincoln is well supplied with car parks at both top and bottom of its hill. You need to be fit for the steep streets of Uphill Lincoln but the area is small and best explored on foot. From May to September you can take a guided walk (lasts about 1½ hours), starting from Exchequergate. The cathedral has its own guides, and there are three tours daily. There are cruises up the river from Brayford Pool, with a taped commentary about its Roman origins.

Excursions

Doddington Hall (5 miles west) A magnificent Elizabethan brick mansion with romantic walled gardens and a turf maze. [*Open May to Sep, pm only; Wed, Sun, Bank Hol (inc Easter) Mons*]
Gainsborough Old Hall (15 miles north west) A late medieval manor house with collections of pictures, furniture, dolls and costumes. [*Open all year, daily except Sun am*]
Tattershall Castle (20 miles south-east) A moated 15th-century castle, of which only the keep remains. [*Open April to Oct, daily except Sun am*]

Belton House (22 miles south) A very fine late 17th century house containing family portraits and furniture and mementoes of the late Duke of Windsor. The park has an adventure playground. (NT) [*Open April to Oct, pm only, Wed to Sun (except Good Friday) and Bank Hol Mons*]

If you want to laze in the sun with a picnic make for **Hartsholme Country Park** (3 miles south-west). [*Open all year, daily*]

When to go

The Lincoln Festival takes place during the first three weeks in May (concerts, plays, exhibitions), preceded by a few days of beer and folk festival. The Lincoln Carnival (stalls, displays, procession with floats) is usually on the first weekend in June, and is followed by a wine festival. In early July there is a weekend celebration of medieval Lincoln with banquets and jousting at the Castle. There are about ten performances of the annual Lincoln Community Play, starting at the end of July. Throughout the year there are various shows (antiques markets, agricultural fairs, horse trials etc) at the Lincolnshire Showground just north of the city. However, Lincoln is never really overcrowded and, especially if you want to visit the country houses in the area, spring or summer is probably the best time to spend a weekend here.

Information

The Tourist Information Centre, 9 Castle Hill, Lincoln; tel: (0522) 29828. Or 21 Cornhill; tel: (0522) 511511.

Lincolnshire Tourist Guide Service, 17 Albion Crescent, Lincoln LN1 1EB; tel: (0522) 30261.

Lincoln Castle, tel: (0522) 511068

Where to stay

Most people would choose to stay in uphill Lincoln rather than in the less interesting part of the city below. There are two comfortable hotels close to the cathedral. There is also plenty of inexpensive bed and breakfast accommodation, especially in the residential area to the west of the cathedral.

LINCOLN
D'Isney Place Hotel
Eastgate, Lincoln   *Tel: (0522) 38881*

A dignified red brick house built in 1735 and extended in Victorian times, D'Isney Place stands in its own large garden of which the 13th-century cathedral close wall forms the south boundary. There are no public rooms and this is really a glorified and rather grand guesthouse. All the bedrooms are individually decorated in mainly pastel shades, varying in size but not in comfort, with a mixture of antique and high quality reproduction furniture. Bathrooms are pristine with luxurious touches; two have jacuzzis, all have towelling bathrobes. The two honeymoon suites have four-poster beds. English or continental breakfast is brought to your room and fresh fruit is also provided.

Bedrooms: *18 bedrooms (single, double, twin and family), 2 with four-poster bed, 16 with bath (2 with jacuzzi), 2 with shower. Direct dial telephone, TV, teamaking*
Facilities: *Parking. Babylistening*
Open: *All year except Christmas*
Credit/charge cards accepted: *Access, Amex, Diners, Visa*
Price category: ££
Special rates: *2 or more nights, B&B £17.50 (single £25) pp per night*

LINCOLN
Minster Lodge Hotel
3 Church Lane, Lincoln LN2 1QJ   *Tel: (0522) 513220*

An attractive Edwardian house with 'Tudor' timbering, Minster Lodge is on the corner of a main road and a quiet residential street five minutes' walk from the cathedral and city centre, with its own car park. The owner converted it to his own specifications and opened it as a hotel in the summer of 1987. Minster Lodge is a clean and simple guesthouse with no frills: white walls and stripped pine doors, built-in furniture and duvets in the bedrooms. Bathrooms are carpeted and windows double-glazed. Evening meals can be provided by arrangement but this is a good central base for those who would prefer to eat out. Lincoln has quite a selection of guesthouses; but perhaps none so clean and convenient as this one.

Bedrooms: *5 bedrooms (double and family) all with bath. Direct dial telephone, TV and teamaking. Bar tray on request*
Facilities: *Parking*
Restrictions: *No dogs*
Open: *All year*
Credit/charge cards accepted: *Access, Visa*
Price category: ££
Special rates: *Children under 8 £5 in parents' room*

LINCOLN
White Hart
Bailgate, Lincoln LN1 3AR   *Tel: (0522) 26222*

In the centre of old Lincoln, overlooking the cathedral, the White Hart could not be better placed. It dates originally from 1320 (the White Hart is that of King Richard II) although the oldest part of the hotel is now the Georgian restaurant, which has a formal but relaxed atmosphere and a French influence in both décor and food. The sitting room and panelled bar have a more old-fashioned, gentleman's club atmosphere with comfortable armchairs, cosy fires and table lamps. Bedrooms are light and pretty, with antique furniture and well-kept bathrooms; some have sitting areas. Half have views over the cathedral, and as traffic is restricted noise is not a problem in the hotel. Breakfasts, buffet lunches and light meals are served in the domed orangery, and drinks can be taken on the roof patio. An efficiently run hotel which retains its charm and has been thoughtfully refurbished.

Bedrooms: *48 bedrooms (single, double, twin and suites), all with bath. Direct dial telephones, TV, teamaking. Suites have minibars*
Facilities: *Parking, lift. Babylistening*
Open: *All year*
Credit/charge cards accepted: *Access, Amex, Diners, Visa*
Price category: *££££*
Special rates: *Thurs to Sun, 2 or more nights (must include Sat) DB&B from £43 (single £49) pp per night. Children under 16 free in parents' room*

London

- More to see and do than most cities, anywhere – with plenty of rainy-day entertainment and nightlife
- Entertaining and educational for older children, but expensive for family outings and tiring with small children
- River trips and picnics in the parks provide an escape from the crowds and the traffic; but avoid the peak tourist season of July and August
- Getting around can be wearing, time-consuming and costly; avoid the rush hours if taking a mid-week break
- Accommodation prices are sky-high; it's worth taking an inclusive package or booking a short break deal through the hotel

L ondon is not the loveliest capital city in Europe but it has a character all its own – and is unbeatable for things to see and do, for all ages and interests. There is scope for many weekends, indeed weeks, of sightseeing, exploring and excursions. Children especially love the double-decker red buses, the beefeaters, Big Ben, the soldiers at Buckingham Palace and the Christmas lights in Regent Street. Although the city is vast, with endlessly sprawling suburbs, most of the major sights can be reached from the Circle Line of the 'tube'. Above ground, there are many distinctive areas and plenty of green spaces. River trips along the Thames are the traditional way to see the cityscape.

Central London area by area

THE WEST END
Covent Garden offers the opera, and shopping and strolling in the old market place – now transformed, and London's nearest equivalent to continental café life. **Soho** is the restaurant (and former 'red-light') district, with London's Chinatown; close by is neon-lit Piccadilly Circus. In addition to the more dubious entertainment of the backstreets, many of London's theatres are in Shaftesbury Avenue, and big cinemas line pedestrianised Leicester Square. Beyond elegant, curved Regent Street (and in complete contrast to Soho) is **Mayfair**, with the most expensive

hotels and clubs, art galleries and shops, notably in Bond Street. Park Lane and Hyde Park beyond it mark the westernmost perimeter of the area; to the north is busy Oxford Street, London's major shopping street.

Top sight: National Gallery

PARKS, PALACES AND PARLIAMENT

West of pigeon-infested Trafalgar Square, **St James's** is a leafier extension of Mayfair, with traditional shops and gentlemen's clubs, its main attractions being the parks (St James's and Green Park) and royal residences (Buckingham Palace and St James's Palace). A stone's throw away are Westminster Abbey, the Houses of Parliament and Big Ben, emblem of London. Otherwise **Westminster** is a fairly dull area, with the solid civil service buildings of Whitehall and the residential streets and squares of Pimlico and Victoria.

Top sights: Buckingham Palace (Changing of the Guard); Houses of Parliament; Tate Gallery

WEST OF PARK LANE

Most of central London's 'villages' have been submerged by supermarkets and shifting populations. But there are still distinct neighbourhoods which retain some charm and interest. **Chelsea,** which has been both bohemian and smart, is famous for the King's Road and Wren's Royal Hospital, home of the red-coated Chelsea pensioners. Neighbouring **South Kensington,** still primarily residential, has many hotels and several museums; to the north are Kensington Gardens and Hyde Park. To the east are the elegant shopping areas of **Knightsbridge** and Sloane Street and the grand ambassadorial squares of **Belgravia**. Further west is scruffy **Earl's Court**, its Australian bed-sit colony earning it the nickname 'Kangaroo Valley'; and **Notting Hill** which has something of a village atmosphere and is known for the Portobello Road market and the annual carnival.

Top sights: Natural History Museum; Victoria and Albert Museum

NORTH OF OXFORD STREET

Beyond Hyde Park are the 19th-century squares and terraces of **Bayswater** and its scruffier neighbour, **Paddington**. Just to the north of Paddington is the area known as **Little Venice**, where elegant stucco houses and gardens overlook a pool of the Regent's Canal. Beyond Oxford Street are several distinct areas: Harley and Wimpole Streets with their clinics, dentists and doctors; bookish **Bloomsbury**; and further east, **Holborn**, with offices and a large legal community around Lincoln's Inn. North of the busy Marylebone Road, grand terraces designed by Nash overlook Regent's Park.

Top sights: British Museum; London Zoo; Madame Tussaud's

THE SOUTH BANK

Although very much part of London from the Londoner's point of view, the area south of the Thames has little to offer the visitor, with the notable exception of entertainment in the South Bank complex which includes the National Theatre, the National Film Theatre and the Festival Hall. The area between London Bridge and Tower Bridge has been developed recently with offices, landscaped riverside walks and a vast new shopping arcade (Hay's Galleria) in the old Victorian warehouses of Hay's Dock. Other attractions include the Gothic Southwark Cathedral and ships on the Thames.

THE CITY

The City is a fascinating area, teaming with workers all week but empty at weekends. Within the square mile are major financial institutions, including the Bank of England and the controversial new Lloyd's building; and between Fleet Street and the Thames are the law courts of the Temple. There are also fine churches, many designed by Sir Christopher Wren after the Great Fire. Nearby Docklands, renovated and up-and-coming as a residential, business and leisure area, is worth exploring; the trip on the Docklands Light Railway gives spectacular views. Famous Fleet Street is no longer the power base of all the national newspapers; several have moved to Wapping, in the Docklands area.

Top sights: St Paul's Cathedral; The Tower of London

Things to see and do

The Changing of the Guard at Buckingham Palace takes place daily at 11.30 am from April to the end of July (rest of year, alternate days) and this event – for which it is advisable to arrive early – dictates the flow of tourists round the major sights. To avoid the crowds see the Tower and St Paul's in the morning and Westminster Abbey in the afternoon.

Almost all museums, galleries and historic buildings open at 10am (the few exceptions are St Paul's Cathedral, Westminster Abbey, the Tower of London, Kensington Palace and London Zoo, which open earlier). Much is closed on Sunday morning; an option then is to visit **Speakers' Corner** (Hyde Park) and hear the soap-box orators.

ART GALLERIES

National Gallery   A huge and well-balanced collection of European paintings from the 13th to the 20th century. It is impossible to do justice to the Gallery in a single visit; better to concentrate on the masterpieces of one school. [*Open all year, daily except Sun am*]

National Portrait Gallery   Paintings and photographs of famous British men and women from Tudor times and including the present Royal Family. [*Same opening days as National Gallery*]

Tate Gallery   British art since the 16th century plus modern European and American art. The Clore Gallery, opened in 1986, is devoted to Turner. [*Same opening days as National Gallery*]

Others:

Courtauld Institute   An important collection of Impressionist and post-Impressionist paintings, plus Italian primitives and some Old Masters [*Open all year, daily except Sun am and Bank Hols*]

Dulwich College Picture Gallery   Old Master paintings in a gallery designed by Sir John Soane. [*Open all year, daily except Sun am, Mons and Bank Hols*]

Queen's Gallery   Masterpieces from the Royal Collection, regularly changed; closed between exhibitions. [*Open all year, daily except Sun am and Mon*]

Wallace Collection   18th-century house with a superb (once private) collection of paintings and furniture, primarily French. [*Open all year, daily except Sun am and Bank Hols*]

There are regular blockbuster special exhibitions at the **Royal Academy**, and the **Hayward Gallery**.

CHURCHES

Visitors are welcome to attend Sunday services but access to parts of churches is restricted then, and sightseers should visit between services.

St Paul's Cathedral   Sir Christopher Wren's masterpiece, with an overwhelmingly rich interior. The vast crypt (interesting tombs; treasury) and the Whispering Gallery are closed on Sundays. There are magnificent views from the dome, but it is a long, hard climb. [*Open all year, daily; crypt and galleries Mon to Sat, closed by mid afternoon*]

Westminster Abbey   Coronation place of the English monarchs since 1066. Tombs and monuments of famous people including Poets' Corner and the Tomb of the Unknown Soldier (a detailed guidebook or guided tour is helpful). The beautiful Henry VII chapel has Gothic fan vaulting and the first Renaissance tomb in England. Undercroft museum. [*Open all year, daily; choir, transepts and Royal Chapels Mon to Sat*]

Other interesting churches, from the architectural and historical points of view, include St Martin-in-the-Fields, Southwark Cathedral and many of the city churches – several were designed by Wren or Hawksmoor.

HISTORIC BUILDINGS
Tower of London A fascinating history lesson, the Tower has been a fortress, palace and prison. Among its highlights are the 'Beefeaters' and the ravens, Traitor's Gate and the execution block on Tower Green, and the superb collection of arms and armour. At popular times there are long queues to enter, and to file past the Crown Jewels. [*Open all year, daily except (Mar to Oct) Sun am and Good Fri, (Nov to Feb) Sun*]

Others:
Apsley House The collections of the Duke of Wellington in splendid house on Hyde Park Corner. [*Open all year, Tues to Sun*]
Banqueting House Famous building by Inigo Jones, with magnificent ceiling painted by Rubens. [*Open (subject to functions) all year, daily except Sun am, Mon and Bank Hols*]
Kensington Palace Royal residence dating from the 17th century; fine state apartments designed by Wren and William Kent. [*Open all year, daily Except Sun am and Good Friday*]

The houses of various Londoners including Dickens, Carlyle, Dr Johnson and Lord Leighton can be visited.

Further afield:
The **Royal Naval College**, Greenwich, is a Baroque masterpiece designed by Sir Christopher Wren, with a famous Painted Hall. [*Open all year, pm, daily except Thurs and Bank Hols*]

MUSEUMS
London museums are almost all closed on Sunday mornings and on Bank Holidays, including all Bank Holiday Mondays, Good Friday, May Day, Christmas (Dec 24-26) and New Year's Day. Any variations are mentioned below.
British Museum The most visited museum in London, with sections devoted to the major ancient civilisations and Early Britain. Exhibits include the Magna Carta, the Sutton Hoo treasure, ancient Egyptian mummies, and the Elgin Marbles. Ancient manuscripts and precious first editions are displayed in the British Library galleries. [*Open standard times*]
Natural History Museum Stuffed animals, fossils and minerals and dinosaurs (models and fossil skeletons). Hall of human biology with working exhibits to show how the body functions. [*Open standard times*]

Science Museum Fascinating displays on the development of space flight, road and rail transport (with historic cars and locomotives) and medicine, plus Children's Gallery of working exhibits. [*Open standard times*]

Victoria and Albert Museum Probably the world's greatest collection of decorative arts from all countries; highlights include the Jones Collection of French furniture, Italian Renaissance sculpture, oriental arts and the Constable Collection (in the Henry Cole Wing). [*Open standard times, plus some Bank Hols (annual variation)*]

Others:

Geological Museum Rocks, gems and models plus simulation of an earthquake. [*Open standard times plus some Bank Hols (annual variation)*]

Imperial War Museum Aircraft, tanks, uniforms, photographs medals and paintings and memorabilia of two World Wars and other 20th century operations. [*Open all year, daily except Sun am, Christmas and New Year*]

London Transport Museum Horse-drawn omnibuses, trolley buses and steam locos displayed in the Victorian hall of Covent Garden's old flower market. Visitors can 'test drive' buses and tubes. [*Open all year, daily except Christmas*]

Museum of London The history of the city from Roman times, with models, sound and light effects, reconstructed interiors, costumes and artefacts. [*Open standard times except closed Mon*]

Museum of Mankind Ethnographic collections of the British Museum. [*Open standard times*]

National Army Museum Army history from 1485-1914. [*Open standard times*]

Sir John Soane's Museum Unusual house designed by Soane, with his collection of works of art. [*Open standard times except closed Mon*]

Theatre Museum Stage ephemera. [*Open standard times except closed Mon; open some Bank Hols (annual variation)*]

Further afield:

National Maritime Museum, Greenwich. The development of ships from earliest times, including 18th-century royal barges and a full-size steam tug. Also marine paintings. [*Open standard times*]

Bethnal Green Museum of Childhood Houses the V&A's vast collection of toys, dolls and dolls' houses. [*Open Mon to Thurs, Sat, pm Sun and some Bank Hols*]

FAMILY OUTINGS

London Dungeon Medieval horrors (the Plague, torture etc) in dark vaults under London Bridge, not for the very young or squeamish. [*Open all year, daily*]

London Zoo A 36-acre site in Regent's Park, including a children's zoo where small children can touch the animals and take rides; feeding times and special displays are during the afternoons. [*Open all year, daily except Christmas*]

Madame Tussaud's Famous waxworks museum with vast collection of portraits and tableaux. The Chamber of Horrors still exerts fascination. [*Open all year, daily except Christmas*]

The Planetarium Armchair viewing of the moving universe; half hourly 'star shows'. There are also evening laser light concerts. Combined tickets with Madame Tussaud's available. [*Open all year, daily except Christmas*]

SHIPS AND THE THAMES

There are several carefully preserved historic vessels open to the public [*all year, daily; Bank Holiday procedure varies*]. In St Mary Overy Dock, close to Southwark Cathedral, is the wooden topsail schooner **Kathleen & May**. Opposite the Tower of London (and linked by ferry) is **HMS Belfast**, a huge Second World War cruiser, bristling with guns, now a floating museum.

At Greenwich are the 19th-century sailing clipper **Cutty Sark** and tiny **Gypsy Moth IV** in which Sir Francis Chichester made the first solo circumnavigation of the globe.

Tower Bridge now has glassed-in walkways with panoramic views, and exhibitions in both the towers. Further down the river is the futuristic **Thames Barrier** and visitors' centre. (See also 'Getting around')

PICK OF THE PARKS

Hyde Park Boating on the Serpentine and riding in Rotten Row.

Kensington Gardens The Albert Memorial, Peter Pan statue and model boats on the Round Pond.

Ranelagh Gardens Chelsea's 18th-century pleasure gardens.

Regent's Park Nash parkland with open-air theatre and zoo.

St James's Park Peaceful park; best for feeding ducks.

Further afield are **Kew Gardens**, with magnificent plant and tree collections and **Richmond Park**, a large natural park with herds of deer.

Shopping

Below we list main shopping areas, streets and shops:

Covent Garden Arts, crafts and fashion on and around the Piazza and in the old market halls. Healthfoods and far-eastern

imports around Neal's Yard
Charing Cross Road Bookshops: Foyles, specialist and second-hand
Tottenham Court Road Hi-fi shops and furniture stores (Habitat, Heals)
Oxford Street Fashion shops and department stores (Selfridges, DH Evans, Debenhams, John Lewis plus London's largest Marks & Spencer); always crowded
Regent Street Smart clothes shops for the 'British' style (Aquascutum, Burberry, Jaeger) and department stores (Austin Reed, Liberty's, Dickens & Jones), jewellers (Garrards, Mappin & Webb) and the famous toyshop, Hamley's
Jermyn Street Traditional shops, notably shirt-makers (Turnbull & Asser, Harvie & Hudson, New & Lingwood) and a cheese shop (Paxton & Whitfield)
Piccadilly Hatchards (books), Fortnum and Mason department store (especially known for food), Simpson's (for clothes), Tower Records
Burlington Arcade Small old-fashioned shops selling antiques, jewellery, smarter souvenirs and traditional British clothes (tartan, Shetland)
Bond Street Smartest clothes and shoe shops (Chanel, Gucci, Hermès, Ferragamo) and jewellers (Asprey, Boucheron, Cartier). Also Sotheby's, the auctioneers, and fine art galleries (Agnew, Colnaghi, Leger) and antiques dealers
South Molton Street Pedestrianised street of chic clothes shops.
Sloane Street Fashion and furnishings (including General Trading Company)
Knightsbridge Harvey Nichols and Harrods, the smartest department stores, plus tartans and Shetland at The Scotch House
Beauchamp Place Expensive boutiques, china and jewellery
Fulham Road Antique and design shops (Conran)
King's Road Boutiques and antiques, punk and Peter Jones department store
Kensington High Street Mid-range department stores (Barkers) and clothes shops
Kensington Church Street Antiques shops

Markets are very much part of London life; some of the best-known and most appealing include:
Bermondsey Antiques (Fri morning; best early)
Berwick Street Food, especially fruit and vegetables
Brick Lane Bric-a-brac and junk (Sun only)
Camden Lock Crafts, clothes and general (Sat and Sun)
Camden Passage Antiques; shops as well as stalls

Chelsea Antiques Market Antiques; but few bargains
Covent Garden Crafts and general, antiques (bric-a-brac) on
Mon in the Jubilee Market and Piazza
Gabriel's Wharf New market; crafts and workshops
Leadenhall Market Meat
Leather Lane Household goods
Petticoat Lane Clothes and household goods; Cockney atmosphere
Portobello Road Antiques and bric-a-brac (Fri and Sat)

Entertainment

Daily quality newspapers and weekly listings magazines (such as
Time Out) give details of what is on, including 'fringe' and
'alternative' entertainment. Theatre listings are found in the
London Theatre Guide, available from Tourist Information
Centres and hotels. You can normally book for concerts, films
and theatres by telephone, giving a credit card number; advance
booking is generally advisable if not always essential. Most major
arts venues do reserve a small allocation of seats for sale on the
day of performance but you will have to queue for tickets for
really successful shows. Tickets for concerts, opera, shows and
other events can be purchased, at inflated prices, through theatre
agencies (see below).

Concerts are held on the South Bank (Royal Festival Hall,
Queen Elizabeth Hall, Purcell Room) and at the Barbican, the
Royal Albert Hall and Wigmore Hall. There are two main **Opera**
companies, the English National Opera at the Coliseum (operas
in English) and the prestigious Royal Opera House at Covent
Garden. **Ballet** is performed both at Covent Garden and Sadler's
Wells; in summer the Royal Ballet have performances in the Big
Top tent in Battersea Park.

Theatre is, of course, one of the great attractions of London's
West End and there is a great variety of productions on offer at
any time, from farces to whodunnits and musicals. You'll have to
go to the South Bank for the National Theatre companies, and the
London headquarters of the Royal Shakespeare Company is at
the Barbican. Other famous non-West End theatres are the Royal
Court (avant garde productions) and the recently restored Old
Vic and the Lyric, Hammersmith (classics, revivals and short
runs). Fringe theatre venues include the Bush in Shepherds Bush;
the Almeida and the King's Head in Islington. Half-price tickets
(plus £1 fee) for same-day performances in the West End can be
purchased by queuing at the kiosk in Leicester Square (from 12
noon for matinees, 2.30pm-6pm for evening shows). Theatre box

offices often have returns. Theatrical ticket agencies often have tickets long after the box office has sold out; but expect to pay 15-25% extra. First Call is a 24-hour credit card booking service which does not always charge fees [telephone 01-240 7200].

First showings of **films** are also normally in the West End (usually Leicester Square); it is cheaper to go to local cinemas when the film is on general release. There are also independent cinemas showing less well-known or classic films; the National Film Theatre on the South Bank has different films every day.

Nightlife

For most people, London nightlife consists of eating and drinking out, or going to plays, concerts and so on. But there are places where you can drink, dance and gamble till the small hours. The smarter West End **nightclubs** are normally membership only, but there are some **discothèques** (such as the Hippodrome, with a spectacular laser show) where entry is at the discretion of 'bouncers' at the door. There are plenty of restaurants with dinner-dancing or floorshows; *What's On* magazine is a useful guide to these. Another evening entertainment organised for tourists is the medieval banquet; there are several places where you can be served by wenches and entertained by wandering minstrels. There's also a 'Cockney Cabaret and Music Hall' and a 'Scottish Banquet', with appropriate entertainment. **Casinos** are membership only and licensing laws mean that it takes at least 48 hours to become a full member; some are run as private clubs.

Getting around

The underground or 'tube' is the quickest method of public transport. The traditional red double-decker buses are a good way of seeing London, but routes are complex. Taxis can be very expensive. If possible, avoid the rush hours (8-9.30am, 5-6.30 pm).

The underground trains and red buses all have the same fare structure based on price zones: the cheapest ticket or a central zone Travelcard covers the journey to most major sights (roughly the same area as our map). The daily Travelcard gives unlimited use of bus and underground; the Capitalcard allows travel by British Rail as well, and is useful if you are staying outside central London or for excursions. Under 5s travel free and children under 16 travel on child fares (children of 14 or 15 need photographs and proof of age, for a child-rate photocard). All children under 16 need child-rate photocards for Travelcards or Capitalcards.

Taxis displaying the lit 'For Hire' or 'Taxi' sign can be hailed in the street; they also congregate in ranks, on main squares and at railway stations. All journeys are metered and you can expect to pay around £2.50 plus tip for a typical two mile trip in central London; but there are surcharges at night and at weekends, for each extra passenger and for luggage carried in the front of the cab. Mini-cabs (booked by telephone) are not metered so it is essential to ask the price when booking and confirm the fare before setting off.

Sightseeing trips are organised by many companies, including London Transport, who use their double-decker buses (open-top in summer) for a 1½ hour, 18-mile itinerary (departures from Piccadilly Circus, Victoria, Marble Arch and Baker Street stations). Most of these short tours cost around £5; many operators feature longer itineraries round the West End and the City, for £11-£15 for a half day. London Tourist Board trained guides are identified by blue badges. There are a few off-beat bus tours such as Literary London. Independent tourists can use the 'Culture Bus', which runs a circuit of London allowing you to stop at major sights and board a later bus on the same ticket. Guided walks with themes like Dickens' London, Haunted London or Historic Pubs are offered by several companies. (See also 'River and canal trips' below)

RIVER AND CANAL TRIPS

A boat trip along the Thames is an enjoyable way to see the city. There are short non-stop round trips, and services stopping at major sights (allowing you to rejoin a later boat when you have looked around). Most tours and cruises embark from Westminster, Charing Cross and Tower piers. There are services to Greenwich and the Thames Flood Barrier, and in the opposite direction to Hampton Court, Kew and Richmond. There are also lunch, supper and disco cruises. Tickets for the boat trip to Greenwich may include entrance to the Maritime Museum, the Old Royal Observatory (museum of astronomy) and the Cutty Sark. The new Thames Line Riverbus service (primarily for commuters) runs between Greenwich and Chelsea using newly developed water-jet-powered catamarans.

The London Waterbus Company operates along the canals of North London from Camden Lock to Little Venice via London Zoo. Jason's Trip is a 1½ hour cruise on an old-fashioned narrow boat from Little Venice to Camden Lock on the Regent's Canal; the same journey in reverse is offered by Jenny Wren Canal Cruises.

Excursions

Within fairly easy reach of central London, mostly close to the Thames, are a number of interesting houses, once the out-of-town homes of nobility or royalty. London Transport and independent firms organise coach excursions.

HISTORIC HOUSES AND GARDENS

Chiswick House Mini mansion in classic Palladian style designed by Lord Burlington. [*Open daily except Sun am*]

Ham House, Richmond A great Jacobean mansion with a Baroque interior and superb furnishings. [*Open daily except Mons (unless Bank Hols)*]

Hampton Court Tudor palace with Wren extension contains state rooms and a Renaissance picture gallery. Mantegna's Triumph of Caesar is in the Orangery. There are gardens with a famous maze. [*Open daily, except Sun am Oct to Mar*]

Kenwood House Classical Adam mansion with fine collection of paintings. Summer concerts. [*Open daily*]

Kew Palace Smallest of the royal palaces, built in 1631, with mainly Georgian interiors. [*Open April to Sep, daily*]

Osterley Park A grand house redesigned by Robert Adam in the late 18th century; splendid Adam interiors. [*Open Tues to Sun and Bank Hol Mons*]

Syon House, Brentford. The severe castellated exterior designed by Adam conceals grand state apartments in classical style and some important paintings. Motor museum, garden centre and Butterfly Farm. [*Open April to Sep, pm, Sun to Thurs, plus Suns in Oct*]

   Marble Hill House, a neat Palladian mansion, and the eccentric Gothick **Strawberry Hill**, both at Twickenham, are also worth visiting.

When to go

Regular annual events include:
February 21: Chinese New Year celebrations
March or April: Oxford v Cambridge Boat Race
April: London Marathon
End May: Chelsea Flower Show (4 days)
June 11: The Trooping the Colour
End June-July: Wimbledon Lawn Tennis Championships (2 weeks)
Mid to end July: The Royal Tournament

End July to mid Sept: The 'Proms'
End August: Notting Hill Carnival (2 days)
Nov: London to Brighton veteran car run (1st Sun)
Mid November: The Lord Mayor's Show
Mid November to early Jan: Christmas lights
   Among the exhibitions at Earl's Court, the most popular are the
Boat Show (early January), Cruft's Dog Show (mid February) and
the Ideal Home Exhibition (March).

Information

London Visitor and Convention Bureau, 36 Grosvenor Gardens,
London SW1W 0DU; tel: 01-730 3488

The main Tourist Information Centre is on Victoria Station
forecourt. There are smaller branches at Heathrow airport, the
Tower of London, Selfridges and Harrods.

London Transport Travel Information; tel 01-222 1234

For recorded information on the day's events telephone 01-246
8041

For recorded information on boat services, telephone 01-730 4812

London Waterbus Company; tel 01-482 2550 (canal trips)

For information on events and entertainment for children,
telephone Children's London 01-246 8007 (recorded message) or
Kidsline 01-222 8070

Where to stay

Accommodation in central London ranges from budget bed-and-
breakfast establishments in the Earl's Court, Victoria, Bayswater
and Paddington areas to luxury hotels in Mayfair and St James's.
There are a lot of purpose-built (Edwardian or modern) business
hotels around Marylebone and Bloomsbury. Converted Victorian
houses in Kensington and Chelsea provide some more personal
small hotels, ranging from middle-price to luxury.
   Midweek prices are generally high, but weekend rates are often
substantially reduced and can be very good value, particularly in
those hotels which cater predominantly for business people
during the week. Many of our recommended hotels fall into the
top two price brackets (££££ and £££££) on their standard rates,
but their weekend break rates – or rates offered by tour operators

at that hotel (see below) – make them compare well with hotels which fall into lower price categories (£££ or even ££), but which do not offer substantial (or any) reductions at the weekend.

Special 'break' rates are offered by hotel groups and tour operators; these are generally very good value, with reductions of up to 50% off the hotel's standard rate. Indeed, some operators offer better prices than the hotel itself. Most 'break' rates are for weekends, and are based on a 2- to 3-night stay; but anything is possible – even if you wish to stay in London for only one night midweek, it's worth checking to see what tour operators can offer. Many include cut price rail travel in the deal, some also offer coach or air travel. 'Children free' offers abound, and unlimited London travel is often included. It's well worth shopping around for the best rate; a hotel may be featured by several operators, at widely differing prices.

In our hotel entries, under '**Special rates**', ∗ precedes the name of a tour operator if the price of its special deal is lower than that offered by the hotel; if a hotel is featured by several operators, we quote the lowest price we could find in summer 1988 (but bear in mind that operators alter their prices in different ways, some putting rates up once a year in autumn, others quoting lower rates for winter and spring, and so on). No one tour operator consistently offered the cheapest rates for all the hotels in its programme, but a few tended to quote higher than average prices for most of theirs. For more information, see page 352 for details of 'Hotel groups and tour operators'.

The British Tourist Authority publishes a leaflet guide to *London Value Hotels* listing hotels offering accommodation for under £25 per person per night (sharing a double room).

∗ followed by the name of a tour operator: this operator's price is the lowest that we could find (in summer '88) for the deal quoted; bookings have to be made through the tour operator, not direct with the hotel. For details of tour operator addresses and telephone numbers, see page 354.

Prices are for b&b per person, sharing a double/twin room with bath

£	= You can expect to pay under £20
££	= You can expect to pay between £20 and £30
£££	= You can expect to pay between £30 and £40
££££	= You can expect to pay between £40 and £55
£££££	= You can expect to pay over £55

Abbey House
11 Vicarage Gate, Kensington, W8 4AG   *01-727 2594*

Situated in a quiet attractive tree-lined side street off Kensington Church Street, near to Kensington Gardens and Kensington High Street, the exterior and entrance of this good-looking and well-maintained house are imposing. A black-and-white tiled floor leads to a fine flight of stairs; all is brightly painted white, with shining brass and plants. The only public room is the basement breakfast room – light and airy, simple and homely. Bedrooms (none with bath or shower) are simple, too, but all is very well cared for. Breakfast is served only in the breakfast room. This does not have the stale and often dismal atmosphere of many of the hotels in this price category, and there are very few jarring notes. A simple and excellent value B&B (unlicensed).

Bedrooms: *15 (single, double, twin, family), none with bath or shower. TV*
Restrictions: *No pets*
Open: *All year*
Credit/charge cards accepted: *None*
Price category: £

Alexander
9 Sumner Place, SW7 3EE   *Tel: 01-581 1591*

In a typical South Kensington residential terrace off Old Brompton Road, the Alexander has recently had a facelift, and all is immaculate. There's a simple basement living room, with TV and 'honesty' bar (guests serve themselves and fill in a card); a pretty, summery, breakfast/dining room, with trellis paper and bamboo style furniture; a lounge area off the reception, in pale mushroom tones; and a patio garden (with pergola). The comfortable bedrooms are all of a similar standard, with pale colours and neat new bathrooms; several have four-poster beds. This is a pleasant hotel for people who don't need copious public rooms.

Bedrooms: *39 (double, twin, family), 4 with four-poster, 36 with bath, 1 with shower. Direct dial telephone, TV (with in-house video)*
Facilities: *Lift*
Restrictions: *Dogs by prior arrangement only*
Open: *All year*
Credit/charge cards accepted: *Access, Amex, Diners, Visa*
Price category: ££££
Special rates: *Children in parents' room £15. ★Best Western Getaway Breaks: Weekends, 2 nights B&B £45 (£50 single) pp per night (does not apply to rooms with four-posters); February 6/7 reduction of £5 pp per night; children up to 16 in parents' room free on break*

Athenaeum
116 Piccadilly, W1V 0BJ   *Tel: 01-499 3464*

Overlooking Green Park, this distinguished hotel prides itself on its service – 24-hour, of course. All is elegant and extremely comfortable: the Windsor lounge, a clubby bar with a renowned collection of malt whiskies, and a subtly lit restaurant. There's piano accompaniment for pre-prandial drinks and dinner. Bedrooms are streamlined with specially made furniture in yew and leather; all are double glazed and air conditioned. Some are reserved for non-smokers.

Bedrooms: *112 (single, double, twin, suites), all with bath. Air conditioning, direct dial telephone, TV with in-house video. Hairdryer in suites and on request*
Facilities: *Lifts, hairdresser. Babylistening*
Restrictions: *Guide dogs only*
Open: *All year*
Credit/charge cards accepted: *Access, Amex, Diners, Visa*
Price category: *£££££*
Special rates: *Weekends, 2 nights B&B £63 pp per night. Children (one to each adult) under 14 free (in parents' room, or own room if available), extra children half price*

Basil Street
Basil Street, Knightsbridge SW3 1AH   Tel: 01-581 3311

An institution, though not institutional, the Basil Street is one of the very few hotels left that has a genuinely English atmosphere, reminiscent of an Edwardian country house, that makes the neo-Edwardian copies seem all the more contrived. Collections of antiques and *objets* assembled over generations abound; there are parquet floors, Oriental rugs, tapestries and paintings; yet it isn't over-grand, and the atmosphere is relaxed, even cosy. Bedrooms (a few doubles and some singles without bath, though a bathrobe is provided for the walk to the public bathroom) are unsophisticated but comfortable in a somewhat old-fashioned way (again in a country-house style). Public rooms are very relaxing and sedate: spacious lounge (for tea or cocktails) and writing areas, dining room with candlelight and piano accompaniment at dinner (and always a trolley of roast beef), an informal lunch restaurant, and a more lively wine bar. There's also a ladies-only club, used by residents and members (many up from the country for the day). A civilised retreat, very near to Harrods, with an almost thirties feel, which will suit those in search of a real English atmosphere, slightly eccentric. The bedrooms without private bathroom offer an opportunity of budget accommodation.

Bedrooms: *103 (single, double, twin), 75 with bath. Direct dial telephone, TV*
Facilities: *Lift*
Open: *All year. Main restaurant closed Sat lunch*
Credit/charge cards accepted: *Amex, Access, Diners, Visa*
Price category: *£££££ (without bath £££)*
Special rates: *Children under 16 free in parents' room*

Beaufort
33 Beaufort Gardens, SW3 1PP   Tel: 01-584 5252

This is a sophisticated bed-and-breakfast hotel in two newly converted Victorian houses in a quiet cul-de-sac off the Brompton Road. It combines the sort of facilities you might expect in a larger business hotel (fax, telex, photocopier, secretarial services, free membership of a health club) with more personal touches (personal stereo, decanter of whisky or brandy, chocolates and so on in the bedroom), and successfully maintains a 'private house' atmosphere. There's only one public room, a reception lounge with an 'honesty' bar for guests to help themselves to drinks. Bedrooms are individually decorated, comfortable and well-coordinated, with much attention to detail. Some have additional sofa beds. Informal luxury in a small and personally-run hotel.

Bedrooms: *28 (single, double, suite), 25 with bath, 3 with shower. Direct dial telephone, TV and video, personal stereo, hairdryer*
Facilities: *Lift*
Restrictions: *Dogs by arrangement only. Some no-smoking bedrooms*
Open: *All year except Dec 23 to Jan 2*
Credit/charge cards accepted: *Access, Amex, Diners, Visa*
Price category: *£££££*
Special rates: *Child free in parents' room*

Berkshire
350 Oxford Street, W1N 0BY   *Tel: 01-629 7474*

In the centre of this major shopping street, opposite Bond Street tube station, this 8-storey building is an oasis of calm. Listen to harp music over tea in the drawing room, look at Stubbs' prints in 'Ascots' restaurant (and more horses in the bar), or relax and watch satellite TV in the very well-appointed bedrooms (with luxurious bathrooms). Public rooms are panelled and plush, with deep Chinese-style fitted carpets and elegant draperies.

Bedrooms: *147 (single, double, twin, suite), all with bath. Air conditioning, direct dial telephone, mini-bar, TV with satellite stations, in-house video, hairdryer, trouserpress. Jacuzzi in suites*
Facilities: *Lifts*
Restrictions: *Guide dogs only*
Open: *All year*
Credit/charge cards accepted: *Access, Amex, Diners, Visa*
Price category: *£££££*
Special rates: *★Embassy Hushaway Breaks, 2 or more nights (must include a Fri, Sat or Sun) B&B £41 pp per night (winter/spring; more in summer); children under 16 in parents' room free on break*

Brown's
Albemarle & Dover Streets, W1A 4SW   *Tel: 01-493 6020*

In the heart of Mayfair, Brown's has been a hotel for 150 years. It's an English institution, well known across the Atlantic (Theodore Roosevelt stayed here, and Franklin and Eleanor had their honeymoon here), with many famous devotees (Rudyard Kipling's desk is preserved). The style still embodies all the things that spell out Englishness: antiques and cut glass displays, wood panelling and stained glass, chintz armchairs and cream teas; although elegant enough, there's a somewhat cosy atmosphere that is reminiscent of a country house. Bedrooms are generally spacious, and very well equipped and decorated; some (connecting rooms) are suitable for family accommodation.

Bedrooms: *133 (single, double, twin, suites), all with bath. Direct dial telephone, TV, minibar. Hairdryer*
Facilities: *Lifts*
Restrictions: *No pets*
Open: *All year*
Credit/charge cards accepted: *Access, Amex, Diners, Visa*
Price category: *£££££*
Special rates: *Weekends, 2-3 nights B&B £68 (£105 single) pp per night*

Bryanston Court

56-60 Great Cumberland Place, W1H 8DD   01-262 3141

Close to Marble Arch, and well placed for Oxford Street shopping and Hyde Park, this smallish hotel is situated in an attractive and reasonably quiet street. Public rooms (lounge and bar) are decorated in a traditional Edwardian style – leather sofas and armchairs, oil paintings and muted colours – which creates a restful and clubby atmosphere. There's a small and pretty pink and red dining room (closed Sat and Sun) with a charcoal grill. Recently refurbished bedrooms (some small) are attractive in pastel shades, modern and well-equipped. Shower rooms tend to be tiny (only seven rooms have bath). The Bryanston Court has a sister hotel, the Concorde, with which it shares its public rooms.

Bedrooms: *54 (single, double, twin, family), 47 with shower, 7 with bath. Direct dial telephone, TV*
Facilities: *Lift*
Open: *All year. Restaurant closed Sat and Sun*
Credit/charge cards accepted: *Acces, Amex, Diners, Visa*
Price category: *£££*
Special rates: *Child's bed in parents' room £12. ★London Travel Service: 2 nights B&B £43.50-£49 pp per night including rail travel (worth it for long-distance travellers); child under 5 in parents' room free on break*

Cadogan Thistle

Sloane Street, SW1X 9SG   Tel: 01-235 7141

This hotel is ideally placed for Knightsbridge and King's Road shopping. It's made up of two late Victorian houses (though it's more likely to be referred to as Edwardian), one the former house of the notorious Lily Langtry. The new owners, the Scottish Thistle group, have restored it well to emphasise the Edwardian atmosphere – panelling, potted palms, swagged chintz drapes, and, of course, Lily Langtry memorabilia. The bar and dining room are attractive and relaxed, with classical background music; the lounge is oak panelled and comfortable. All is subdued and elegant. Bedrooms vary in size, though most are generously proportioned. They too are plushly refurbished in Edwardian themes, well equipped, with some real and reproduction mahogany antiques; some suffer from traffic noise. One of the 'Turret Rooms' was favoured by Oscar Wilde. The 'traditional English breakfast' can include lemon sole, finnan haddock, eggs Benedict, or minute steak and potatoes.

Bedrooms: *69 (single, double, twin, suites) all with bath and shower. Direct dial telephone, TV and in-house video, hairdryer, trouserpress, minibar*
Facilities: *Lift*
Restrictions: *No dogs. One floor reserved for non-smokers*
Open: *All year*
Credit/charge cards accepted: *Access, Amex, Diners, Visa*
Price category: *£££££*
Special rates: *★Highlife Breaks: 2 or more nights (must include a Friday, Saturday or Sunday) B&B £39-£43 (single £43); children under 14 in parents' room free on break*

Chesterfield

35 Charles Street, W1X 8lX   *Tel: 01-434 1771*

Sample gracious living just off Berkeley Square. In well-converted Georgian houses, this hotel has an atmosphere which belies its size. The public rooms are elegant – panelled library for clotted cream teas, clubby bar, restaurant and neighbouring glassed-in 'Terrace', rich in hanging plants. Bedrooms are comfortable, though not very large, with good floral fabrics; bathrooms are luxurious. During the week it caters for the executive businessman; at weekends, couples are encouraged to sample an 'English weekend in Mayfair', with champagne and chocolates, and in-house movies. It's understandably popular with North American visitors.

Bedrooms: *113 (single, double, twin, suite), all with bath. Direct dial telephone, TV and in-house video, hairdryer. Minibar in suites. Trouserpress on request*
Facilities: *Lifts*
Restrictions: *No dogs*
Open: *All year*
Credit/charge cards accepted: *Access, Amex, Diners, Visa*
Price category: *£££££*
Special rates: *Fri to Sun, 2 nights B&B, £39 (£50) pp per night. Children free in parents' room*

Claverley

14 Beaufort Gardens, SW3 1PS   *Tel: 01-589 8541*

Three minutes' walk from Harrods, off the Brompton Road, this is a well-maintained Victorian town house (actually two houses), with overflowing window boxes and shining brass handrail. Public rooms consist of a comfortable wood-panelled lounge with leather chesterfield sofas, another spacious and cosy seating area by the reception, and a simple and pleasant country-style breakfast room on the lower ground floor. Bedrooms are well decorated in pastels, with cottage-style spriggy wallpapers; there aren't always two armchairs, or two bedside lamps. Bathrooms are neat and simple. This is an excellent and good-value bed-and-breakfast hotel, very conveniently situated for museums and shopping.

Bedrooms: *36 (single, double, twin, family), 30 with bath or shower. Direct dial*

telephone, TV. Hairdryer on request
Facilities: *Lift*
Restrictions: *Dogs by arrangement*
Open: *All year*
Credit/charge cards accepted: *Visa*
Price category: ££
Special rates: *Child under 13 sharing parents' room free (including breakfast)*

Cranley Place

1 Cranley Place, SW7 3AB   *Tel: 01-589 7944*

In a quietish terrace off the Old Brompton Road, this is a pretty half-brick, half-painted house which has been under the present management for only a year or so. Staff are young and enthusiastic rather than polished and professional, and the atmosphere is consequently informal. Public rooms consist of a large front room which doubles as reception and lounge, and a breakfast room with one large table and a kitchen on one side. There's also a small paved garden, described in the brochure as 'cozy' (sic). Furniture is varied, mostly antique, and bedrooms – recently refurbished – are individually decorated and furnished, with thickly lined curtains and bedspreads in good fabrics, period features and interesting touches. Bathrooms are on the small side. This is a stylish little hotel of character, for people who don't need much in the way of comfortable public areas.

Bedrooms: *10 (double, twin), 6 with bath, 4 with shower. Direct dial telephone, TV. Hairdryer on request*
Restrictions: *No dogs*
Open: *All year*
Credit/charge cards accepted: *Access, Amex, Diners, Visa*
Price category: ££££-£££££
Special rates: *Child in parents' room free*

Dorset Square

39 Dorset Square, NW1 6QN   *Tel: 01-723 7874*

A fine Regency town house on a garden square (guests have access), near to Marylebone and Baker Street. Recently restored and opened (1985), it has been very tastefully decorated and furnished, giving the feel of an English country house. Public rooms – spacious drawing room, small lounge – are restful and pleasing, with comfortable sofas, chintz and flowers. There's an 'honesty' bar, from which guests help themselves to drinks. Bedrooms, too, are very well decorated and furnished, with chintz, rag-rolled paper, good carpets and many pleasing touches, including bathrobes. Bathrooms are marble, with very good quality fittings. The restaurant, under separate ownership, has a welcoming tea-room atmosphere, with pine and bamboo; it's less luxurious than the hotel itself. Staff are friendly and well trained. A very stylish hotel, very different from most in its price category.

Bedrooms: *47 (single, double, twin, suites), all with bath or shower. Direct dial telephone, TV, minibar, hairdryer*

Facilities: *Lift*
Restrictions: *No children under 12*
Open: *All year*
Credit/charge cards accepted: *Access, Amex, Visa*
Price category: ££££
Special rates: *Children in parents' room £25*

Ebury Court

26 Ebury Street, SW1W 0LU   *Tel: 01-730 8147*

At the edge of Belgravia, three minutes' walk from Victoria Station, this Victorian hotel has been run for over 50 years by Mrs Topham (her brother started it with one house, and over the years it has grown to five). The Ebury Club (temporary membership is available to hotel guests) uses the plush bar and an ex-conservatory (opening out to a York stone paved patio) as their club rooms. Hotel guests have the use of a small traditional sitting room area – Regency stripes and chintz – by the front door, and a basement dining room with rather eclectic décor and a '50s feel. The 'sandwich room' is a corridor to the bar, with TV; there's another TV room and seating area with writing desk. Bedrooms (with a large proportion of good-value singles) make good use of limited space. They do not have central heating (extra blankets in the cupboard) or TV (though you can rent one at £1 a night); but they are fresh and comfortable, in a gracious old-fashioned style. Few have private bathrooms. Breakfast in bed costs extra. Meals are straightforward – baked ham with madeira sauce, Scotch salmon, roast beef salad, apple crumble. This is a home-from-home for many country-based ex-Londoners, and it has a genteel charm all of its own. It won't suit those looking for modern sophistication.

Bedrooms: *38 (single, double, twin), 11 with bath. Direct dial telephone. TV available (£1)*
Facilities: *Lift. TV in lounge*
Restrictions: *Small dogs only. No children under 5 in restaurant*
Open: *All year*
Credit/charge cards accepted: *Access, Visa*
Price category: £££
Special rates: *Child's bed in parents' room £20*

Eccleston

Eccleston Square, SW1V 1PS   *Tel: 01-834 8042*

The Eccleston is a tidy 1900s building in a fairly quiet area close to Victoria Station and Belgravia. A friendly welcome takes the chill off the bland marble foyer; at one end is a cool spacious lounge area, at the other a cosier small bar. The blue and white restaurant is Italian in everything but décor, and fun. Bedrooms vary in size and are by no means stylish – some wear and tear suggests limits to the 1987 refurbishment – with pleasant colours and plain but adequate furniture. Good value for a central location.

Bedrooms: *107 (single, double, twin, family), 74 with bath or shower. Direct dial telephone, TV (pay for video), teamaking. Minibar in 'premier' rooms. Hairdryer on request*
Facilities: *Lift*
Restrictions: *No-smoking area in restaurant. Dogs by prior arrangement*
Open: *All year*
Credit/charge cards accepted: *Access, Amex, Diners, Visa*
Price category: *£££*
Special rates: *Children in parents' room £10. ★Superbreak, one or more nights B&B £29 (single £48.25 during week, £29 at weekends) pp per night (winter/spring price; more in summer); children under 16 in parents' room free on break*

Elizabeth

37 Eccleston Square, SW1   *Tel: 01-828 6812*

Very near to Victoria Station, off Buckingham Palace Road, this early 19th-century building houses an old-fashioned family-run B&B (unlicensed). Guests have the use of the mature gardens in the square, and of a tennis court. Public rooms consist of a pleasant lounge with wing chairs and chesterfield, TV, and magazines and travel books; and a basement breakfast room (no smoking here) with polished tables and dresser. Breakfast (English) is served between 8am and 9.30am. Bedrooms are old fashioned but not uncomfortable; only 7 have bath. A good-value, simple B&B

Bedrooms: *24 (single, double,twin, family), 7 with bath. Some rooms with TV and fridge*
Facilities: *Tennis*
Restrictions: *No dogs. No smoking in breakfast room*
Open: *All year*
Credit/charge cards accepted: *None*
Price category: *££*
Special rates: *Children under 4 in parents' room free*

Fielding

4 Broad Court, Bow Street, WC2B 5QZ   *Tel: 01-836 8305*

In the heart of Covent Garden, close to Bow Street police station, and just across the road from the Royal Opera House, this pleasant little hotel with shutters and window boxes is quietly situated in a pedestrianised lane. Bedrooms are simply decorated with spriggy cotton fabrics; all but one have a shower room (some rather small), but no bath. There is a small and basic basement dining room where breakfast is served, and a very small bar which doubles as a lounge. There's no lift. The atmosphere is homely and friendly.

Bedrooms *26 (single, double twin, family), 23 with shower, l with bath. Direct dial telephone, TV*
Facilities: *Babylistening*
Restrictions: *No dogs*

Open: *All year except Christmas*
Credit/charge cards accepted: *Access, Amex, Diners, Visa*
Price category: £££

The Gore
189 Queen's Gate, SW7 5EX   *Tel: 01-584 6601*

Just a stone's throw from the Albert Hall and Kensington Gardens, this small hotel has been decorated with great flair by its owners. All is splendidly maintained, outside and in, with masses of flowers and plants and shining brass. Walls have subtle paint effects in muted tones, there are paintings and interesting objects everywhere. The two very comfortable public rooms are the informal but stylish Coffee House, for breakfast and lunch (and dinner from Sunday to Friday nights), and a fine sitting room/bar, with deep sofas and dark green walls. Bedrooms have cane furniture and fine fabrics; they are well equipped and very comfortable, with good bath or shower rooms; a few are extra special.

Bedrooms: *54 (single, double, twin, family), 36 with bath, 18 with shower. Direct-dial telephone, TV, minibar, safe, hairdryer*
Facilities: *Lift. Babylistening*
Restrictions: *Dogs by prior arrangement*
Open: *All year. Coffee House closed Sat dinner*
Credit/charge cards accepted: *Access, Amex, Diners, Visa*
Price category: ££££
Special rates: *Child's bed in parents' room £15, cot £2 ★Best Western: autumn and winter, weekends 2 nights B&B £32.50 ('87/'88 rate)*

Goring
Beeston Place, SW1W 0JW   *Tel: 01-834 8211*

Near to Buckingham Palace and Victoria Station, sandwiched between very busy streets, The Goring looks out over a neat courtyard garden (sadly not accessible to guests), and its front rooms are double glazed. It would be hard to find a more solidly traditional hotel than this. Mr Goring's grandfather built it in 1910, and it was the first hotel in the world to have a private bathroom and central heating for each bedroom. The current Mr Goring confidently predicts that 'there will always a Mr Goring at The Goring to welcome you'. Certainly the owner's personal care and attention shows – all is impeccably maintained, staff are attentive, and nothing is too much trouble. It's all very English, quiet and subdued, and not lacking in any comfort; from the first step into the entrance, one is transported into a bygone era.

Bedrooms: *90 (single, double, twin, suite), all with bath. Direct dial telephone, TV, hairdryer*
Facilities: *Parking. Lift*
Restrictions: *No dogs*
Open: *All year*
Credit/charge cards accepted: *Access, Amex, Diners, Visa*
Price category: £££££
Special rates: *Child in parents' room £30*

Green Park

Half Moon Street, London W1Y 8DP　　　　　　　　*Tel: 01-629 7522*

Well situated in a quiet street just of Piccadilly, this stylish hotel has a comfortable lounge area off reception, a bar, and a very attractive Monet-inspired restaurant – with prints of the well-known paintings. Bedrooms are light, designer-decorated in pastel tones. Some have kingsize beds and whirlpool baths; 15 rooms are reserved for non-smokers.

Bedrooms: *160 (single, double, twin, family, suite), all with bath. Direct dial telephone, TV. Hairdryer, trouserpress*
Facilities: *Lifts*
Restrictions: *No dogs*
Open: *All year*
Credit/charge cards accepted: *Access, Amex, Diners, Visa*
Price category: ££££
Special rates: *Children under 18 in parents' room free. ★Gold Star: 1 night B&B £39 pp per night, £33.25 each extra night. £2.50 pp per night supplement June-Oct*

Hazlitt's

6 Frith Street, W1V 5TZ　　　　　　　　　　　　*Tel: 01-434 1771*

Indicative of the changing nature of London's former red-light district – now thoroughly rejuvenated, with well-regarded restaurants – this new hotel, in three early 18th-century terrace houses, is understated outside and in. Bedrooms are interesting and individual, without being luxurious, and many have original details such as fireplaces; there are pine washstands, Victorian baths with brass fittings, mahogany pieces and lots of prints; beds have duvets. There's a comfortable sitting room, but no bar or restaurant (breakfast is served in the bedroom). This is an atmospheric and good-value home from home – it doesn't really feel like a hotel – very near to the heart of theatreland.

Bedrooms: *23 (single, double, twin and suite), all with bath. Direct dial telephone, TV. Hairdryer on request*
Facilities: *Babylistening*
Restrictions: *No dogs*
Open: *All year except one week at Christmas*
Credit/charge cards accepted: *Access, Amex, Diners, Visa*
Price category: ££££
Special rates: *Children: £10 per bed, £5 per cot in parents' room*

Hospitality Inn

39 Coventry Street, W1V 8EL　　　　　　　　　　*Tel: 01-930 4033*

The situation may not suit everyone – just by Leicester Square and Piccadilly Circus – but it's plainly an advantage for some. This recently opened hotel has few public rooms (a basement dining room, and an airy reception/bar) but that's hardly the point in this area. Bedrooms – all in American walnut, with attractive furnishings and lamps – are very comfortable, and bathrooms are well equipped. One floor (out of seven) is reserved for non-smokers.

Bedrooms: *92 (single, double, twin), all with bath. Air conditioning, direct dial telephone, TV, in-house video, teamaking, hairdryer, trouserpress.*
Facilities: *Lifts*
Restrictions: *No dogs*
Open: *All year*
Credit/charge cards accepted: *Access, Amex, Diners, Visa*
Price category: *££££*
Special rates: *Thurs to Sat, 2 nights or more B&B £36.50 pp per night. Children under 16 in parents' room free*

Knightsbridge Green
159 Knightsbridge, SW1X 7PD   *Tel: 01-584 6274*

Right in the centre of Knightsbridge, near Hyde Park, this former Georgian coaching inn and 'gentlemen's chambers' is now a family-owned bed-and-breakfast hotel which has recently been refurbished, and offers surprisingly quiet and excellent value accommodation. Bedrooms (almost two-thirds are suites, with their own pretty sitting room) are spacious, well decorated – brass, chintz, good wardrobes; bathrooms are pristine. There's a first-floor 'club room', light and airy with pink sofas, newspapers and coffee percolator; and a small kitchen where you can make tea. Breakfast is served in the bedroom; the hotel is unlicensed. It's a thoroughly likeable and charming place, with friendly service and good housekeeping.

Bedrooms: *22 (single, double, twin, suites), all with bath and shower. Direct dial telephone, TV, teamaking. Hairdryer, trouserpress*
Facilities: *Lift*
Restrictions: *No dogs*
Open: *All year*
Credit/charge cards accepted: *Access, Amex, Visa*
Price category: *££££*
Special rates: *Child's bed in parents' room £12.50*

L'Hôtel
28 Basil Street, SW3 1AT   *Tel: 01-589 6286*

A well-situated town B&B (convenient for Knightsbridge shopping), prettily decorated in Franco/American rustic/folk art style (stencilled walls, French pine furniture, fabric wall coverings). Bedrooms are stylish and comfortable, though they vary in size; most have a gas coal-fire. The only public room is a basement wine bar/brasserie, open to non-residents, where breakfast is served; food here is way above that of the average wine bar, as it shares its kitchen with the highly rated Capital Hotel (same ownership).

Bedrooms: *12 (double, twin, suite), all with bath. Direct dial telephone, TV, minibar. Hairdryer on request*
Facilities: *Lift*

Open: *All year*
Credit/charge cards accepted: *Amex, Visa*
Price category: ££££
Special rates: *Children in parents' room £10*

Marlborough Crest

Bloomsbury Street, WC11B 3QD   *Tel: 01-636 5601*

This medium-sized hotel has recently been taken over by the Crest group, and is yet another of the London hotels that has been refurbished to 'recapture the gracious days' of the Edwardian era. Bedrooms, though standardised, do not lack charm and are very well decorated and comfortably furnished; bathrooms, too, are of good standard. Public areas are stylish: all wood, brass and prints. There's a brasserie with mirrored columns, potted palms, an art deco feel and good atmosphere; a cocktail bar (piano from 7pm except on Sunday) and a pub-style bar. The lounge area is by the reception, so not completely restful. The hotel is well situated for the British Museum, and theatreland.

Bedrooms: *169 (single, double, twin, family), all with bath. Direct dial telephone, TV (pay for video), minibar, teamaking. Hairdryer, trouserpress*
Facilities: *Lifts. Babylistening*
Restrictions: *No smoking on two bedroom floors*
Open: *All year*
Credit/charge cards accepted: *Access, Amex, Diners, Visa*
Price category: £££££
Special rates: *Weekends (must include a Friday, Saturday or Sunday night), 2 to 4 nights B&B £42 pp per night. One child in parents' room free*

Mountbatten

Seven Dials, WC2 9HD   *Tel: 01-836 4300*

Situated in something of a backwater, though very near to theatres and opera house, this member of the 'Edwardian Hotels' Group commemorates Lord Louis. Photos, a Mountbatten exhibition, the Burma Restaurant, Viceroy suite and Broadlands Drawing Room (with harp player) leave you in little doubt, as do the occasional viceregal decorative touches. All is peaceful and very comfortable; there's a choice of two bars, and snacks and tea are available in the deep carpeted drawing room, with its gas log fire. Bedrooms are very well appointed, with many mod cons.

Bedrooms: *127 (single, double, twin, suites), all with bath. Direct dial telephone, TV with satellite stations and video, hairdryer, trouserpress. Minibar in suites*
Facilities: *Lift*
Restrictions: *Dogs at manager's discretion*
Open: *All year*
Credit/charge cards accepted: *Access, Amex, Diners, Visa*
Price category: £££££
Special rates: *★Embassy Hushaway Breaks: 2 or more nights (must include a Fri, Sat or Sun) B&B £41 (winter/spring; more in summer); children under 16 in parents' room free on break*

Observatory House
37 Hornton Gardens, W8 7NS   *Tel: 01-937 1577*

In an attractive residential area near Kensington Church Street, Kensington Gardens and Kensington High Street, this Italianate late 19th-century brick building is impeccably maintained, with a very welcoming air. Inside, it has just been refurbished, with good quality carpets and furnishings, and all is bright and very pleasing. The only public room is a slightly formal basement breakfast room, airy and pretty, with sofas and low tables, which can be used as a lounge. Bedrooms are comfortable and well equipped. A good-value and pleasing B&B.

Bedrooms: *26 (single, double, twin, family), 2 with bath, 22 with shower. Direct dial telephone, TV, teamaking. Hairdryer, trouserpress, safe*
Restrictions: *No pets*
Open: *All year*
Credit/charge cards accepted: *Access, Amex, Diners, Visa*
Price category: *££*
Special rates: *Weekends, 2 nights B&B £23.50 (single £33.15) pp per night. Child in parents' room £14*

Plaza on Hyde Park
Lancaster Gate, W2 3NA   *01-262 5022*

This Victorian hotel occupies a corner position on the Bayswater Road, overlooking Hyde Park and close to Lancaster Gate tube station. It has recently been almost completely refurbished (and new parts are currently being added). Public rooms are open-plan, decorated in a smart modern style and pastel tones; the restaurant has a café atmosphere and murals depicting the 'golden age of Hyde Park'. Bedrooms are reasonably spacious, with co-ordinated and stylish décor; bathrooms tend to be small. This hotel offers very good value, particularly for long weekend stays.

Bedrooms: *350 (single, double, twin), all with bath. Direct dial telephone, TV with in-house video, teamaking. Hairdryer, trouserpress, teletext in 'executive' rooms*
Facilities: *Lifts*
Restrictions; *No dogs in public rooms. Some no-smoking tables in restaurant, and 60 no-smoking bedrooms*
Open: *All year*
Credit/charge cards accepted: *Access, Amex, Diners, Visa*
Price category: *££££*
Special rates: *Thurs to Sun, 2 nights (must include Sat), B&B £30 pp per night; additional Sunday, £12.50. Children under 16 free in parents' room (up to 4 children in their own room £5 per child per night)*

The Ritz

Piccadilly, W1V 9DG   *Tel: 01-493 8181*

The turn-of-the-century creation of César Ritz; the name itself conjures up the appropriate image. It's decorated throughout in the style of Louis XVI: opulent and grand, with ornate marble fireplaces and pillars, heavy chandeliers, mirrors and gold leaf decoration. Here is a chance to capture the atmosphere of a more gracious age, with a Palm Court and Sunday tea-dancing, cabaret over dinner, and fashion shows in the Long Gallery. You'll be required to dress the part, too, and jeans are 'not permitted in any public area'. Bedrooms are lavish, most still with the original brass beds. It's a fine place for a really special weekend break.

Bedrooms: *130 (single, double, twin, suite), all with bath. Direct dial telephone, TV with in-house video, minibar. Hairdryer in suites and deluxe rooms*
Facilities: *Lifts. Shops. Hairdresser/barber*
Restrictions: *No pets*
Open: *All year*
Credit/charge cards accepted: *Access, Amex, Diners, Visa*
Price category: *£££££*
Special rates: *Weekends, 2 or 3 nights B&B £75 pp per night*

Royal Court

Sloane Square, SW1W 8EG   *Tel: 01-730 9191*

Handy for the eponymous theatre and the King's Road, the Royal Court spans four 1890s houses beautifully re-designed in the 1980s. It is something of a rendezvous – locals appreciate the lively Tavern Bar (real ale), the good-value basement bistro and the tranquilly sophisticated restaurant called The Old Poodle Dog. The pale-panelled foyer lounge is comfortably spread with fawn velvet sofas under its chandeliers, and upstairs the linking corridors are a pleasure to walk. Bedrooms – each has a doorbell – are attractive ensembles of gentle colour, good lighting, elegant beds and shapely furniture. An enjoyable hotel: lively below, peaceful above, stylish throughout.

Bedrooms: *102 (single, double, twin, family, suites), all with bath or shower. Direct dial telephone, TV (with in-house video). Minibar, hairdryer, trouserpress in some rooms*
Facilities: *Parking for 6 cars. Lift*
Restrictions: *No dogs*
Open: *All year*
Price category: *£££££*
Special rates: *Weekends, 2 nights B&B £49.50, DB&B £67 pp per night; weekdays, 2 nights B&B £51, DB&B £68.50 pp per night. Reductions for children*

Royal Horseguards Thistle

Whitehall Court, SW1A 2EJ   *01-839 3400*

Part of a large, imposing Victorian Gothic building, set among offices and ministries and overlooking the Thames, the Royal Horseguards occupies what was once part of the Liberal Club. It is well placed for the major sights – Westminster, Buckingham Palace, the National Gallery – and theatres. Inside, the public rooms are undergoing refurbishments; the new look is stately and a little stark. There are ample public rooms. The restaurant is club-like, the theme emphasised by bookshelves; the bar has a jolly brasserie atmosphere, with marble-topped tables, mirrored ceiling and potted palms; the coffee shop leads into a terrace garden; and the split-level lounge is restful and refined. Bedrooms are of two types, standard and superior; they tend to be small. The 'superior' décor is traditional with chintz drapes and bedcovers; some have river views. Standard rooms may face into a well, with little natural light. Bathrooms, too, may be small. Two floors of bedrooms are reserved for non-smokers. This large hotel is a good option for people who want to be near the big sights, but don't mind some compromise on bedroom comfort.

Bedrooms: 287 (single, twin), all with bath. Direct dial telephone, TV (pay for video films), teamaking. Hairdryer, trouserpress
Facilities: Lifts. Babylistening
Restrictions: No dogs, except guide dogs
Open: All year
Credit/charge cards accepted: Access, Amex, Diners, Visa
Price category: ££££
Special rates: ★Highlife Breaks: 2 or more nights (must include a Fri, Sat or Sun) B&B £33-£41 pp per night; children under 14 sharing parents' room free on break

Waldorf
Aldwych, WC2B 4DD   *Tel: 01-836 2400*

Situated between Fleet Street and Covent Garden, this is a purpose-built 1908 hotel, now faithfully restored by Trusthouse Forte to bring out the best of its Edwardian features, particularly in the public areas. The *pièce de résistance* is the classic Palm Court, where tea dances take place on Friday, Saturday and Sunday; there's also a harmonious and elegant dining room with minstrel gallery, a Club Bar, and a recently added atmospheric French-style brasserie. Bedrooms vary in size and to some degree in style; the most recently refurbished play on an Edwardian theme, with appropriate bathware. Some bathrooms await their turn at refurbishment. The Waldorf is an excellent base for those who value copious and stylish public rooms.

Bedrooms: 310 (single, double, twin, family, suites), one with 4-poster, all with bath and shower. Direct dial telephone, TV, minibar. Hairdryer, trouserpress
Facilities: Lifts
Restrictions: Dogs at manager's discretion. Some no-smoking tables in brasserie; one floor of no-smoking bedrooms
Open: All year
Credit/charge cards accepted: Access, Amex, Diners, Visa
Price category: £££££
Special rates: Weekends (must include a Sat), 2 or more nights B&B £47 (single £59) pp per night. Children under 16 free in parents' room

Stakis St Ermin's

Caxton Street, SW1H 0QW   *Tel: 01-222 7888*

Close to parks and palaces and entered through a courtyard car park, this 1887 building (on a site once a chapel and nunnery) has a ground floor of Baroque magnificence, all balconies and balustrades and sumptuous ceilings. There are peaceful nooks and corners in the lounge area, piped music and mahogany in the big clubby bar, two vast and elegant restaurants (plus a light lounge menu). Bedrooms are well-appointed, with restful décor, some good city views and a pleasing attention to detail – the fruitbowl replenished daily. A comfortable hotel, big but friendly.

Bedrooms: *296 (single, double, twin, family), all with bath. Direct dial telephone, TV (with in-house video), teamaking, minibar. Hairdryer, trouserpress*
Facilities: *Parking, lifts*
Restrictions: *Dogs by arrangement*
Open: *All year*
Credit/charge cards accepted: *Access, Amex, Diners, Visa*
Price category: £££££
Special rates: *Weekends, 2 nights B&B £40 pp per night. Children under 16 sharing parents' room free*

Wilbraham

Wilbraham Place, Sloane Street, SW1X 9AE   *Tel: 01-730 8296*

An oasis of calm, the Wilbraham consists of two late Victorian houses in a small side street close to Sloane Square and Knightsbridge. It has been family-run since the war, and combines good old-fashioned comfort and a welcoming atmosphere with professional service. There's a small, light and airy lounge, and a bay-windowed buttery/bar with wood panelled walls and a clubby atmosphere. Breakfast (with fresh orange juice) is served only in the bedrooms. All is clean, comfortable and in good repair; not surprisingly, guests return again and again.

Bedrooms: *50 (single, double, twin), 38 with bath or shower. Direct dial telephone. TV and hairdryer on request*
Facilities: *Lifts. TV in lounge*
Restrictions: *No dogs in bedrooms*
Open: *All year. Restaurant and bar closed Sun and Bank Hols*
Credit/charge cards accepted: *None*
Price category: £££
Special rates: *Children in parents' room £10 (bed), £3 (cot)*

Norwich

- Enough to see and do for a weekend: a fine cathedral, good museums and some charming old streets with interesting old houses and churches – and good shops
- One of the better cities for a break in high summer – it is seldom overrun with tourists
- A city to suit keen theatre or concertgoers
- A disappointing range of hotels; accommodation is unlikely to be a major feature of your stay and modern chain hotels are as good as any

Norwich is well off the main tourist track, unsophisticated but not sleepy and offering some surprises to the newcomer. Its charms include quaint, twisting, sometimes steep and often cobbled streets with ancient houses. In addition there are some thirty medieval churches, a striking clue to the prosperity of the place in the 14th and 15th centuries, when the wool trade based there established Norwich as the commercial heart of East Anglia.

Norwich is more or less contained within a circle described by the remains of the old town walls and the course of the River Wensum to the north and east. Despite this the centre is confusing; there is a complex layout of streets (a legacy of their Saxon origin) and it is easy to lose your sense of direction. However, much of the pleasure of the place comes from pottering around the old streets with their mellow brick-and-timber cottages, their Georgian and Regency houses and their flint-faced Perpendicular churches, some floodlit at night. Of the many pretty streets cobbled Elm Hill, tiny Bridewell alley and elegant Colegate are the most deservedly famous. The Cathedral Close, hidden behind buildings bounded by old gateways, has a quiet, village-like atmosphere and gives good views of the soaring spire of the Cathedral.

All is not peaceful and picturesque however. Norwich is a busy commercial centre with many modern buildings and there is a lot of traffic in the streets which have not been pedestrianised. Parks and green spaces are limited. By Sunday, you may feel in need of an excursion to Blickling or the Broads.

Top sight

The Cathedral   Although Norman in origin (it was founded in 1096), the Cathedral has had much later decoration added. A particular feature is that the roofs of the nave and the cloisters are covered in gilded carved bosses (binoculars are essential to examine them in detail). Other points of interest include the carved stone vaulting, painted stonework, splendid stained glass, carved misericords in the choir and the beautiful semicircular east end.

Other sights

THE CASTLE
All that remains of the **Norwich Castle** is the ornate Norman keep (conspicuously well-preserved as it was refaced with Bath stone in 1834). Inside there are small displays of archaeology and arms and armour, and an exhibition relating to links between Norwich and the Continent. There are guided tours of the battlements (good views) and dungeons. The area south of the castle keep is now being excavated: visitors can watch an audio-visual display explaining the historical significance of the project. (*Open as Castle Museum, see below*)

HISTORIC BUILDINGS
The many historic buildings in Norwich are labelled with circular green plaques, giving their date and other information. They include the Georgian **Assembly House**, the medieval **Guildhall** (now the Tourist Information Centre), **Pulls Ferry** (an ancient watergate) and the remains of the 14th-century **city walls**.

MUSEUMS AND GALLERIES
Castle Museum   An exceptional range of paintings of the 19th-century Norwich School, plus pottery and porcelain (with a collection of some 600 teapots). There are also natural history galleries and sections on local history, geology and archaeology. [*Open all year, daily except Sun pm, Good Friday, Christmas and New Year*]
Bridewell Museum   A museum devoted to exhibits of local crafts and industries – a surprisingly diverse collection of skills very effectively shown (boat building, mustard making, clock making, brewing, printing and more). [*Open all year, daily except Sun and Bank Hols*]
Strangers Hall   A rambling house dating from 1320, added to

and remodelled over about 400 years. The rooms are decorated and furnished in various period styles, mostly corresponding to the age of each room itself. There are also exhibitions of toys and costumes. [*Open all year, daily except Sun and Bank Hols*]

On the western fringe of the city, on the campus of the University of East Anglia, is the highly regarded **Sainsbury Centre**, housing an intriguing collection of primitive, tribal and modern art, beautifully displayed in juxtaposition. There are also regular temporary exhibitions. [*Open all year, pm only, Tues to Sun except Bank Hols*]

CHURCHES

Norwich has many ancient churches, some of which are kept locked (their exteriors are worth at least a passing glance) or have been converted to other uses (including a museum, Scouts' hut, badminton hall, puppet theatre and antiques market).

Essential viewing is the lovely church of **St Peter Mancroft**, large and light in the Perpendicular style. The medieval church of **St Peter Hungate** has a fine hammerbeam roof with gilded angels and some 15th-century painted glass. It contains a small but appealing museum with illuminated religious books, church plate and other treasures.

Entertainment

Norwich has a good range of theatres for a city of its size, including the Theatre Royal, the Maddermarket theatre and the Da Silva puppet theatre. There are regular concerts and recitals in various historic buildings, notably the cathedral and the Assembly House.

Shopping

Norwich is a good town for shopping. Everyday needs are met by a range of chain and department stores and the large open market which forms the focal point of the town centre. The main shopping streets are London Street, one of the first in the country to be paved for pedestrians, and Pottergate. Visitors may be more interested in the many antiques, crafts and other specialist shops to be found in the narrow backstreets, also often closed to traffic. In Bridewell Alley is Colman's mustard shop (incorporating a small museum). Royal Arcade, a jolly piece of art nouveau town planning, is another attractive shopping street.

Getting around

Visitors staying south of the river will find it simpler to use the bus service than to tackle central Norwich by car – though there are many car parks. The centre is not very well-defined or compact but walking is probably the best way to explore it. There are guided tours (including some with themes) from the Tourist Information Centre during July to September, all lasting about 1½ hours. The Tourist Information Centre also supplies town trails, following streets of historic interest. Southern River Steamers offer one-hour boat trips along the attractive River Wensum from Foundry Bridge Quay (opposite the railway station) and from Elm Hill Quay. Traffic along the outer bank can mar the enjoyment.

Excursions

Beeston Hall, Beeston St Lawrence (11 miles north-east)   A flint Georgian house in 'Gothick' style with classical interiors containing family portraits and furniture. [*Open early April to mid Sep, Fri and Sun; also Wed in Aug, and Bank Hols pm*]
Norfolk Wildlife Park and Play Centre, Great Witchingham (12 miles north-west)   A huge collection of European mammals and birds in natural conditions, plus a play area for children. [*Open all year, daily*]
Blickling Hall, Blickling (16 miles north)   An exceptionally fine red brick Jacobean mansion with state rooms and 18th-century formal garden. (NT) [*Open April to Oct; daily except Mon (unless Bank Hol), Thur and Good Friday*]
Other houses and gardens in the area have limited opening dates and times.
Southern River Steamers offer 1- to 3-hour boat trips (April to September) to the network of rivers and small lakes known as **The Broads**. Alternatively, Wroxham (12 miles north-east) is a good centre from which to cruise the Broads. Cruises may include cream teas or conducted tours of a bird reserve.

When to go

Norwich is not over-crowded even in summer. The Royal Norfolk Show takes place at the end of June or beginning of July (one mile outside the city). The Lord Mayor's Procession, followed by entertainment and fireworks, is in mid July. The Norfolk and

Norwich Festival, a cultural festival with several themes, is held every third year in October (next in 1991). The best time to tour the Broads is in spring (for wildlife and lack of crowds) and early summer (May and June have the driest weather).

Information

The Tourist Information Centre, The Guildhall, Gaol Hill, Norwich, NR2 1NF; tel: (0603) 666071

Where to stay

The majority of hotels are relatively modern and designed for business travellers, and few are really central. One traditional (but much modernised) hotel is the main exception. There is a concentration of guesthouses in the area near the station and along the western approaches to the city, notably in Earlham Road and Unthank Road, both within a few minutes' walk of the centre.

NORWICH
The Beeches
6 Earlham Road, Norwich NR2 3DB   *Tel: (0603) 621167*

An enthusiastically run family hotel, on the edge of Norwich but quite well-placed for the centre. The family who took over the concern in 1984 have been gradually extending and improving it. The main house which is Georgian in style but dates from the mid-19th century, has quiet, freshly painted bedrooms with cheerful cotton duvets, and floral curtains. There is also a second, larger house where the family now lives. This is 'Plantation House', once Norwich's maternity home, set in suitably peaceful surroundings with an overgrown 'secret' garden. Plantation House has been converted to provide more bedrooms, all with bathrooms en suite. Bedrooms in a simpler annex building are more basic and mostly singles. In the main house the dining and breakfast room is sunny and light with white bentwood chairs, marble tables and views over the garden. The lounge has less charm and some traffic noise. A good base, especially for those who like to have a garden. Dinner is available from Monday to Thursday only; weekenders are offered a free buffet supper from 6pm-9pm.

Bedrooms: *20 bedrooms (single, double, twin and family) 12 with bath in 2 houses. Plus 12 without bath in annexe. TV, teamaking except in annexe*
Facilities: *Parking. Teamaking facilities in kitchen (24 hours)*
Restrictions: *No dogs*
Open: *All year except two weeks at Christmas*

Credit/charge cards accepted: *Access, Visa*
Price category: £
Special rates: *Children under 10 free in parents' room*

NORWICH
The Maids Head Hotel
Tombland, Norwich, Norfolk NR3 1LB   *Tel: (0603) 761111*

The Maids Head dates from 1272 and claims to be the oldest continuously operated hotel in the country. It is very much changed in character with a mixture of decorative styles: one bedroom, the Queen Elizabeth, and a tiny panelled bar are almost all that remain of the old coaching inn. The modern bedrooms at the back are generally smaller and quieter than the traditional bedrooms at the front, where furniture is old rather than antique. Little extras include fruit on arrival and newspapers. There are two restaurants: the stone-flagged courtyard carvery and the rather boudoir-like Georgian 'Minstrel' restaurant upstairs. There are also three bars and a lounge which is something of a passage; piped music in the public rooms can be irritating. The Maids Head is the most comfortable and convenient hotel in Norwich for a short break, close to the cathedral, shops and museums. Special interest weekends (Christian Heritage, Historical Houses, Norfolk Windmills, Gun-dog training) are a feature.

Bedrooms: *79 bedrooms (single, double, twin and family), 4 with 4-poster beds, all with bath or shower. Direct dial telephone, TV (with video), teamaking. Hairdryer, trouser press*
Facilities: *Parking, lift. Babylistening*
Open: *All year*
Credit/charge cards accepted: *Access, Amex, Diners, Visa*
Price category: £££
Special rates: *Weekends, 2 or 3 nights, DB&B £34-£36 (single £40-£42). Children under 14 free in parents' room*

Oxford

- A seat of learning since medieval times, with very fine colleges and university institutions, several designed by Wren
- Good for serious museumgoers but also for more lighthearted entertainment with plenty going on, especially during term-time
- The centre is usually too busy for leisurely pottering but the green areas surrounding the city are ideal for strolling, punting and picnicking
- A poor selection of hotels in the centre, but some excellent ones within striking distance
- Some very good restaurants
- Lots of scope for excursions; you could consider staying outside and visiting Oxford on a day trip

The romantic idea of Oxford as a city of 'dreaming spires' is far removed from the reality of a busy city with industrial outskirts. Here, to a great extent, 'town' takes precedence over 'gown', making Cambridge seem sleepy and provincial by comparison.

Yet escape the main roads and much of Oxford is unspoilt: lanes and alleys lead to ancient inns, courtyards and historic colleges, some with lovely gardens of their own, a few in open green settings or close to peaceful meadows or the river. Most of the interest is concentrated to the east of the Carfax crossroads, either side of the curving High Street which runs to Magdalen bridge. 'The High' is dominated by university buildings and colleges, some medieval, most in the familiar yellowish Cotswold stone. To the north is the monumental Radcliffe square with the classical domed Radcliffe Camera and beyond it the famous Bodleian Library; to the south Christ Church and the cluster of colleges in and around picturesque, cobbled Merton Lane. The Ashmolean Museum is only a short walk west of the busy Cornmarket street, housed in a splendid neo-classical building.

When traffic, noise and intensive sightseeing take their toll you can drift along the Cherwell in a punt and picnic in the meadows. And a short way away, you can visit Cotswold villages, cruise along the Thames or see Blenheim Palace, itself something of a tourist trap.

Top sights

Ashmolean Museum   Britain's oldest public museum is a vast and important collection basically comprising Asian and Mediterranean antiquities (ground floor) and European fine and decorative arts (first and second floors) – with some overlap. The great strengths of the museum include oriental porcelain, Islamic artefacts and coins, as well as Italian Renaissance paintings and works by the French Impressionists and English Pre-Raphaelites. Unusual treasures include such diverse objects as Guy Fawkes' lantern, a priceless Stradivarius violin, Henry VIII's stirrups and the robes of a North American Indian chief (most in the Trandescant Room, a 'closet of rarities' collected by the original founder in the 16th century). [*Open all year, Tues to Sat, and pm Sun and Bank Hol Mons*]

Christ Church   The grandest college, reflecting the pretensions of Cardinal Wolsey who founded it in 1525. It has the largest quadrangle in Oxford (Tom Quad). Tom Tower was designed by Wren and **Christ Church Cathedral**, the smallest cathedral in the country, heads a distinguished list of college chapels. **Christ Church Picture Gallery** contains important Old Master paintings and drawings, mostly Italian. The drawings, displayed in rotation, include works by Leonardo da Vinci and Michelangelo, Dürer and Van Dyck. The most famous painting is Carracci's *Butcher's Shop*. [*Open all year, Mon to Sat, and pm Sun*]

Other sights

COLLEGES AND UNIVERSITY BUILDINGS

Oxford has about 35 colleges of which about 20 are ancient and close to the city centre. You can normally wander around the courtyards (quadrangles or 'quads') and into the chapels; and you can sometimes peep into college dining halls. Opening times are displayed by the college gates; about half the colleges are open in the afternoons only. Apart from Christ Church, two colleges should be at the top of your list, especially if time is short:

Magdalen   Magdalen (pronounced 'Maudlin') has a lovely riverside setting with meadows and a deer park. The graceful Great Tower dominates the east end of the High Street. The oldest parts of the college date from the mid-15th century; between them stands a grand 18th-century building in formal grounds.

New College   Despite its name, one of the oldest colleges, founded in 1379. The castle-like buildings include a magnificent chapel with some good early stained glass and a statue of Lazarus by Jacob Epstein. Behind the 14th-century cloisters is a peaceful sunken garden, bounded by the ancient city wall.

Close to Christ Church are **Oriel** and, in a pretty cobbled lane parallel to the High Street, **Merton**, one of the oldest colleges in Oxford with a 14th-century quadrangle and a very old library, and tiny **Corpus Christi**. Back on the High are **Queen's**, an ultra classical building with an Italianate cupola designed by Hawksmoor, and **All Souls**, founded in 1438, with a quad also by Hawksmoor. **Trinity** and **St John's** are both rather like grand manor houses transported from the nearby Cotswolds, St John's with a very lovely garden. Other colleges worth seeing include **Brasenose**, with an ornate chapel roof; **Keble**, a riot of High Victorian fantasy with streaky-bacon brickwork; and the sleek modern **St Catherine's** where the Danish architect Arne Jacobsen designed everything down to the teaspoons. Some of the other colleges commemorate their famous students: Samuel Johnson at **Pembroke** (his teapot and a portrait by Reynolds), Shelley at **University College** ('Univ'); William Morris at **Exeter** where the chapel contains one of his tapestries; and John Wesley, the famous Methodist, at **Lincoln**, where his room is open to the public.

Two important university (as opposed to college) buildings are regularly opened to the public. The **Sheldonian Theatre** is a horseshoe-shaped building designed by the young Wren on the model of a Roman theatre; climb up to the cupola for a splendid view of Oxford's dreaming spires. At the **Bodleian Library** there are regular exhibitions of some of the rarest books and manuscripts. You can visit the main courtyard and the adjacent **Divinity School**, a 15th-century vaulted lecture room which houses a selection of treasured manuscripts. Another famous Oxford landmark – to be admired from the outside only – is James Gibbs' circular **Radcliffe Camera**, now a reading room for the Bodleian. The **Botanic Gardens**, the oldest in Britain (founded in 1621), which also belong to the University, are well worth a visit. **The Oxford Story** A new attraction (opened March 1988), The Oxford Story presents historical scenes in a series of effective tableaux – medieval to modern – complete with contemporary sounds and even a few smells. Visitors can listen to Alec Guinness's explanatory comments on a personal stereo.

MUSEUMS

Most of Oxford's museums belong to the university and there are some small museums for rather specialised interests. The other main museums are the **Museum of Oxford** with imaginative displays illustrating the history of the city, the **University**

Museum, devoted mainly to natural history displayed in an elaborate Victorian vaulted gallery, and the **Pitt-Rivers Museum** (anthropology and ethnography). The **History of Science Museum**, **The Bate Collection of Musical Instruments** and the **British Telecom Museum** are open from Monday to Friday only. The **Rotunda Museum** of antique dolls' houses is open only on Sunday afternoons May to September or by appointment.

CHURCHES
St Mary the Virgin, the university church (on 'the High'), is built in an intriguing mixture of ornate styles from Gothic to Baroque. The Saxon tower of **St Michael at the North Gate** is the oldest building in Oxford.

Shopping

In general, shopping in Oxford is much like shopping in any other busy town, with the usual High Street shops and chain stores. Two Oxford institutions are the covered central market, open Monday to Saturday and known for its cafés, and Frank Cooper's original shop, selling the famous Oxford marmalade, with a small museum. Bookshops of course are plentiful – notably Blackwell's in Broad Street, one of the largest in the world.

Getting around

The main sights of Oxford are within fairly easy walking distance of each other and you won't really need a car. Motorists from hotels outside Oxford can use the free 'Park and Ride' car parks on the edge of the city (with frequent bus services to the centre); parking in the city centre is very restricted. Local buses can be used for excursions (there are regular buses from Cornmarket to Blenheim).

The Oxford Information Centre organises various daily walking tours from Easter to October and can provide details of sightseeing tours by bus (some open-top). From May to September bus tours can be combined with a river cruise.

Like Cambridge, Oxford has made punting part of its culture. You can hire punts (and other boats) at Folly Bridge on the Thames – known in Oxford as the Isis – and at Magdalen Bridge and Cherwell boathouse (a good starting point) on the Cherwell. A deposit is required.

Excursions

Salter's organise boat trips along the Thames throughout the summer. (See also 'The Thames Valley' chapter).

Blenheim Palace (8 miles north) Grandiose home of the Dukes of Marlborough and birthplace of Winston Churchill. Built by Vanbrugh to commemorate the first Duke's victory at the Battle of Blenheim, the palace contains magnificent state rooms with fine paintings and furniture. There is an exhibition of 'Churchilliana'. In the park, landscaped by Capability Brown, is an adventure play area and butterfly house, reached by narrow gauge railway. [*House open mid Mar to Oct, daily*]

North Leigh Roman Villa (9 miles west) The remains of a Roman villa including a fine mosaic patterned floor. [*Open April to Sep, daily except Sun am, Thurs, and alternate Fridays*]

Rousham House (12 miles north) Much less commercial than Blenheim, Rousham is famous for the lovely landscaped garden by William Kent, which includes cascades, temples, contrived vistas and a false 'ruin'. Kent also made some alterations to the house (which dates from 1635) and decorated some of the rooms. [*House open April to Sep, pm only, Wed, Sun and Bank Hol Mons*]

Minster Lovell (17 miles west) Romantic riverside ruins of a large 15th-century manor with a medieval dovecote. [*Open all year, daily except Sun am, Christmas and New Year*]

Gardens worth visiting include **Waterperry Gardens**, 9 miles east [*open all year, daily except Sun am, Christmas and New Year*] and **Pusey House Gardens**, 12 miles west [*open April to Oct, pm only, Tues to Thurs, weekends and Bank Hol Mons*]

When to go

Throughout university term time and during summer there's plenty in the way of plays and concerts. Annual events include the Torpids, inter-collegiate boat races, in February; Eights Week (more boat races) at the end of March; May Day celebrations; and St Giles' Fair in early September. July and August are usually crowded with foreign tourists. *This Month in Oxford* gives details of events, entertainment and current opening hours.

Information

The Oxford Information Centre, St Aldgate's, Oxford OX1 1DY; tel: (0865) 726871

Thames and Chilterns Tourist Board, The Mount House, Church Green, Whitney, Oxon OX8 6D2; tel: (0993) 778800 (information on the surrounding countryside)

Where to stay

Oxford has several reasonable city hotels, but no very charming small ones and we thought the range poor for a place of this size and importance. Guesthouses are cheap but very few are central. It's worth considering staying outside Oxford, perhaps at Woodstock.

GREAT MILTON
Le Manoir aux Quat' Saisons
Great Milton, Oxfordshire, OX9 7PD   *Tel: (08446) 8881*

Dating from the 14th century, Raymond Blanc's magnificent manor is in a world of its own. A harmonious blend of grey and yellow stone with mullioned windows, the house is set in 27 acres of beautifully maintained grounds. The atmosphere throughout is sedate and comfortable, neither stuffy nor informal. Attention to every detail has made the bedrooms unusually gracious and comfortable (although they vary in size), with extravagant use of chintz fabrics, large beds and many square pillows, some lovely antiques, a sizeable sofa and three sorts of coathanger; the wide range of goodies includes a decanter of madeira, fresh fruit and flowers daily. There is no bar but guests may be served drinks wherever they choose. The two sitting rooms are stylishly decorated with lots of inviting sofas and chairs, oil paintings, antiques and open fires. Outside, the splendid grounds include a stable yard, a herb garden (14 different kinds of mint), an extensive vegetable garden and a water garden. Raymond Blanc's cooking is legendary (this has been among the top restaurants in *The Good Food Guide* for several years), and this is a superlative and secluded place in which to forget the outside world. It doesn't, of course, come cheap.

Location: *On Church Road, off A329*
Bedrooms: *10 (double, twin, suite), 2 with 4-posters, 2 with jacuzzis, all with bath. Direct dial telephone, TV, hairdryer*
Facilities: *Parking. Swimming pool, tennis court, riding*
Restrictions: *No children under 7 in restaurant. No smoking in restaurant. Dogs in kennels and on leads in garden*
Open: *Last week in Jan-mid Dec*
Credit/charge cards accepted: *Access, Amex, Diners, Visa*
Price category: *£££££*
Special rates: *Oct to April, midweek, 2 or more nights DB&B £80 pp per night. Children in parents' room £40*

HORTON-CUM-STUDLEY
Studley Priory
Horton-cum-Studley, Oxford OX9 1AZ   *Tel: (086 735) 203/254*

A long private drive leads to this fine Elizabethan building overlooking pasture. The house dates from the 12th century and is steeped in history. With much of its architectural detail intact, the hall makes a fine seating area with an open fireplace and an impressive panelled ceiling; the windows have stained glass coats of arms. This and the lounge have both been recently decorated with a bold scheme of cream, blue and maroon, and provide comfortable seating (there are books and magazines). Although the bar retains its fine oak panelling and the restaurant its beamed ceiling, both would benefit from similar redecoration. Bedrooms vary in size and décor from the rather basic to the reasonably comfortable. With 13 acres of rather neglected (erstwhile formal) gardens and grounds, tranquillity is assured.

Location: *7 miles out of Oxford, about 3 ½ from A40*
Bedrooms: *19 (single, double, twin, suite), 1 with four-poster, all with bath/shower. Direct dial telephone, TV, teamaking*
Facilities: *Parking. Grass tennis court, croquet. Clay pigeon shooting for parties of more than 10*
Open: *All year except one week in Jan*
Credit/charge cards accepted: *Access, Amex, Diners, Visa*
Terms: £££
Special rates: *Children sharing parents' room £11 per bed, £3 per cot*

OXFORD
Eastgate Hotel
The High, Oxford, OX1 4BR   *Tel: (0865) 248244*

Part Cotswold stone, part rendered, with stone mullions and leaded lights, this hotel was built at the turn of the century. The traditional pub – wood panelled bar with books above it – is at the High Street end; the back of the hotel extends along Merton Street and is reasonably quiet. The entrance hall (gas log fire) and restaurant (including carvery) are pleasantly decorated with attractive fabrics; the piped music seems unnecessary. The lounge is small with no natural light. Upstairs are a lot of steps and levels and bedrooms which are well, if not extravagantly, decorated, again using fine fabrics. A good central location with the advantage of a car park.

Location: *Just off the High Street in centre of Oxford*
Bedrooms: *42 (single, double, twin), 1 with 4-poster, all with bath/shower. Direct dial telephone, TV, teamaking. Hairdryer on request*
Facilities: *Parking. Babylistening*
Open: *All year*
Credit/charge cards accepted: *Access, Amex, Diners, Visa*
Price category: ££££
Special rates: *Weekends, 2 nights DB&B £42 (£47) pp per night. Children in parents' room free. Children under 16 in own room 25% discount*

OXFORD
The Randolph Hotel
Beaumont Street, Oxford OX1 2LN   *Tel: (0865) 247481*

This hotel is something of an Oxford institution, a sturdy Victorian Gothic building (recently cleaned) opposite the Ashmolean Museum. Bedrooms (could be noisy but for the double glazing) are adequately comfortable, with co-ordinated use of fabrics. The public rooms (due for extensive refurbishment) are a little impersonal. Osbert Lancaster's illustrations for *Zuleika Dobson* are displayed in the traditional dining room – a light room with panelled walls and a piano. The unimaginative arrangement of furniture in the lounge is partly compensated for by the panelled bar with vaulted ceiling and fine carved stone fireplace. The splendid entrance hall has a great staircase and maintains its original Victorian Gothic features. This hotel provides solid accommodation in a central location.

Bedrooms: *109 (single, double, twin, suites), all with bath. Direct dial telephone, TV, teamaking. Mini bar in suites. Hairdryer, trouserpress in some rooms and suites*
Facilities: *Parking. Babylistening*
Open: *All year*
Credit/charge cards accepted: *Access, Amex, Diners, Visa*
Price category: *££££*
Special rates: *April to Oct, 2 nights DB&B £44-£46 (single £49-£51) pp per night. Children in parents' room free. Children in own room 25% discount*

OXFORD
Willow Reaches
1 Wytham Street, Oxford OX1 4SU   *Tel: (0865) 721545*

This guesthouse is a white-painted Edwardian building, quietly situated about seven minutes' drive from the centre of Oxford. Clean and simple accommodation is provided: little is co-ordinated, but it doesn't really matter. A TV lounge downstairs with leather patchwork chairs doubles up as a bar with drinks dispensed over a stable door. Down some steps is the dining room with deep pile carpet, exposed brickwork and plain wooden furniture. Here guests may choose from a limited but varied menu and the wine list is unexpectedly extensive. Outside is a long garden with a rockery and small pond. A good little unpretentious guesthouse.

Bedrooms: *9 (single, double, twin, family), 4 with bath/shower. Direct dial telephone, TV, teamaking. Hairdryer on request*
Facilities: *1 garage. Video library*
Restrictions: *No dogs*
Open: *All year*
Credit/charge cards accepted: *Amex, Diners, Visa*
Price category: *£*
Special rates: *Weekends, 2 nights B&B £18 pp per night. Children under 4 in parents' room £4; children in family room £10*

STANTON HARCOURT
The Harcourt Arms
Stanton Harcourt, Oxfordshire OX8 1RJ   *Tel: (0865) 881931*

A creeper-covered, Cotswold stone pub in a quiet village setting with comfortable accommodation in a separate cottage-style building a short distance from the pub. Bedrooms are cosy and decorated in a mixture of styles; there is an appealing disregard for co-ordination. The pub dining room seats a great many in interconnecting rooms. With a beamed ceiling, Windsor chairs, lots of pictures, and a rare inglenook fireplace with smoking oven, it is a cosy place. Fish and steaks are the specialities and the jokey wine list debunks any stuffy approach to drinking. Informal, enjoyable and welcoming.

Location: *On main road through the village*
Bedrooms: *9 (single, double, twin), all with bath. Direct dial telephone, TV, teamaking*
Facilities: *Parking*
Restrictions: *No dogs in bedrooms*
Open: *All year except Christmas Day*
Credit/charge cards accepted: *Access, Amex, Diners, Visa*
Price category: *££*
Special rates: *Weekends, 2 nights B&B (and reduction of £9 on dinner) £29.50 pp per night. Reductions negotiable for children in parents' room*

WESTON-ON-THE-GREEN
Weston Manor
Weston-on-the-Green, Oxfordshire OX6 8QL   *Tel: (0869) 50621*

A large Elizabethan/Victorian Cotswold stone hall, set well back from the road and surrounded by 13 acres of formal and rough gardens. The bedrooms, many of which are in the recently converted coach house away from the main building, are comfortably furnished – mainly with reproduction furniture and co-ordinated fabrics – but the result is a little impersonal. The fine dining room with panelling, a minstrels' gallery and a vaulted and beamed ceiling is let down by a dull arrangement of tables and 'function' chairs; but candles on the tables add a warmer touch. The lounge on the first floor suffers from strip lighting, and although there is a bar on the ground floor (due for refurbishment), guests tend to use the main hall. This is large and impressive with fine plasterwork, corniced ceiling and a welcome open fire. A fine building with good facilities and a secluded setting.

Location: *8-9 miles north of Oxford, on A43*
Bedrooms: *37 (double, twin, suite), 2 with 4-posters, 14 in Coach House, all with bath. Direct dial telephone, TV, mini-bar, teamaking. Trouser press and hairdryer in Coach House rooms*
Facilities: *Parking. Squash court. Swimming pool, croquet, clay pigeon shooting, fishing. Babylistening*
Restrictions: *No dogs. No smoking in bedrooms*
Open: *All year*

Credit/charge cards accepted: *Access, Amex, Diners, Visa*
Price category: £££
Special rates: *2 nights DB&B £38.75 pp per night. Children under 16 free in parents' room*

WOODSTOCK
The Feathers Hotel
Market Street, Woodstock, Oxfordshire   *Tel: (0993) 812291*

Predominantly 17th-century and situated in the centre of Woodstock, this is a charming hotel with an unforced approach to elegance and hospitality. Bedrooms (those at the front could be noisy) are individually furnished and decorated with pleasant fabrics and antique furniture. Even the smaller rooms have an airy brightness and extra touches include books, magazines and fresh flowers. Spread over three buildings, the inside is on different levels, off an unusual staircase. Fresh flowers are arranged with real flair in the public rooms, which manage to combine cosiness with elegance. There is a panelled drawing room with an open fire and lots of books, and a 'morning room'. The bar has antiques and collections of stuffed birds and animals. Outside is a pretty walled garden with teak furniture. A delightful and naturally welcoming hotel – fresh and bright and comfortable.

Bedrooms: *16 (single, double, twin), all with bath. Direct dial telephone, TV*
Open: *All year*
Credit/charge cards accepted: *Access, Amex, Diners, Visa*
Price category: £££
Special rates: *Nov to Mar, 2 nights DB&B £42.50-£52.50 pp per night. Children in parents' room £10*

Prices are for b&b per person, sharing a double/twin room with bath	
£	= You can expect to pay under £20
££	= You can expect to pay between £20 and £30
£££	= You can expect to pay between £30 and £40
££££	= You can expect to pay between £40 and £55
£££££	= You can expect to pay over £55

Stratford-upon-Avon

- Stratford is right in the centre of England and makes a good weekend break from most places. But it is very touristy
- The main if not the sole reason for coming here is to go to the Royal Shakespeare Theatre, or at least visit the Bard's birthplace. A good place to take older children
- Special weekend-break deals including rail fares and theatre tickets as well as meals and hotels make Stratford a labour-saving 'package' weekend
- If you are without a car, you can see some of the countryside and visit some of the sights outside Stratford on a guided coach tour
- There's plenty of accommodation of all types

A small prosperous market town, known principally as the birthplace of our greatest playwright, Stratford is a place of pilgrimage for every self-respecting Englishman and theatre-goer. But it is also an interesting town in its own right, with a great concentration of well-preserved historic buildings, notably Tudor timber-framed houses. Stratford makes a good base for touring the surrounding countryside, and there are several fine stately homes and castles within easy reach. Punts, canoes and rowing boats can be hired for trips on the Avon.

SHAKESPEARE

Several properties associated with Shakespeare and his family can be visited. The most famous is **Shakespeare's birthplace**, a half-timbered house with contemporary furniture and an small exhibition, where Shakespeare was born in 1564. Also in Stratford are **New Place** (or Nash's House), site of Shakespeare's retirement and death in 1616; and **Hall's Croft**, his daughter's house. Both have contemporary furniture and fine Elizabethan gardens. Just outside Stratford at Shottery (1 mile, signposted footpath) is **Anne Hathaway's Cottage**, picturesque home of Shakespeare's wife; and at Wilmcote (3 miles) **Mary Arden's House**, home of his mother, with a small countryside museum. Combined tickets for all the properties can be bought from the Shakespeare Birthplace Trust in Church Street and coach tours of all five properties can be booked locally.

The World Of Shakespeare is a 25-minute sound and light presentation covering aspects of life in Shakespearean England with tableaux illustrating a Royal progress, bear baiting, the Plague etc.

The Royal Shakespeare Company has three theatres in Stratford. There are regular backstage tours of the main **Royal Shakespeare Theatre**, lasting 45 minutes. The RSC collection (theatre portraits, props and memorabilia) is in the new **Swan Theatre**.

FAMILY OUTINGS

There are two museums in the centre of Stratford: the **Arms and Armour Museum** and the **Motor Museum** (vintage cars of the '20s and '30s).

The **Stratford Brass Rubbing Centre** and the **Butterfly Farm** (hundreds of different species in a jungle setting) provide alternative entertainment.

EXCURSIONS

Charlecote House (5 miles east)   An Elizabethan house with mainly Victorian interior. (NT) [*Open Apr to Oct daily except Mon and Thurs; open Bank Hol Mons, closed Good Friday*]

Warwick Castle (8 miles north-east)   An impressive early castle on the edge of medieval Warwick, overlooking the Avon. The 17th- and 18th-century State Rooms contain a fine collection of pictures and furniture. Other attractions include the torture chamber (with gruesome exhibits), the armoury, dungeons and Ghost Tower. The castle now belongs to Madame Tussaud's and there is a waxwork recreation of 'A Royal Weekend Party' in 1898 in the Victorian private apartments. [*Open daily all year*]

Ragley Hall, Alcester (9 miles west)   Fine 17th-century house with magnificent Baroque plasterwork in the Great Hall. The park, landscaped by Capability Brown, now has an adventure wood, maze and country trail. [*Open April to Sep, daily except Mon and Fri; open Bank Hol Mons*]

Upton House, nr Banbury (10 miles south-east)   Fine collections of old master paintings and porcelain, and lovely gardens. [*Open pm only: May to Sep, Sat to Wed; April and Oct, Sat, Sun and Bank Hol Mon*]

Coughton Court, nr Alcester (11 miles west)   Historic house with Catholic associations; fine furniture and family portraits. [*Open pm only: May to Sep, daily except Mon and Fri; April and Oct, weekends plus Easter Mon to following Thurs*]

Getting around

There is ample parking space in the centre, including two big car parks in Rother Street. Stratford is small enough to explore comfortably on foot, but there are guided bus tours of the town and its outlying sights (some on open double-deckers) and bus tours to nearby stately homes (see 'Information' below).

When to go

Stratford is extremely popular with overseas tourists and it is advisable to avoid summer crowds. The season of the Royal Shakespeare Company lasts from April until the end of January. On 23rd April there are celebrations to commemorate Shakespeare's birthday. The Stratford Festival (carnival, firework displays, poetry readings etc) takes place in the second half of July.

Information

The Heart of England Tourist Board, Old Bank House, Bank Street, Worcester WR1 2EW; tel: (0905) 613132

Guide Friday (Stratford Centre of Tourism), Civic Hall, The Market Place, 14/15 Rother Street, Stratford-upon-Avon, CV37 6LU; tel: (0789) 294466 (guided tours)

The Box Office, Royal Shakespeare Theatre, Stratford-upon-Avon, Warwickshire, CV37 6BB; tel: (0789) 295623 (tickets for performances at the Royal Shakespeare Theatre, the Swan or The Other Place; enclose large s.a.e.); (0789) 414999 (bookings for 'stop-over' packages – see below); (0789) 296655 (back stage tours). Telephone (0789) 69191 for 24-hour ticket availability information

The Shakespeare Connection; tel: (0789) 294466 (a 'Guide Friday' coach connects at Coventry with trains from London. The last departure from Stratford is after the theatre performance)

Stratford-upon-Avon Festival; tel: (0789) 67969

Where to stay

Stratford has a very good range of accommodation of all types, with a total number of hotels and guesthouses quite out of proportion to its size. They include some grand establishments set in parkland just outside the town, several old timbered inns in the centre, and plenty of guesthouses, particularly along the Shipston Road.

The Royal Shakespeare Company organises 'Stop-over' packages with accommodation (in a choice of 18 hotels and guesthouses), discounted rail fares and theatre tickets. Accommodation is for one night, but an extra night's stay with dinner and breakfast can be arranged (with payment direct to the hotel); for details telephone (0789) 414999. The packages are divided into various categories: luxury, deluxe, A, B and C. Accommodation in package C does not include private facilities. All hotels offer free accommodation for children under 14 sharing their parents' room, and some will arrange babysitting on request.

STRATFORD-UPON-AVON
Caterham House
58/59 Rothers Street, Stratford, Warwickshire CV37 6LT   *Tel: (0789) 67309*

A delightful B&B/guesthouse in two knocked-through Georgian houses about five minutes' walk from the theatre. Although on a moderately busy road, many bedrooms are at the back of the house and quiet. They are charmingly decorated in rustic style with brass bedsteads, white cotton bedspreads and pine furniture; magazines add to the homely touches. Only two have their own shower; nine others share two bath/shower rooms. The breakfast room is welcoming, with stone flagged floor and rugs and two big tables for communal eating. A comfy sitting room, with rich yellow walls and a rather heavy three-piece suite, also houses the TV. The whole place has a friendly and inviting feel and is decorated with flair and simplicity; it's run by a Frenchman and his English wife. It is heartening to find such good-value accommodation so near to the theatre.

Bedrooms: *13 (double, twin, family), 2 in annexe, 2 with shower*
Facilities: *Parking. TV in lounge*
Open: *All year except a few days over Christmas*
Credit/charge cards accepted: *None*
Price category: £
Special rates: *Children under 10 in parents' room, half price*

STRATFORD-UPON-AVON
The Shakespeare
Chapel Street, Stratford, Warwickshire CV37 6ER   *Tel: (0789) 294771*

In the centre of town, this ancient black-and-white and much-gabled building dates from 1637. Trusthouse Forte have given it the familiar ingredients – a refined house style which includes comfortable bedrooms – but it's the building itself which provides the charm; there are beams everywhere, and a maze of passages upstairs. The restaurant is pleasantly decorated with chintzy curtains and orange upholstery, and a more pub-like bar serves snacks. The lounge is made up of a series of interconnecting areas with a large fireplace and comfortable chairs. Nothing can detract from the historic appeal of the building and its central location.

Bedrooms: *70 (single, double, twin, suite), 2 with four-posters, all with bath. Direct dial telephone. TV, teamaking. Hairdryer. Iron on request*
Facilities: *Parking. Lift*
Restrictions: *No dogs in restaurant*
Open: *All year*
Credit/charge cards accepted: *Access, Amex, Diners, Visa*
Price category: *££££*
Special rates: *Weekends, 2 nights (must include Sat) DB&B £48-£56 (£54) pp per night. Children under 14 free in parents' room, under 16 in own room, 75% of adult rate*

STRATFORD-UPON-AVON
Stratford House
Sheep Street, Stratford, Warwickshire, CV37 6EF   *Tel: (0789) 68288*

This small hotel is a town house behind a pretty red brick façade of Georgian appearance. The obvious advantage of its proximity to the theatre compensates for the lack of car parking (although strictly limited space is available by arrangement). There is a small rear garden. Bedrooms at the front are noisy (but double glazed); others are in the extension leading away from the road. Mostly quite small, they have painted or sprig-patterned paper, cottagey fabrics, simple furniture, and duvets. The room with the most character is in the attic, right up in the beams. The serviceable lounge provides adequate seating, while the restaurant is part conservatory, with cane and wicker furniture and trailing plants. Run as a separate establishment, it doubles as the breakfast room.

Bedrooms: *10 (double, twin, family), all with bath/shower. Direct dial telephone, TV, teamaking. Hairdryer and iron on request*
Facilities: *Some parking at nearby hotel*
Restrictions: *No dogs*
Open: *All year except 4 days at Christmas*
Credit/charge cards accepted: *Access, Amex, Diners, Visa*
Price category: *£££*
Special rates: *Winter, 2 nights DB&B £37.50-£40 pp per night. Children under 10 in parents' room £10*

STRATFORD-UPON-AVON
Welcombe
Warwick Road, Stratford, Warwickshire CV37 0NR   *Tel: (0789) 295252*

This vast, red brick Jacobean-style hotel was built in 1869; since 1983 it has been owned by Venice Simplon (they of the Orient Express), whose careful and extensive refurbishment results in a luxury establishment. Approached via a half-mile drive, it is surrounded by 153 acres of undulating parkland including a golf course. Public rooms are especially grand with panelled walls, huge marble mantelpieces and close attention to detail – to the extent that the pattern of the lounge carpet mirrors the plasterwork ceiling. Lots of tangerine-coloured sofas and contrasting chairs in the lounge give way to starker seating in the Trevelyan Terrace, which has Victorian décor, a piano and a large covered bar. The sumptuousness of the dining room is marred slightly by tables set rather close to each other, but it is a fine room with lovely views down the valley and golf course. A few of the old-fashioned bedrooms were due for refurbishment when we inspected; the redecorated style is grand, with antiques, chintzy fabrics and sophisticated co-ordinated schemes. This is a splendid hotel in the traditional manner, with staff at every turn to pamper guests. Lap up the luxury.

Bedrooms: *79 (single, double, twin, suites), 4 with four-poster, all with bath. Direct dial telephone. TV, teamaking. Hairdryer, trouser press*
Facilities: *Parking. Snooker, table tennis, darts in games room. Croquet, golf. Babylistening*
Restrictions: *Dogs in bedrooms only*
Open: *All year except over New Year*
Credit/charge cards accepted: *Access, Amex, Diners, Visa*
Price category: ££££
Special rates: *Weekends, 2 or more nights, DB&B £55 (single £60) pp per night, including golf*

Prices are for b&b per person, sharing a double/twin room with bath	
£	= You can expect to pay under £20
££	= You can expect to pay between £20 and £30
£££	= You can expect to pay between £30 and £40
££££	= You can expect to pay between £40 and £55
£££££	= You can expect to pay over £55

York

- A great all-rounder for all ages, with plenty to see and do, rain or shine, including two major cultural festivals in summer
- There's a wide choice of accommodation, from homely guest-houses to elegant Georgian town house hotels
- A good place for pottering: pedestrian streets with pretty old houses, enticing shops and tearooms galore
- The chief snag of visiting York is that it is firmly on the international tourist track, and very crowded in summer

York is a city of great charm and character, with much evidence of layers of history: Roman foundations and Viking street names, medieval walls and buildings – including the mighty Minster – and red brick Georgian town houses. Although much expanded, within the walls the city retains its compact medieval scale. Around the Minster is an area of narrow crooked lanes and well-preserved old streets (closed to traffic) lined with picturesque houses and shops; see the Shambles, a narrow lane where the overhanging upper storeys of the houses almost meet in the middle. There are plenty of tearooms where you can restore aching feet and revive energies. You can walk round the remains of the walls with their gateways (known as 'bars') or amble by the slow-flowing River Ouse.

There are several sights which should not be missed – from the spectacular Minster itself to some excellent museums which would be well worth a special journey on their own merits. There is plenty to occupy even the most voracious sightseer for a weekend; if you have any extra time there are several important country houses to visit near the rolling countryside of the Howardian hills.

Top sights

York Minster   A magnificent Gothic cathedral, largest of its kind in England. Among the many points of interest are the outstanding stained glass dating from 1150, the painted roof of the nave, the carved stone choir screen and the early Norman crypt (containing modern paintings of ancient northern saints).

Sightseeing is restricted during services (there are five services on Sundays).

The chapter house has a beautiful soaring painted ceiling and a display of new and restored and damaged bosses from the 1984 fire. In the undercroft (below the cathedral) you can see the huge new concrete foundations, along with remains of earlier buildings found during the excavations – a bewildering array of masonry from almost every century since Roman times.

✿ **Jorvik Viking Centre** *Holiday Which? Weekend Break Award* Not so much a museum as an experience, the Jorvik Viking Centre aims to bring archaeology to life. Visitors are transported in special 'time cars' through reconstructions of Viking life, complete with sounds and smells. At the end of the tour you can wander through the site of the excavation of Coppergate itself. Currently one of the most popular tourist sights in the country – you will probably have to queue. [*Open all year, daily*]

Other sights

HISTORIC BUILDINGS

Fairfax House An 18th-century aristocratic townhouse, recently restored and opened to the public. The elegant interior makes a fitting home for the very fine Terry Collection of Georgian furniture, clocks and carpets. [*Open Mar to Dec, daily except Sun am and Fri*]

Merchant Adventurers' Hall Built in the 1350s, this is one of the finest surviving medieval guild halls in Europe. [*Open all year, daily except Suns Nov to mid-Mar*]

Treasurer's House Originally the home of the medieval Treasurer of York Minster, this fine house dates mainly from the 17th century (a video in the basement relates the history of the house). Rooms contain period furniture and paintings and there is a small collection of antique glasses. (NT) [*Open April to Oct, daily*]

Other buildings of interest include the shell of **Cliffords Tower** (near the Castle Museum), the rebuilt **Guildhall** with its replica coloured bosses and jolly grotesques in the wooden roof and the **Assembly Rooms**, an elegant 18th-century ballroom.

You can walk (2 ½ miles) around the medieval **city walls** which pass close to the Minster, giving fine views both of the Minster itself and of the houses and gardens around it.

MUSEUMS AND GALLERIES

Castle Museum A fascinating and extensive folk collection, the main attractions being the period rooms and replica streets using shop fronts rescued from demolition work. Other exhibits include domestic and farm equipment, toys, costumes, armour and a water-driven corn mill [*open all year, daily*]. The same entrance ticket gives admission to **The York Story** [*open all year, daily except Sun am*], a permanent audio-visual exhibition interpreting the social and architectural history of the city (in the Heritage Centre).

City Art Gallery A small selection of European paintings, mainly Old Masters. There are also works by Yorkshire artists, notably William Etty, and a collection of modern stoneware pottery. [*Open all year, daily except Sun am, Good Friday, Christmas and New Year*]

National Railway Museum Another big attraction (a million visitors a year), the Railway Museum appeals to the layman as well as the buff – you'd have to be pretty unromantic not to be fascinated by the display of trains including steam locomotives and the immaculately preserved Royal Saloons. [*Open all year, daily except Sun am, Good Friday, Christmas and New Year*]

Yorkshire Museum Extensive collections of Roman, Anglo-Saxon and Viking antiquities with a 'Roman Life' gallery (including wallpaintings, jewellery and a lock of auburn hair). Also medieval sculpture and Yorkshire pottery. The museum is situated in the 10-acre Museum Gardens, where there are the ruins of a medieval abbey, remains of Roman walls and defences and an observatory. [*Open all year, daily except Sun am, Good Friday, Christmas and New Year*]

CHURCHES

Of the dozen or so city churches, three are particularly worth visiting: **All Saints**, North Street, famous for its stained glass (look out for the medieval spectacles-wearer) and a beautiful painted hammer-beam roof; **Holy Trinity**, Goodramgate, which has interesting inward-facing box pews; and **St Martin Le Grand**, a fine blend of old and new, the south aisle having been gutted in the war and restored to form a separate church with modern pews, organ and west window – and the original early 15th-century west window.

Shopping

There is a market daily except Sundays, off Parliament Street. The most appealing shopping streets for tourists are the pedestrian streets in the centre, especially Petergate, Stonegate, the Shambles and the modern precinct at Coppergate. Fudge and toffee are specialities.

Getting around

Cars should be parked in one of the city centre car parks; even outside the walls parking is restricted. Most of the major sights are within the old walls – or only just outside – and can be seen on foot. Some of the old centre of York is closed to traffic; just wandering through the picturesque streets is one of the delights of a visit. Walking tours, organised by several companies, include evening guided walks of 'haunted' streets and buildings. The York Association of Voluntary Guides offers free daily walking tours lasting two hours (start from Exhibition Square). You can also take bus tours: the Jorvik Tour Bus has regular stops all over the city centre and passengers can re-join on the same ticket after visiting sights. Boat trips along the River Ouse can be arranged from Hills Boatyard, Lendal Bridge; cruises last one hour. Or you can hire motorboats or rowing boats from York Cruiser Hire. There are also some evening city cruises.

Excursions

Beningbrough Hall (8 miles north-west)   A grand early Georgian house with fine plasterwork and wood carving and a collection of 100 portraits on permanent loan from the National Portrait Gallery. There is a Victorian laundry, and an adventure playground in the park. (NT) [*Open May to Oct, pm only, Tues to Thurs, weekends and Bank Hol Mons; weekends April and Nov*]

Sutton Park (10 miles north)   An early Georgian house in a park landscaped by Capability Brown. It contains fine English and French furniture, Italian plasterwork decoration and a collection of porcelain. [*Open April to Sep, pm only; Suns, Tues (from May), and Bank Hol weekends*]

Castle Howard (15 miles north-east)   This magnificent stately home is now almost as famous for its role in the televised 'Brideshead Revisited' as for being the masterpiece of the Baroque architect John Vanbrugh. It contains fine collections of Dutch and Italian paintings and of furniture and ceramics. Hawksmoor's Mausoleum is the main feature of the park. [*Open daily late Mar to Oct*]

When to go

If you visit York in spring or autumn you avoid the peak tourist season, but you also miss some of York's traditional events. The flat racing season – a total of just 15 days – begins with a three-day meeting in May, and ends in October. The annual York Early Music Festival takes place during the first week in July with concerts in York Minster, the Guildhall and other historic buildings and associated events (plays, exhibitions etc) elsewhere. Every four years (next in June/July 1992) the city hosts a major cultural Festival at the heart of which are the traditional Mystery Plays, performed nightly in the ruins of St Mary's abbey. Most of the historic houses in (and around) York are closed in mid-winter, but at any time of year there is plenty to do. Most hotels offer reduced rates and weekend break deals in winter.

Information

The Tourist Information Centre, De Grey Rooms, Exhibition Square, York YO1 2HB; tel: (0904) 21756/7

The York Race Committee, the Racecourse, York YO2 1EX; tel: (0904) 20911 (credit card bookings accepted by telephone)

The Festival Office, 1 Museum Street, York YO1 2DT; tel: (0904) 58338 (York Early Music Festival). Tickets can be purchased by post from late April/early May. After May apply to Ticket World, 6 Patrick Pool, Church Street, York YO1 2BB; tel: (0904) 644194

York (four-yearly) Festival, 1 Newgate, York YO1 2LA

Where to stay

It is convenient to stay in the centre of York, but the quieter residential area of the Mount (near the racecourse) is an attractive alternative with a wide range of accommodation. The hotels we recommend include moderately-priced guesthouses and small hotels, two grander establishments and two unpretentious country houses outside the city.

ACOMB
Hill Hotel
60 York Road, Acomb, York YO2 5LW   *Tel: (0904) 790777*

A detached 19th-century house in the highest part of this residential suburb of York, with views over the city and a delightful ¾ acre garden of lawns and flowerbeds. This is a traditional family hotel which has been modernised inside. Public rooms are comfortable with views of the garden. Bedrooms are spacious and high-ceilinged, with mainly unit furniture and conservative décor. A comfortable, well-kept place, suitable for families with children.

Location: *2 miles west of York on B1224 (towards Wetherby)*
Bedrooms: *10 (double, twin, family), 2 with four-poster beds, all with bath.*
Direct dial telephone, TV (with video), teamaking
Facilities: *Parking. Children's playground. Babylistening*
Restrictions: *No dogs. No smoking in dining room*
Open: *Mid Jan to mid Dec*
Credit/charge cards accepted: *Access, Amex, Diners, Visa*
Price category: *££*
Special rates: *2 nights DB&B, Nov to Mar £28 (single £33), April to Oct £31
(single £36). Children under 3 free in parents' room; 3-10, £3 B&B, £7 DB&B*

SHERIFF HUTTON
Rangers House
The Park, Sheriff Hutton, York   Tel: (034 77) 397

Built in 1639 as a brewhouse and stable for the Royal Hunting Lodge in
the Park, and retaining the original mullioned windows, the Rangers
House is now an unusual, even eccentric country guesthouse within 20
minutes' driving distance of York. The main entrance carries the coat of
arms of King James I, a former frequent visitor to the Hunting Lodge.
There is a grand hall on a small scale, used as a lounge; a gallery for
reading; and a 'conservatory' extension with old Lloyd loom chairs and
games for children. Furniture is old, if not always antique, and the
bedrooms, comfortable but simple, retain original features such as beams.
There is an elegant dining room, serving 4-course dinners; the establishment is licensed, but guests may bring their own spirits and wine. Meal
times are flexible.

Location: *In the park, ½ mile south-east of Sheriff Hutton (1 mile from
Strensall/Sheriff Hutton junction); 10 miles from York*
Bedrooms: *6 (single, double, twin, family), 3 with bath, single with shower only*
Facilities: *Parking. Playroom. Lawn darts and boules. Babylistening.*
Restrictions: *No dogs*
Open: *All year*
Credit/charge cards accepted: *None*
Price category: *££*
Special rates: *Oct to March, weekends, 2 nights DB&B £27 pp per night.
Children in parents' room £3.50 to £10 depending on age, including high tea*

YORK
Abbots Mews
6 Marygate Lane, Bootham, York YO3 7DE   Tel: (0904) 34866

A comfortable and very convenient hotel just outside the town walls in its
own quiet cul-de-sac. Abbots Mews was originally a coachman's cottage
with a 19th-century coachhouse and stables and was converted a decade
ago. Like Topsy, it just growed. Extensions include the lounge where the
original walls have become inside walls, and bamboo seating, plants and
windows give the feeling of sitting outside. The dining room is
traditional, with brocade walls and chandeliers; sliding doors lead to an
outdoor seating area with a lawn and shrubs. There is also a cosy beamed

bar. Bedrooms vary in size and have white fitted furniture, velvety upholstery and flowery wallpaper. Menu and cooking are straightforward, service is good.

Bedrooms: 42 *(double, twin and family), 30 in annex, all with bath. Direct dial telephone, TV, teamaking. Hairdryer on request*
Facilities: *Parking. Babylistening*
Restrictions: *No dogs*
Open: *All year*
Credit/charge cards accepted: *Access, Amex, Diners, Visa*
Price category: ££
Special rates: *Winter, 2 or more nights DB&B £32 (single £40) pp per night. Children under 12 in parents' room half price*

YORK
Bootham Bar Hotel
4 High Petergate, York YO1 2EH   *Tel: (0904) 658516*

A pretty 18th-century house, just by Bootham Bar – one of the fortified city gateways. Bedrooms are decorated with a light touch, most with views of the Bar or the garden. The tea room is a mixture of Victorian parlour and French bistro, serving light meals till 8pm. There is nowhere else to sit; but this wouldn't matter to keen sightseers wanting a central, spotless and inexpensive base.

Bedrooms: 10 *(double and twin), all with bath. TV, teamaking. Hairdryer on request*
Facilities: *Luggage lift*
Restrictions: *No dogs*
Open: *All year*
Credit/charge cards accepted: *None*
Price category: ££
Special rates: *Children in parents' room half price*

YORK
Grasmead House Hotel
1 Scarcroft Hill, The Mount, York YO2 1DF   *Tel: (0904) 29996*

A delightful small bed and breakfast hotel with romantic appeal, in a quiet corner of the Mount, five minutes' walk from the city centre. All bedrooms have four-poster beds (the oldest circa 1730). There is a pleasant lounge, a simple cottagey breakfast room and a well-kept small garden. Opposite are a bowling green and tennis courts, and an ancient right of way to the centre of York runs outside the house. The friendly owners have a motto: 'Anything from advice to an aspirin – just ask'; they will show you videos of York, supply maps and recommend restaurants. There is on-street car parking.

Bedrooms: 6 *(double), all with four-poster beds and bath (extra beds available). TV, teamaking*
Restrictions: *No dogs*
Open: *All year*

Credit/charge cards accepted: *Access, Amex, Diners, Visa*
Price category: ££
Special rates: *Children in parents' room £10*

YORK
The Judges Lodging
9 Lendal, York YO1 2AQ   *Tel: (0904) 38733*

A fine Grade I listed town house, built around 1710 and later used as the
official residence of the Assize Court Judges. In 1979 it was restored in
rather florid style and opened as a hotel. The dining room is the finest of
the public rooms, and food is ambitious, with a French accent. The
vaulted cellar bar is rather ordinary and the hall, though with some fine
period features, is too small to serve as a sitting room. Bedrooms are
comfortable, with antique and reproduction furniture; gold taps, fake
flower arrangements and extravagantly draped beds are not to everyone's
taste, but fruit and sherry may compensate. Notices request that guests
should not remove antique knick-knacks displayed for their pleasure.

Bedrooms: *14 (single, double and twin, several combining as family suites),
4 with four-poster beds, all with bath except single (shower only). Direct dial
telephone, TV. Hairdryer on request*
Facilities: *Parking. Babylistening*
Open: *All year*
Credit/charge cards accepted: *Amex, Diners, Visa*
Price category: ££££
Special rates: *Children in parents' room £10 to £15*

YORK
Middlethorpe Hall
Bishopthorpe Road, York YO2 1QP   *Tel: (0904) 641241*

A William III country house, once the home of the famous diarist Lady
Mary Wortley Montagu and later of the Terry family, now restored by
Historic House Hotels. It stands in a superb landscaped garden close to
York race course. The interior has been lovingly furnished with antiques
and oil paintings in keeping with the period and style of the house. In
addition to a gracious drawing room there is a cosier library; and there are
three intimate dining rooms, one oak-panelled. Simpler food is served in
the downstairs Grill. Bedrooms are elegant and individually decorated
with great taste; bathrooms, Edwardian in style, have modern luxuries.
The bedrooms in the attractive stable courtyard have been decorated to
the same standard. All in all, a most civilised and special hotel.

Location: *1½ miles outside York, by the racecourse*
Bedrooms: *31 (single, double, twin and suite), 20 of them in courtyard annexe
and cottages, one with four-poster bed, all with bath. Direct dial telephone, TV*
Facilities: *Parking, mini lift. Croquet. Chauffeur service*
Restrictions: *No dogs. No children under 8*
Open: *All year*
Credit/charge cards accepted: *Access, Amex, Diners, Visa*
Price category: ££££
Special rates: *Oct to Mar, 2 nights DB&B £65 (single £67.50) pp per night*

YORK
Mount Royale
The Mount, York YO2 2DA   *Tel: (0904) 628856*

Near the race course, about 15 minutes' walk from the Minster, the Mount Royal consists of two William IV houses and a modern extension. There's a large, beautiful and immaculately kept garden, and a fine secluded swimming pool. Inside all is full of character and the public rooms (including two sitting rooms and a small bar) are cosy. The spacious dining room, looking out over the gardens, has a formal atmosphere. The cooking is ambitious and portions are reputed to be large. Bedrooms are spacious, individually furnished and very comfortable; four new annexe rooms opening out onto a patio have just been added.

Bedrooms: *22 (double, twin, family), all with bath. Direct dial telephone, TV, teamaking. Hairdryer, trouserpress. Fridge in some rooms*
Facilities: *Parking. Heated outdoor swimming pool. Babylistening*
Restrictions: *Small dogs only*
Open: *All year except Christmas and New Year*
Price category: £££
Special rates: *2 nights (except Bank Hol weekends) DB&B £45 (single £55.00 B&B) pp per night. Children in parents' room: under 5 free, over 5 £10*

YORK
The Town House Hotel
Holgate Road, York YO2 4BB   *Tel: (0904) 643051*

A terrace of early Victorian brick houses in a reasonably quiet residential area near the Mount and within about 15 minutes' walk (or a short bus ride) of the city centre. The most appealing room is the flagstoned conservatory, a veritable hanging garden of runaway greenery with cane furniture. Reception is in an unobtrusive corner and a mynah bird says 'hello' in three different voices. There is a comfortable lounge, with elegant antique and reproduction Victorian furniture and a cosy and relaxing bar. The dining room is the Grapevine restaurant, open to non-residents, light and spacious with cane-back bentwood armchairs and potted palms. Food is fresh, fillet steaks are a speciality and there is a reasonably priced table d'hôte menu. The separate Town House Lodge offers bed and breakfast at slightly cheaper rates.

Bedrooms: *23 (single, double and twin), 18 with bath or shower. Town House Lodge has 10 bedrooms. Direct dial telephone, TV. Hairdryer on request*
Facilities: *Parking*
Restrictions: *Dogs in bedrooms and conservatory on lead only*
Open: *All year except Christmas week*
Credit/charge cards accepted: *Access, Amex, Diners, Visa*
Price category: £
Special rates: *Winter, 2 nights (except Bank Hol weekends) DB&B £25.65 (single £31.50) pp per night. Reduced rates for children in parents' room*

GENTLE
COUNTRYSIDE

The Cotswolds, The Scottish Borders, The Stour Valley,
The Thames Valley, Upland Dorset, The Welsh Marches

The Cotswolds

- Hills, woodland and gentle farming country characterised by appealing villages and market towns
- No great sights but some handsome medieval churches, fine domestic architecture, and lovely gardens to visit
- A good area for children – especially if they're keen on wildlife and Roman history. Local museums are good for wet days
- Best for people with cars. Touring at random is likely to be more rewarding than homing in on the main tourist areas
- A wide choice of comfortable hotels, many in typical Cotswold manor houses or old inns, but few cheap. Plenty of places to eat out too
- The main snag is the summer crowds, bringing traffic, higher prices and a slightly trippery atmosphere to some of the villages

The Cotswold hills run for about forty miles between Stratford-on-Avon and Bath, just east of the broad valley of the River Severn, where the abrupt escarpment gives way to undulating open farmland divided by wooded river valleys. The honey-coloured local limestone lends a particular charm to the prosperous, neatly-kept villages with their picturesque stone-tiled cottages, bridges and drystone walls, and their fine medieval churches, built from the profits of the wool trade. Exploring the villages themselves could keep most people happy for much of a weekend. On the edge of the Cotswolds, Bath and Stratford-on-Avon have plenty to offer active sightseers and theatre-goers.

The North

Broadway must once have been an imposing village, with its rich mixture of architecture down the wide main street, but now it's very touristy and there's not much to see – except antique shops. Smaller and less crowded villages include **Buckland** and **Stanton**, which has good cottages in orderly layout below the scarp, and tiny **Snowshill** with its manor house perched above. The handsome market town of **Winchcombe** has a fine wool church, pretty shops and old pubs. West of Broadway and towards the spa town of **Cheltenham** are outlying hills, of which the biggest is Bredon Hill.

The ancient market town of **Chipping Camden** is a tourist showpiece with a classic Cotswold wool church combined with a row of almshouses and a well-preserved High Street. In the valley to the south is the steep, elegant village of **Blockley**, leading nowhere and therefore unspoilt. **Stow-on-the-Wold**, on a little plateau of its own, is subject to heavy through traffic but has an attractive green and antique shops around the central square. Around Stow, in the river valleys, are picture postcard villages such as **Naunton** and **The Slaughters** (Upper and Lower), well-known beauty spots which are often crowded but not over commercialised. The tourist attractions of nearby **Bourton-on-the-Water**, in a pretty setting on the River Windrush, include a trout farm, a model village, a motor museum and a perfumery exhibition. There are hordes of visitors in summer but it is a good place to take children.

HISTORIC BUILDINGS AND GARDENS

nr Chipping Camden, Hidcote Manor Garden   Famous garden with formal vistas, oriental-style gazebos and cottage-style walled parts. [*Open April to Oct*]

Moreton-in-Marsh, Batsford Arboretum   A 19th-century arboretum with an oriental emphasis. Informal visits, garden centre. [*Open April to Oct, daily except Tues and Fri*]

Snowshill Manor   An eccentric collection including samurai dummies, exotic furniture, toys, bicycles; lovely gardens and village. (NT) [*Open May to Sep, Wed to Sun; plus weekends in April and Oct*]

Winchcombe, Sudeley Castle   A half-ruined stately mansion with royal connections (tomb of Queen Katherine Parr) and the inspiration for Blandings in P.G. Wodehouse's novels. State rooms with paintings by Constable, Turner, Rubens and Van Dyck. Toy museum, adventure playground, falconry displays. [*Open April to Oct; daily, pm only*]

FAMILY OUTINGS

Broadway Tower Country Park   Organised nature trail and country walks in a park around an 18th-century folly. Adventure playground and picnic area. [*Open April to early Oct, daily*]

Bourton-on-the-Water, Birdland   A large aviary with many exotic and colourful species, some flying wild. [*Open all year, daily*]

Bourton-on-the-Water Model Railway   Display of over 40 British model trains. [*Open Mar to Oct, daily*]

Guiting Power, Cotswold Farm Park   Rare breeds of farm

animals. Pets corner for small children. [*Open Easter to Sep, daily*]
Winchcombe Railway Museum   A well-kept outdoor site with
signal box, railway signs, points etc in a garden setting. [*Open all
year, daily, pm only*]

The Centre and South

Burford, sloping down to the River Windrush, has a fine church
and interesting buildings. To the south-west are **Bibury**, with
squat cottages scattered around a bend in the River Coln, and
Fairford where the grand medieval wool church has a complete
series of 16th-century painted windows. **Cirencester** has a good
claim to be the capital of the Cotswolds and is a fine old market
town with Roman origins. To the west are the attractive hamlets
of the **Duntisbournes**, the village of **Slad**, immortalised in *Cider
with Rosie*, and **Painswick**, the grandest village of the Cotswolds,
with fine ashlar mansions and a churchyard with ornate tombs.
Stroud itself has little to offer, but the steep wooded valleys
nearby provide some of the best walking in the whole area. There
are also wide expanses of high, flat common land around the
typical market town of **Minchinhampton**.

   In the southernmost part of the Cotswolds, the upland area is
only a few miles wide, and tree-lined valleys alternating with flat
woodland are characteristic. **Tetbury** is a lively market town with
modern outskirts and traffic problems but with some pretty
features, like the cottages along the 'Chipping' steps. **Wotton-
under-Edge** and **Dursley** are pleasant but not really Cotswold
towns: timber frames, brick and stucco are as much in evidence
as limestone. Yet **Castle Combe**, on the south side of the M4, is a
typical and perfectly preserved Cotswold village with picturesque
gabled cottages; draconian parking restrictions are evidence of its
popularity.

HISTORIC BUILDINGS AND GARDENS
Chedworth, Roman villa   The finest Roman villa in the west of
England. Extensive remains of the bathing system, mosaics and a
small museum. (NT) [*Open Mar to Oct, Tues-Sun and Bank Hol
Mons; Nov to mid Dec, Wed-Sun. Closed Good Friday*]
Painswick Rococo Garden   A mid 18th-century garden, being
restored to its original design. [*Open May to Sept, Wed-Sun*]
Westonbirt Arboretum   A landscaped collection of trees and
shrubs, founded in 1829 and now run by the Forestry Commission. Informal layout makes for pleasant walks. [*Open all year,
daily*]

MUSEUMS

Bibury, Arlington Mill   The Cotswold Country Museum, in an atmospheric old corn mill. Exhibits include farm tools, domestic bygones, reconstructed craftsmen's shops, clothes, toys, Arts and Crafts furniture and period rooms. [*Open Mar to Oct, daily, plus winter weekends*]

Cirencester, Corinium Museum   Cotswold history, concentrating on the Romans with mosaics, masonry and reconstructions of rooms. [*Open all year, daily except Sun am and (Oct to Mar) Mons*]

Northleach, Cotswold Countryside Collection   A museum of rural life and social history, housed in an 18th-century 'House of Correction'. Agricultural implements, reconstructed blacksmiths' and wheelwrights' workshops and a display on the history of prison reform. [*Open April to Oct, daily except Sun am*]

FAMILY OUTINGS

✿ **Burford, Cotswold Wild Life Park**   *Holiday Which? Weekend Break Award*

A varied collection of wild animals in 120 acres of parkland. Fringe attractions include pony and train rides in summer and a brass rubbing centre in the manor house. [*Open all year, daily*]

Prinknash Bird Park   Waterfowl, exotic pheasants and peacocks in the parkland of Prinknash abbey. Also pygmy goats, deer and the Monks' fish pond. [*Open Easter to Oct, daily*]

Crickley Hill Country Park   Gentle walking with special interest trails (archaeology, geology, ecology) and spectacular views over the Severn Vale. [*Open all year, daily*]

Walking

Nearly all the most attractive scenery in the region lies on the western escarpment; here too, big views open out westwards towards the Malvern Hills and beyond them into Wales. The long-distance Cotswold Way, running 100 miles from Chipping Campden to Bath, is carefully designed to take in much of the best of a landscape characterised by secluded narrow valleys and bold grassy slopes. Recommended areas for short or full-day walks are the Frome Valley (east of Stroud), Shenberrow Hill (near Buckland), Broadway Hill, Painswick Beacon, Cleeve Hill and the Devil's Chimney (both near Cheltenham). The last four of these are all good viewpoints which can be reached by a short walk from a car park.

Away from the escarpment, much of the scenery is rather bleak and unvaried; the villages are their obvious attraction, but a ramble encompassing some of them is likely to include road-walking and some plodding over uninviting-looking flattish arable fields. A few oases of lusher, more interesting countryside exist however, for example Chedworth Woods.

See *Holiday Which? Good Walks Guide* walks 86-89.

When to go

The Cotswolds do get very crowded in summer, especially at weekends. Spring and early autumn are more peaceful. If you just want to relax by an open fire, go for walks and browse in antique shops without too many tourists you could choose winter – but many of the sights are closed to the public.

Information

The Heart of England Tourist Board, 2/4 Trinity Street, Worcester WR1 1BR; tel: (0905) 613132

Cotswold Publicity Association, c/o Tourist Information Centre, Corn Hall, Market Place, Cirencester, Glos. GL7 2NW; tel (0285) 4180. Many Cotswold villages publish their own regularly up-dated tourist information booklets (notably the free '*Roundabout*' series) with maps, potted histories, lists of events and so on.

Cotswold Warden Office, c/o County Planning Department, Shire Hall, Glos GL1 2TN; tel: (0452) 425674 (programme of guided walks)

Where to stay

Hotels in the Cotswolds are not cheap. This is a good area to choose if you want country-house comforts like drawing rooms with log fires, interior-designed bedrooms and gastronomic treats. However, some hotels are pretentious and overpriced. Local tourist offices can provide lists of the many guesthouses and farms which offer bed and breakfast accommodation.

BAMPTON
University Farm
Lew, Bampton, Oxfordshire OX8 2AU   *Tel: (0993) 850297*

A working farm offering plain and comfortable accommodation in a tiny village, main-road but very rural. Bedrooms, many with low ceilings, are fair-sized and regularly repainted white. They are clean and tidy and simply furnished in cottage style. There is a cosy sitting room with a wood-burning stove set in a stone inglenook fireplace, William Morris fabrics and fresh flowers; a small bar for pre-dinner drinks; and a conservatory, added to provide more space and a breakfast room. With its brick walls, cream paint, and lace cloths, it is fairly traditional; but a dresser with plates adds to the farmhouse feel. Pride is taken in the claim that no frozen food is used. Outside is an attractive farmyard and a lawned and paved garden. A cosy and unfussy place.

Location: *On the A4095, 3 miles from Witney*
Bedrooms: *6 (double, twin and family), all with bath/shower and TV*
Facilities: *Parking*
Restrictions: *No children under 4 years. No dogs. No smoking in bedrooms*
Open: *All year except Dec 24-Jan 7*
Credit/charge cards accepted: *None*
Price category: £
Special rates: *2 nights DB&B £25.50 pp per night. Children sharing parents' room £8.50*

BIBURY
Bibury Court
Bibury, Nr Cirencester, Gloucestershire GL7 5NT   *Tel: (028574) 337*

Set in a secluded position beside the river Coln and surrounded by seven acres of lawns and an orchard, this is a large and rather stark Cotswold stone house with gables, built in 1633. It is supremely old-fashioned but nonetheless comfortable with old and slightly battered furniture, a miscellany of floral fabrics that don't match (taken to extremes in the lounge), hot water bottles and huge old-fashioned baths. Bedrooms vary in size, atmosphere and furnishing. Many have four posters (old or new); brocade, Sanderson or Laura Ashley fabrics; candlewick bedspreads and large Victorian wardrobes. The lounge is large and panelled with a pink and white plasterwork ceiling, a large open fire and lots of chairs; TV can be watched in a smaller room with lots of books. There is a bar with 1920s' panelling and strident gold and black wallpaper, but the dining room (with tables rather close together) is pleasant and harmonious.

Location: *On the main road through Bibury to Burford; follow signposts*
Bedrooms: *16 (single, double, twin, family, suite), 9 with 4-poster, 9 with bath. Direct dial telephone. Hairdryer. TV in suite*
Facilities: *Parking. Pool table in bar. TV room. Fishing. Babylistening*
Restrictions: *Dogs by prior arrangement*
Open: *All year except 10 days over Christmas*
Credit/charge cards: *Access, Amex, Diners, Visa*
Price category: ££
Special rates: *Winter, 2 nights, DB&B £34-£36 pp per night. Children in parents' room, £5-£10, depending on age*

BLOCKLEY
Lower Brook House
Blockley, Moreton-in-Marsh, Gloucestershire GL56 9DS   Tel: (0386) 700286

Set on the road in a remarkably unspoilt village, this charming Cotswold stone house has a delightful garden and offers plain, comfortable accommodation and above average food. Up steep stairs, the cottage style bedrooms are decorated with small print papers and jolly colours (which don't always match but it doesn't matter) while magazines and a whole bottle of Radox add to the comfort. The welcoming lounge, decorated with horse brasses and dried flower arrangements, has an impressive inglenook fireplace complete with bread oven. The floor is stone flagged and the old furniture is comfortable. The dining room is smallish without being cramped; linen napkins and fresh flowers on the tables are indications that trouble will also be taken with the food and service – both are excellent. Outside is the delightful picture-book country cottage garden, at the bottom of which is car parking and the brook (from which the hotel takes its name) enjoyed by ducks. An unpretentious village hotel in a tranquil setting where relaxation and good food are more important than modern gadgetry.

Bedrooms: *8 (double, twin), all with bath/shower. TV, teamaking*
Facilities: *Parking*
Restrictions: *No dogs in public rooms*
Open: *Feb to Dec*
Credit/charge cards accepted: *Access, Diners*
Price category: *£££*
Special rates: *Winter, 2 nights DB&B £41.50 pp per night. Children in parents' room £5 (B&B), £15 (DB&B)*

BROAD CAMPDEN
The Malt House
Broad Campden, Chipping Campden,
Gloucestershire GL55 6UU   Tel: (0386) 840295

Dating from the 17th century, this attractive string of cottages with diamond-paned windows is set by a quiet village road. The wisteria-covered garden side of the houses looks out over five acres of lawns, orchards and paddocks with Jacob sheep and bantam hens. Bedrooms are quite small but have a country charm – pretty fabrics and antique furniture. There are two comfortable sitting rooms downstairs – one has a wood-burning stove and access to the garden. Antiques, china, knick-knacks, books, magazines, Scrabble and Trivial Pursuit add to the private house atmosphere. Fruit and vegetables from the kitchen garden are served in the cheerful dining room, with beamed ceiling and antique furniture including a grandfather clock. Guests may eat at one big table if they like. Neither lavish nor luxurious but cosy and comfortable, this will appeal to those who enjoy the implicit invitation to 'join in'.

Location: *Past the 'Baker's Arms' which is about 1 mile from Chipping Campden*
Bedrooms: *5 (single, double, twin), 2 with bath. TV. Teamaking. Iron and hairdryer on request*

Facilities: *Parking. Croquet*
Restrictions: *Children in dining room, preferably over 12. No dogs*
Open: *All year except 24-26 Dec*
Credit/charge cards accepted: *Access, Visa*
Price category: £££
Special rates: *Children in parents' room free*

Nr BROADWAY
Collin House

Collin Lane, Broadway, Hereford and Worcester WR12 7PB   Tel: (0386) 858354

Down a gravel drive with trees to either side is this unspoilt double-fronted T-shaped Cotswold stone house, surrounded by nine acres of informal gardens which include a pool. The comfort of the bedrooms (named after flowers) should be measured more by touches such as home-made biscuits and magazines rather than sophistication of décor – they are enjoyably 'un-designer' with some antique furniture and cotton fabrics. Downstairs is a large and welcoming bar with bare boards and rugs, inviting sofas and chairs, and an open fire. Food is undeniably English; at lunchtime you may choose from the interesting bar menu, but dinner is served in the more traditional dining room, with its Victorian prints, and flowers and candles on the tables. The sitting room is slightly reminiscent of a waiting room; guests tend to congregate in the bar. A pleasant country house in which to relax, altogether uprentious and rather appealing.

Location: *Off the A44 towards Evesham*
Bedrooms: *7 (single, double, twin), all with bath, single with separate WC, 2 with four poster. Teamaking. TV on request*
Facilities: *Parking. Lounge with TV. Outdoor pool with solar cover*
Restrictions: *No dogs in bedrooms*
Open: *All year except 24-26 Dec*
Credit/charge cards accepted: *Access, Visa*
Price category: ££
Special rates: *Nov to Mar, 2 nights DB&B £35 pp per night. Children in parents' room £15*

BROADWAY
Mill Hay

Broadway, Hereford and Worcester WR12 7JS   Tel: (0386) 852498

Bed-and-breakfast accommodation in an attractive 18th-century Cotswold country house, in a tranquil setting near Broadway, surrounded by old English gardens including a mill pond. That said, this is not a typical quaint retreat because the atmosphere is distinctly 'continental'. The medium size bedrooms are spotless and comfortable with duvets. Bathrooms are shared (apart from the family suite in the attic). Breakfast is prepared in front of guests and served over a breakfast bar in the kitchen with modern oak units. There are two sitting rooms, one panelled, one with a stone carved frieze; both are furnished with some antiques and leather Chesterfield sofas. A well-run establishment for those with European tastes.

Location: *¼ mile out of Broadway towards Snowshill*
Bedrooms: *5 (single, double, twin, family), 2 with four-poster. No private bathrooms. Teamaking*
Facilities: *Parking. TV in lounge*
Restrictions: *No pets. No smoking in bedrooms*
Open: *Mar to Dec*
Credit/charge cards accepted: *None*
Price category: £
Special rates: *Children in parents' room £8-£17.50 depending on age*

BURFORD
The Bay Tree
Sheep Street, Burford, Oxfordshire OX8 4LW   *Tel: (0993) 823137*

Quietly situated off and away from the High Street is this 16th-century Cotswold stone house complete with mullioned windows and leaded panes. Accommodation is spread between the main building, the nearby cottage and the recently built 'garden rooms' overlooking the pretty terraced lawns. Bedrooms are comfortably if plainly furnished with antiques and floral pattern curtains, refined cottage-style. The main house, with many different levels and steps, contains the public rooms – the largest of which is the dining room with a rug-covered stone flagged floor. Whitewashed stone walls hung with tapestries, wooden tables and Windsor chairs look gently rustic. There is a small bar with beamed and vaulted ceiling by the main staircase, and further seating is available in a number of intimate rooms with fireplaces, leather Chesterfields and William Morris curtains, newspapers, books and magazines. The new conservatory and tea shop should prove to be both sympathetic and useful.

Bedrooms: *22 (single, double, twin, suites), 3 with 4-posters, 2 with half-testers, 8 in cottage, 4 garden rooms; all with bath. Direct dial telephone, TV, teamaking. Hairdryer*
Facilities: *Parking. Conservatory*
Restrictions: *No dogs. No smoking in restaurant. No children under 7 in dining room during dinner*
Open: *All year except Christmas and Boxing Day*
Credit/charge cards accepted: *Access, Amex, Diners, Visa*
Price category: £££
Special rates: *Winter, 2 nights DB&B £40 pp per night. Children sharing parents' room half price*

BUCKLAND
Buckland Manor
Buckland, Gloucestershire WR12 7LY   *Tel: (0386) 852626*

A very fine example of the English country house hotel, this magnificent gabled Elizabethan manor house with mullioned windows is secluded, elegant and spacious. Situated at the end of a cul de sac in a hamlet near Broadway, the sensation that it is in a world of its own is enhanced by being set in a south-west facing bowl of land surrounded by higher ground. Ten acres of beautiful landscaping includes lawns and formal gardens, swimming pool and tennis court. The dining room is almost stately with Elizabethan style furnishings, and the panelled drawing room (beamed ceiling, parquet floorings and rugs) has grand but comfortable sofas and a discreet drinks table. There is a smaller, elegant 'writing room'. Throughout the hotel flowers, books and magazines abound. Bedrooms are luxuriously furnished with rich fabrics, antiques and a sofa. Expensive, but wonderful for a special treat. *Holiday Which? Weekend Break Award*

Location: *Off the A46 two miles south west of Broadway*
Bedrooms: *11 (double, twin, family), 2 with four-poster, all with bath. Direct dial telephone, TV*
Facilities: *Parking. Heated outdoor swimming pool, tennis court. Croquet, putting*
Restrictions: *No dogs. No children under 12. No pipes or cigars in dining room*
Open: *Second week in Feb to mid-Jan*
Credit/charge cards accepted: *Access, Visa*
Price category: £££££

CHADLINGTON
Chadlington House
Chadlington, Oxfordshire OX7 3LZ   *Tel: (060 876) 437*

This is a 17th-century house, with later Victorian/mock Tudor additions, set in a small village overlooking rolling arable land. The atmosphere is that of a genteel and well-run guest house; good-sized bedrooms decorated with little flower patterns, lacy fabrics and loo paper hidden in knitted dolls. All the public rooms are reasonably spacious, with browns and oranges the predominant colours; the emphasis is on comfort rather than co-ordination of décor. In the traditional dining room the only picture is a reproduction of Annigoni's portrait of the Queen; in the hall is a picture of Churchill. This is a very English place.

Location: *Off A34 on to B4022/or off A361 from Burford*
Bedrooms: *12 (single, twin, double, family cottage), all with bath. TV, teamaking. Hairdryer*
Facilities: *Parking*
Restrictions: *No children under 8. No dogs*
Open: *Feb 18-Dec 7*
Credit/charge cards accepted: *Access, Visa*
Price category: ££
Special rates: *Nov to Mar, 2 nights DB&B £52-£65 pp per night. Children in parents' room half price*

CHIPPING CAMPDEN
Kings Arms
Chipping Campden, Gloucestershire GL55 6AW   *Tel: (0386) 840256*

Overlooking the market square in the centre of Chipping Campden, this hotel is a predominantly 18th-century building of Cotswold stone. There is country hotel charm in all the bedrooms, which have some antique furniture and chintzy co-ordinated décor. The dining room has modern ladderback chairs, and old photographs and framed wine labels on the walls. Cream-painted panelling and pink and green old fashioned fabrics make the lounge restful; there are fresh flowers, books, television and many indoor games. The bar is very fine – as comfortable as a sitting room, with ample sofas; there's a large open fireplace, bridles and bits and horseshoes hang on the hessian walls, and newspapers on poles. It makes a relaxing place to enjoy a good lunch. When fine, you can take your food out into the large grassy garden at the back.

Location: *Right in the middle of Campden, above the main square*
Bedrooms: *14 (single, twin, double), 2 with bath*
Facilities: *TV in sitting room*
Restrictions: *No dogs in public rooms*
Open: *All year*
Credit/charge cards accepted: *Access, Visa*
Price category: *£££*
Special rates: *Winter weekends, 2 nights DB&B £37.50 pp per night. Children in parents' room £7-£11*

GREAT RISSINGTON
The Lamb Inn
Great Rissington, Gloucestershire GL4 2LJ   *Tel: (0451) 20388/20724*

In a quiet village with big views out over farmland, this friendly pub (some 350 years old) has many levels and some low ceilings. The bar has old village photographs and a wide range of draught beer; guests can eat here, or in a smaller buttery, or in the bistro-style restaurant. Magazines and games are provided in the cosy beamed lounge, the (smallish) bedrooms are prettily decorated and all is very clean and bright. Outside is a pleasant west-facing sloping garden and a covered heated pool for which a small charge is made. A charming and fresh country, where a lot of loving care has gone into everything.

Location: *On eastern edge of village*
Bedrooms: *8 (double, twin), 5 with bath. 1 with 4-poster*
Facilities: *Parking. Lounge with TV. Covered heated swimming pool*
Restrictions: *No dogs except by prior arrangement*
Open: *All year except Christmas Day*
Credit/charge cards accepted: *Access, Visa*
Price category: *£*
Special rates: *Winter, 2 nights DB&B £25 pp per night. Children in parents' room £8.50, travel cot £1.50*

KINGHAM
Mill House Hotel
Kingham, Oxfordshire OX7 6UH   *Tel: (060871) 8188*

Surrounded by flat pastureland through which runs an old mill stream, this well-modernised Cotswold stone house dates from the 17th century (with many subsequent and sympathetic additions). Bedrooms are comfortable, with contrasting traditional fabrics; some are a little more lavish, but all are pretty and fresh with co-ordinated bathrooms. The pleasant dining room has soft colouring, festoon blinds and frivolous pictures which should not distract one from the serious business of eating well. The lunch menu is displayed on a blackboard in the bar (open fireplace, pictures and copper pans on the walls). A large and airy lounge is equipped with board games, books and magazines; French doors lead to a patio. A well-run establishment in a peaceful setting.

Location: *On western outskirts of Kingham, off B4450*
Bedrooms: *21 (double, twin, family), all with bath. Direct dial telephone, TV, teamaking. Hairdryer*
Facilities: *Parking. Croquet, trout fishing*
Restrictions: *No children under 5. No dogs. Pipes and cigars discouraged in restaurant*
Open: *All year*
Credit/charge cards accepted: *Access, Amex, Diners, Visa*
Price category: *£££*
Special rates: *2 or more nights DB&B £46 (single £56) pp per night. Children in parents' room free*

MINCHINHAMPTON
Burleigh Court Hotel
Minchinhampton, Nr Stroud, Gloucestershire GL5 2PF   *Tel: (0453) 883804*

A large Georgian house with superb views over its old-fashioned country-house gardens which follow the contour of a steep slope. Beds are often huge in the unusually large bedrooms, which are freshly decorated with plain papers and floral curtains. Predominant colours are cream or white, except in the stable rooms where the furniture is cane or pine. The emphasis is on comfort and guests are provided with various goodies depending on whether the purpose of their stay is business or pleasure. Vegetarian and low-calorie dishes are included on the menu, served in the plain dining room decorated in beige and blue. It is a big room and trouble is taken to remove surplus tables so that one is not surrounded by empty tables if the hotel is not full. The bar and lounge are combined in one large panelled reception room with lovely views of the gardens; there is a friendly atmosphere with an open fire and comfy armchairs. Outside is an original Victorian plunge pool, now heated. It is all fresh, bright, light and spacious and older people will feel at home in the gentle hospitality of this family-run hotel.

Location: *Off A419, towards Burleigh and Minchinhampton; then a left turn following signpost to Burleigh Court*
Bedrooms: *16 (double, twin, family), 5 in annexe, all with bath/shower. Direct dial telephone, TV, teamaking*
Facilities: *Parking. Outdoor heated swimming pool, putting green*
Restrictions: *No dogs*
Open: *All year, except 25-30 Dec*
Credit/charge cards accepted: *Access, Amex, Diners, Visa*
Price category: *£££*
Special rates: *2 or more nights DB&B £38 pp per night. Children in parents' room £6-£10*

NORTH CERNEY
The Bathurst Arms
North Cerney, Cirencester, Gloucestershire GL7 7BL   *Tel: (028583) 281*

A pink-and-black 17th-century coaching inn with converted blacksmith's forge and stables, set back from the road behind a front lawn with a large barbecue. It is run as a traditional country pub, and has very cosy cottage bedrooms. The pub bar doubles as lounge: stone-flagged floor, Turkish carpet, wood-burning stove, settle benches, horse brasses and lots of photographs, both old and new, make it warm and welcoming. The dining room is a tiny cottage room, part panelled with tongue and groove. A fireplace, floral curtains, flowers and candles on the tables add to the cosy intimacy. The stables have been turned into an additional and unusual bar, with its original stone floor and the mangers used as side tables. Electric heaters are provided in the bedrooms where the bright and sometimes bold floral papers generally reflect the flower after which each is named; blankets *and* duvets are provided. Cosy comfort and good value.

Location: *On A435 (Cirencester to Cheltenham Road); 3 miles from Cirencester*
Bedrooms: *6 (double, twin), 1 with 4-poster, 4 with bath/shower. TV, teamaking*
Facilities: *Parking. Shooting. Fishing*
Restrictions: *No dogs in public rooms*
Open: *All year except on Christmas Day*
Charge/credit cards accepted: *Visa*
Price category: *£*
Special rates: *Children in parents' room, £5 (depending on age)*

SHIPTON-UNDER-WYCHWOOD
The Lamb Inn
Shipton-under-Wychwood, Oxfordshire OX7 6DQ   *Tel: (0993) 830465*

An L-shaped Cotswold stone house dating from the 13th century, quietly situated away from the through road and run as an inviting combination of pub/B&B/restaurant. Up a steep staircase, bedrooms (with names) are comfortable, with plain curtains and matching headboards. The spacious main bar, with exposed stone walls, polished parquet flooring and Windsor chairs, is decorated with old photographs; here you can browse through newspapers on poles. The open fireplace is a back-to-back arrangement and is shared by the small sitting area at the foot of the stairs. The dining room with a low, beamed ceiling is similar in style and has an inglenook fireplace. With a small garden, mostly used for *al fresco* bar meals, this is a cheery and welcoming small hotel.

Location: *Signposted in Shipton-under-Wychwood*
Bedrooms: *5 (double, twin), all with bath/shower. TV, teamaking. Hairdryer on request*
Facilities: *Parking*
Restrictions: *No children under 14. No dogs*
Open: *All year except week after Christmas*
Credit/charge cards accepted: *Access, Amex, Diners, Visa*
Price category: *££*
Special rates: *Winter, 2nd and subsequent nights, B&B £12.50 (single £15)*

SHIPTON-UNDER-WYCHWOOD
The Shaven Crown
Shipton-under-Wychwood, Oxfordshire OX7 6BA   *Tel: (0993) 830330*

An unusual H-shaped Cotswold stone house, the oldest part built in 1350. Situated on the through road, rooms at the front may suffer from traffic noise but rooms at the back are set round a courtyard garden. The pride and glory is the spectacular double collar braced roof in the hall, a fine array of beams said to be the same as at Berkeley Castle. It's now used as a lounge with a gas log fire and comfortable seating. The Buttery Bar, with loose box seating and horse brasses, serves bar food for both lunch and dinner; there's also a traditional parquet floored dining room. Bedrooms are rather old-fashioned but not uncomfortable, and furnished with some antiques. An unpretentious family-run hotel.

Location: *4 miles north of Burford on A40. Signposted in Shipton-under-Wychwood*
Bedrooms: *8 (single, double, twin, family), 5 with bath. TV, teamaking*
Facilities: *Parking. Bowling green*
Restrictions: *No dogs. No children under 4 in dining room in the evening*
Open: *All year*
Credit/charge cards accepted: *Access, Visa*
Price category: *££*
Special rates: *Oct to Mar, and midweek April to Sep, 2 or more nights B&B (plus £10 dinner allowance) £33 (single £31.50) pp per night. Children in parents' room £12*

Nr STOW-ON-THE-WOLD
Wyck Hill House
Stow-on-the-Wold, Gloucestershire GL54 1HY   *Tel: (0451) 31936*

An impressive stone house of indeterminate age with later Georgian and Victorian additions in a quiet setting, with 33 acres of ground and gardens and superb views over surrounding farmland. It has been sumptuously decorated in grand designer style. Bedrooms, with king-size beds, are large and light, extravagantly decorated with co-ordinated everything – even the luggage rack straps contrast with the bold floral fabrics and plainer pastel walls – and acres of fabric have gone into cushions, pillows, drapes and screens. Each room is supplied with fruit, mineral water, bathrobes and even a built-in security box. Bathrooms (simpler) match the rooms and have telephones. The grand public rooms with fine architectural detail are pleasant, varied and spacious. The finest has an Adam ceiling and fireplace and is a magnificent room with bold chintz chaircovers and cream moirée swagged curtains at the large bow window. The panelled library, with lots of books and magazines, the oak-panelled bar or the large entrance hall provide a wide choice of comfortable seating, with open fires. The dining room has five full-lengh windows overlooking the gardens and is formally decorated in green and pink with good reproduction antique chairs. A fine, lavish and sophisticated country house hotel. (It has recently changed hands – reports welcome.)

Location: *2 ½ miles from Stow*
Bedrooms: *24 (double, twin, family), 4 in Coach House, 4 in cottages; all with bath. Direct dial telephone, TV*
Facilities: *Parking. Library. Croquet. Clay pigeon shooting. Woodland walks*
Restrictions: *No children under 6*
Open: *All year*
Credit/charge cards accepted: *Amex, Access, Diners, Visa*
Price category: *££££*
Special rates: *Winter, 2 nights DB&B £49 pp per night. Children in parents' room £25*

Nr TETBURY
Calcot Manor

Nr Tetbury, Gloucestershire GL8 8YJ   Tel: *(066 689) 227/355*

Dating from the 14th century, this old Cotswold farmhouse (with extensive outbuildings) has been cleverly converted to provide a comfortable hotel. Bedrooms are of a good size and individually decorated. Co-ordinated chintzy fabrics and papers in pastel shades extend to the valances, headboards, bedcovers and, in some cases, coronets. Furniture is a harmonious blend of antique and repro and bathrooms are well-appointed, many with jacuzzi. The restaurant (pale orange walls and pale green upholstery) is a restful room and sufficiently plain to keep one's mind on the food, which has a good reputation. There's an informal 'open' bar in the lounge, and an elegant drawing room with books, games and watercolours; guests are encouraged to feel at home. The owners plan to improve and extend their attractive property still further – which should not detract from the pleasant atmosphere .

Location: *3 miles outside Tetbury, on A4135. Signposted*
Bedrooms: *12 (double, twin, family), 3 in annexe, 1 with 4-poster, all with bath, 3 with jacuzzi. Direct dial telephone, TV. Hairdryer. Irons on request*
Facilities: *Parking. Heated outdoor swimming pool, croquet*
Restrictions: *No children under 12. No dogs. No smoking in restaurant*
Open: *All year except first week in January*
Credit/charge cards accepted: *Access, Amex, Diners, Visa*
Price category: *££££*
Special rates: *Winter, 2 nights DB&B, £66-£77 pp per night; summer, 2 nights midweek, DB&B £63.50-£74.50 pp per night*

TETBURY
The Close Hotel
8 Long Street, Tetbury, Gloucestershire GL8 8AQ   Tel: (0666) 52272/52777

An attractive 17th-century stone town house, with subsequent Georgian and Victorian Gothic additions. Set on the main road in Tetbury, bedrooms on the front are noisy during the day (though double glazed) while those at the back are quiet and overlook a secluded garden. Extensive refurbishment (as we went to press) will up-date the décor and add a further eight bedrooms overlooking the garden. The standard of comfort and thoughtfulness is high and bedrooms are attractively decorated ; the new look will incorporate sophisticated pastel schemes using chintzy fabrics and contrasting textures. Guests are provided with many extras: the forgetful packer should be well pleased with bottled toiletries, bathrobes, flannels, curling tongs and so forth, quite apart from the sherry, sweets, fruit, biscuits and mineral water. Spectacular arrangements of dried flowers decorate many of the rooms and passage areas. The dining room and garden room, with marble effect walls and fine plaster mouldings, are lovely light and elegant rooms overlooking the garden. They are approached via the lounge which inevitably ends up being rather passage-like but it, too, has fine plasterwork and comfortable seating. Complete with car parking and a delightful garden, this is a surprisingly restful and elegant retreat in the middle of a town.

Bedrooms: *10 (single, double, twin) 3 with 4-poster, all with bath/shower. Direct dial telephone, TV. Hairdryer, curling tongs, trouser press*
Facilities: *Parking. Croquet*
Restrictions: *No children under 10. No dogs. No smoking in dining room*
Open: *All year*
Credit/charge cards accepted: *Access, Amex, Diners, Visa*
Price category: *££££*
Special rate: *2 or more nights DB&B £51 (£70) pp per night. Children in parents' room £6*

UPPER SLAUGHTER
Lords of the Manor
Upper Slaughter, Bourton-on-the-Water,
Gloucestershire GL54 2JD   Tel: (0451) 20243

Owned by the Witts family for more than 200 years, this low-built Cotswold stone house, 17th-century with Victorian additions, has a charming and peaceful setting – surrounded by seven acres of park-like grounds including a small lake, well-kept lawns and a walled garden laid out and bordered with box hedges. Bedrooms (named after families Witt-connected by marriage) are light and airy and well-decorated in traditional English style, with some antique furniture, engravings on the walls and chintzy or cottage-style fabrics. The drawing room and bar overlooking the front garden have fine cornices, Victorian etchings and photographs. Coats of arms ornament the stone fireplace in the drawing room, and the dining room with mellow yellow walls divides into four areas of antiques and Victorian chairs. The atmosphere is serene and gently old-fashioned.

Location: *Signposted in Upper Slaughter*
Bedrooms: *15 (single, double, twin), 2 with four-poster, all with bath, Direct dial telephone, TV, Hairdryer*
Facilities: *Parking. Garden room with TV. Fishing. Croquet. Babylistening*
Restrictions: *Dogs in bedrooms only*
Open: *All year*
Credit/charge cards accepted: *Access, Amex, Diners, Visa*
Price category: *££££*
Special rates: *Children in parents' room £15*

WILLERSEY
The Old Rectory
Church Street, Willersey, Nr Broadway,
Hereford and Worcester   *Tel: (0386) 853729*

It is six years since the Jones carried out extensive renovations to this house to provide carefully decorated, spotlessly clean and thoroughly genteel B&B accommodation. Situated just by the church in a small and tranquil village, the house dates back some 300 years with exposed beams to prove it, but, with later additions, it is quite Georgian in character. The spacious bedrooms (named after towns and villages in the vicinity) have extras worthy of a higher ranking hotel – such as the loan of a dressing gown and electric blankets (although double glazing throughout should reduce the necessity for their use). Each bedroom has its own hot water tank so there is no risk of a cold bath. With floral fabrics and walls of painted woodchip or textured papers, co-ordination extends to the colour of sheets and blankets; furniture is mostly mahogany. There is a light and airy first-floor lounge, decorated quite plainly, and a spacious dining room, with patterned carpet and brick fireplace. Outside is a well-kept garden with sloping lawn, borders and stone walls. Comfortable, sedate, a little refined.

Bedrooms: *6 (double, twin), all with baths, 2 with separate WC*
Facilities: *Parking*
Restrictions: *No children under 12. No dogs. No smoking in bedrooms*
Open: *Feb 6-Dec 7; and New Year's Eve*
Credit/charge cards accepted: *Access, Visa*
Price category: *££*
Special rates: *Children in parents' room £10*

The Scottish Borders

- Varied scenery of undulating hills and river valleys, with some wild moorland and rugged peaks in the west
- A good area for touring by car with excellent, uncrowded main roads (but beware hairpin bends and sheep on minor ones)
- Plenty of outdoor activities from fishing on the Tweed to riding and shooting, with some hotels offering organised special breaks
- Some splendid stately homes to visit, plus ruined abbeys, most within easy driving distance of each other in the centre of the area
- Hotels tend to be old-fashioned and quite expensive. But there are some good choices for families, 'foodies' and fishermen
- Ideal for those seeking a quiet break, and for outdoorsy teenagers. Less good for families with young children

This is a very beautiful and unspoilt part of Britain, often ignored by visitors hurrying north to the Highlands. Rolling hills and the grassy valleys of the Tweed and the Teviot create a peaceful and pastoral landscape in the centre. To the east is the coast; to the west, remote hills of around 2,000 feet and moorland inhabited mainly by sheep (but with some favourite beauty spots). Ruined abbeys and grim castles merge with the landscape as reminders of the turbulent past when most were repeatedly attacked by the English, and it is this common heritage which has linked the four original counties (Berwickshire, Roxburghshire, Peebleshire and Selkirkshire) as the Borders. This is the country romanticised by Sir Walter Scott as wild and lawless, now peaceful and mostly uncrowded.

There are some handsome old royal burghs with market place and town cross, though the dark grey stone is severe and most are spoilt by industrial outskirts. The textile industry still flourishes, and visitors are encouraged to follow various craft trails, visiting mills with shops. But it is more rewarding to explore the valley of the meandering River Tweed (which gave its name to the famous fabric) from the east where it forms the border with England, through the fertile lowlands of the Merse where it is overlooked by historic houses and castles, to the more remote and rugged west.

The Centre

The central plain, with most of the larger towns and four ruined abbeys, is mainly agricultural. For those who want to tour the area and do some sightseeing, this is the best base. In the middle of the plain at the confluence of the Tweed and the Teviot is **Kelso**, undoubtedly the most attractive town in the area, with its elegant market square, cobbled streets and distinguished houses. You can walk by the river, wander through the ruins of the Romanesque abbey, potter about the streets and visit Floors Castle. Further along the Tweed is **Melrose**, which also grew up around a 12th-century abbey; the extensive and splendid ruins are in a lovely setting beside an orchard garden below the abruptly rising Eildon hills. At **Jedburgh** there is a High Street and market square of colourful houses, with several sights of some interest, including the abbey church, almost entire but roofless. To the south there is a fine drive to Hawick, over wooded hills. **Hawick** itself is a busy, mainly Victorian town of comparatively little interest to the visitor – but the circuit to Melrose or Kelso can be completed via **Selkirk**, a former county town famous for its bannocks (buns) which has the best local museum in the area.

HISTORIC BUILDINGS

Dryburgh Abbey The most secluded of the ruined Border abbeys, in a loop of the Tweed; it houses the graves of Field Marshal Haig and Sir Walter Scott. [*Open all year, daily*]

Gordon, Mellerstain A fine Adam mansion with characteristic pastel and plaster interiors and a collection of 18th-century furniture and paintings. Half formal, half landscaped gardens. [*Open Easter weekend then May to Sep, pm daily except Sat*]

Jedburgh, Mary Queen of Scots' House Fortified town house with mementoes of the Queen. [*Open Easter to Oct, daily; closed Sun am except July and Aug*]

Kelso, Floors Castle Palatial home of the Dukes of Roxburghe with a suite of state rooms containing mainly French furniture and family portraits. Displays of costumes and stills from *Greystoke* which was filmed here. [*Open May to Sep, Sun to Thurs; plus Bank Hol Mons, and Fri in July and Aug*]

Melrose, Abbotsford Sir Walter Scott's home, a 19th-century gothic mini-castle on the Tweed. Atmospheric library and collections of armour and weaponry. [*Open mid Mar to Oct, daily except Sun am*]

Selkirk, Bowhill Home of the Duke of Buccleugh, with a superb picture collection, including works by Holbein, Canaletto,

Reynolds and Gainsborough. [*Open early July to mid Aug, pm daily*]
Smailholm Tower   Fortified farmhouse where the young Walter
Scott spent his holidays, well kept and guided. [*Open April to Sep,
daily except Sun am*]

MUSEUMS

Most towns have a museum of local history housed in an
interesting building. These include **Halliwell's House** at Selkirk
and **Kelso Museum** in Turret House, Kelso, both with reconstructed old shops; **Hawick Museum** at Wilton Lodge; and the
Castle Jail at Jedburgh, which also offers an insight into Victorian
prison life. Other small museums include the **Motor Museum** at
Melrose.

FAMILY OUTINGS

Selkirk, Bowhill   The grounds of Bowhill include an adventure
playground with woodland and riverside walks and pony
trekking. [*Open May to Aug, pm daily except Fri*]

The North and East

The ranges of the Moorfoot and Lammermuir hills are separated
by Gala Water and Leader Water, dominated by two towns.
Galashiels is primarily industrial, with little to offer the tourist
except a small wool museum and a working mill. **Lauder** is a
good example of a Borders town which has lost its glory: a former
royal burgh with little to show for it except the splendour of
nearby Thirlestane castle. East of Lauderdale, the Lammermuirs
continue almost unbroken to the coast. At the southern edge lies
Greenlaw, another town of decayed grandeur and further east is
Duns, a market centre for the agricultural lowlands to the south,
with some attractive 18th- and 19th-century buildings and shops
in interesting back alleys. A country park above the town
provides lakeside walks and a climb up Duns Law. To the
south-east is **Coldstream**, prettily situated on the Tweed – for
many visitors from the south the first town in Scotland.

HISTORIC BUILDINGS

Duns, Manderston   Vast Edwardian country house in classic
Georgian style, but with a silver staircase. Formal gardens and a
grand stable block. [*Open mid May to mid Sep, pm only; Thurs, Sun
and Bank Hol Mons*]
Lauder, Thirlestane Castle   An exuberant exterior edged in pink
sandstone, and an astonishing interior with ceilings and furnishings of great grandeur. Historic toy collection in the old

nurseries and Border country life exhibition in the south wing. [*Open Easter weekend, then May to Sep, pm Wed, Thurs and Sun; July and Aug, pm daily except Sat*]

FAMILY OUTINGS

Coldstream, The Hirsel The grounds of the Hirsel (which belongs to the former Prime Minister, Lord Home) include nature walks along the valley of the River Leet, round the lake and through the woods. There is a homestead museum and craft centre. [*Open all year, daily*]

The South and West

In the West the terrain is rougher and there is more typically Scottish heather and thistle scenery than in the central area around Kelso. To the south of Jedburgh are wooded hills, and there is also extensive Forestry Commission planting to the west of Hawick. The two are separated by a naked expanse of rough moorland between the Teviot and Liddesdale, penetrated by narrow burns and narrow roads. Here is the superbly isolated Hermitage Castle to which Mary Queen of Scots rode from Jedburgh to visit her lover, the Earl of Bothwell, in 1566.

Further west is **St Mary's Loch**, with sailing and fishing; nearby are the celebrated natural features of the **Grey Mare's Tail**, a rugged waterfall draining Loch Skeen, and **The Devil's Beef Tub**, a dry hollow. Between the valleys of the Ettrick, the Yarrow and the Upper Tweed rise bleak grassland hills – the Moorfoots – with drystone walls and sheep. Most roads follow the river valleys, sometimes wooded, sometimes surrounded by open, unfenced moorland. Minor hill roads can be hair-raising, but give exhilarating views. The main town in the area is **Peebles**, a prosperous market town with many features of its considerable age, like the ruins of Cross Kirk. There are no large towns upriver of Peebles, only the increasingly wild hills, divided by burns with the odd dark grey stone-built village. This is the countryside associated with author John Buchan (later Lord Tweedsmuir) and at **Broughton** there is a small museum dedicated to his life and works. The highest peaks are in the south-west and include Lochcraig Head (2,625 feet).

HISTORIC HOUSES

Innerleithen, Traquair House A very old and well-preserved house with exhibits including ancient charters and furniture used by Mary Queen of Scots. Also an 18th-century brewhouse with home brewed ale. Regular events and adult painting weekends.

[Open Easter weekend then daily May to Sep, pm only until July]
nr Jedburgh, Ferniehirst Castle A small border fortress, now
open to the public after restoration. *[Open May to Oct, pm Sun; plus
pm Wed in July and Aug]*
Newcastleton, Hermitage Castle Sir Walter Scott's favourite
castle is a grim, roofless, but romantic ruin, in a remote setting in
Liddesdale. *[Open all year, daily except Sun am]*
Peebles, Neidpath Castle A medieval tower house above the
Tweed with a bare but atmospheric interior. *[Open Easter weekend
then May to mid Oct, daily except Sun am]*

Museums

Peebles has a **Tweeddale Museum**, Walkerburn the **Scottish
Museum of Woollen Textiles** and Broughton a museum devoted
to John Buchan.

Family outings

Jedburgh, The Woodland Centre A varied collection of all
things woody; giant wooden games and play area, plus suggested walks and trails, mostly through woods. *[Open April, May,
Oct, Sun, Wed and Bank Hol Mons; June to Sep daily]*
Peebles, Kailzie Gardens and Wildfowl Pond A well-kept and
varied garden with woodland and walled areas, and a small
aviary. *[Open April to mid Oct, daily]*

Walking

The Borders contain some very good and only moderately taxing
hill walks, and you can walk in most of the countryside: there is a
tradition of unrestricted access for walkers in the hills (except in
shooting seasons), and you can assume that you are allowed to
follow any path unless there is a sign to the contrary. But a major
problem is that very few paths are mapped, and the path network
in any case is rather sparse; this can mean that it is often difficult
to devise round walks.

The region is crossed by the Southern Upland Way, one of only
two long-distance paths in Scotland, a 212-mile route from
Portpatrick on the south-west coast to Cockburnspath on the east
coast. It takes in some fine scenery, and is a good basis for day
walks.

Relatively ambitious climbs include Grey Mare's Tail, Broad
Law, Culter Fell, Tinto and White Coomb, all good viewpoints; a
compass is essential. Also recommended is an expedition on to
the Cheviot Ridge, taking in one of the summits such as Windy
Gyle or The Cheviot itself. From the top there are huge views

over the Pennines and the Southern Uplands, but in all but the driest weather be prepared for boggy conditions.

For easier rambles, good bets include the Eildon Hills, which are laced with paths and are just elevated enough to get some magnificent views; the river valleys, notably Tweeddale which contains some pleasant riverside paths (you can't follow the river all the way however); and there are many areas of forestry planatation, some of which have self-guided trails, including the vast Kielder Forest.

See *Holiday Which? Good Walks Guide* walks 143, 162.

When to go

Events in summer include The Great Tweed Raft Race, starting from Kelso, held on a Sunday in late May, the Mosstroopers Race meeting in June at Hawick and the Braw Lads Gathering at Galashiels (last week in June). The traditional Common Ridings are held in June (Hawick, Selkirk) and July (Jedburgh, Lauder) – colourful displays of horsemanship which are performed by (and primarily for) the townspeople. Throughout the summer there are various local games and festivals, agricultural shows, horse trials and so on; they include Melrose Summer Festival (June), Games at Kelso, Jedburgh and Innerleithen (July), Peebles Agricultural Show and Hawick Summer Festival (August) and Peebles Highland Games and Arts Festival (September). The Kelso races are in October.

The Borders Festival of Ballads and Legends takes place from late September to mid October, with many events at weekends. Many performances are held in historic houses and ancient inns.

Salmon fishing on the Tweed takes place in February/March and October/November.

The Tourist Office publishes a guide (monthly in summer) to 'What's On'.

Information

The Scottish Borders Tourist Board, Municipal Buildings, High Street, Selkirk TD7 4JX; tel: (0750) 20555. There are Tourist Information Centres in the main towns, April to October.

The Countryside Ranger Service, Borders Regional Council, Regional Headquarters, Newtown St Boswells TD6 4SA; tel: (0835) 23301 (information on guided walks, picnic sites and waymarked trails)

A fishing permit can be obtained from tackle and sports shops, hotels or the tourist information centres.

Where to stay

There is a shortage of good, reasonably priced traditional hotels but for cheap accommodation there are plenty of bed and breakfast establishments (look out for the distinctive blue and white B&B sign, indicating Tourist Board classification). If you want to concentrate on touring and sightseeing, then the central area around Kelso is the best base, but those who want to be in, or close to, remote countryside could head further west around Peebles or Selkirk. All three towns have some very comfortable establishments; Peebles has the best range of cheaper but acceptable accommodation. Most hotels operate a sliding tariff, with cheaper rates out of the fishing season.

ECKFORD
Marlefield Country House Hotel
Eckford, Near Kelso, Roxburghshire TD5 8ED   *Tel: (05734) 561*

A handsome house in a lovely, peaceful location with four acres of parkland and views of the Cheviot hills. The interior does not quite live up to the promise of the outside as finely proportioned rooms with original features (fireplaces in every room) have been altered in character by modern furniture and fabrics; colour schemes are not always in keeping either. However all the bedrooms (except no 28) are very large. Easily the most appealing room is the pine-panelled dining room with elegantly laid tables. A Swiss chef presides and fruit and vegetables are mostly home-grown. The hotel is often used by fishing and shooting parties.

Location: *½ mile from Eckford (between Jedburgh and Kelso)*
Bedrooms: *6 (twin and family), all with bath. Direct dial telephone, TV (with video) and teamaking*
Facilities: *Parking. Babylistening*
Open: *All year*
Credit/charge cards accepted: *Access, Amex, Diners, Visa*
Price category: *£££*
Special rates: *2 or more nights DB&B £40 pp per night. Children £5 in parents' room*

ETTRICKBRIDGE
Ettrickshaws Country House Hotel
Ettrickbridge, Selkirkshire TD7 5HW   *Tel: (0750) 52229*

If getting away from it all is your main priority, and luxury is low on the list, this could be the ideal place for a weekend. Ettrickshaws is small and uninstitutional, in remote, hilly countryside. Inside it is traditionally furnished, with some modern additions already beginning to show their age. It is comfy enough if in places slightly shabby: but this is the sort of place where contrived interior décor would be beside the point. There is a friendly, informal atmosphere and if you do stay in for the day, a peaceful sitting room with a writing desk and shelves full of books. Otherwise, there are plenty of lovely walks and some private fishing on the Ettrick; packed lunches can be provided. The food here is good enough to raise the hotel out of the ordinary, unfussily presented.

Location: *Off the A7, 1½ miles west of Ettrickbridge*
Bedrooms: *6 (double and twin), all with bath/shower. Direct dial telephone, TV (with video) and teamaking. Hairdryer on request*
Facilities: *Parking. Packed lunches. Private fishing on the Ettrick*
Restrictions: *No dogs in public rooms or two bedrooms. No children under nine. No smoking in drawing room*
Open: *Mid Feb to mid Dec*
Credit/charge cards accepted: *Access, Amex, Diners, Visa*
Price category: *££*
Special rates: *2-3 nights, reduction of £1 pp per night; 4-6 nights, reduction of £3. Children £22.50 in parents' room*

INNERLEITHEN
Tighnuilt House Guest House
Peebles Road, Innerleithen, Peeblesshire EH44 6RD   *Tel: (0896) 830491*

An attractive white roughcast house set in well-kept formal gardens and woodland above the Tweed. Dating from the 1920s, the house retains Art Deco and Art Nouveau features and is impeccably maintained inside and out. Bedrooms and public rooms are large and comfortable, most with splendid views across the hills. A delightful place, offering good value for those who do not object to the lack of private bathrooms.

Location: *Between Innerleithen and Peebles, on the A72*
Bedrooms: *6 (single, double, twin and family), none with private bath. Teamaking*
Facilities: *Parking. TV and pool table in lounge.*
Restrictions: *No smoking in dining room*
Open: *Easter to mid-Dec*
Credit/charge cards accepted: *Visa*
Price category: *£*
Special rates: *Reductions for children, depending on age*

KELSO
Ednam House
Bridge Street, Kelso, Roxburghshire   *Tel: (0573) 24168*

A fine Georgian mansion in the centre of Kelso but with lawns sloping down to the Tweed. The hotel has been in the same family since 1928 and the glass-walled restaurant extension dates from the 1930s. Public rooms are comfortable but dowdy; refurbishment has been piecemeal over the years but period features, fine views and fresh flowers save the day. Food is quite good, with old-fashioned service. Bedrooms at the back have river views; those at the front are larger. Ednam House caters chiefly for keen fishermen for five months of the year and the hotel will cook your catch for you. A sound old-fashioned hotel with a certain eccentric charm.

Location: *Just off the main square of Kelso*
Bedrooms: *32 (single, double, twin and family), all with bath. Direct dial telephone. TV. Teamaking on request. Hairdryer, trouser press*
Facilities: *Parking. Snooker table. Fishing by arrangement. Babylistening*
Restrictions: *No dogs in dining room*
Open: *12 Jan to 23 Dec*
Price category: *££*
Special rates: *2 nights DB&B, £28.50-£35 (single £35) pp per night. Reductions for children under 14, depending on age*

KELSO
Sunlaws House Hotel
Kelso, Roxburghshire TD5 8JZ   Tel: (05735) 331

A Victorian country house of grand proportions, owned by the Duke of Roxburghe. This is a very comfortable and civilised place to stay, well placed for the natural and architectural delights of the Borders, but also with much to offer in its own extensive grounds. Sunlaws is very much the country house and most people could happily spend a weekend here with walks and the odd excursion (for instance to Floors Castle, the Duke's rather larger home). Bedrooms are traditional and comfortable, with lots of thoughtful extras, including magazines, fruit and biscuits. Younger people and families might prefer the slightly cottagey stable block with freshly decorated rooms in co-ordinating fabrics and wallpapers, with rattan furniture. The drawing room is elegantly furnished and decorated; flowers, photographs and glossy magazines contribute to the country house effect. The dining room is slightly less grand but comfortable, and food, especially the fish, has been highly praised. The Library, a panelled room lined with leatherbound books, is just the place for a post-prandial dram.

Location: *On A698, 3 miles south-west of Kelso*
Bedrooms: *21 (single, double and twin), 20 with bath (1 with shower only). 6 in stable courtyard. Direct dial telephone, TV and teamaking. Hairdryer on request*
Facilities: *Parking. Croquet, tennis, fishing, shooting (full range and clay pigeon). Packed lunches. Babylistening*
Restrictions: *No dogs in public rooms*
Open: *All year*
Credit/charge cards accepted: *Access, Amex, Diners, Visa*
Price category: *£££-££££*
Special rates: *Winter, 2 nights DB&B £44.50 pp per night (£47.50 in spring, £50 in summer). Fishing breaks, DB&B £55 (single £65) pp per night, shooting breaks full board £52.50 (single £62.50) pp per night. Reduced rates for children in parents' room*

PEEBLES
Cringletie House Hotel
Peebles EH45 8PL   *Tel: (072 13) 233*

A 19th-century turreted mansion standing in 28 acres of grounds two miles from Peebles (and only 20 miles from Edinburgh). It is well maintained and comfortably furnished with antiques and good traditional furnishings. The sitting room is spacious and panelled with a fine painted ceiling, the two dining rooms are high-ceilinged and light. Bedrooms (some in the turrets) are comfortable, with fine views. A walled kitchen garden supplies some of the produce for the table; very good eating here, and an interesting wine list. Cringletie was built by David Bryce for the Wolfe Murray family in 1861 and has been a hotel since 1963.

Location: *Off the A703, two miles north of Peebles*
Bedrooms: *16 (single, double, twin and family), 11 with bath/shower. Direct dial telephone, TV, hairdryer*
Facilities: *Parking, lift. Tennis, croquet, putting*
Restrictions: *No dogs in public rooms or unaccompanied in bedrooms. Smoking discouraged in dining rooms*
Open: *Mid Mar to Dec*
Credit/charge cards accepted: *Access, Visa*
Price category: £££
Special rates: *Autumn and spring, 2 or more nights DB&B £35 (£34 single) pp per night; weekends, 2 or more nights DB&B £41 (£40 single) pp per night. Child in parents' room £10.50 (£7.50 for second child or child under 5), teenagers £15.50, cot £2.50*

PEEBLES
The Cross Keys
Northgate, Peebles EH45 8RS   *Tel: (0721) 20748*

A delightful old coaching inn with its own courtyard, set back from a quietish street, the Cross Keys was a favourite haunt of Sir Walter Scott and is featured in several of his novels. Bedrooms are simple, clean and comfortable – most are at the back of the building and therefore quiet. The lounge, with television, is more basic but the breakfast area leading off it has french windows onto the garden. The restaurant, called the Kings Orchard, is a comfortable beamed room, once the stables. Meals and drinks are served in the courtyard in fine weather.

Location: *Off High Street in centre of Peebles*
Bedrooms: *7 (single, double, twin and family), none with bath. Teamaking on request*
Facilities: *Parking. Pool tables in bar. Games room in bar*
Open: *All year*
Credit/charge cards accepted: *Amex, Diners, Visa*
Price category: £
Special rates: *Children under 6 in family room free*

PEEBLES
Peebles Hotel Hydro
Peebles EH45 8LX   *Tel: (0721) 20602*

A vast spa hotel, much rebuilt and extended since the late 19th century, with fine views and 30 acres of manicured lawns and wooded grounds, the Peebles Hydro offers a weekend break in itself. The range of recreation facilities, both indoor and outdoor, is vast and includes a luxurious pool complex with jacuzzi, sauna and a gym. There is dancing to a live band on Friday and Saturday nights in the ballroom. The public rooms are traditional and institutional, with an aura of Edwardian elegance; bedrooms are simple, modern and well-equipped if rather anonymous. A good choice for the gregarious and active.

Location: *Off the A72 a mile west of Peebles*
Bedrooms: *137 (single, double, twin and family), all with bath. Direct dial telephone, TV, teamaking, hairdryer, trouser press*
Facilities: *Parking. Tennis, riding, squash, putting, mini-golf, archery, croquet, pitch and putt. Indoor swimming pool, gym, sauna, solarium, badminton, billiards, snooker, table tennis. Hairdresser. Babylistening. Playground, adventure playground and children's playroom. Nature trail*
Restrictions: *No dogs*
Open: *All year*
Credit/charge cards accepted: *Access, Amex, Diners, Visa*
Price category: £££
Special rates: *3 nights midweek DB&B £44.66 (single £48) pp per night. Children in parents' room £7.50*

SELKIRK
Philipburn House Hotel
Selkirk, TD7 5LS   *Tel: (0750) 20747*

There is little very typically Scottish about Philipburn House, but it is a welcoming hotel, ideal for families and with a good reputation for cooking and an impressive wine list. It makes a good base for exploring the Ettrick and Yarrow valleys and Bowhill, as well as the better-known area around Kelso. But it is perhaps ideal for people who want to take advantage of the hotel's own assets, especially for those who want to take their children away for the weekend; there's a swimming pool, an adventure playground and a games room and tuition can be arranged for riding and fishing. In the evening first-growth clarets, fine burgundies and candlelit poolside dining keep adults happy too. Specialities include local lamb and venison, Mull prawns and salmon from the Ettrick. There are dinner dances on Saturday nights. Almost half the bedrooms are suites, designed for family use – most are spacious with rustic pine furniture and floral cotton fabrics; two with sliding glass doors overlook the pool and are more modern in style. Public rooms are informal, again with lots of pine furnishings which give the place a slightly Austrian feel.

Location: *Above the junction of the A707 and A708, about ½ mile from the centre of Selkirk*

Bedrooms: *16 (double, twin, suites, family, cottages), all with bath/shower. Direct dial telephone, TV, teamaking, hairdryer, trouser press*
Facilities: *Parking. Swimming pool. Playground. Games room. Babylistening*
Restrictions: *Dogs in outside suites only. No smoking in restaurant*
Open: *All year*
Credit/charge cards accepted: *Access, Amex, Diners, Visa*
Price category: *£££*
Special rates: *Weekends (except Christmas), 2 nights DB&B (including teas and Sun lunch) £37.50 pp per·night. Children under 10 in parents' room free*

Prices are for b&b per person, sharing a double/twin room with bath	
£	= You can expect to pay under £20
££	= You can expect to pay between £20 and £30
£££	= You can expect to pay between £30 and £40
££££	= You can expect to pay between £40 and £55
£££££	= You can expect to pay over £55

The Stour Valley

- Gentle landscape and charm on a small scale; no need to drive for miles
- Good for pottering around picturesque villages; plenty of antique shops, craft shops and cosy tearooms
- Few really important sights but some fine medieval 'cloth' churches and Tudor houses, from timber-framed cottages to country mansions
- Not very much to do on wet days and few sights of particular interest to children
- Prime beauty spots and places associated with Constable can be crowded in summer and the busy A12 is never far away
- Some civilised small hotels and very good restaurants; an ideal area for 'foodies' or city dwellers who want to unwind

The River Stour forms the boundary between Suffolk and Essex. About 6 miles north-east of Colchester it bisects the tiny area known as Dedham Vale, where Constable grew up and which his paintings made famous. If you are looking for the originals of Constable's vistas you'll probably be disappointed; the lie of the land has often altered and modern farming methods and major roads have left their mark. But some of the landmarks – mills, locks and church towers – are still there and the watermeadows, the ruminative cattle and the sleepy villages with thatched cottages are very evocative. There are some even prettier, picture postcard villages beyond Dedham Vale itself but included within the officially designated 'Area of Outstanding Natural Beauty' and close to the valley of the Stour.

Dedham Vale

The heart of Constable country, **Dedham** is deservedly the area's most popular village, with a broad High Street of elegant 18th-century houses and ancient inns facing a 15th-century flint-built church, and rowing boats for hire on the river. Castle House, the home of the late Sir Alfred Munnings, is now a showcase for many of his paintings and drawings. **East Bergholt** (where Constable was born and spent most of his youth) is marred by dull modern housing but the village is still interesting, particularly around the church with its unfinished tower and ground-level bell cage. Just down the valley is Flatford Mill, featured in Constable's most popular paintings, now with a large paying car park.

There are other, quieter villages, not as well-groomed as Dedham, but less crowded and well worth a visit. **Nayland** is a down-at-heel small town on the Stour, centred on the old market square; the church contains an altarpiece by Constable. **Higham** is an attractive hamlet with cottages sloping gently down to a bridge across the River Brett. **Boxford**, with its riverside church and jettied, timber-framed houses is scruffily picturesque and **Polstead**, with a big village pond, is pleasant. But perhaps the finest village is **Stoke-by-Nayland**, where the lovely 16th-century Guildhall and Maltings crouch below the lofty church tower, itself often a landmark in Constable's paintings.

VISITING CONSTABLE'S VIEWPOINTS

Many of the painter's original viewpoints are now on private land. Flatford Mill and Willy Lott's cottage (which features in 'The Haywain') are used as a Field Studies Centre and not open to casual visitors. However you can visit **The Bridge Cottage** at **Flatford**, also depicted in several of his works; there is an exhibition, plus a tea garden and boats for hire. (NT) [*Open Apr to Oct, Wed to Sun; daily June to Aug*]

In and around Dedham you can buy detailed walking maps of Constable's haunts, showing the viewpoints of his paintings (which were, however, not usually strictly topographic).

Further afield

Beyond Dedham Vale the countryside expands into rolling valleys and open arable fields on a larger scale. Here medieval wool wealth has given towns and villages their distinguished character and notably fine churches – usually of flint, often decoratively alternated with stone. Many buildings have timber frames, often plastered and painted in 'Suffolk pink' (which seems to cover shades from puce to light orange) and with thatched roofs. Some houses are decorated with pargeting – ornamental bas-relief in plaster.

We list below (in a circuit order) the most attractive villages and towns in the area; many other villages, off this well-beaten track, are worth exploring and likely to be less crowded.

Hadleigh, a very attractive town along the River Brett, has a High Street of pretty old-fashioned shopfronts. By the church is a delightful square, made up of churchyard, medieval guildhall and Tudor gatehouse – known as the Deanery Tower. **Kersey** is a classic English village with one street of cottages running across the valley of a little stream. At the bottom is the 'splash', a ford which doubles as a duckpond. Something of a medieval showcase, **Lavenham** is a remarkably well-preserved assortment of timber-framed buildings, including the guildhall, the priory and old inns and shops. The most obvious landmark is the superb church in exemplary Suffolk style. Lavenham is, inevitably, popular with coach parties and tourists. **Long Melford** really is long – well over a mile of inns, shops and restaurants along the broad and busy main street. There are many antique shops, with merchandise varying from bric-a-brac to fine furniture; over the bridge is the large green, with a magnificent church and, nearby, the two great houses, both dating from the 16th century (see 'Historic buildings'). **Cavendish** is a picturesque little village where tiny pink cottages with heavy fringes of thatch surround a green with a graceful 14th-century church tower. Nearby **Clare** is a small town spoilt by the main road; merchants' houses with Georgian façades and timber-framed inns and shops surround the market place. Next to the church is the Ancient House, now a little museum with pargeting on its gables. There are remains of an Iron Age fort (on the common), a Norman castle, and an abandoned railway station (both in a small country park). **Castle Hedingham**, another notably well-kept village, is still dominated by a Norman castle keep. Off the main road, its streets are unwidened, its buildings low and clustered around an odd-looking church (with a Norman interior). Church Ponds and Falcon Square both have a pronounced medieval feel. **Sudbury** is a market town, with little provision for tourists. If you go to see Gainsborough's House (see below), look out for Friar Street (near the river) with some good timber-framed houses.

HISTORIC BUILDINGS

Cavendish, Nether Hall A 15th-century manor house with a small collection of paintings. There are tours of the house and surrounding vineyards, in production since 1972. [*Open all year, daily*]

Hedingham Castle A square Norman keep still in exceptionally good order despite school visits and other, earlier, marauders. The interior, with a banqueting hall and minstrels' gallery, is packed with souvenirs. [*Open Easter, then daily May to Oct*]

Lavenham, The Guildhall One of the noblest façades in Lavenham. Inside there are historical displays of local crafts and industry, notably the wool trade. (NT) [*Open April to Oct, daily*]

Lavenham, The Priory A former Benedictine priory, later home of a wealthy medieval wool merchant. Recent restoration has uncovered much original detail and a traditional herb garden has been created. [*Open April to Oct, daily*]

Long Melford, Kentwell Hall   A lovely moated manor house dating from the 16th century, recently restored after a long period of neglect. Money-raising activities include a week-long Tudor festival in summer, with authentic costumes, sports and banquets. The brick maze, modelled on a Tudor rose, is an odd addition. [*Open Mar to Sep, pm, Wed, Sun and Bank Hols*]

Long Melford, Melford Hall   Standing in its own parkland, opposite the village green, Melford is a large and very fine red-bricked Tudor mansion with turrets and characteristic barley-twist chimneys. It contains fine collections of furniture, porcelain and paintings, plus a room devoted to Beatrix Potter who often visited the house. [*Open April to Sep, pm, Wed, Thurs, weekends and Bank Hols*]

Sudbury, Gainsborough's House   Gainsborough's birthplace and childhood home is a Georgian town house containing period furniture and some of his lesser-known works. [*Open all year: Tues to Sat, and pm Sun and Bank Hol Mons*]

MUSEUMS

Cavendish, Sue Ryder Museum   A small but highly evocative museum showing the origins and principles of the philanthropic Sue Ryder Foundation. [*Open all year, daily*]

RAILWAYS

Nr Castle Hedingham, Colne Valley Railway   A short stretch of track, privately restored, with some smart locos and rolling stock. There's a good picnic site; and a dining car serves food and teas. Regular steam days, mostly in summer. [*Open all year, daily; telephone (0787) 61174 for details*]

Chappel, East Anglian Railway Museum   Victorian station with signalbox and goods shed used for exhibitions and a buffet car for refreshments. Comprehensive collection of rolling stock and steam locomotives. Regular steam days. [*Open all year, daily; telephone (07875) 2571 for details*]

Walking

Despite the obvious charms of its villages, the Stour Valley is chiefly unspectacular, flattish agricultural landscape – not ideal walking country. There are a handful of attractive and very easy rambles, notably along the Stour between Manningtree and Stratford St Mary (including the classic Constable country between Flatford and Dedham, a walk alongside quiet meadows;

the path can get flooded after heavy rain, however), and the Stour and Orwell estuaries near Shotley Gate (itself an ugly village, but there are good views across the water to Harwich). Further north is a pleasant riverside path by the Gipping near Needham Market.

But unquestionably the best walking in this region is found at least 30 miles north-east, along the Suffolk coast between Walberswick and Aldeburgh, a designated Area of Outstanding Natural Beauty, which includes some of East Anglia's finest scenery. Its undulating heathlands, semi-open pine forests and a genuinely remote coast are best explored on foot; there is a dense network of paths and tracks.

See *Holiday Which? Good Walks Guide* walks 120-122.

When to go

The annual Tudor recreations at Kentwell Hall, Long Melford, run from the end of June for three weeks and are open to the public at weekends. The East Anglian Summer Music Festival, based at Hadleigh, runs from late July until mid August with concerts on Saturday mornings and Sunday afternoons. At Sudbury, there is a carnival in June, a regatta in July and an open-air arts and crafts exhibition on Sundays from July to September. Most hotels are open all year round.

Information

The East Anglia Tourist Board, Toppesfield Hall, Hadleigh, Suffolk; tel: (0473) 822922. Tourist Information Centres in the Public Library at Sudbury, tel: (0787) 72092, and in the Guildhall at Lavenham, tel: (0787) 248207, supply more detailed local information

East Anglian Summer Music Festival, The Old School, 5 Bridge Street, Hadleigh, Suffolk IP7 6BY (tickets from mid June)

Where to stay

Several of the larger villages have traditional inns, often on the road. More appealing are several small, personal establishments, and a few luxurious, and expensive, hotels – both generally offering a very high standard of cooking. There is also a concentration of Wolsey Lodges (see chapter on 'Alternative accommodation') in this part of East Anglia.

DEDHAM
Dedham Vale
Stratford Road, Dedham, Colchester, Essex CO7 6HW   *Tel: (0206) 322273*

A Victorian country house, the main feature of which is the Terrace Restaurant, a large and light conservatory-style dining room with hanging plants; Indian or international food is served from a buffet and *rôtisserie*. The theme is reflected in the bar with its *trompe d'oeil* mural of garden scenes. There is a small comfortable lounge. The bedrooms are decorated carefully but not elaborately and comfortably furnished with some antique pieces. There's a terrace, and sloping lawned gardens. If the cuisine appeals, one would be quite comfortable here.

Location: *Off the A12, 2 miles south of Dedham*
Bedrooms: *6 (double, twin and 1 family suite), all with bath. Direct dial telephone, TV*
Facilities: *Parking*
Restrictions: *No dogs*
Open: *All year. Restaurant closed Sat lunch and Sun dinner*
Credit/charge cards accepted: *Access, Amex, Diners, Visa*
Price category: *££££*
Special rates: *Reduced rates for children in parents' room*

DEDHAM
Dedham Hall
Dedham, Colchester, Essex CO7 6AD   *Tel: (0206) 323027*

Well known by many for its painting courses, this charming rural working farmhouse dates from the 14th century. The bedrooms are dotted around in various parts of the house and outbuildings and are comfortably rather than lavishly furnished with plain painted walls, floral curtains and some antiques. The two comfortable sitting rooms have lots of books, and pictures on the walls painted by students and teachers. The dining room is reached by walking through the farmhouse kitchen complete with Aga, which adds to the pleasant informal no-nonsense spirit of the place. The six acres of paddock and English country garden are delightful. The energetic hostess provides dinner-party-style menus, usually including her home-made cheese. A friendly and unpretentious place in which to encounter kindred spirits; but not really suitable for families with small children. Weekend painting courses are offered. *Holiday Which? Weekend Break Award*

Location: *5 minutes' walk from the centre of Dedham village*
Bedrooms: *12 (single, double, twin), 3 in converted farm building; 3 with bath, 5 with shower. Teamaking*
Facilities: *Parking. Croquet*
Restrictions: *No dogs. No smoking in dining room*
Open: *Mar to Nov*
Credit/charge cards accepted: *None*
Price category: *££*
Special rates: *Children in parents' room £10*

DEDHAM
Maison Talbooth
Stratford Road, Dedham, Colchester, Essex CO7 6HN   *Tel: (0206) 322367*

A Victorian country house which is run as a grand B&B. Bedrooms, named after poets, are lavishly decorated and are furnished with large beds plus a mixture of antique, reproduction and modern furniture. Televisions with teletext and an array of miniatures and mixers add to the personal comforts. Breakfast is served in your bedroom and dinner may be eaten at either of the two sister establishments in the area (Dedham Vale Hotel or Le Talbooth restaurant). Play croquet or chess (on the large scale 'board') in the lawned gardens, or flip through magazines in the sitting room with its fine plaster trellis ceiling and large cream chairs. Perhaps a little too contrived and slightly impersonal to be truly 'English', this is a place to be thoroughly pampered with modern comforts.

Location: *Off the A12 1½ miles south of Dedham*
Bedrooms: *10 (double, twin, suites), all with bath. Direct dial telephone, TV with teletext, minibar*
Facilities: *Parking. Croquet, outdoor chess, fishing*
Restrictions: *No dogs*
Open: *All year*
Credit cards accepted: *Access, Amex, Diners, Visa*
Price category: *££££*
Special rates: *Children in parents' room £10*

HADLEIGH
The Gables
Angel Street, Hadleigh, Suffolk   *Tel: (0473) 827169*

For the past eight years, week-long painting courses have been run by the artist owner, and now non-painting guests are welcome for shorter stays. Set on a surprisingly busy road, this is a pink-painted gabled house some five or six hundred years old with lots of exposed beams. The bedrooms, named after local artists, are plainly decorated and provide simple comfort. A set-menu dinner is served at one big table. There is a comfortable lounge with bare boards and rugs, leather Chesterfields, and books; drinks are dispensed from a dresser. Outside is a courtyard patio, a cottage garden and, of course, the studio. It's a homely establishment, with an undemanding atmosphere.

Bedrooms: *5 (double, twin, 1 family room), 2 with bath, 1 with shower. Teamaking*
Facilities: *Parking. Studio*
Restrictions: *No dogs. No smoking in bedrooms or dining room*
Open: *All year except two weeks at Christmas*
Credit cards accepted: *None*
Price category: *££*
Special rates: *2 nights, 10% reduction. Children half price in parents' room*

HINTLESHAM
Hintlesham Hall
Hintlesham, Ipswich, Suffolk IP8 3NS　　　　　　　*Tel: (047 387) 268*

A splendid Elizabethan house with Georgian façade set in 18 acres of ground with Jersey cows, and chickens supplying produce for the kitchens. The sedate grandeur of the decoration – antique furniture in most of the rooms – belies the surprisingly young and informal atmosphere here. The entrance hall has a stone flagged floor with lots of plants in baskets and pots. The elegantly painted and panelled dining room is candlelit at night and the large bar, with panelling and oil paintings, has a drawing room atmosphere with tasteful and fashionable decoration. The first-floor bedrooms in the main house are huge and extravagantly draped and swagged; the bedrooms in the extension are slightly box-like, but they are carefully decorated. In either type you will welcome the creature comforts – which include home-made biscuits, books and magazines, and extra duvets. Famous for its cooking under the previous owner, Robert Carrier, Hintlesham's reputation is justifiably high; food is delicious and beautifully presented.

Location: *Five miles west of Ipswich on the A1071*
Bedrooms: *17 (double, twin and suites), one with four-poster bed, all with bath. Direct dial telephone, TV, minibar*
Facilities: *Parking. Snooker, table tennis. Tennis*
Restrictions: *No cigars or pipes in dining room. No dogs. No children under 10. Minimum stay of 2 nights if including Saturday*
Open: *All year*
Credit cards accepted: *Access, Amex, Diners, Visa*
Price category: *£££*
Special rates: *Oct to April, 2 nights DB&B £52.50 (£87.50 in suite) pp per night (additional Sunday night at half normal room rate)*

LAVENHAM
The Swan
High Street, Lavenham, Suffolk CO10 9QA　　　　　　*Tel: (0787) 247477*

This is a large, low, timber framed old coaching inn on a corner site in the centre of the village. Downstairs is a labyrinth of interconnecting lounges, pleasantly and comfortably furnished. It is a surprise to find that the splendid dining room with a very fine oak beamed and vaulted ceiling was added only in the 1960s. There is a pub-style bar with beamed ceiling and signatures of World War II pilots who were stationed nearby. Beams (some very low) upstairs too, in passages and bedrooms – where oak furniture and chintzy fabrics do not make a radical departure from hotel decoration. Bathrooms, although modernised, may still have lino flooring. But it is a good solid Trusthouse Forte hotel with imaginative menus and traditional facilities and services. There are occasional special-interest weekends (horse racing, chamber music).

Bedrooms: *48 (single, double, twin, suites), 2 with four-poster beds, all with bath. Direct dial telephone, TV, teamaking*
Facilities: *Parking. Babylistening*

Open: *All year*
Credit cards accepted: *Access, Amex, Diners, Visa*
Price category: ££££
Special rates: *2 nights DB&B £47.50-£50 (£52-55) pp per night. Children up to 16 free in parents' room, 75% of room rate in own room*

LONG MELFORD
The Black Lion
The Green, Long Melford, Suffolk CO10 9DN   *Tel: (0787) 312356*

There is a young and friendly spirit at this cream painted Georgian coaching inn, and although it occupies a corner site it is reasonably quiet and away from the main route through Long Melford. It's decorated throughout in fashionable 'rustic' style with sea-grass carpeting, some antiques and pine, and here and there a bust or a stuffed bird – falling short of luxury only by being slightly sparse. The dining room with Hogarth prints, pine chairs and green damask cloths is pleasant, simple and spacious and gives on to a walled garden; the sizeable sitting room has comfy Chesterfield sofas and antiques. Bedrooms are quite plain and tend to have brass bedsteads, chintzy curtains and covers and televisions hidden discreetly below round tables. In the food department, soups, sauces and puddings have been praised.

Bedrooms: *9 (double, twin and family), all with bath. Direct dial telephone, TV, tea-making*
Facilities: *Parking. Babylistening*
Open: *All year*
Credit cards accepted: *Access, Amex, Diners, Visa*
Price category: ££
Special rates: *Reduced rates for children in parents' room, £7.50 in separate adjoining room*

The Thames Valley

- English traditions from the playing fields of Eton to Henley regatta, Ascot races to the Changing of the Guard at Windsor Castle
- Some great houses to visit, several with royal – or at least ducal – connections
- Not good for touring by car; much of the area is built up and the Thames itself is rarely visible. Better to take a boat trip
- Few cheap or even very charming places to stay along the Thames itself. But Windsor is a good town base, and the whole area is within day-trip distance of London or Oxford
- A good area for gastronomic treats – there are several accoladed restaurants

The area normally regarded as the Thames Valley is the relatively small section between Windsor and Oxford. This is Berkshire, or, as the signs say, Royal Berkshire and it is an area of great Englishness and tradition. The gently meandering river recalls regattas and The Boating Song and lazy summer picnics or the antics of Three Men in a Boat. Windsor Castle, at least as much as Buckingham Palace, is a symbol of royalty and tradition. Typical of the area are cottages of flint or diapered brickwork, half-timbered inns and Georgian town houses. Unfortunately, heavily built-up areas and roads encroach on the rural charm; this is commuter belt and it shows.

Windsor and Eton

Windsor and Eton, separated by a pedestrian bridge across the Thames, have much to offer those who love English tradition and history. The famous school dominates Eton – which consists mainly of one long High Street – while the massive castle is the focal point of the old town of Windsor, now much expanded but with some cobbled streets and old houses. In both towns old inns and houses have been converted into antique shops and tearooms. Inevitably Windsor is the more touristy; during term time at least, Eton seems populated mainly by the boys, in their distinctive tail coats.

HISTORIC BUILDINGS AND GARDENS

Eton College The 16th- and 17th-century School Yard, the gothic Chapel and the cloisters are the main areas of the school open to the general public; there's also a Museum of Eton Life. [*Open April to Sep, daily except 1 June and 17 Sep, pm only during term time, all day otherwise*]

Windsor Castle Said to be the largest and oldest inhabited castle in the world, Windsor Castle has been a royal residence since the time of William the Conqueror, though much rebuilt. The grand **State Apartments** contain some magnificent paintings, including masterpieces by Van Dyck, Rubens and Canaletto. A separate ticket is required for the Old Master drawings – including works by Leonardo da Vinci, Raphael, Michelangelo and Holbein – and for Queen Mary's Dolls' House, a masterpiece of reduction designed by Lutyens. There are often long queues and it is advisable to arrive just before opening time to avoid them. Also well worth seeing is the coach museum. There are splendid views over the Thames Valley from the terrace behind the Horseshoe Cloisters. The Changing of the Guard can be seen in the morning. [*Castle precincts: open all year, daily except Good Fri and 13 June. State Apartments: open Jan to mid Mar and mid Oct to early Dec Mon to Sat; May to Oct also Sun pm; closed 3 weeks in June. Drawings, Dolls' House: open all year Mon to Sat (except Good Fri and Christmas) plus Sun pm May to mid Oct*]

Also within the castle precincts is **St George's Chapel**, often considered the finest example of Perpendicular architecture in England, with remarkable fan vaulting and wood carving. It is the burial place of ten monarchs, including the founder, Edward IV. There are conducted tours on Saturdays.

Windsor Great Park Windsor Castle is best seen from the three mile Long Walk. Other parts of the Great Park worth including in a walk are the Savill Garden and Valley Gardens.

Guildhall This 17th-century building has royal portraits.

FAMILY OUTINGS

Windsor, Royalty and Empire A re-creation of Queen Victoria's Diamond Jubilee celebrations of 1897 with a theatre show that brings famous Victorians to life. Housed in the original royal waiting room of the station. [*Open all year, daily except 25 Dec*]

Windsor Safari Park A pleasant, well laid out safari route with a surprisingly rural feel, close as it is to built-up areas. A variety of shows and exhibitions including performances with sealions, killer whales and dolphins and falconry displays; plus a nature trail, adventure playcentre and tropical plant and butterfly house. Regular half-hourly bus services from Windsor town centre. [*Open all year daily except 25 Dec*]

The Thames Valley

Maidenhead, Marlow and, most famous of all, Henley are riverside towns with expensive houses and lawns leading down to the Thames, old bridges and handsome red brick Georgian houses lining the main streets. Between these towns are a number of pretty villages: Cookham, birthplace of Stanley Spencer, with a High Street of old inns and half-timbered buildings; Bisham, with picturesque low cottages and overgrown gardens and Hurley, a peaceful backwater where a fine flint church, an ancient rectory and a priory surround the village green. Beyond Henley there is more rural charm to the landscape; wooded between Remenham and Wargrave (a pretty village on the Thames), open and agricultural between Sonning and Shiplake. The area around Reading is built up but Pangbourne, Goring and Streatley are typical elegant riverside towns. The most interesting and unspoilt town, however, is Dorchester-on-Thames where flint cottages, antique shops and old inns line the curving main street and the peaceful abbey seems miles from anywhere. There is little through traffic and Dorchester feels like the end of the road. In fact, the Thames meanders on via Abingdon, a market town with some interesting old buildings, to Oxford and the Cotswolds.

HISTORIC BUILDINGS AND GARDENS

Henley-on-Thames, Stonor   Stonor is a lovely red brick manor tucked away in the Chiltern hills. The extensive mainly Georgian façade conceals a much earlier interior, including a medieval solar and Catholic chapel; the house has been in the same family for over 800 years. [*Open pm; May to Sep, Sun, Wed and Thurs; plus Sun and Bank Hol Mon in April, Sat in Aug*]

Mapledurham House   An Elizabethan mansion in the secluded and peaceful village of the same name. It contains fine Tudor interiors and 17th- and 18th-century furniture and paintings. Mapledurham can be visited by boat from Caversham. [*Open Easter Sun to Sep, pm; Sat, Sun and Bank Hol Mons*]

Pangbourne, Basildon Park   A classical house built in 1776. The main feature is the Octagon room; there are fine paintings and furniture. (NT) [*Open April to Oct, pm, Weds to Sun*]

nr Reading, Stratfield Saye   Home of the Dukes of Wellington since 1817, the house is now something of a shrine to the Iron Duke. The gardens contain a wildfowl sanctuary and splendid trees, including a Turkey Oak, under which the Duke's famous horse Copenhagen lies buried. [*Open May to Sep, daily except Fri; plus April weekends*]

Taplow, Cliveden A very grand 19th-century house, with wooded parkland, formal gardens and fine views of the Thames. Cliveden is now a luxury hotel but the three rooms open to visitors give a feeling of its colourful past as home of a Prince of Wales, various Dukes and the Astor family. (NT) [*House open April to Oct, pm Thurs and Sun, grounds daily Mar to Dec*]

nr Windsor, Dorney Court An atmospheric manor house dating from the early 16th century. Romantic associations with Charles II whose mistress, Barbara Palmer, was an ancestor of the present owners. [*Open pm; Easter (inc Good Fri) to mid Oct, Sun and Bank Hol Mons; plus Mon and Tues June to Sep*]

(See London chapter for details of Chiswick House, Ham House, Hampton Court, Kew Gardens and Syon House)

GALLERIES

Cookham, Stanley Spencer Gallery A tiny gallery devoted to the famous painter with his powerful, unfinished 'Christ Preaching at Cookham Regatta'. [*Open Easter to Oct, daily; Nov to Easter Sat, Sun and Bank Hol Mons*]

CHURCHES

Dorchester Abbey Founded in 634, but dating mainly from the 12th century, the abbey church is famous for its lead font, the 14th-century painted reredos and extraordinary Jesse window. It also contains interesting old tombs and the remains of frescoes. There is a cloister garden on the Thame, and a little museum in the monastery guest house.

FAMILY DAYS OUT

Maidenhead, Shire Horse Centre Home of the Courage Shire horses; guided tours, playground, small animals area. [*Open daily Mar to Oct*]

BOATING

There are various passenger cruises along the Thames from centres such as Reading and Windsor, between Easter and October. A launch plies between Reading and Mapledurham, leaving Caversham promenade at 2.15pm when Mapledurham house is open.

Boats and cruisers can also be hired by the hour or day from many places along the river. Several companies will book boats for short breaks of 3 or 4 nights, though usually not at weekends in high season.

Walking

The river's classic beauty, fine trees and waterside buildings can be enjoyed by a level and very easily managed towpath. Well-frequented and almost too easy as it is, it is nevertheless essential viewing; the best sections are west from Maidenhead to Henley-on-Thames, and around Goring. Until the Countryside Commission's Thames Walk is developed, in a year or two, it is not possible to follow the entire route of the river. Where the hinterland is undeveloped, there is scope for good round walks, as in the southern end of the unspoilt Chiltern hills – in particular the area north of the stretch of the Thames from Marlow to Goring. Hambleden and Cookham are both deservedly popular bases for shorter routes. West of the river at Goring are the Berkshire Downs, a rolling expanse of chalk downland, traversed by a number of wide tracks and the long-distance Ridgeway Path (which follows metalled farm roads in places in this area). Further north, the scenery flattens out, but the towpath is still pleasant; the Sinodun Hills are a small isolated group of low grassy hills on the west side of the river from Dorchester-on-Thames and are particularly attractive for short walks.

See *Holiday Which? Good Walks Guide* walks 68, 96-8.

When to go

Summer is the traditional time to enjoy the Thames Valley, especially if you are exploring by boat (book well ahead for weekends). You'll need tickets for the major social events.

The Royal Meeting at Ascot races is held in mid June and Henley Royal Regatta from late June to early July – followed by Henley Festival of Music and the Arts ('floating' concerts and fireworks).

Those wanting to explore Eton and Windsor could avoid the tourists by taking their weekend out of season – except when the State Apartments of Windsor Castle are closed (*see above*). The Royal Windsor Horse Show is held in Home Park in mid May and The Windsor Festival (classical music) takes place from late September to October.

Information

The Thames and Chilterns Tourist Board, The Mount House, Church Green, Witney, Oxon OX8 6DZ; tel: (0993) 778800

Beautiful Berkshire, Shire Hall, Shinfield Park, Reading RG2 9XD; tel: (0734) 875444 (information on country hotels offering weekend breaks)

Henley Festival of Music and the Arts, Box Office: 27 Hart Street, Henley-on-Thames, Oxon RG9 2AR; tel (0491) 575751. General enquiries: tel 01-734 2505

Thames Hire Cruiser Association, 19 Acre End Street, Eynsham, Oxford OX8 1PE; tel: (0865) 990107 (list of boatyards; advice on hiring for short breaks)

Windsor Tourist Information Centre, Thames Street, Windsor, Berks; tel: (0753) 852010.

Where to stay

Most towns have a pub with traditional accommodation, but there is a distinct shortage of simple country hotels in this area. There are several hotels on the river, most with immaculate lawns, large restaurants and well-equipped rooms; the few more characterful hotels are mostly further from the river. Hotels recommended in our chapter on Oxford are worth considering.

DORCHESTER-ON-THAMES
The White Hart
Dorchester-on-Thames, Oxfordshire OX9 8HN   *Tel: (0865) 340074*

An attractive village hotel in a whitewashed building dating from the 17th century. The restaurant and bar are in a separate building reached by a covered walkway and across the car park is the sympathetic addition of a cottage providing two suites. Bedrooms, named after villages and towns, are decorated with pretty traditional fabrics; they are comfortable rather than lavish, with fresh fruit provided every day. The restaurant has lots of beams and some exposed stone walls, copper pots and pans, fresh and dried flowers; the Abbey Bar is more informal with wood burning stoves and sporting prints. The lounge, with wing chairs round a central refectory table, is a little staid. A pleasant, clean and comfortable hotel.

Bedrooms: *20 (single, double, twin, suites), 2 in annexe, 2 with four-posters, all with bath. Direct dial telephone, TV, teamaking. Hairdryer, trouserpress. Minibar on request*
Facilities: *Parking*
Restrictions: *Dogs by prior arrangement*
Open: *All year except 4 days over Christmas*
Credit/charge cards accepted: *Access, Amex, Diners, Visa*
Price category: £££
Special rates: *Oct to Mar (and some summer weekends), 2 nights DB&B £37.50 (£50) pp per night*

HENLEY-ON-THAMES
Regency House
River Terrace, Henley-on-Thames, Oxfordshire RG9 1BG   Tel: (0491) 571133

In a fine position by the edge of the river, behind a small front garden and away from the through traffic of Henley, the Regency House is run as a B&B. Bedrooms (with names) are almost cottage-like in atmosphere and décor, with floral print paper and lace bedspreads; they are equipped with a cocktail tray. The lounge and dining room are divided by doors; they have unobtrusive décor and large brocade-covered sofas. Pictures, books and a drinks tray make guests feel at home. A lovely riverside position, remarkably quiet for this part of the world.

Bedrooms: *5 (single, double, twin), all with bath. Direct dial telephone. TV, teamaking. Minibar*
Facilities: *Mooring (1 boat)*
Restrictions: *No dogs. No children under 12*
Open: *All year except 4 days over Christmas*
Credit/charge cards accepted: *Access, Amex, Visa*
Price category: ££
Special rates: *Weekends, 2 nights DB&B £37.50 pp per night*

HURLEY
Ye Olde Bell
High Street, Hurley, Nr Maidenhead, Berkshire SL6 5LX   Tel: (062 882) 5881

Recently acquired by Trusthouse Forte, this is not really the small pub one might imagine from the initial impression. Situated in a no-through-road, the original black and white building dates from the 12th century; the hotel also includes a Victorian/mock Tudor house next door, a modern annexe and a converted beamed and vaulted tithe barn, used mainly for functions. Bedrooms in the Victorian part are decorated with stencilled fabrics and papers; those in the oldest part are harmoniously floral. The old part is very up and down and the inn-style public rooms with beams are decorated with horse brasses and Hogarth prints. The dining room, while a bit dark, has lots of character; it leads to the very large English country-house garden.

Bedrooms: *26 (single, double, twin, family), 4 with 4-poster, 8 in Malt House, 8 in annexe, all with bath. Direct dial telephone, TV, teamaking. Hairdryer, trouser press. Minibar*
Facilities: *Parking*
Restrictions: *Pets by prior arrangement*
Open: *All year*
Credit/charge cards accepted: *Access, Amex, Diners, Visa*
Price category: £££
Special rates: *Children under 16 free in parents' room*

PANGBOURNE
The Copper Inn
Pangbourne-on-Thames, Reading, Berkshire RG8 7AR   *Tel: (07357) 2244*

A red brick building with a black and white 'Tudor' façade in the centre of Pangbourne. The dining room is large and light with French doors opening onto a patio area and the garden beyond. It is decorated in French style, with ladder-back chairs, trellis screens, tapestries, plates, coppers and paintings. The lounge has some antique furniture; further seating is provided in the entrance hall, which has a writing desk and books, and a restful colour scheme. The bar is more pub-like, with banquette seating. The spacious bedrooms are comfortable but less imaginative; passing traffic may be noticeable. This inn has good bar food, and has earned a reputation for its cuisine.

Bedrooms: *21 (single, double, twin, family), 7 in annex, 1 with four-poster, all with bath. Direct dial telephone. TV, teamaking. Hairdryer, trouserpress and minibar in some rooms*
Facilities: *Parking. Babylistening*
Restrictions: *No dogs*
Open: *All year*
Credit/charge cards: *Access, Amex, Diners, Visa*
Price category: *£££*
Special rates: *Weekend, 2 nights B&B (and allowance towards dinner of £15.85) £31.25 pp per night. Children under 14 in parents' room free*

SONNING
The White Hart
Thames Street, Sonning-on-Thames, Berkshire RG4 OUT   *Tel: (0734) 692277*

This black and white gabled hotel has gardens leading down to the river. It offers a variety of accommodation: bedrooms are either in the main house, above the 'Hideaway Bistro', or in 'Palace Yard'. Those away from the main house are cottagey, with pine furniture; the 'Standard' has candlewick and cotton, 'Premier' has recently been redone with chintzes, cushions and trimmings. Those on the road suffer a bit from noise. The restaurant and cocktail bar are stylishly decorated, all swagged curtains and chintz; the bar lounge has a beamed ceiling and a welcoming fire; the overall effect is both smart and restful. Outside is a spacious but slightly over-furnished terrace, with lawns beyond.

Bedrooms: *25 (single, double, twin, family), 6 in Palace Yard, 7 in Hideaway Bistro, 8 with four-poster, all with bath. Direct dial telephone. TV, teamaking. Trouserpress. Hairdryer in superior rooms*
Facilities: *Parking. Mooring. Babylistening*
Open: *All year*
Credit/charge cards accepted: *Access, Amex, Diners, Visa*
Price category: *££££*
Special rates: *Weekends, 2 nights DB&B £37.50 pp per night*

STREATLEY
The Swan at Streatley
Streatley-on-Thames, Berkshire RG8 9HR   *Tel: (0491) 873737*

This pleasant old hotel has a marvellous waterside setting: the interconnecting public rooms open to a terrace and the river, where a splendid Oxford college barge is moored below the lawn. Extensive new building includes a Leisure Centre to add to the already considerable attractions. Bedrooms are mostly spacious and comfortable, traditionally decorated and supplied with fresh fruit and mineral water.

Location: *By the river bridge between Goring and Streatley*
Bedrooms: *44 (single, double, twin), all with bath. Direct dial telephone. TV, teamaking*
Facilities: *Parking. Mooring. Indoor swimming pool, multi-gym, sauna, solarium*
Restrictions: *Dogs by prior arrangement. Cigars discouraged in dining room*
Credit/charge cards accepted: *Access, Amex, Diners, Visa*
Price category: *£££*
Special rates: *Weekends, 2 nights DB&B £49.75 pp per night. Children under 10 in parents' room free; over 10, £15*

WATLINGTON
Well House
34-40 High Street, Watlington, Oxfordshire OX9 5PY   *Tel: (049 161) 3333*

Ten years ago, this was a restaurant in one building; it has since spread into four houses, and now provides accommodation, too. The houses date back several centuries; there are beams and some low ceilings, and in the red brick bar the well from which the house takes its name. Bedrooms are plainly decorated with chintzy curtains and matching bedcovers; the beamed sitting room and the attractive restaurant with Victorian chairs are relaxed and unfussy. A restful place to stay, well-run and welcoming.

Bedrooms: *8 (double, twin), all with bath/shower. Direct dial telephone. TV, teamaking. Hairdryer and iron on request*
Facilities: *Parking*
Restrictions: *No dogs*
Open: *All year*
Credit/charge cards accepted: *Access, Amex, Diners, Visa*
Price category: *££*
Special rates: *Cot in parents' room £5; children in adjacent room to parents, £12.50*

YATTENDON
The Royal Oak
Yattendon, Newbury, Berkshire RG16 OUF   *Tel: (0635) 201325*

This is a charming 16th-century red brick country inn, on the square of a quiet village. The emphasis is on good food and the dining room, a lovely room with warm tangerine walls, has Regency-style chairs at four or five tables beautifully decorated with arrangements of fresh flowers and fruit. An extensive and varied menu is also offered in the more informal beamed bar (quarry tiled floor, Windsor chairs and newspapers on poles). The entrance hall doubles as a sitting room; there's an open fireplace, sofas and chairs in soft colours, pictures and prints. Bedrooms are charming; they have pretty paint effects, co-ordinated fabrics, and homely touches including books (and bathrobes) in the bathroom. There is a pretty cottage-style garden at the back, and car parking nearby. A fine blend of easy-going sophistication and homely hospitality. *Holiday Which? Weekend Break Award*

Bedrooms: 5 *(single, double, twin), all with bath. Direct dial telephone. TV. Hairdryer*
Facilities: *Parking*
Restrictions: *Dogs by prior arrangement only*
Open: *All year*
Credit/charge cards accepted: *Access, Amex, Visa*
Price category: £££
Special rates: *Weekends, 2 nights B&B (including champagne and allowance of £10 towards dinner) £40 pp per night. Children under 8 in parents' room £10.50; over 8, in own room, £25 B&B*

Upland Dorset

- Rolling downs and sheltered valleys for walks, views and picnics but the most scenic walks are along the coast
- Attractive market towns and many pretty villages to explore
- A weekend's worth of places children will enjoy
- A scattering of historic houses and gardens, though they close in winter
- Accommodation ranges from rooms in pubs to comfortable country house hotels – but with few traditional mid range hotels

North of the A35 and west of the A350, in a rectangle roughly between Dorchester, Beaminster, Sherborne and Blandford, lies the heart of Dorset. Its hills swell from gentle tumps in the farming vales to the huge chalk curves of the downs, where the villages nestle in steep intervening valleys. Thomas Hardy's Wessex can still be filmed here from thatched cottages and mellow manor houses, pockets of unspoilt Old England; while on high ground you find Ancient Britain – Bronze-Age barrows and Iron-Age forts contour every vantage point. This part of Dorset has some distinguished market towns and beautiful country houses, but its really grand 'architecture' is the green immensity of Maiden Castle.

The busy county town of **Dorchester** has a Georgian core, Victorian outskirts and ancient origins: when the Romans built a garrison town they had the Maumbury Rings, a Neolithic monument, to hand for an amphitheatre. Remnants of a Roman townhouse have been uncovered in the grounds of County Hall. Dorchester is as full of pubs and restaurants as a venerable market town should be, including the half-timbered Judge Jeffrey's Lodging (he of the 'Bloody Assize' in the 17th century). Thomas Hardy called it Casterbridge, and the town cherishes landmarks from his novels. Hardy's heart is buried in Stinsford churchyard to the east, and his cottage is at Bockhampton. A mile or so south of Dorchester, Maiden Castle rises from flat fields as a grassy wall, exhilarating to scale on a fine day, and enormously impressive as its size and complexities are revealed.

Between main routes north-west of Dorchester there are Roman-straight downland roads, plunging lanes and villages of varying appeal. The eagle of **Wynford Eagle** perches in stone on the porch gable of the manor; **Cattistock** has a hairpin bend and a 19th-century church with some striking interior features; **Power-stock** spreads winsome thatched cottages across a hillside not far from **Eggardon**, one of the bleakest hill forts. Radio masts intrude on the scene hereabouts, and also near appealing little **Rampisham** in its narrow valley. **Evershot** has the prettiest High Street, all thatch and flowers and bow-windowed frontages between the Acorn Inn and lion-decorated Melbury Gate: pleasant (if muddy) walking in the vicinity includes the parkland round Melbury House. Further west, **Stoke Abbot** nestles in a wooded combe, an enjoyable farming village of ornate cottages and a church with some medieval character left. From **Pilsdon Pen**, at 908 feet the highest point in Dorset, there are sea views out across Marshwood Vale. Honey-coloured **Beaminster** is a pleasant small town to wander round, much of it rebuilt all of a piece in local stone after 18th-century fires. It has a handful of inns and antique shops, a market square with a market cross, and a magnificent 16th-century church tower with pinnacles and much sculpture.

Two routes follow river valleys north of Dorchester. The A352 takes you swiftly to postcard-pretty **Cerne Abbas**, well-visited and worth it, a pleasing mixture of stone and thatch, flint and red brick and visible timber frames, rare in Dorset. It has a graceful church, elegantly restored, and some splendid remnants of the Benedictine Abbey. On a hillside just north the chalk-cut Cerne Giant is famously nude and aggressive, and these days protected from eroding feet. You can look from a lay-by but you're discouraged from approaching his fence. The other route is the Piddle (or Trent) Valley. Downstream is **Tolpuddle**, where a solemn little cottage museum tells the story of its Martyrs transported for forming a trade union, and **Puddletown** where behind the busy main road junction hide some peaceful pretty houses and a lovely church. Upstream, the Piddle villages are amiably workaday; for more intensive charm, fork east to **Plush**. Out of the downs and across well-watered Blackmore Vale, **Sherborne**'s magnificent abbey and school give it the feeling of a small cathedral city. Many other medieval buildings survive in its streets and side-lanes, among the Tudor, Stuart and Georgian flavours; it's a showpiece country town to explore in detail. Its two Castles stand outside to the east – the Old one interestingly ruined, the New a stately home. In the surrounding country there are several fine manor houses – notably at **Sandford Orcas** and **Purse Caundle**, both occasionally open to the public.

The dairy farming landscape of Blackmore Vale, much more open than Marshwood's, is richly and spaciously mapped out;

you can appreciate it best from the big wooded hills to the south. From **Bulbarrow Hill** in the central downs the views extend to the Quantocks and the Mendips; from Hambledon or Hod, twin hill-forts, you look across the winding Stour valley. **Sturminster Newton** (locally known as 'Stur') is a small market town and a major livestock centre. From the south you approach across the river, and the old bridge still bears a plaque threatening transportation to enemies of the town. Across the water meadows, 17th-century Sturminster Mill has been restored to working order, grinding oats and flour with a 19th-century water turbine and open on milling days. About a mile along the river – a lovely summer walk – the mill near **Fiddleford** is also restored and sometimes open: it has a fine medieval hall with an elaborate timber roof.

The centre of **Blandford Forum**, rebuilt after a great fire in 1731, is still almost completely 18th-century, elegant and well proportioned. The market place is particularly pleasing. The parish church, oddly topped with a cupola, has fine old box pews; near it is the Fire Monument, a classical portico suitably inscribed. The town was rebuilt by the brothers Bastard, local architects and craftsmen – their 'Blandford school' was characterised by the use of many different shades of brick and stone. West of Blandford, a series of 'Winterborne' villages begins to follow the course of a stream whose source emerges in winter but drops below the chalk in summer; there's another series further south-west, sometimes spelt 'Winterbourne'. The northern villages include **Winterborne Clenston**, where you pass a Tudor manor with some splendid barns, and a Victorian church; and tiny **Winterborne Tomson**, downstream near the A31, whose little 12th-century church next to the farmhouse was perfectly restored in the 1930s in memory of Thomas Hardy.

In the next dip of the downs, **Milton Abbas** is the 18th-century planned village which replaced what Lord Milton considered an unsightly former settlement around medieval Milton Abbey. Its street curves down to an artificial lake, and its two rows of thatched white cottages behind grassy verges form a picturesque model housing estate. The church of Milton Abbey survives, lofty and impressive – it would have been enormous if the nave had ever been built. Next to it Lord Milton built his massive long mansion with Gothic pinnacles, now a public school; the 15th-century Abbot's hall with its splendid, complex timber roof is open in school holidays.

HISTORIC HOUSES AND GARDENS

Athelhampton   Impressive medieval house five miles north-east of Dorchester, built around 1500 for a Lord Mayor of London; enclosed formal gardens, laid out in 1890s. [*Open Easter to Oct, Wed, Thurs and Sun and all Bank Hols; in Aug, also Mon and Tues, pm*]

Beaminster, Mapperton Charming hillside garden of tranquil small manor house (not open), with orangery, fountain and fishponds. [*Open mid Mar to early Oct, Mon to Fri*]

Beaminster, Parnham House In immaculate gardens, an Elizabethan mansion much enlarged and restored and now a furniture workshop and school, full of craftsmen's work in wood. [*Open April to Oct, Wed, Sun and all Bank Hols*]

Chard, Forde Abbey Just inside the Dorset-Somerset border, a serene 17th-century house originally a 12th-century monastery, with 30 acres of beautiful varied gardens. [*Open April to mid Oct, gardens daily except Sun am and Sat, house pm only Wed, Sun and Bank Hols*]

Charminster, Wolfeton House Appealing and unusual Elizabethan manor with much older gatehouse; some fine interior stonework. [*Open May to Sep: in Aug, pm except Sat; otherwise pm Tues, Fri, Sun and Bank Hols*]

Minterne Magna, Minterne Gardens of elaborate 1900s country house (not open) include rhododendrons, rare trees, 18th-century landscaping. [*Open April to Oct, daily*]

Sherborne, Compton House West of Sherborne on the A30, manor with grandiose 19th-century-Tudor frontage houses the collection of Worldwide butterflies; also Lullingstone Silk Farm. [*Open April to Oct, daily*]

Sherborne, Sherborne Castle Mansion built for Sir Walter Raleigh, home of the Digby family since 1617, in landscaped grounds by Capability Brown; fine furniture, porcelain, pictures. [*Open Easter to Sep, pm only, Thurs, Sat, Sun and Bank Hol Mons*]

MUSEUMS

Dorchester, Dorset County Museum Splendid coverage of Maiden Castle in archaeology section; also Thomas Hardy's study, farming bygones, temporary exhibitions. [*Open all year, Mon to Sat*]

Dorchester, Dinosaur Museum Fossils, skeletons, lifesize reconstructions; audio-visual displays. [*Open all year, daily*]

Dorchester, Tutenkhamun Exhibition Dim corridor with spotlit displays leads to reproduced tomb-chambers with taped commentary. [*Open all year, daily*]

Dorchester, Dorset Military Museum Weapons, uniforms, badges, photographs, histories, on display in the Keep. [*Open all year: July to Sep, Mon-Sat; Oct to June, Mon-Fri*]

FAMILY OUTINGS

Dorchester, Maiden Castle Enormous grassy concentric earthworks with complicated entry routes, paths high and low, good views. Tough going for toddlers but fine for energetic children, especially combined with a visit to the County Museum. [*Open all year, daily*]

Milton Abbas, Park Farm Museum Friendly and family-run: village history and interesting bygones collected in the thatched stables, plus lots of animals outdoors to feed and pet, and a play area. [*Open April to Oct, daily*]

Walking

Walking in the chalk country of inland Dorset is something of a mixed bag. Its best aspect is rolling downland, punctuated by small copses of beech trees and patches of landscaped parkland, and dissected by smooth-sided valleys; the areas between Blandford Forum and Cerne Abbas, and around Beaminster are good examples of this, and contain some very pretty villages. A fine ramble can be made taking in Bulbarrow Hill, where there is an impressive view over Somerset, and Milton Abbas.

Unfortunately agricultural 'improvement' has turned a lot of the once herb-rich grassland into featureless prairie, and quite a lot of public rights of way have been ploughed out. After rain, the chalk tracks can become a mud-bath.

EXCURSIONS TO THE COAST

Some of the most enjoyable walking is along Dorset's varied coast, followed for nearly all of its length by a well-waymarked coastal path. Be prepared for fierce gradients and hair-raising, unfenced drops; in the chalk sections especially, the ground is prone to become sticky and slithery.

Lovers of Hardy will be pleased to find some surviving heathlands, mostly on the Isle of Purbeck in the east; the finest is on the south side of Poole Harbour, and can be explored through many enjoyable paths and tracks. Magnificent views of it and over Swanage Bay can be obtained from the path along the crest of the Purbeck ridge between Swanage and Corfe Castle. A little further west, Wareham Forest is a huge pine plantation offering easy walking on level sheltered sandy tracks; a nature trail begins from the Forestry Commission car park on a minor road leading north-west from Wareham.

East of Lulworth Cove as far as Kimmeridge is Ministry of Defence property, and the public only has access to the coast path at most week-ends throughout the year and daily at Easter and in

August. Despite the obvious military presence, it's worth making a special effort to sample what is probably the wildest part of the entire south coast. An excellent and well-signposted 3½ mile walk, starting from the Cove and taking in the remains of a fossilised forest, Mupe Bay and Bindon Hill, gives you a good idea of this. East of Kimmeridge, it soon becomes a tough but exhilarating switchback to St Aldhelm's Head; for a less exhausting taster, start from Worth Matravers and follow the lane south-west until St Catherine's Chapel, where you can pick up the coast path for a little. Just west of Swanage, there is easy walking at Durlston Head, while closer to Poole Harbour is Studland, from where you can take paths over the heath, along the grassy whaleback ridge of Ballard Down (getting sea views on three sides) and along the top of chalk cliffs.

East of Osmington Mills (south-east of Dorchester) all the way to Poole Harbour is consistently beautiful walking country. Most popular of all is the cliff path west of Lulworth Cove; it's an easy short mile to the natural arch of Durdle Door, and it's worth continuing to Burning Cliff. A track runs parallel inland across dullish farmland but unless you're in a hurry to return, it's better to retrace your steps along the cliff-top.

Near the western end of Dorset's coast, Golden Cap is most easily reached from Seatown or Chideock; good circular routes can be devised taking in the heathland of Eype Down nearby.

When to go

In summer, Dorset's main roads are usually crammed with holiday traffic heading for the coast or forging west to Devon or Cornwall. Dorchester too gets packed out. For a peaceful break, explore a small locality in depth – on lesser routes and country lanes. Out of season, the historic houses are shut but you can travel much more freely to pretty villages, market towns and a relatively uncrowded Dorchester.

Information

The West Country Tourist Board, Trinity Court, 37 Southernhay East, Exeter EX1 1QS, tel: (0392) 76351. The information centres at Dorchester and Blandford Forum are open all year.

Where to stay

Inland Dorset doesn't have a great deal of middle-range accommodation; there are one or two beautiful country house hotels, and some small and personal places. The area also has many traditional inns: several in our area have rooms, usually quite simple, as well as good food.

BEAMINSTER
Hams Plot
Beaminster, Dorset DT8 3LU   *Tel: (0308) 862979*

Near the market square of this small country town, Hams Plot is a white-painted Regency house with front veranda, surrounded by a peaceful garden with room to walk by the brook, sit under venerable trees or sunbathe by the small pool. A sitting room with graceful antiques opens onto the veranda, and another is a library of maps and local lore. Bedrooms are light and spacious, individually furnished in country style; the bathrooms were originally their dressing rooms. Dinner is served at one big Victorian table and the cooking uses good things from the kitchen garden. In an organised but easy-going atmosphere, Mr and Mrs Dearlove offer comfort and excellent value.

Bedrooms: *5 (double, twin), all with bath/shower. Teamaking*
Facilities: *Parking. TV in library. Swimming pool. Tennis, croquet*
Restrictions: *No children under 10. No dogs. Dinner served Sun, Mon, Wed and Fri only*
Open: *April to Oct, and Christmas*
Credit/charge cards accepted: *None*
Price category: £
Special rates: *3 nights, 5% discount*

CHEDINGTON
Chedington Court
Chedington, Beaminster, Dorset DT8 3HY   *Tel: (093589) 265*

Splendid Jacobean-style country house built in 1840, with vast views over Dorset and Somerset and ten acres of elegant grounds. The richly comfortable, handsomely proportioned public rooms and the big high-ceilinged bedrooms are all appropriately furnished with English antiques and good English style. It's formal and very peaceful: Mr and Mrs Chapman are reserved but attentive hosts, pampering personal touches abound, and the food is excellent.

Location: *¼m off the A356 (about 3 miles north of Beaminster) at Winyard's Gap*
Bedrooms: *10 (double or twin), one with a four-poster bed, all with bath and/or shower. TV, teamaking*
Facilities: *Parking. Billiards, putting, croquet. Babylistening*
Restrictions: *No small children in dining room. No dogs*

Open: *All year, except Christmas and 4 weeks Jan/Feb*
Credit/charge cards accepted: *Amex, Visa*
Price category: £££
Special rates: *Nov to 24 Mar (when open), 2 nights DB&B £44-£55 (single £54-£65) pp per night. Children in parents' room, under 8 DB&B; £22.50; 8-14, DB&B £27.50*

DORCHESTER
Casterbridge Hotel
49 High Street East, Dorchester, Dorset DT1 1H0   *Tel: (0305) 64043*

Very convenient for sightseeing; but traffic noise is a snag at the front of this Georgian guesthouse on a busy street, and some of the pretty bedrooms are small. It's an attractive house, scattered with family antiques and paintings; there's no restaurant but breakfasts are generous, tea is served (in the conservatory in summer) and a small bar opens off the well-appointed lounge.

Bedrooms: *16 (single, double, twin), 15 with bath and/or shower; 6 are in courtyard annexe. Direct dial telephone, TV. Hairdryer*
Facilities: *Parking. Babylistening*
Open: *All year except Christmas*
Credit/charge cards accepted: *Access, Amex, Diners, Visa*
Price category: £
Special rates: *Nov to Mar (except Easter) 3 nights B&B, 10% discount. Children sharing parents' room £6*

EVERSHOT
Summer Lodge   🏨
Evershot, Dorset DT2 0JR   *Tel: (093 583) 424*

In the centre of one of Dorset's most attractive villages, a most attractive house (18th-century and later) with a walled garden of lawns, flowers and pleasant pool area. There's a lovely big drawing room – desirable sofas, log fire – a small TV room also amply cushioned, an inviting bar and dining room; all is in relaxed good taste, with masses of fresh flowers. Bedrooms are of a very high standard, the food is excellent, and the caring hospitality of the owners is outstanding – a legendary country house welcome. *Holiday Which? Weekend Break Award*

Bedrooms: *12 (single, double) all with bath. Direct dial telephone, teamaking. Hairdryer*
Facilities: *Parking. Heated outdoor swimming pool. Croquet, tennis court*
Restrictions: *No children under 8*
Open: *All year*
Credit/charge cards accepted: *Access, Visa*
Price category: ££££
Special rates: *Winter, 3 nights midweek, DB&B £47 pp per night. Children in parents' room 40% discount*

MAIDEN NEWTON
Maiden Newton House
Maiden Newton, nr Dorchester, Dorset DT2 0AA   *Tel: (0300) 20336*

Off a quiet corner of a main-road village, a Victorian-rebuilt Dorset manor that really looks the part – romantic mellow stone and mullioned windows – in 17 acres of woods and gardens by the river Frome. Its atmosphere is both super-thoughtful hotel and instant house-party: first name terms are compulsory and set dinner (excellent food) is *en famille* with your hosts. The house is beautifully furnished in merging English styles – Regency armchairs and William Morris chintz in the big drawing room, chinoiserie and art deco drapes in the library – and the very individual bedrooms are sumptuous. Bathrooms vary from large to huge. Books and magazines are liberally spread, but conviviality is the thing.

Location: *12 miles north-west of Dorchester, just off A356*
Bedrooms: *7 (double and twin), one with four-poster bed, all with bath. TV and teamaking on request. Hairdryer, trouserpress*
Facilities: *Parking, stabling. Croquet, fishing*
Restrictions: *No children under 12 in dining room. Dogs by prior arrangement*
Open: *All year except Jan*
Credit/charge cards accepted: *Access, Visa*
Price category: *££££*
Special rates: *Nov to March, 2 or more nights, 12% reduction*

STURMINSTER NEWTON
Plumber Manor
Sturminster Newton, Dorset DT10 2AF   *Tel: (0258) 72507*

This fine Jacobean manor in peaceful farming country (with a trout stream running through the gardens) has been the home since the 17th century of the Prideaux-Brunes, who run it as a restaurant-with-rooms. The restaurant is relaxed and attractive with the emphasis on the quality of the food, including excellent vegetarian cooking. Bedrooms in the main house have a lived-in, flowered-wallpaper general style; those in the annexe are 'superior' which means both bigger and better furnished, comfortably modern. Bathrooms throughout are neat and no-nonsense. Very good value.

Location: *Off the Hazelbury Bryan road, 2 miles south-west of Sturminster*
Bedrooms: *12 (double and single); 6 are ground floor in converted stable block; all with bath. Direct dial telephone, TV, teamaking. Hairdryer*
Facilities: *Parking. Tennis, croquet*
Restrictions: *No children under 12. No dogs*
Open: *All year except 2 weeks in Feb*
Credit/charge cards accepted: *Access, Visa*
Price category: *£££*
Special rates: *Nov to Mar, 2 or more nights, 10% discount; Oct and April, midweek, 2 nights 10% discount, 3 or more 15% discount*

The Welsh Marches

- Good touring country with varied landscape and unexploited rural charm; a very rewarding area for walks and pottering around
- Unspoilt, picturesque towns and showcase villages with quaint black-and-white buildings, handsome Georgian houses and fine medieval churches
- Few major sights, or places for family outings. The remains of border castles and some interesting churches provide the main sightseeing interest. Apart from a handful of local museums there's not much to do on a wet day
- A good area for a quiet, relaxing weekend break even in season. Only Ludlow and Hay-on-Wye get crowded
- Accommodation is easy to find but rarely luxurious: farms and country inns offer the best value

The area of the Welsh Marches from the Wye Valley to the Shropshire Hills offers a tranquil landscape of moorlands, meadows, rolling farmland, hedgerows, woodland and green hills. There are attractive towns, peaceful picturesque villages of timber-framed buildings – and castles to remind us that this is border country. Less wild than the Scottish Borders, the Marches have a parochial old-fashioned charm and are still well off the beaten track, unlike the Lower Wye Valley whose more spectacular landscape has been much exploited.

The English/Welsh border bisects the area – which includes the counties of Shropshire, Hereford and Worcester, Powys and Gwent. Its countryside is varied and splits naturally into three distinctive parts.

The South

The countryside north and west of Monmouth is predominantly farmland, the pleasures of this part being castle spotting and hill walking, both with fine views if carefully chosen. Red sandstone gives character and colour to soil and buildings alike. To the west the **Black Mountains** are high narrow ridges reaching 2,660 feet, divided by rivers; they have a remote air, with tiny farmsteads in the lush valleys, but are easily crossed by narrow roads. To the north the secluded, rural **Golden Valley** leads to the River Wye. Above Hay, the Black Mountains broaden into wild open slopes; you can strike into them by road via Gospel Pass, a spectacular viewpoint.

Monmouth stands at the confluence of the Rivers Wye and Monnow, with its fortified bridge (over the Monnow) and its castle ruins at either end of a long High Street. It is a well-kept, attractive town, with a good museum containing Nelson memorabilia, and a magic lantern theatre. In the lee of the mountains is **Abergavenny**: busy, crowded and mostly Victorian in character. There is a small but densely-packed museum at the site of its ruined castle. Smaller market towns like **Crickhowell** and **Talgarth** can be used as a base for steep hill walking. **Hay-on-Wye**, between the mountains and the river, is remarkable for the number of second-hand bookshops crammed into a tiny area, and is pretty in its own right. Across the river is **Clyro**, where the diarist Francis Kilvert was curate. The city of **Hereford** has been much spoilt by traffic systems and sprawling outskirts, but it does have a fine cathedral and a pleasant stretch of the River Wye with a riverside walk between the two bridges.

HISTORIC BUILDINGS AND GARDENS

Abbey Dore Court Gardens   Intimate riverside gardens in the Golden Valley. [*Open mid Mar to mid Oct, daily*]

nr Abergavenny, White Castle   Mostly 13th-century remains, once limewashed, in a quiet setting with lovely views to the west. [*Open all year, daily*]

Raglan Castle   The extensive remains of this 15th-century castle give an air of having been lived in and are fun to explore. [*Open mid Mar to mid Oct, daily except Sun am*]

Tretower Court and Castle   A well-preserved courtyard house in stone and timber; the castle is a shell. [*Open mid Mar to mid Oct, daily except Sun am*]

Even tiny villages have their own ruins or castle mounds. At both **Skenfrith** and **Grosmont**, castles are well sited above villages. Skenfrith is the prettier site with river and church adjoining.

CHURCHES

The area has some outstanding churches. **Kilpeck** is famous for the red sandstone carvings of pagan celtic figures, dating from Norman times. **Dore Abbey** is a large abbey church in a quiet valley setting. In the Black Mountains are the spectacular 13th-century remains of **Llanthony Abbey** (see 'Where to stay'). The church at nearby **Partrishow** has a lovely carved rood screen, a rare survival of the musicians' gallery. Other churches worth seeing include St Margaret's and Vowchurch.

The Centre

North of the Wye is fruitful countryside, divided by brooks and planted with woods and orchards. There are picture-postcard villages of black and white timber-framed buildings and ancient churches. To the west are the uplands known as **Radnor Forest**. There are some expanses of Forestry Commission conifers here and further north but most of the area survives as rough and unreclaimed moorland hills or grassy sheep pasture. By the Shropshire border, the area is all hills and wide river valleys.

The most outstanding villages with black and white buildings are **Pembridge**, **Weobley** and **Eardisland**; all are worth exploring. Radnor is reduced to a tiny pair of villages: **New Radnor** is the larger, with a castle mound and a sleepy High Street while **Old Radnor** is a cluster of mostly modern hillside cottages with a fine church and an ancient stone inn at the top. There are several market towns of some interest: **Presteigne** on the Lugg and **Kington** on the Arrow are both in fine countryside. Nearby **Knighton** is steeply set on one side of the Teme Valley, astride Offa's Dyke. To the west is the former spa town of **Llandrindod Wells** with a pump room, tall Victorian and Edwardian houses and, on the central square, old-fashioned hotels. **Leominster**, to the east, has some fine black and white buildings (notably the Grange), the odd medieval alley, an interesting local museum and several stately Georgian houses.

Ludlow is the finest town in the Marches. The extensive ruins of the castle, the market place which retains its medieval plan, the typical Tudor inns and the elegant Georgian houses leading down towards the river are the main attractions. In particular, Broad Street, a near-perfect blend of 17th- to 19th-century houses sloping down to a gateway, is one of the finest streets in England. There is a small museum, and a number of shops selling antiques and expensive clothes.

Historic Buildings and Gardens
Kington, Hergest Croft Gardens   About 50 acres of rare trees and shrubs, with an old-fashioned kitchen garden. Best seen in May and June when the rhododendrons are out. [*Open May to Sep, daily; Oct, pm Sun*]
nr Leominster, Berrington Hall   A Georgian courtyard house in red sandstone with grounds landscaped by Capability Brown. Elaborate period décor. (NT) [*Open pm; April and Oct weekends,*

May to Sep Wed to Sun; plus Bank Hol Mons]
nr Leominster, Croft Castle Turreted and battlemented with a mostly 18th-century interior in Gothic style. (NT, joint tickets with Berrington Hall) [*Open as above*]
Ludlow, Ludlow Castle A Norman castle on a commanding site above the River Teme, used as a theatre during the July festival. Good views from the tower. [*Open all year, daily*]

CHURCHES
Presteigne and Leominster have grand churches and that of **Ludlow** is almost cathedral-like, with a fine organ and outstanding misericords. **Old Radnor** has a superb 15th-century church with an ancient carved organ case, a remarkable medieval rood screen and a font probably carved from a pre-Christian standing stone. Most other churches in the area are medieval and have not suffered from over-zealous restoration; they include those at Pembridge and Eardisland. Shobdon church is in 'Strawberry Hill Gothic' style.

The North

Around Ludlow are the whalebacks of the **Shropshire Hills**. To the east is the abrupt outline of the Clee Hills; to the north-east **Wenlock Edge** shoots off towards the Wrekin. To the west grassland and pasture are interspersed with tracts of forest and green river valleys; further north rises the sudden mass of the **Long Mynd** – high rough moorland, deeply cut by many little streams to form smooth hills. Continuing westwards over the spine of the Long Mynd, unexpectedly green valleys are quickly overshadowed by the even higher ridge of the Stiperstones. The hills here have a thin acid soil and classic moorland patterns of wildlife; at the summit are strange rocky outcrops and superb views in fine weather.

Clun is a surprisingly prosperous market town, given its seclusion; it has an old bridge over the river Clun and castle ruins. **Bishop's Castle** slightly further north is a fascinating relic with a steep main street and an atmosphere of earlier importance – but there is no longer a castle. **Montgomery** is a former county town which has retained a graceful Georgian main square. There are good views of the surrounding countryside from the neatly kept castle ruins. The former industrial town of **Welshpool** has a pleasant centre with old buildings; you can take a day trip on the Shropshire Union Canal or the steam railway to Llanfair Caerinion. **Church Stretton** is a pleasant little Shropshire town and a good base for walks. At **Snailbeach** the curious remains of the lead mining industry and old spoil heaps create a desolate lunar landscape. **Much Wenlock** is lovely, an unspoilt town with fine priory ruins.

HISTORIC BUILDINGS
Craven Arms, Stokesay Castle A fortified manor; a superb collection of buildings round a central courtyard, parts dating from the 13th century. [*Open Mar to Oct, daily except Tues; Nov, weekends*]
Welshpool, Powis Castle A huge pink sandstone pile with celebrated terraced gardens plunging down to the Severn. It now houses the Clive collection of treasures from India. [*Open April to June, Sep and Oct, pm, Wed to Sun and Bank Hol Mons; July and Aug, daily except Mon (unless Bank Hol)*]

MUSEUMS
Church Stretton, Acton Scott Working Farm Museum Designed to be a typical old Shropshire hill farm with working dairy, saddlery and shire horses as well as static exhibits. [*Open April to Oct, daily*]

Walking

With such an outstanding variety of hill and unspoilt lowland, the Marches deserve to be better known for walking. The most frequented areas are the Black Mountains and the Shropshire Hills. The former's long ridges and abrupt slopes provide some exhilarating, but no more than moderately demanding, rambles. Church Stretton is a good base for exploring the Shropshire Hills; the Long Mynd has some rewarding routes taking in a remote-feeling upland mass – the steep-sided valley of Ashes Hollow is one of its highlights. Also recommended is the ascent of Caer Caradoc, east of Church Stretton, which gets huge views to the north and east; it can be approached from Church Stretton itself or from Hope Bowdler. The Stiperstones ridge is a little further south, and provides the most exciting hill-top walk in the county; the path along the ridge is quite easy, but circular walks incorporating it will include a fair amount of well-graded ascent. The other main attraction is the Offa's Dyke Path – a sizeable section of the 168-mile long-distance route runs through this area south to north. It roughly follows the border, making the most of the excellent scenic variety of the Marches; two of its finest parts are along the east flank of the Black Mountains and the stretch from Gladestry (south-west of Kington) and Clun. Most of the Path is well waymarked, but it is advisable to carry a map.

Elsewhere, you will encounter few walkers. Among the almost undiscovered parts of the region are the upland of Radnor Forest, an area of bold grassy and afforested hills and steep-sided valleys, and the moorland and remote sheep farming country south of it on the Welsh side of the border.

See *Holiday Which? Good Walks Guide* walks 93, 94, 100, 101, 102, 201, 211, 212.

When to go

Ludlow, Hay-on-Wye and the Gospel Pass are places to avoid in high season; otherwise this is a good area to choose for a peaceful weekend break in summer.

There are several arts festivals in June and July and the most popular places can be crowded at this time. Leominster Festival is held during the first two weeks of June as is the Much Wenlock Arts Festival. Ludlow Festival (late June for two weeks) includes theatre performances in the castle, fringe events and guided historical tours; it is not the best time to visit Ludlow unless you have tickets. Abergavenny Carnival and Fête begins three weeks of music and drama in July. In early September Llandrindod Wells Victorian Festival has become a colourful annual event.

Information

This area is the responsibility of many separate local and tourist authorities.

The Heart of England Tourist Board, 2/4 Trinity Street, Worcester WR1 1BR; tel: (0905) 613132 (covers Hereford and Worcester, and Shropshire)

The Wales Tourist Board, PO Box 1, Cardiff CF1 2XN; tel: (0222) 27281

Cadw: Welsh Historic Monuments, Brunel House, 2 Fitzalan Road, Cardiff CF2 1UY; tel: (0222) 499909 (details of castles and ancient sites)

The Offa's Dyke Association, West Street, Knighton, Powys; tel: (0547) 528753 (information on walks and other aspects of the area)

Box Office, Castle Square, Ludlow, Shropshire SY8 1AY; tel: (0584) 2150 Festival Secretary, tel: (0584) 2448 (Ludlow Festival)

Where to stay

For those who want to tour the area, a fairly central base like Ludlow, Presteigne or Pembridge is probably best and each has at least one traditional black and white inn. But for keen walkers and others who want to concentrate on a particular area (like the Black Mountains or the Shropshire hills) there are some cosy farmhouses and small country house hotels in remoter areas.

GLASBURY ON WYE
Llwynaubach Lodge
Glasbury on Wye, Powys, via Hereford HR3 5PT   *Tel: (04974) 473*

A distinctively converted L-shaped stone stable block in the gently undulating pastures of the Wye Valley, Llwynaubach once served the horse-drawn tramway from Hay to Brecon. It is now a small hotel of some character with exposed beams and brickwork and barn-like public rooms. In the bedrooms modern white furniture contrasts quite happily with the rustic feel. However in some areas, like the restaurant and lounge, the reproduction furniture and patterned floral carpets are not quite in keeping. There is a bar in the old mill where the original machinery is a feature. The garden, with croquet lawn, swimming pool and a trout pond, has views over the hills and paddocks full of Jacob sheep. A good choice for those seeking peace and quiet – although there is some slight traffic noise if you are sitting in the garden.

Location: *Off the B4350 between Hay-on-Wye (3 miles) and Glasbury village (½ mile)*
Bedrooms: *6 (double and twin) with bath. Direct dial telephone, TV, teamaking, minibar*
Facilities: *Parking. Swimming pool, croquet. Fishing on Wye*
Restrictions: *No dogs in public rooms. No children under 6*
Open: *All year*
Credit/charge cards accepted: *Access, Visa*
Price category: *££*
Special rates: *Weekends (except Bank Hols or high season), 2 nights DB&B (including Sunday lunch) £28.50 pp per night; also midweek reductions for 3 nights. Children £10 in parents' room*

GOVILON
Llanwenarth House
Govilon, Abergavenny, Gwent NP7 9SF   *Tel: (0873) 830289*

A 16th-century manor house modified in Victorian 'Gothick' taste, Llanwenarth House is set down a bumpy drive in farmland within the Brecon Beacons National Park. The owners rightly consider it is more of a family home than a hotel and are sceptical about hotel guides and concepts like 'short breaks'. It is the almost theatrical country house spirit and the enthusiasm of the Weatherill family which make it such a captivating place to stay. The elegant drawing room (emphatically not a lounge) and dining room have restrained décor and antique furniture and bedrooms (not numbered) are also tasteful and uncluttered. Mrs Weatherill (Amanda) is a Cordon Bleu cook and uses farm and local produce. A civilised place for civilised adults.

Location: *3 miles south-west of Abergavenny*
Bedrooms: *5 (double and twin), all with bath. TV, teamaking*
Facilities: *Parking. Croquet*
Restrictions: *No dogs in house. No children under 5*
Open: *Mar to Jan*
Credit/charge cards accepted: *None*
Price category: ££
Special rates: *2 nights B&B £20.50 (£33.50 single) pp per night. Children £15.70 in parents' room, £13.70 on 2-night stays*

LLANTHONY
Abbey
Abergavenny, Gwent, NP7 7NN   Tel: (0873) 890487

In the middle of the ruins of a 12th-century priory, in a remote valley in the Black Mountains, this hotel is ideal for those prepared to forgo creature comforts in exchange for an experience. Apart from its splendid setting, the antique character of the hotel has survived apparently unaltered from the 18th century or even earlier. Many people will find it huge fun; tiny spiral staircases, knee-high windows overlooking the priory and 'secret' passages (one with 19th-century guest's graffiti, another blocked off by a 'danger' sign and a metal hip bath). There is no lounge, but a simple authentic dining room (the abbot's parlour) and a vaulted bar in the cellar. Bedrooms are full of character: simple and homely with period features and old furniture, some with canopied beds. It is all highly eccentric and the basic sanitary arrangements, illogical layout and total lack of any modern facilities ('62 stairs to the top room, no lift!') may be too monastic for some people. But the menu is promising; healthy starters and rich main courses (rabbit casserole; salmon or guinea fowl in a cream sauce).

Location: *Turn off A465 at Skirrid Mountain, then follow signposts*
Bedrooms: *5 (double and family); 1 public bathroom*
Facilities: *Parking*
Restrictions: *Children under 10 discouraged*
Open: *Mid Mar to mid Dec*
Credit/charge cards accepted: *None*
Price category: £

PEMBRIDGE
The New Inn
Market Square, Pembridge, Leominster,
Hereford and Worcester HR6 9DZ   Tel: (054 47) 427

A rambling half-timbered building on an ancient market square, the New

Inn is anything but new; it dates from 1311 when it was a courthouse (where the last treaty of the Wars of the Roses is said to have been signed in 1461). The young owner, Jane Melvin, has been careful to preserve its ancient character. Bedrooms, beamed and whitewashed, are simply furnished with old armchairs and rustic modern pine. Facilities are basic and rooms on the road can be (intermittently) noisy. There are two bars, one flagstoned with an open fire and settles, the other carpeted, with comfy old-fashioned furniture. In the restaurant pretty tablecloths and china, candles and terracotta wine coolers add a touch of rustic sophistication. Food is carefully prepared and bar meals are especially good value. A delightful, unpretentious place to stay for those who prefer simple comforts.

Bedrooms: 7 *(single, double and family), 1 with shower. 1 public bathroom*
Facilities: *Parking*
Open: *All year*
Credit/charge cards accepted: *None*
Price category: £
Special rates: *Children under 5 £3 in parents' room*

PRESTEIGNE
The Radnorshire Arms
High Street, Presteigne, Powys LD8 2BE   *Tel: (0544) 267406*

The Radnorshire Arms is an Elizabethan manor turned coaching inn of the typical 'Magpie' appearance. The public rooms are all cosy and panelled (which makes them rather dark) and filled with oak furniture, some antique, some pub-like. The bar is very much a pub, but a comfortable, genuine, traditional one with beams, an open fire and a friendly atmosphere. Nor have the bedrooms altogether lost their character; the Weobley is the best with its panelled walls and oak furniture but others, both standard and superior, are comfortable enough and 'they all have squeaky floorboards' and mullioned windows which give a cottagey feel. Bathrooms tend to be functional. Most rooms have a view over the spacious garden. A solid traditional Trusthouse Forte hotel, good for families.

Bedrooms: 16, 8 *in annexe (double, twin and family), all with bath. Direct dial telephone, TV, teamaking*
Facilities: *Parking, lift. Climbing frame in garden. Babylistening*
Open: *All year*
Credit/charge cards accepted: *Access, Amex, Diners, Visa*
Price category: £££
Special rates: *2 or more nights DB&B £36 (single £44) pp per night. Children under 16 free in parents' room (75% in own room)*

VOWCHURCH
The Croft
Vowchurch, Hereford and Worcester HR2 0QE   *Tel: (098 160) 226*

A self-styled 'country guest house' in the Golden Valley, set back from a fairly quiet B road. The house dates from 1780 but was enlarged and redesigned at the turn of this century and is externally plain and unassuming. Inside it is airy and the décor is stylish and cleverly chosen to complement the Edwardian feel. There is a small dining room, with a conservatory, and a comfortable lounge with cosy corners and homely touches including a piano and board games. Most rooms have fine views across the lawns towards the eastern fringes of the Black Mountains. The annexes, in the adjoining mews and the old coach house, have slightly less character but are still comfortable. The daily menu has a choice of starters and homemade puddings and one main course; most of the vegetables come from the garden.

Location: *On the B4348 (Hay-on-Wye to Ross-on-Wye) at the junction with the B4347 from Pontrilas*
Bedrooms: *7, 4 in annexe (double and twin), all with bath. TV and teamaking*
Facilities: *Parking. Croquet*
Restrictions: *No dogs. No children under 10. No smoking in bedrooms or dining room*
Open: *All year except Christmas*
Credit/charge cards accepted: *None*
Price category: £
Special rates: *Oct to Mar, 2 nights DB&B £22.50-£24 pp per night*

WHITNEY-ON-WYE
Rhydspence Inn
Whitney-on-Wye, nr Hay-on-Wye,
Hereford and Worcester HR3 6EU   *Tel: (04973) 262*

This exceptionally fine medieval building is itself almost enough for a recommendation. It dates at least from the 16th century and was once an inn for Welsh drovers taking livestock to the English markets. Inside, exposed beams and half-timbered walls are a feature and some thought has gone into enhancing the character of the inn ('genuine creaks, groans, draughts and atmosphere' boasts the brochure). Cottagey bedrooms have been carefully and tastefully furnished and the restaurants and bars are cosily rustic too. There are fresh flowers in the bedrooms and on the dining tables and an open fire in the bar. The one drawback of the hotel is its position: 100 yards from the A438 and with only distant views of real countryside. Traffic noise is not very noticeable inside the hotel, but does spoil the potentially pleasant garden area.

Bedrooms: *5 (single, double and twin), all with bath except single (shower). TV and teamaking*
Facilities: *Parking*
Restrictions: *No dogs*
Open: *All year*
Credit/charge cards accepted: *Access, Amex, Visa*
Price category: £
Special rates: *Mid Nov to Mar, 2 nights DB&B £25 pp per night, 3 nights DB&B £23. Child's bed in parents' room £10*

NATIONAL PARKS

Dartmoor, Exmoor, The Lake District,
The North York Moors, The Peak District, Snowdonia,
The Yorkshire Dales

Dartmoor

- The remotest countryside in south-west England, ideal for rugged walking. But it can get crowded in high summer
- A wide range of things to see and do, with a unique collection of archaeological sites, some interesting small country museums and charming villages for pottering and cream teas
- A good place to take the children: ponies, railway rides and several places for family outings
- Comfortable secluded country hotels and traditional village pubs

The National Park of Dartmoor is the largest area of wilderness left in southern England, a vast tract of empty moorland where wild ponies roam. Ancient stone circles and menhirs contribute to a sense of awe (as does the existence of the notorious top-security prison). Much of Dartmoor consists of rounded grassy hills, with exposed granite crags known as tors. The valleys bear marks of earlier inhabitation: medieval clapper bridges of flat granite stones, and old mineral workings served by water channels (leats).

On the edge of the moor the lush and intricate countryside provides a fine contrast and there are some famous and spectacular beauty spots, notably Lydford Gorge in the the west and Teign Gorge, Lustleigh Cleave and Becky Falls in the east. The fringes of Dartmoor have a character all of their own with narrow, steep country lanes, high hedges and cosy villages of thatched houses. To the north and east, in particular, the landscape is an appealing mixture of small, secluded valleys lined with ancient woodland, small hedged fields, forestry planting, and occasional patches of heathland.

Pretty villages with thatched cottages, medieval stone farmhouses and neat greens include **North Bovey, Drewsteignton** (with a medieval packhorse bridge), **Lustleigh** and **Throwleigh**. **Widecombe** has a fine church, the so-called 'Cathedral of the Moor'. The market towns around the edge of Dartmoor are a mixed bag: of most interest are **Ashburton**, which has several attractive streets of slate-hung houses, and **Chagford**, unspoiled and intimate, clustered round a modest market square. **Moretonhampstead** has several high-quality craft shops and an unusual row of 17th-century almshouses owned by the National Trust.

ARCHAEOLOGICAL SITES
There are a number of antiquities including neolithic burial chambers, standing stones (menhirs), and cairns. Pride of place goes to **Grimspound**, an outstandingly impressive collection of Bronze Age hut circles.

HISTORIC BUILDINGS
Buckfastleigh, Buckfast Abbey   A restored Benedictine monastery in the Dart valley. [*Open all year, daily*]
Drewsteignton, Castle Drogo   Britain's newest castle, completed in 1930 to a witty and innovative design by Sir Edwin Lutyens, overlooks the river Teign. (NT) [*Open April to Oct, daily*]
nr Tavistock, Buckland Abbey   A 13th-century Cistercian abbey turned country house, once the home of Sir Francis Drake. [*Open July to Oct, daily; and Nov to Mar, pm Wed, Sat and Sun*]

Also impressive are the ruins of Norman **Okehampton Castle**, on a narrow ridge above the town. Just outside the National Park is **Ugbrooke**, a fine Adam house with family collections of furniture and paintings.

MUSEUMS
The most interesting local museums are the **Finch Foundry Museum** at Sticklepath (a 19th-century water-powered edge tool works) and the **Museum of Dartmoor Life**, housed in a converted mill at Okehampton. Just outside the National Park is the **Morwellham Quay Museum**, a recreation of the Victorian copper-mining port, with a community in costume.

FAMILY OUTINGS
The **Dartmoor Wildlife Park** at Sparkwell has a falconry centre and a collection of big cats; children can play with the tamer animals and take pony rides. There is a miniature pony centre at North Bovey, a butterfly farm at Buckfast, and a rare breeds farm at Parke, near Bovey Tracey. **Buckfastleigh Steam and Leisure Park** has a modest loco shed and a small museum among other attractions.

The large **River Dart Country Park** near Ashburton, offers adventure playgrounds, nature trails, swimming, fishing and riding. The **Canonteign Falls and Country Park** near Chudleigh is organised around the spectacular waterfall and other natural features.

There are several pony trekking centres, mainly on the fringes of the moor, and several craft centres – including the Devon

Guild of Craftsmen at Bovey Tracey and the Moorland Craft Centre at Haytor, both with exhibitions and demonstrations as well as retail shops.

RAILWAYS

The Dart Valley A steam-hauled line with splendidly restored Victorian saloon carriage and observation coach. The line passes through very pretty valley scenery between Buckfastleigh and Totnes.

An attraction for small children is the **Gorse Blossom Miniature Railway Park**, near Newton Abbot.

Walking

The higher parts of the moors offer fine scenery and solitude, but have few clear paths, and you will need to carry a compass in case the mist comes down. The ranges of the enormous military training area which occupies most of the northern moors are generally not used at weekends (when they are in use, red warning flags are flown).

Even in the more varied and less taxing areas on the edges of the moor the going can be rough, though route-finding is helped by clear signposting and waymarking. Two particularly fine walks are along the steep wooded Teign Gorge between Chagford and Dunsford and through Lustleigh Cleave on the River Bovey. The southern extent of the moor, for example near Harford, is worthwhile for some impressive views over the South Hams and into Cornwall. There are short easy walks to and around beauty spots, such as along the grassy banks of the River Dart by the so-called New Bridge down to Becky Falls, a pretty cascade in a wooded glen; along the River Teign from Fingle Bridge; or along dramatic Lydford Gorge. Several of the tors can be reached quite easily from the road: Hay Tor is the most visited, nearby Hound Tor more impressive.

See *Holiday Which? Good Walks Guide* walks 15-19.

When to go

Most of the roads in the Park get very busy on fine days in July and August and you can expect large crowds at beauty spots, especially to the north and east of the moor. There are some summer bus services to the central area. Local festivities include May Day celebrations in Lustleigh and the Sticklepath Midsummer Revel. There are Carnival weeks in July at Buckfastleigh and

Chudleigh (just beyond the National Park). Moretonhampstead carnival is in late August, followed by Kingsteignton. Widecombe fair is in mid September.

Dartmoor is a good area for autumn walking, generally staying warm longer than national parks in the north. Many hotels are open all year, and some offer winter breaks

Information

The Dartmoor National Park Information Service, Parke, Bovey Tracey, Devon TQ13 9JQ; tel: (0626) 832093. During the season there are information centres at various points.

The Dartmoor Centre at 3 West Street, Okehampton, Devon EX20 1HQ [tel: (0837) 3020] is also run by the National Park Authority and can help with booking accommodation, advise on walks and rainy day activities and provide details of local events.

Where to stay

On Dartmoor itself there are some very comfortable hotels, most in converted country houses. Many visitors choose to stay in the nearby coastal resorts including Torquay and Teignmouth. Bed and breakfast accommodation is available in many small towns around the edge of Dartmoor and in some farmhouses.

Nr ASHBURTON
Holne Chase
Nr Ashburton, Devon TQ13 7NS   *Tel: (036 43) 471*

This attractive 16th-century hunting lodge, set in 26 acres of grounds and surrounded by trees, overlooks sloping meadows leading down to the River Dart. Much of the interior has recently been refurbished: the new bedrooms are spacious and pleasant, with traditional fabrics, mahogany or pine furniture, and well-appointed bathrooms; older bedrooms show scant attention to co-ordination, and are homely rather than stylish. Public rooms are unremarkable and have a lived-in atmosphere; a wood-burning stove and lots of games in the lounge will cheer you up on a wet afternoon. The recently extended dining room is light and pretty (and very spacious), but Provençal cotton curtains and red hessian give it a warm look. It's an unpretentious and peaceful hotel.

Location: *3 miles west of Ashburton, on Two Bridges road*
Bedrooms: *14 (double, twin, suite), 2 in annexe, 1 with four-poster, all with bath. Direct dial telephone, TV, teamaking. Hairdryer on request*
Facilities: *Parking. Croquet, putting, cricket, fishing. Babylistening*
Restrictions: *Dogs by prior arrangement. No smoking in restaurant*

Open: *All year*
Credit/charge cards accepted: *Access, Amex, Diners, Visa*
Price category: ££
Special rates: *2-5 nights, DB&B £311.50-£44 (single £46) pp per night. Winter (except Christmas to New Year), 2-5 nights DB&B £28-£40.50 (single £42.50). Children in parents' room: £5-£10, depending on age; cot £3.50*

CHAGFORD
Gidleigh Park
Chagford, Devon TQ13 8HH　　　　　　　　　*Tel: (064 73) 2367/2225*

In the most secluded setting (directions are essential), this is a 1920s country house in Tudor style, surrounded by some 50 acres of grounds and formal gardens. The American owners ensure that all is perfectly maintained, and accommodation is first class: bedrooms have antiques, fine fabrics used for bedspreads, canopies and bedside table cloths, comfortable sofas and chairs and well-appointed (some marble) bathrooms. Bathrobes, pot pourri and a thermos of chilled water are the kind of extras that welcome you. The reception rooms leading off the central hall include an elegant (if slightly formal) drawing room with bold chintz fabrics, magazines and fresh flowers, and a dining room panelled in pale oak. The cooking is highly rated, and there is a very extensive and interesting wine list. The gardens are glorious; there's a newly created water garden, fed by the River Teign, and there are plans for a cricket pitch. Perfection does not, of course, come cheap.

Location: *Approach from Chagford, not Gidleigh. From Chagford village square, turn into Mill Street (next to Lloyds Bank); 150 yards on, fork right. At Factory Crossroads go straight across to Holy Street, and follow lane 1½ miles to end*
Bedrooms: *14 (double, twin), all with bath. Direct dial telephone, TV, hairdryer*
Facilities: *Parking. Tennis, croquet, fishing*
Restrictions: *Dogs by prior arrangement. Older children only. No pipes or cigars in dining room*
Open: *All year*
Credit/charge cards accepted: *Access, Amex, Diners, Visa*
Price category: £££££
Special rates: *Children in parents' room £15 (£40 including dinner)*

DODDISCOMBSLEIGH
The Nobody Inn
Doddiscombsleigh, nr Exeter EX6 7PS　　　　　　*Tel: (0647) 52394*

In a small and quiet village two miles from the National Park, this is a charming country pub in a semi-detached 16th-century cottage. The beamed bar is a bit dark during the day, but cosy at night; there are antique tables and Windsor chairs, smoke-stained walls and a large open fireplace, warming-pans, horse brasses, firearms and photos. The inn is well known for its exceptionally large wine and whisky list – some 40 pages long. Bedrooms are quite basic, but there's a drinks tray in each (whole bottles of whisky, gin, brandy and sherry). In the main pub, breakfast (even full English) is served in the bedrooms, too.

Bedrooms: *7 (single, twin, double), 3 in annexe. 6 with bath/shower.*
Teamaking. Payphone, hairdryer on request. Fridge and TV in annexe rooms (TV on request in others)
Facilities: *Parking*
Restrictions: *No dogs. Children under 14 in annexe only*
Open: *All year, except Christmas Day*
Credit/charge cards accepted: *Access, Visa*
Price category: £
Special rates: *4 or more nights, B&B £16 (single £18.50) pp per night*

EASTON CROSS
Easton Court
Easton Cross, Chagford, Devon TQ13 8JL   *Tel: (064 73) 3469*

A picturesque thatched cottage (plus a 1920s addition) with a pretty garden, where Evelyn Waugh wrote many of his novels. The old part is quaint and charming; there are two sitting rooms (beams, large open fireplace and bread oven, snug armchairs, books). The pleasant and unfussy dining room has oak tables and Windsor chairs. Bedrooms are a little old-fashioned and generally un-coordinated, though they have a cottage charm. Most are away from the road and have views over fields. This is an appealing base from which to explore Dartmoor.

Location: *On the A382 just east of Chagford*
Bedrooms: *8 (single, double, twin, family), 2 with four-poster, 4 with bath, 4 with shower. Teamaking. TV on request*
Facilities: *Parking. Babylistening*
Restrictions: *No children under 14. No dogs. No smoking in dining room*
Open: *All year except Jan*
Credit/charge cards accepted: *Access, Amex, Diners, Visa*
Price category: ££
Special rates: *2 nights DB&B £37.50; 3-6 nights DB&B £35*

FRENCHBEER
Teignworthy
Frenchbeer, nr Chagford, Devon TQ13 8EX   *Tel: (064 73) 3355*

A Lutyens-style 1920s stone house, built by the same craftsmen as Castle Drogo, in a very secluded position near Forestry Commission land. The emphasis is on relaxation: furniture is comfortable rather than particularly stylish. In the large lounge there is a huge granite fireplace, board games and books; there is a smallish bar. The dining room (coffee-coloured panelled walls, wooden bow-backed chairs) has fine views over the gardens; the cooking has a good reputation – short menu, first-class ingredients, and a simple modern style. Bedrooms are individually decorated, spacious and comfortable (white or cream walls, textured wool bedspreads, chintzy curtains); they are supplied with chocolates and fruit. You can explore the 14 acres of sloping gardens, or go fishing in the Teign or the Dart.

Bedrooms: *9 (double, twin), 3 in annexe, 1 with four-poster, all with bath. Direct dial telephone, TV. Teamaking on request*

Facilities: *Parking. Tennis (grass), croquet. Sauna, sunbed. Babylistening*
Restrictions: *No dogs. No children under 10. Smoking discouraged in dining room*
Open: *All year*
Credit/charge cards accepted: *Access, Visa*
Price category: *££££*
Special rates: *Nov to Easter (except Christmas and New Year), 2-3 nights DB&B £63.50 (single £66.50) pp per night*

HAYTOR
Bel Alp House
Haytor, Dartmoor, Devon TQ13 9XX   Tel: (036 46) 217

This is an Edwardian house in Italianate style, set in 8 acres of well-kept gardens and woods, with marvellous views over Dartmoor. It is run along the lines of a private house-party where guests are introduced to one another (though they sit at separate tables). The bedrooms are not lavishly decorated – colours are muted, bedspreads are candlewick or wool and furniture is antique or repro – but they are comfortable, and most have views. Two of the bathrooms are the original Edwardian ones with marble floors. The dining room and sitting room are furnished in similar style with plain colours and some antique furniture; the bar, off the hall, has a large stone and slate fireplace. There's a basement games room. This is a friendly and peaceful hotel.

Location: *Off the B3344, 1½ miles west of Bovey Travey*
Bedrooms: *9 (double, twin, suite), 8 with bath, 1 with shower. Direct dial telephone, TV, teamaking. Hairdryer on request*
Facilities: *Parking. Tennis, croquet. Billiards. Babylistening*
Restrictions: *Dogs by prior arrangement. No children under 7 in dining room at dinner. No smoking in dining room*
Open: *Mar to Oct. Advance bookings in winter*
Credit/charge cards accepted: *Access, Visa*
Price category: *£££*
Special rates: *2-4 nights, DB&B £48-£60 (single £57-£69) pp per night. Children in family suite, half price*

HAYTOR VALE
The Rock Inn
Haytor Vale, nr Newton Abbot, Devon TQ13 9XP   Tel: (036 46) 205/305

A charming 18th-century coaching inn in a row of cottages, in a quiet hamlet high up on Dartmoor. Public rooms are mostly in traditional pub style: the main bar has beams, fireplaces, Windsor chairs; the lounge has sofas and chairs, and armour on the walls. There's a bistro atmosphere in the restaurant – red-and-white seersucker cloths, wood-burning stove and hunting prints on the white painted stone walls. Bedrooms vary; despite duvets (blankets on request) and new floral fabrics and papers, they are old-fashioned in style. In some rooms, an unusual fixture on the wall dispenses a phial of whisky or gin which is charged automatically at reception. Across the road is a pretty lawned garden. An informal place, also enjoyable for a pub lunch.

Bedrooms: *9 (double, twin), 6 with bath. Direct dial telephone, TV, teamaking. Drinks machine in some*
Facilities: *Babylistening*
Restrictions: *No dogs. No smoking in restaurant*
Open: *All year*
Credit/charge cards accepted: *Amex, Visa*
Price category: ££
Special rates: *Dec to Mar (except Christmas, New Year and Bank Hols), Thurs and Fri, DB&B £21.50 pp per night*

LYDFORD
The Castle Inn
Lydford, Okehampton, Devon EX20 4BH   Tel: (082 282) 242

Beside Lydford Castle and Gorge, on the edge of Dartmoor, this is very much a traditional pub-with-rooms. Many less authentic places try to copy the style: slate floors, battered Turkey carpet, round-back settles, lots of Victorian pictures and plates on the walls and pots and pans in the open inglenook fireplace. There are two bars: one public, another a large room which doubles as restaurant and lounge. Food is simple, but the standard is high. Bedrooms are fairly basic and décor not necessarily co-ordinated. This is a friendly place run by an energetic couple.

Bedrooms: *7 (double, twin), 2 with bath, 1 with shower. TV, teamaking*
Facilities: *Parking. Darts in bar*
Open: *All year*
Credit/charge cards accepted: *Access, Visa*
Price category: £
Special rates: *Summer, 2 nights DB&B £31 (single £41) pp per night; 3 nights £27.70 (single £37.50) pp per night. Reductions available in winter*

SANDY PARK
Mill End Hotel
Sandy Park, Chagford, Devon TQ13 8JN   Tel: (064 73) 2282/2406

An old white-painted mill on the river, set in two acres of gardens. Bedrooms are comfortable and decorated either with bold chintzes and antiques or (in the newer addition) in more modern style with built-in furniture. Public rooms are traditional and homely, with patterned carpeting, comfortable old sofas and chairs covered in floral linen union in the drawing room, antiques and open fireplace. The dining room is spacious and inviting (though the chairs are a bit spartan). Food is good, portions generous. There's an unusually wide choice at breakfast. The friendly and efficient service is all part of the old-fashioned atmosphere. You will be well looked after.

Location: *Off the A382, two miles north-east of Chagford*
Bedrooms: *17 (single, double, twin, family), all with bath (2 not en suite). Direct dial telephone, TV, hairdryer*

Facilities: *Parking. Fishing. Babylistening*
Restrictions: *No dogs in public rooms. No children under 5 in dining room at dinner*
Open: *All year except one week in Dec*
Credit/charge cards accepted: *Access, Amex, Diners, Visa*
Price category: ££
Special rates: *Children free in parents' room*

SOUTH ZEAL
The Oxenham Arms
South Zeal, Devon EX20 2JT   *Tel: (0837) 840244*

This ancient granite building (12th-century and incorporating two monoliths which were in situ) has a peaceful village setting on the edge of Dartmoor. There are lots of beams, worn stone floors, and white-painted stone walls; it's far from smart, and the décor is rather old-fashioned. The bar (lino flooring and a large granite fireplace) is very much 'the local'. The lounge has a granite fireplace, too, together with miscellaneous old-fashioned furniture, and cupboards with a display of china. The bedrooms are quite interesting, though their fabrics and furniture are fairly dull. The pretty, grassy garden is approached via uneven steps (not for the infirm).

Bedrooms: *10 (double, twin, family), 2 in annexe, 8 with bath. Direct dial telephone, TV, teamaking*
Facilities: *Parking. Darts in bar*
Restrictions: *No dogs in dining room. No children in bar*
Open: *All year*
Credit/charge cards accepted: *Access, Amex, Diners, Visa*
Price category: ££
Special rates: *3 nights B&B £18.50 (single £28.50) pp per night. Reductions in winter*

SOUTH ZEAL
Poltimore
South Zeal, Okehampton, Devon EX20 2PD   *Tel: (0837) 840209*

A picturesque white-painted thatched cottage with a delightful garden, offering simple guest-house accommodation. The beamed sitting room has a large stone fireplace, lots of comfy seating, and a wall full of photos; in one corner is an informal bar area. Next door is the TV room, jolly and bright, with shelves full of bottles and knick-knacks. Bedrooms are simply furnished, co-ordinated in cottagey fabrics; beds have orthopaedic mattresses. Vegetables for the evening meal are home-grown. A homely and good-value guest house.

Bedrooms: *7 (single, double, twin), 5 with bath. Teamaking*
Facilities: *Parking. TV in lounge*
Restrictions: *No children under 12. No smoking in dining room. Dogs by prior arrangement*
Open: *All year*

Credit/charge cards accepted: *None*
Price category: £
Special rates: *Winter, 3 nights DB&B £20.35 (single, without bath, £19.70) pp per night*

TWO BRIDGES
Cherrybrook Hotel

Two Bridges, Yelverton, Devon PL20 6SP   *Tel: (0822) 88260*

This is an unspoilt family-run guesthouse hotel, in an early 19th-century white-painted cottage set high up on the moor. Accommodation is comfortable and homely: the dining room has miscellaneous Victorian and Windsor chairs, a dresser which houses the wine and other bottles, and a map of the area. The old cow shed and barn are now the lounge and bar: there's a varnished slate floor, beamed ceiling and wood burning stoves. Floral patterned chairs and rugs, and the owners' collection of pink-and-white china, add colour. Bedrooms are generally tastefully decorated. The garden is mostly rough grass with an abundance of wild flowers; there are free-range hens.

Location: *½ mile north-east of Two Bridges on B3212*
Bedrooms: *7 (single, double, twin, family), all with shower. Teamaking. TV and electric blanket on request*
Facilities: *Parking*
Restrictions: *Smoking discouraged in dining room*
Open: *All year except 2 weeks over Christmas and New Year*
Credit/charge cards accepted: *None*
Price category: £
Special rates: *3 or more nights, B&B £16 pp per night. Children under 12 in parents' room, half price*

Exmoor

- Despite its small size, very varied scenery, which includes a superb stretch of coast. Very broad appeal for walking and pony trekking
- Even in high summer you can escape the crowds and, unlike on Dartmoor, much of the scenery can be appreciated from a car – but beware steep hills and sharp bends
- Limited sights apart from picture postcard villages but there are some good possibilities for family outings
- A reasonable range of hotels, mostly middling in price and standards; Dartmoor has cosier pubs and more comfortable country house hotels

Much of Exmoor consists of smooth sheep-strewn moorland, criss-crossed by little valleys and rivers, with some pretty picture postcard villages. The coast is wild and exhilarating, with the classic Lorna Doone country between Lynmouth and Porlock. A grand range of rounded hog's back cliffs runs all along the coast, including the highest in England (over 900 feet at Countisbury). Most cliffs are covered with vegetation, and some are thickly wooded; precipitous combes cut through the cliffs at intervals and there are some pretty coves.

The ancient royal hunting preserve of Exmoor Forest is now an area of open moorland at the centre of a National Park. Here wild ponies and sometimes red deer can still be seen. The landscape is one of broken, rounded heather- and bracken-covered hills alternating with farmland and small valleys with rushing streams. Dunkery Beacon, the Park's highest point at 1705 feet, has superb panoramic views of the West Country and across to Wales. The other areas of high ground lie to the south and east, rising as broad heather-topped ridges with gentle valleys in between.

There are many pretty villages dotted around the Park. Tiny **Selworthy** is a perfectly preserved group of 19th-century thatched cottages and tithe barn (owned by the National Trust), with a green and a fine church. Other particularly appealing villages are **Luccombe, Nettlecombe and Wootton Courtenay**. Hump-backed packhorse bridges are a feature of many places, including **Allerford** and **Winsford**, which has seven. **Dunster** is an exceptionally attractive small town, its unspoilt (though crowded) main street punctuated by an unusual circular 17th-century Yarn Market. The castle (see below) looms at one end, while tucked away at the back is a fine working medieval water-mill. **Dulverton** is the main town of Exmoor, and features in *Lorna Doone* as the place where Jan Ridd first set eyes on the heroine (motorists can follow the Lorna Doone Trail from Dulverton, visiting the locations of the main events of the novel). **Exford** , with a village green and traditional inns, is at the heart of Exmoor hunting country.

The only coastal settlements of any size are the strikingly set twin towns of Lynton and Lynmouth. **Lynton**, a small resort, is perched on the 400-foot cliffs; **Lynmouth**, largely rebuilt after a disastrous flood in 1952, is spread around the wooded slopes and valley floor below. They are linked by a funicular railway, operated by water gravity, which was the steepest in the world when it was built in 1890. Two of the prettiest villages are **Porlock**, with its famous hill, and **Porlock Weir**, a small group of colour-washed cottages clustered round a tiny harbour and a beach of purple pebbles. There's some boating at Porlock Weir and at Lynmouth.

Most of the more conventional sights are in the east of the Park (and those of Dartmoor are within easy driving distance). There are splendid cliff viewpoints at Berrynarbor, Hangman Point, Martinhoe, Wringcliff Bay and Foreland Point. The Valley of Rocks is a treeless valley with peculiar rock formations, a spot beloved of Shelley, its romanticism now somewhat tarnished by the conspicuous car park and road. Watersmeet is a popular picnic spot at the confluence of two swift rivers.

Parts of the coast are best appreciated from a boat. There are no large sandy beaches, although the holiday beaches of North Devon are close to the edge of Exmoor. The most attractive beaches are at **Heddon's Mouth** and **Woody Bay**, both approached by a longish walk through picturesque steep-sided valleys, and at **Lee Bay** and **Wringcliff Bay**. All these coves have sand at low tide.

HISTORIC BUILDINGS

nr Barnstaple, Arlington Court A 19th-century neo-classical house, with a carriage museum. (NT) [*Open April to Oct, Sun to Fri and Bank Hol weekends inc Sats*]

Dunster Castle A huge crenellated castle, part 13th century, part 19th, with magnificent staircase and ceilings, terraced shrub garden and fine views over Exmoor (NT) [*Open April to Sep, Sun to Thurs; Oct pm only*]

Ilfracombe, Chambercombe Manor A small manor house with medieval origins and furniture of the 16th and 17th centuries. [*Open April to Sep, Mon to Fri and pm Sun*]

Monksilver, Combe Sydenham Hall A 16th-century house, linked historically with nearby Cleeve Abbey (see below) and with Sir Francis Drake whose wife lived here. Fine gardens, monastic fishponds and woodland trails. [*Open Easter Mon to Oct, Mon to Fri*]

Washford, Cleeve Abbey Unusually complete 13th-century Cistercian abbey, with particularly good heraldic tiles and wall paintings. [*Open all year, Mon to Sat and pm Sun*]

Interesting churches include those at Dunster, Martinhoe, Monksilver and Nettlecombe; Oare church is famous for its Lorna Doone connections and nearby is tiny Culbone. Between Exmoor and Dartmoor are **Knightshayes Court**, near Tiverton, **Tiverton Castle** and **Bickleigh Castle**.

FAMILY OUTINGS

For children there is a theme park, **Watermouth Castle**, between Combe Martin and Ilfracombe and a working farm at nearby Bodstone Barton. The **Wildlife Park** at Combe Martin, the **Exmoor Bird Gardens** at Bratton Fleming and **Quince Honey Farm** at South Molton show animals in their natural habitat. The **Exmoor Brass Rubbing Centre** at Lynton is very enterprisingly run. The 23-mile long **West Somerset Railway** claims to be Britain's longest privately owned passenger railway and runs a variety of steam and diesel trains. The **Cobbaton Combat Vehicles Museum** is for those who like tanks and armoured cars, with a children's mini assault course.

Walking

Within a relatively small area, Exmoor offers some of the most varied walking in Britain, from easy strolls to more energetic cliff and moorland rambles, though the region does not contain any rugged mountain scenery. The most obvious attraction is the South-West Peninsula Path, 35 miles of which run along the Exmoor coast. With such good scenery just inland it is not hard to devise interesting round walks which include sections of it, taking in the cliffs themselves, wooded valleys, moorland and quiet pasture.

A good general starting point is County Gate, where the A39 coast road crosses Countisbury Hill; there are fine walks inland from here to Malmsmead, Oare and the Lorna Doone valley, as well as towards the coast.

Further inland, the paths crossing the moors can get boggy,

but many of the valley routes are both straightforward and enjoyable; the scenery is empty and very quiet. Particularly worthwhile is the Barle valley in the area of Tarr Steps, a fine ancient stone bridge in a beautiful woodland setting.

The choice of easy walks is wide, including some on the higher ground which give huge views, such as Hollerday Hill (overlooking the Valley of Rocks), Dunkery Hill and Selworthy Beacon; and the riverside path in the wooded Lyn Valley around Watersmeet is very attractive. Some paths – for example down the Heddon Valley from Hunter's Inn and at Cloutsham on the Holnicote Estate – have been set up as self-guided nature trails. There are also easy walks around Wimbleball Lake, a reservoir in the south-east popular for fishing and sailing.

The coast path is easy to follow throughout, and most other paths and tracks are excellently waymarked or signposted.

See *Holiday Which? Good Walks Guide* walks 20-22, 30-32.

When to go

Most places, particularly Dunster, Tarr Steps and the Doone valley, are busy in July and August, although not impossibly so. The A39 coast road can also be very slow. The Minehead and Exmoor Arts Festival takes place at various venues in the district in the last two weeks of July, and Dulverton has a festival lasting two weeks in the second half of August. The trout fishing season on Wimbleball Lake is from May to October.

Like Dartmoor, Exmoor is a good area for autumn walking, staying warm longer than many national parks in the north.

Information

Exmoor National Park Authority, Exmoor House, Dulverton, Somerset TA22 9HL; tel: (0398) 23665. There are also National Park Information Centres at Dunster, County Gate, Lynmouth and Combe Martin, all open from Easter to September.

Where to stay

Accommodation on Exmoor is either in simple village inns, or in converted country houses, farmhouses or hunting lodges. Several hotels offer fishing. There are some more expensive hotels recommended in the *The Good Food Guide*, just beyond the National Park limits. The coastal resorts offer guest-house and

B&B accommodation; there is a considerable amount at Lynton, a good base for exploring the Park.

Nr DULVERTON
Ashwick Country House
Dulverton, Somerset TA22 9QD   *Tel: (0398) 23868*

This is a very secluded Edwardian country house set in six acres of grounds and gardens, high up on Exmoor. The entrance hall is impressive: a gallery, marble fireplace, parquet flooring with rugs and original William Morris paper; it's also a comfortable sitting area, with large sofas. There's a library and a lounge, too, a little less stylish. Bedrooms are well equipped, and have personal touches such as bathroom scales and mineral water; the 'superior' rooms are supplied with magazines and fruit as well. A peaceful retreat where guests are encouraged to feel at home.

Bedrooms: *6 (double, twin), all with bath. Direct dial telephone on request. TV. Trouserpress, minibar in some rooms*
Facilities: *Parking. Croquet*
Restrictions: *No dogs. No children under 8*
Open: *All year*
Credit/charge cards accepted: *None*
Price category: *££*
Special rates: *2 or more nights, DB&B £34-£40 (single £43-£49) pp per night*

DULVERTON
The Carnarvon Arms
Dulverton, Somerset TA22 9AE   *Tel: (0398) 23302*

This large hotel was purpose-built in 1873 to serve the now disused Dulverton Station. It is old-fashioned, and comfortable rather than lavish; but it offers good facilities (games room, hairdresser, swimming pool, tennis, and opportunities for fishing, shooting and so on) and good English food. There are three or four lounges (one with TV) with comfy old armchairs and predominantly Victorian furniture. The dining room is pretty and bright with co-ordinated wallpapers, linen cloths and fresh flowers. Bedrooms are quite spacious, many recently decorated with floral or bold stripe papers. This hotel can cater for many tastes, but the emphasis is on outdoor activities.

Bedrooms: *25 (single, double, twin, suite), 22 with bath. Direct dial telephone, TV. Hairdryer on request*
Facilities: *Parking. Heated outdoor swimming pool, tennis, shooting, fishing, stabling, sandpit. Billiards, games room (table tennis), bar billiards. Hairdresser. Babylistening*
Open: *All year except three weeks in Feb*
Credit/charge cards accepted: *Access, Visa*
Price category: *££*
Special rates: *4-6 nights, DB&B £37 (single £39.50) pp per night. Children in parents' room £7 (over 11 £22)*

EXFORD
The Crown
Exford, Somerset TA24 7PP   *Tel: (064 383) 554*

This 17th-century gabled and tile-clad hotel is well known among the
hunting fraternity: hounds meet here and if you haven't brought your
horse, a hireling hunter can be arranged. The building is on the roadside
with a stable yard and smallish garden. Inside the furnishing and décor
are rather functional. There's a large entrance hall with a stone fireplace,
dresser, and lots of magazines; a beamed bar with sepia photographs; a
sitting room with chintz curtains; and a jolly dining room (pictures of
Exmoor for sale). Bedrooms are mostly decorated with floral patterns;
there are duvets as well as sheets and blankets, and a welcoming glass of
sherry. The atmosphere is friendly, with locals popping in for a chat.

Bedrooms: *15 (single, double, twin), all with bath. Direct dial telephone. TV,
teamaking. Hairdryer*
Facilities: *Parking. Stabling*
Open: *All year*
Credit/charge cards accepted: *Access, Amex, Visa*
Price category: *£££*
Special rates: *Weekends, 3 nights DB&B £41.70 (single £50) pp per night.
Children in parents' room: babies and toddlers £7.50; under 12 £15 (not including
meals)*

HAWKRIDGE
Tarr Steps Hotel
Hawkridge, Nr Dulverton, Somerset   *Tel: (064 385) 293*

This Georgian house with sympathetic 1920s additions is set at the bottom
of a very steep hill. People come here to stay put and fish, shoot or ride.
There's an uncontrived country-house atmosphere (rods and waders in
the hall); all the rooms are reassuringly well-lived-in with faded fabrics
and almost threadbare carpets. The bar feels like a sitting room (stags'
heads, hunting prints and otter and fox masks on the walls); faded green
hessian and oil paintings decorate the dining room. The light drawing
room has an open fireplace, and a gently ticking clock. Bedrooms are
equally old-fashioned, with traditional fabrics; some have pine furniture
and lace bedspreads. There is no television anywhere. A tranquil and
idiosyncratic hotel.

Location: *Signposted from Hawkridge. Not accessible from Liscombe/Winsford
direction*
Bedrooms: *15 (single, double, twin), 2 with four-poster, 7 with bath*
Facilities: *Parking. Stabling. Fishing, shooting, clay-pigion shooting*
Restrictions: *No dogs in public rooms*
Open: *Mid Mar to mid Nov*
Credit/charge cards accepted: *Amex, Visa*
Price category: *££*
Special rates: *Weekends, 3 nights DB&B £32 pp per night; Mon-Thurs DB&B
£28 pp per night. Children in parents' room half price*

LYNMOUTH
The Rising Sun
The Harbour, Lynmouth, Devon EX35 6EQ   Tel: (0598) 53223

On a steep slope by the harbour, this pub/hotel is in a pretty row of white cottages with roses round the door and a cottage garden at the back. Thatched roofs and beams add to the charm (the oldest part is 14th-century). The traditional pub bar has a welcoming fire set in a stone wall; the panelled dining room is a little cramped but freshly decorated with bold chintzy curtains. Bedrooms, too, are on the small side: some have brass bedsteads and pine furniture. More chintzy curtains add a touch of sophistication to their otherwise cottage style. The last on the row is 'Shelley's Cottage' – where you may either self-cater or use the hotel facilities. A friendly pub in an attractive coastal setting.

Bedrooms: *16 (single, double, twin, family), 1 in cottage, 5 with bath, 11 with shower. Direct dial telephone, TV, teamaking. Hairdryer on request*
Facilities: *Fishing. Babylistening*
Open: *All year*
Credit/charge cards accepted: *Access, Amex, Visa*
Price category: *££*
Special rates: *Autumn and spring, 2 nights DB&B £31-£34 pp per night. Children in parents' room: under 2, 15% of tariff; 2-12 half price; over 12, 75%*

MIDDLECOMBE
Periton Park
Middlecombe, Nr Minehead, Somerset TA24 8SW   Tel: (0643) 5970

A fine Victorian country house set in 30 acres of woodland, fields and gardens. It's furnished and decorated throughout in Victorian style. The comfortable drawing room has brocade-covered chairs, a club fender, and lacy lampshades (there's also a record player, a drinks tray and lots of books); the billiard room has a full-size table, bare floorboards and a large stag's head. Bedrooms are spacious and sympathetically decorated (William Morris papers and antique lace panels) with attention to period detail and mouldings; there's a table for breakfast, and magazines and mineral water. This is a well-run hotel, organised along 'house-party' lines, in a tranquil setting.

Bedrooms: *6 (double, twin, suite), all with bath. Direct dial telephone, TV, teamaking. Hairdryer on request*
Facilities: *Parking. Croquet, boules. Riding. Billiards. Babylistening*
Restrictions: *No dogs in public rooms. Young children by arrangement only*
Open: *All year*
Credit/charge cards accepted: *Access, Amex, Diners, Visa*
Price category: *£££*
Special rates: *2 nights DB&B £46 pp per night. Children under 12 in parents' room £10*

Nr PARRACOMBE
Heddons Gate
Heddons Mouth, Parracombe, Devon EX31 4PZ   *Tel: (05983) 313*

A large hotel surrounded by 20 acres of terraced gardens and grounds, in a lovely peaceful setting. The house and the décor combine contemporary with antique, but the general effect is Victorian. There's plainly a nostalgia for the 'old days': bedrooms have names such as 'Grandma's Room' or 'Servants' Quarters'. They are mostly spacious with some Victorian furniture, brass or mahogany beds, lace or crochet bedcovers; biscuits, milk in a thermos and fruit make you feel well looked after. The conscientious service extends to the turning down of beds, place names on the dining tables and making sure you know the name of your waitress. Good English food is served in the large, rather plain, dining room. There are a number of comfortable sitting rooms, a bar and a 'snug' with card table. Down the drive are some self-contained cottages with spacious family accommodation. This well-run hotel is popular with its predominantly middle-aged guests who return year after year.

Bedrooms: *14 (single, double, twin, suites), 3 in cottages. 1 with four-poster. 13 with bath, 1 with shower. Direct dial telephone, TV, teamaking*
Facilities: *Parking*
Restrictions: *No children under 8*
Open: *Easter to beginning Nov*
Credit/charge cards accepted: *None*
Price category: *££*
Special rates: *3-6 nights DB&B £31-£40 pp per night. Children in parents' room, 8-16 half price*

PORLOCK WEIR
The Anchor Hotel & The Ship Inn
Porlock Weir, Somerset TA24 8PB   *Tel: (0643) 862753*

Quietly situated overlooking the tidal Bristol Channel, this hotel/inn (the result of a merger some ten years ago) offers two different styles of accommodation. The Anchor is mid 19th-century and run as a traditional hotel: public rooms are old-fashioned and a little sombre, bedrooms are plainly decorated with chintz fabrics and some antiques (and paper bathmats in the bathrooms). A grand piano at the foot of the stairs and pictures of Exmoor and staghounds add a certain homeliness. The early 16th-century Ship Inn is a pretty white-painted pub, the main feature of which is the beamed bar with large open fireplace. Bedrooms here are simply decorated in cottage style. At the back is a pretty, sloping garden up steep steps. Friendly service and a pleasant setting make it a comfortable place to stay.

Bedrooms: *30 (single, double, twin, family), 1 with four-poster. 4 in annexe. 27 with bath. Direct dial telephone, TV, teamaking. Hairdryer on request*
Facilities: *Parking. Shooting. Babylistening*
Restrictions: *Dogs in bedrooms only*
Open: *All year*

Credit/charge cards accepted: *Access, Amex, Visa*
Price category: *££*
Special rates: *2 nights, DB&B £33.75-£42.75 (single £41.25-£50.25). Children in parents' room £10 (cot £5); in own room, under 15, half price*

SIMONSBATH
Simonsbath House
Simonsbath, Nr Minehead, Somerset TA24 7SH   *Tel: (064 383) 259*

This charming long and low white-painted hotel overlooks the river Barle as it sweeps away down a gentle Exmoor valley. It's a comfortable country house with rather less emphasis on hunting and fishing than many places in this part of the world. The entrance hall is a cosy English sitting room with panelling and an open fire; in the evenings, the door is opened through to the adjoining bar/library. The dining room is more modern – pale orange walls and stylishly set tables. Bedrooms vary a bit – cheerful and sophisticated, or panelled and stately. Bathrooms are more than adequate and guests are supplied with flannels, books and mineral water. There's a pretty, sloping lawned front garden. A quiet rural hotel for a restful stay.

Location: *Centre of Simonsbath*
Bedrooms: *7 (double, twin), 2 with four-poster, all with bath. Direct dial telephone, TV, hairdryer*
Facilities: *Parking*
Restrictions: *No dogs. No children under 10*
Open: *Feb to Nov*
Credit/charge cards accepted: *Access, Amex, Diners, Visa*
Price category: *£££*
Special rates: *2 nights DB&B £45 (single £47) pp per night; 3 nights DB&B £44 (£46)*

WINSFORD
Royal Oak Inn
Winsford, Exmoor National Park, Somerset TA24 7JE   *Tel: (064 385) 455*

A picturesque thatched pub/hotel in a quiet village at the heart of Exmoor. The pub part is straightforward with a large open fireplace, horse brasses and pictures of moor and hounds; the rest of the ground floor is taken up by a number of cosy low-ceilinged lounges. One room has a mural of hunting scenes (including caricatures of the locals), and the dining room is rather dominated by a brick fireplace displaying a collection of plates and goblets. Bedrooms in the main building have a cottage atmosphere with co-ordinated floral papers and fabrics. Some more modern-style bedrooms are in the converted outbuildings. A pleasant country hotel.

Bedrooms: *14 (double, twin, family), 5 in annexe, 1 family cottage, all with bath. Direct dial telephone, TV. Hairdryer*
Facilities: *Parking. Fishing*
Restrictions: *Dogs in kennels only*
Open: *All year*

Credit/charge cards accepted: *Access, Amex, Diners, Visa*
Price category: ££
Special rates: *2 or more nights, DB&B £42.75 (single £59.40) pp per night. Children in parents' room free*

WITHYPOOL
The Royal Oak Inn
Withypool, Somerset TA24 7QP *Tel: (064 383) 506*

A roadside pub in a small village at the heart of Exmoor. There are two bars: one (with beams, open fireplaces and antlers on the walls) is used as a lounge in the evenings for residents and diners; the other is a traditional pub bar (bench seating, a fine shove-ha'penny table, pictures of Exmoor and hunting scenes, and a large collection of hunt buttons). The dining room also has a country pub atmosphere, plain and fresh with white walls and pink candles. The cottage-style bedrooms are not very spacious; pot pourri and a thermos of iced water are unexpected touches. A comfortable and well-run pub with character.

Bedrooms: *8 (double, twin, family), all with bath (though 2 not en suite). Direct dial telephone, TV, teamaking. Hairdryer*
Facilities: *Parking, stabling. Clay pigeon shooting. Fishing*
Restrictions: *No children under 10*
Open: *All year except Christmas*
Credit/charge cards accepted: *Access, Amex, Diners, Visa*
Price category: ££
Special rates: *Children 10-14 in parents' room half price*

The Lake District

- Beautiful and amazingly varied scenery which can be enjoyed even from a car
- Wonderful walking country – 1,500 miles of paths and bridleways – and some serious mountains
- Abundant accommodation, from renowned hotels with gourmet cooking to comfortable B&Bs
- A fair sprinkling of sights to visit
- Crowds are a problem in summer, but not everywhere

Britain's most popular National Park is a compact area – about 30 miles across – of such intricate and varied scenery that it feels much larger. Its lakes lie in the valleys formed by an outward thrust of ice-age glaciers, radiating from the ancient central rocks; this geological freak has folded ridges and saddles and peaks into a landscape of concentrated drama. Rain all too frequently blots it out, but even a gleam of sunlight reveals the watercolour magic that attracts admirers – 12 million a year, many of them regulars. Whether you explore by car or on foot, the chances are you'll develop an addiction – to favourite places, favourite seasons, favourite hotels. It is an area ideal for gentle touring with the leisure to take a walk on impulse or change your route according to the weather. In the most accessible southern part traffic and crowds file up roads and centres all summer, but further north is much less busy and over in the west you can find true isolation.

The Southern Lakes

An easy drive from the M6 through the pleasant market town of **Kendal** and some rolling farmland brings you to **Windermere**, England's largest lake. It's over ten miles long and much used for watersports – the only lake in the District that has (in parts) no speed limit. Steamers travel its length, a ferry plies across, speedboats and waterskiers zoom around. Woodland along the sloping east shore half conceals grand Victorian villas (many now hotels) and luxury timeshare developments. **Windermere town**, Lakeland's railhead, is a sprawling residential accumulation with high terraces of B&B; **Bowness**, its lakeside extension, is the most commercialised place in the Lake District, filled with souvenir shops, fast food outlets and seasidey hotels. Both are to be avoided on summer weekends. The western shore is tranquil and hardly visited: there's a maze of minor roads south of **Far Sawrey** and the tiny car ferry from Bowness.

At the lake's northern end several tourist routes converge on little stone-built **Ambleside**; in spite of clogged summer traffic it's an excellent place for shopping (walking gear, knitwear and sheepskin) and having tea. North of Ambleside, **Rydal Water** and **Grasmere** are small much-visited lakes, with many paths from main road parking places. This is Wordsworth country: he loved all Lakeland but lived here, in Dove Cottage and in Rydal Mount. Pretty Grasmere village gets swamped by literary tourism. The scenery around is charming, with a local Alpine neatness, and there are spectacular further views – up the **Langdale** valleys you reach famous climbing country with several peaks approaching 2,500 feet.

In gentler wooded country west of Windermere, little **Esthwaite Water** is Beatrix Potter territory with a literary following of its own. Cars are kept out of **Hawkshead**, a tidy showpiece village with coaching-inn pubs and a fine church. Paths and Forestry Commission tracks lead through the Lake District's largest woodland area, **Grizedale Forest**, to the eastern shore of **Coniston Water**. This is the straight five-mile stretch where world waterspeed records were broken, and Donald Campbell died in 1967. The subtle colours of its southern fells are best appreciated from the quiet east road, or from a trip on the Victorian steam yacht *Gondola*, rebuilt and run by the National Trust. At the northern end Coniston village – part Lakeland slate, part modern bungaloid – is steeply set against quarry-scarred brown hillsides and the looming 2,635 feet of Coniston Old Man. In complete contrast is **Tarn Hows**, the photogenic little beauty spot east of the road to Ambleside, a chocolate-box composition of shapely trees on a promontory mirrored in brilliant water.

HISTORIC BUILDINGS
Coniston Water, Brantwood   On the lake's quiet eastern shore, the home of John Ruskin sheds a sympathetic light on the eminent Victorian. Memorabilia, gardens, exhibitions – including one about A.W. Wainwright and his handwritten fell-walking books. [*Open all year, daily, except Mon and Tues mid Nov to mid Mar*]
Grasmere, Dove Cottage   Tiny home of the Wordsworths from 1799 to 1808; adjacent museum displays personal belongings (including William's socks). [*Open daily except mid Jan to mid Feb*]

Kendal, Levens Hall Elizabethan mansion incorporating Norman pele tower: fine panelling, plasterwork and furniture; grounds include topiary garden and steam model collection. [*Open Easter to mid Oct, Sun to Thurs; steam models pm only*]

Kendal, Sizergh Castle (NT) Norman pele tower, Tudor great hall, linenfold panelling and attractive contents; rockery and rose garden. [*Open April to Oct, pm only; Sun, Mon, Wed and Thurs*]

Rydal, Rydal Mount Wordsworth's much more imposing last home: mementoes and portraits. [*Open all year, daily except Tues Nov to Feb*]

Troutbeck, Townend 17th-century farmhouse, as lived in by many generations of a Cumbrian yeoman family. (NT) [*Open April to Oct, daily except Mon and pm Sat*]

Hill Top, Near Sawrey Home of Beatrix Potter, much-visited by fans of *Peter Rabbit*; her original drawings are now displayed not here but in Hawkshead. [*Open April to Oct, Mon to Thurs, Sat, and pm Sun*]

MUSEUMS

Bowness, Windermere Steamboat Museum Victorian and Edwardian steam pleasure craft, lovingly restored to working order. [*Open Easter to Oct, daily*]

Kendal, Abbott Hall Museum Dignified Georgian complex with themed displays of Lakeland life and exhibitions of painting and sculpture; fine 18th-century furniture, paintings and porcelain [*Open all year, Mon to Fri and pm weekends*] **Kendal Museum**, in the town centre, has archaeology and natural history, largely local. [*Open all year, Mon to Fri and pm weekends*]

FAMILY OUTINGS

Lakeside and Haverthwaite Railway Standard gauge steam railway running 3 ½ miles through the Leven Valley. Steamboat connections at Lakeside, engines and rolling stock to be seen at Haverthwaite.

Newby Bridge, Fell Foot Country Park Eighteen acres of parkland on the south-east shore of Windermere: safe bathing, rowing boats, picnic site. (NT) [*Open all year, daily*]

The Northern Lakes

Four of the five lakes radiating north can be reached quickly from **Penrith** and the M6, as well as by more scenic routes from Windermere and Grasmere. The fifth, **Haweswater**, is awkwardly remote – a long trek through small lanes from Penrith or over a shoulder of Shap Fell. Its stark dam and hard white waterline make it the most obvious reservoir in the Lakes; it has a dead-end road and a lone hotel, but no villages, sights or sports. Its appeal is the grand and lonely setting – and the drifts of cowslips in the spring. Westward across wild fells and the Roman ridgeway path called High Street lies **Ullswater**, the lake that has everything – size, beauty, setting – and rivals Windermere in popularity. From the lush Eamont valley meadows it bends seven and a half miles to the dramatic fells below Helvellyn: the scenery and walks are wonderful. The villages are not; **Pooley Bridge** is very commercialised, **Patterdale** and **Glenridding** pleasanter but congested all summer. The lake is busy with steamers, sailing, windsurfing and assorted small boats – though a 10mph speed limit keeps most powered craft away – and the action is along the west shore where hotel lawns reach the water's edge. The main road is a traffic-crawl in summer but does have splendid views. There's a succession of waterfalls, culminating in the much-visited **Aira Force**; and somewhere near Gowbarrow Wordsworth met his dancing crowd of daffodils.

Keswick, attractively set, is a sturdy market town with a broad main street, a moot hall and a bustle of pubs and chip shops. Just north is the great bald dome of Skiddaw (3,053ft) and just south **Derwent Water**, pretty from every angle and accessible all round. It's a squarish lake of reedy shores, wooded islets, little promontories, many paths, and popular fell walks with viewpoints. Up the river Derwent romantic **Borrowdale** winds through dense woods and under rugged heights, and past the giant 'glacial erratic' Bowder Stone, deposited here during ice-age upheavals. Pretty villages worth a detour include Watendlath and Seatoller. For huge open views of the northern fells make for **Castlerigg Stone Circle**, on flat uplands off the road from Keswick to Grasmere. This main north-south route of the Lake District runs by **Thirlmere**, a long narrow reservoir-lake formed by combining two small ones, very quiet and shrouded in woodland. Access is good all round; forest footpaths and stiffer walks lead off from both sides. It's prettiest from the minor road along the west bank where there are viewpoints and some tiny pebble beaches.

Bassenthwaite is the nondescript blur on your right as you speed along the flat road towards Cockermouth. It's much more attractive from the road set high on its eastern side, giving a panorama of the lake and surrounding hills. Waymarked walks lead through Dodd Wood, and there's a route up Skiddaw. On Bassenthwaite only 'quiet' watersports are permitted, and public access is discouraged at the marshy southern end, an important wetland nature reserve.

HISTORIC BUILDINGS AND GARDENS

Bassenthwaite Lake, Mirehouse Small manor house on the eastern shore: Wordsworth and Tennyson associations. Attractive gardens, walks, nature trail. [*Open all year; grounds daily; house pm, Sun, Wed and Bank Hol Mons*]

Dacre, Dalemain Two miles north of Ullswater, a medieval and Elizabethan mansion with a Georgian façade. Deer park and gardens, furniture and family portraits, small museum of agricultural bygones. [*Open Easter Sun to mid Oct, Sun to Thurs*]

Derwent Water, Lingholm Gardens Imaginative formal and woodland gardens below the fells west of the lake: rhododendrons and azaleas, walks and views. [*Open April to Oct, daily*]

MUSEUMS

Keswick, Pencil Museum Unexpectedly fascinating: the Cumberland Pencil Company displays development, manufacture and artwork. [*Open all year, daily except am at weekends*]

FAMILY OUTINGS

Lowther Park Extensive grounds of Lowther Castle (now mostly demolished): adventure playgrounds, assault courses, jousts, circus ('acres of pure fun'). [*Open Easter to mid Sep, daily*]

The Western Lakes

The central mass of mountains round Scafell Pike blocks north-south access, and the east-west roads are mountain passes. Winlatter Pass and Newlands Valley (from Keswick) are differently pretty and relatively undemanding; Honister Pass (from Borrowdale) has gradients of one-in-four and fine views over scree-covered fells. Any of these gets you over to the National Trust's threesome of Buttermere, Crummock Water and Loweswater – a popular excursion, but not in the Windermere league for crowds. **Buttermere** is small and tranquil, surrounded by steep but friendly hummocky fells and scattered trees. **Crummock Water** is wilder and more bare, twice as big and half as pretty. There are easy walks round both – the Buttermere circuit is a particularly agreeable family stroll – and a path strikes off uphill to **Scale Force**, the Lake District's highest waterfall. Roadside parking places are few: leave the car in Buttermere village between the lakes. Further down the valley little **Loweswater** is worth seeking out, down some quiet lanes, for its gentle scenic mixture of pine trees, pasture and varied hillsides. There are fine views of steep sugar-loaf fells, and good walks on the west side away from the road.

The only approach by road to **Ennerdale Water** in the next valley is from the west, through flat farmland at the far edge of the National Park. Nothing disturbs the silence of this reservoir lake in its craggy setting; fishing from the shore is the only sport permitted and it has no road beside it. A Forestry Commission track follows the north shore from the car park at Bowness Knott and a path (mostly easy) allows you to complete the circuit in two hours or so. Waymarked walks among the conifers go east up the Liza valley, towards the climbing challenges of Pillar, Steeple and Red Pike.

Of all the lakes, the deepest, coldest and most spectacular is **Wast Water**, brooding below the great east walks of scree which shadow its sunface. You can reach it across the mountains from Ambleside by Wrynose and Hard Knott, the most difficult passes in the Lake District, or from further south by relatively deserted roads across sheep strewn moorland. Then deceptively gentle lanes bring you to the superb drive along the lake towards Great Gable, whose symmetrical pyramid takes visual precedence over the highest peaks in England, Scafell (3,162 ft) and Scafell Pike (3,210 ft). The road ends at **Wasdale Head**, barely a village— there's an inn, a mountain rescue centre and a tiny church with a graveyard full of memorials to climbers. Wasdale is a magnificent base for serious climbing and walking, but perilous at all times and in all weathers for the inexperienced.

HISTORIC BUILDINGS AND GARDENS

Cockermouth, Wordsworth House Graceful Georgian house where the poet was born, furnished in period. Also attractive walks round this lively old market town set where two rivers meet. (NT) [*Open April to Oct, daily except Thurs, and Sun am*]

Muncaster, Muncaster Castle A mile east of Ravenglass, the Pennington family seat dates from the 14th century with additions up to the 19th; furniture and paintings mostly 16th and 17th. Grounds have famous rhododendrons, a bird garden, views over the Esk valley [*Open Easter to Sep, pm only, daily except Mon (unless Bank Hols)*]. Nearby **Muncaster Mill** is a restored 18th-century watermill producing stone-ground flour. [*Open April to Sep, Sun to Fri*]

FAMILY OUTINGS

Ravenglass and Eskdale Railway Seven miles of narrow-gauge track, originally linking mines and quarries with the coast; steam and diesel engines. At Ravenglass the **Railway Museum** has relics, models and a slide show.

Walking

There can be no doubt that the Lake District offers the best range of walking anywhere in the country. There are all sorts of mountain climbs from very easy to fairly difficult; interesting passes which take you from one valley to the next; paths round lakes; and walks in the gentler areas on the fringes, particularly to the south. In all the more popular areas, paths are well-used and clearly marked (though unhappily footpath erosion has scarred the landscape in many places, particularly on the slopes). And walkers' needs are widely catered for – whether with cups of tea at farmhouses on the way or with drying rooms at the end of the day. The main problem you're likely to encounter (apart from the weather) is choosing which walk to take.

For serious walkers, the biggest attraction is the area between Eskdale (to the south), Wasdale, Borrowdale and Great Langdale (to the east). This contains several of the Lakes' most imposing mountains giving outstanding walking, much of it on high, exposed ridges. They can be climbed from any of these valleys, though the routes from Eskdale are tough; and Scafell Pike, the highest, is a long haul from any direction. The road up Wasdale gets closer to the summits than any of the others. As well as mountain climbs, this is a good area for interesting valley-to-valley walks: there are good paths connecting each of these valleys from the point where the roads come to an end.

There are of course many other areas – such as the fells round Robinson and Grisedale Pike in the north-west, and the mountains of the Helvellyn range in the centre – with nearly as great a claim on the keen walker's attention. But a different approach altogether would be to follow one of the two (unofficial) long-distance paths which pass through the Park. Both take in some impressive scenery. The Cumbria Way runs from south to north through the middle of the Park, taking in Coniston, Great Langdale and Borrowdale, on its way from Ulverston to Carlisle. The Coast-to-Coast Path crosses the Park from west to east on its way to Robin Hood's Bay in Yorkshire, via Borrowdale and Grasmere.

If you're not quite so heroically-minded but still want to try some modest fell-walks, Borrowdale and the area around Grasmere and Ambleside are good places to aim for, as is the southern end of Ullswater round Glenridding. All three have a very good variety of not-too-difficult walks taking in lakes and valleys as well as hills. Borrowdale in particular has a very fine ridge walk along Cat Bells, just west of Derwent Water. If you feel like graduating to something harder, all three areas have some impressive taller mountains to climb – such as Great Gable from Borrowdale, Fairfield from Grasmere or Ambleside, and Helvellyn from Glenridding (with or without Striding Edge on the way). There are very attractive easy walks in the area between Windermere and Coniston Water – for example around Hawkshead, around Tarn Hows, and in Grizedale Forest where there is a forest trail. There are also some very attractive paths in the area just south of Ullswater, around Howtown. And a great attraction throughout the Park, even for those who don't normally count themselves as walkers, is the very large number of level paths round the shores of the lakes; every lake has at least one quiet side.

See *Holiday Which? Good Walks Guide* walks 125-138.

Boats and buses

The lake boat services are good ways of getting about, as well as useful outings. Windermere stops are Lakeside, Bowness and Waterhead, and the car ferry across the lake (just south of Bowness) saves a long trek round. Ullswater steamers stop at Glenridding, Howtown and Pooley Bridge. Derwent Water has the Keswick Launch Service to seven landing stages, all good starting points for walks. As well as the main bus companies (Ribble for east and central areas, Cumberland Motor Services for Keswick and west), the Mountain Goat minibus company runs between the main centres. There's also a Fell Bus service along the Buttermere and Borrowdale valleys, which walkers can 'hail and ride'.

Shopping

Like any other popular tourist area, the Lake District has plenty to sell you. Edible souvenirs are Grasmere gingerbread, Cumberland rum butter and Kendal mint cake. Apart from walking and climbing gear, there are sheepskin, knitwear, tweed and rugs; things made of green Lakeland slate; a local perfume industry and endless local art. Besides shops, the area has many good studios and craft centres – these are as much entertainment as retail outlets, and some make a small entrance charge, refundable if you buy. Interesting places include Kirkstone Gallery, Skelwith Bridge (specialising in slate); Wetheriggs Pottery, Penrith; Adrian Sankey Glass, Ambleside; Lakeland Rural Industries, Grange-in-Borrowdale; Thornthwaite Galleries (local artists); and Heaton Cooper Studio, Grasmere (watercolour prints).

When to go

Spring is, obviously, the season for daffodils and attracts many visitors. The central and southern parts of the Lake District are busy throughout the summer and on Bank Holidays; the traffic normally keeps moving but parking can be very difficult in Ambleside and Keswick. Great Langdale and Borrowdale can also get crowded. The outlying areas to the east, north and west – particularly the west – are generally much quieter. Autumn tints on the fellsides are spectacular, and the crowds ease up – especially mid-week. Winter always brings snow.

The Cumbrian Games are held each summer in Grasmere and Ambleside. The Theatre-in-the-Forest at Grizedale offers plays, concerts and talks all summer.

Information

The Cumbria Tourist Board, Ashleigh Holly Road, Windermere, Cumbria LA23 2AQ, tel: (096 62) 4444. The Lake District is liberally scattered with Tourist Information Centres, some open Easter to October only.

The National Park Information Centre, Brockhole, Windermere, Cumbria LA23 1LJ, tel: (096 62) 2231 (splendid grounds on the north-east shore of the lake; audio-visual displays, exhibitions and films as well as books and information). Other centres include Keswick and Seatoller.

The Forestry Commission runs Grizedale Forest Visitor Centre, near Scatterthwaite: it has forestry and wildlife exhibitions, and lots of waymarked trails start here.

Where to stay

The Lake District has easily the best range of accommodation in any National Park, though most of it is in and around the best-known areas such as Windermere, Derwent Water, Borrowdale and Ullswater. The choice of hotels is enormous. At the top end you can spend a small fortune soaking up the luxury of some of the smartest hotels in the country; but there are also some family-run places offering very good value. B&Bs are concentrated mainly in the towns, especially Windermere, Ambleside and Keswick. If you don't mind roughing it a bit the youth hostel network is well worth considering; most are splendidly located.

AMBLESIDE
Wateredge
Borrans Road, Waterhead, Ambleside, Cumbria LA22 OEP   Tel: (053 94) 32332

Peacefully set at the head of Lake Windermere, Wateredge consists of two 17th-century fishermen's cottages with later additions, and lawns leading down to the lake. Public rooms are light and well-furnished, make excellent use of lake views and are relaxing and stylish. There are some interesting nooks and crannies in the older part of the house which includes an oak-beamed dining area, serving good 6-course dinners. Bedrooms are comfortable, if slightly less spacious than might be expected, and nearly all face the lake (avoid the rooms on the road side). A new extension, not quite in keeping with the rest of the house, has been added to provide five new luxury suites. Wateredge is a friendly place, offering excellent service.

Location: *½ mile south of Waterhead, on A591*
Bedrooms: *23 (single, double, twin, family), 5 suites in annexe, all with bath or shower. Direct dial telephone, TV, teamaking*
Facilities: *Parking, private jetty. Rowing boats*
Restrictions: *No children under 7. No dogs in lounge. No smoking in dining room*
Open: *Early Feb to early Dec*
Credit/charge cards accepted: *Access, Amex, Visa*
Price category: ££
Special rates: *3 to 6 nights DB&B, £41 (single £42.50) pp per night. Feb to mid-May (excluding Easter, and Bank Hol in May), DB&B £32 (single £33.50). Children half price in parents' room*

AMBLESIDE
Nanny Brow
Clappersgate, Ambleside, Cumbria LA22 9NF   *Tel: (0966) 32036*

An Edwardian country house turned immaculate country house hotel, set in five acres of gardens and woodlands at the foot of Loughrigg Fell. Public rooms are comfortably traditional. Bedrooms have all been individually decorated in tasteful chintzy style. The garden wing extension contains luxury suites with sitting rooms; these are modern and rather bleaker in style.

Location: *One mile west of Ambleside on A593*
Bedrooms: *18 (double and suites), 17 with bath, 1 with shower. Direct dial telephone, TV, teamaking. Hairdryer. Some suites with kitchen and dining area*
Facilities: *Parking. Spa bath, solarium. Billiards. Babylistening*
Restrictions: *No dogs in public rooms. No smoking in dining room*
Open: *All year*
Credit/charge cards accepted: *Access, Visa*
Price category: ££
Special rates: *Winter weekends, 2 nights DB&B (and including Sun lunch) from £26.50 pp per night; rest of year, reductions on midweek and weekend stays. Children under 12 half price in parents' room, free in suites*

AMBLESIDE
Kirkstone Foot Country House
Kirkstone Pass Road, Ambleside, Cumbria LA22 9EH   *Tel: (053 94) 32232*

A 17th-century manor house in two acres of gardens above the village of Ambleside. Rooms are decorated in traditional hotel style: patterned carpets, brocade and velour chairs and a mixture of reproduction and antique furniture. There are plenty of books, magazines and board games in the lounge; in winter there is a log fire. In fine weather tea is served on the verandah or lawns. But at anytime, the highpoint of a stay here is the simple set dinner served at 8pm; leave room for the splendid choice of puddings, with second helpings encouraged. A homely but well-run hotel.

Bedrooms: *15 (double and single), all with bath or shower. Direct dial telephone, TV, teamaking. Hairdryer*
Facilities: *Parking. Croquet. Babylistening*
Restrictions: *No dogs*
Open: *7 Mar to beginning Dec*
Credit/charge cards accepted: *Access, Amex, Diners, Visa*
Price category: *££*
Special rates: *3 nights DB&B £33.50 pp per night. Children 2-7 sharing parents' room, one-third price; 7-12, two-thirds price*

AMBLESIDE
Rothay Manor
Ambleside, Cumbria LA22 0EH   *Tel: (0966) 33605*

Rothay Manor is a handsome listed Regency building, in its own grounds on the Langdale side of Lake Windermere. The lounges and restaurant are elegantly furnished and the atmosphere is welcoming and relaxing if slightly exclusive and genteel. Bedrooms have been neatly and subtly decorated and have all mod cons. Food is very good and the afternoon teas are legendary. Eminently recommendable at the top of the range, for those in need of a treat.

Location: *On A593 south-west of Ambleside*
Bedrooms: *15 (single, double, twin), 2 suites in annexe, all with bath. Direct dial telephone, TV*
Facilities: *Parking. Croquet. Bridge and cookery courses, wine tastings in winter*
Restrictions: *No dogs*
Open: *Mid Feb to early Jan*
Credit/charge cards accepted: *Access, Amex, Diners, Visa*
Price category: *£££*
Special rates: *Nov to Mar, reduced rates, particularly for midweek stays. Children sharing parents' room £20*

BASSENTHWAITE LAKE
The Pheasant Inn
Bassenthwaite Lake, Cockermouth, Cumbria CA13 9YE   *Tel: (059 681) 234*

A good choice for visiting the northern part of the Lakes, with rapid communications via the A66 to most other parts. The inn, which dates from around 1600, has cosily furnished rooms including the atmospheric old bar (serving real ale) and several comfortable lounge areas. The long shape of the beamed dining room dictates rather regimented rows of fairly close tables, but food is good, service friendly and efficient and the atmosphere informal. Bedrooms are well-equipped and fairly modern. There is a small but very well-kept garden. The Pheasant is suited to anyone who appreciates some informal comfort and character in a quiet location – though non-residents do make the Pheasant busy at all times.

Location: *Just off the A66, 6 miles north-west of Keswick and 5 miles east of Cockermouth*
Bedrooms: *20 (single, double, twin), 18 with bath, 2 with shower. Teamaking. Hairdryer, electric blanket*
Facilities: *Parking*
Restrictions: *No dogs in bedrooms or dining room. No smoking in dining room*
Open: *All year except Christmas Day*
Credit/charge cards accepted: *None*
Price category: *££*
Special rates: *Nov to Mar, DB&B £34 pp per night*

CONISTON
Sun
Coniston, Cumbria LA21 8HQ   *Tel: (053 94) 41248*

A 16th-century inn attached to a turn-of-the-century house, The Sun stands in its own gardens, at the foot of the 'Coniston Old Man'. It has been refurbished recently, in fairly opulent taste. The main lounge is comfortable with floral suites and fine views over the crags; the dining room has similar views and a similar, predominantly blue colour scheme. The bar, serving as a public inn, is traditional and cosy. Bedrooms are generally stylish, all with different décor and most with fine views; the two without views have four-poster beds as compensation. A good base for walking, fishing and riding.

Location: *200 metres above Coniston village*
Bedrooms: *11 (single, double, twin), 2 with four-posters, all with bath. TV, teamaking. Electric blanket*
Facilities: *Parking*
Restrictions: *No smoking in dining room. No dogs in public rooms. No small children in dining room*
Open: *Mar to Dec*
Credit/charge cards accepted: *Access, Visa*
Price category: *££*
Special rates: *Winter and spring (excluding Bank Hol weekends), 2 nights DB&B £33 pp per night. Children sharing parents' room £13*

GRANGE-IN-BORROWDALE
Borrowdale Gates

Grange-in-Borrowdale, Keswick, Cumbria CA12 5UQ   *Tel: (059 684) 204*

The quiet, beautiful location in the grand, wooded Borrowdale Valley is possibly the main appeal of this comfortable Victorian manor house. It has the relaxed atmosphere of a country house – slightly dowdy in parts, with cottagey, chintzy armchairs, log fires and lots of personal touches. Picture windows overlook well-established gardens. Bedrooms are pleasant enough and well-equipped and the food is competently prepared and generously served.

Location: *Just north of the hamlet of Grange*
Bedrooms: *23 (single, double, twin and family), all with bath or shower. TV, teamaking*
Facilities: *Parking. Babylistening*
Restrictions: *No dogs in public rooms*
Open: *All year*
Credit/charge cards accepted: *Access, Amex, Diners*
Price category: *££*
Special rates: *Nov to Mar, 2 nights at weekends DB&B £30 (£32 single), during week £27 (£28.50 single)*

GREAT LANGDALE
The Old Dungeon Ghyll

Great Langdale, Ambleside, Cumbria LA22 9JY   *Tel: (096 67) 272*

A traditional dalehead inn in a dramatic situation with the sheer face of the Stickleback ridge towering behind it, the Old Dungeon Ghyll is mainly suited to walkers and climbers and to families. The lounge and dining room are spacious, relaxing and traditional, with open fires; there is a cosy residents' bar and a spartan climbers' bar. Bedrooms are cottagey with stripped pine furniture and quilted duvets; only four have private facilities (showers). Food is generous and filling but not particularly polished or refined; this is the sort of place where no one expects you to dress up for dinner. Single rooms, without shower, are very cheap. A bus runs four times a day to and from Ambleside.

Location: *7 miles north-east of Ambleside, off B5343*
Bedrooms: *14 (single, double, twin, family), 4 with shower*
Facilities: *Parking. Indoor games. Play area (trampoline, swing)*
Open: *All year except Christmas*
Credit/charge cards accepted: *None*
Price category: *£*
Special rates: *Midweek, DB&B £27 (single £16.25 without shower) pp per night. Children half price in parents' room*

HAWKSHEAD
Field Head House
Hawkshead, Cumbria LA22 0PY   *Tel: (096 66) 240*

An unpretentious country house, dating from the 17th century, Field Head House stands in six acres of mature gardens. The van Guliks treat their guests like guests, offering a warm welcome and really excellent and imaginative home cooking, with the emphasis on fresh vegetables from the garden. English breakfasts and traditional puddings are substantial. Public rooms are comfortable, with log and woodburning fires. Bedrooms, most with good views of the garden and valley, are quite varied in size but well-furnished, well-equipped, light and pleasant. Field Head House is just outside Hawkshead where William Wordsworth was at school, and a few minutes' from Hill Top where Beatrix Potter wrote her stories. It is just the place, as the brochure says, to curl up in front of the fire with a book.

Location: *1 mile north of Hawkshead*
Bedrooms: *8 (single, double, twin and family), 4 with bath, 3 with shower. TV (on request), teamaking. Hairdryer. Some rooms with telephone*
Facilities: *Parking, stabling. Croquet*
Restrictions: *No smoking in bedrooms or dining room. Well behaved children only*
Open: *All year*
Credit/charge cards accepted: *Amex, Diners, Visa*
Price category: ££
Special rates: *Nov to Mar, reduced rates at weekends; also Christmas, New Year and 'Gardening' breaks. Children £10 in parents' room*

HAWKSHEAD
Queen's Head
Hawkshead, Cumbria LA22 0NS   *Tel: (096 66) 271*

A popular olde-worlde village pub offering simple accommodation. The Queens Head is a whitewashed inn dating from 1667, with a newer rear extension containing the residents' lounge. Breakfast is served in the oak-panelled restaurant; bar meals and the local Hartley's real ale are served in the cosy pub itself. Bedrooms are small and neatly furnished with creaking floorboards and some charm. Hawkshead is a pedestrian area; guests are given free passes to the village car park.

Bedrooms: *8 (double or twin), 3 with bath. Teamaking*
Restrictions: *No dogs. No children under 10*
Open: *All year*
Credit/charge cards accepted: *Access, Amex, Diners, Visa*
Price category: £
Special rates: *From Nov, winter weekends, B&B about £13-£16.50 pp per night*

HOWTOWN
Howtown Hotel
Howtown, Ullswater, Penrith, Cumbria CA10 2ND   *Tel: (085 36) 514*

A homely family-run 19th-century farmhouse quietly situated on Ullswater, providing a reasonably-priced alternative to the luxurious Sharrow Bay just up the road. The interior is cosy and comfortable, with open log fires in the public rooms which include a cheery restaurant, several lounges and a separate TV room. Most rooms have excellent views of the fells and there is a small, steep garden at the rear. The main drawback is the difficulty in getting a booking; the owners claim 99% occupancy – a common cry, but at these prices, a believable claim.

Location: *3½ miles south of Pooley Bridge on east shore of Ullswater*
Bedrooms: *16 (single, double), 2 in annexe with bath*
Facilities: *Parking. Private foreshore on lake*
Restrictions: *No children under 8. No dogs in public rooms and at manager's discretion only in bedroooms*
Open: *End Mar to 1 Nov*
Credit/charge cards accepted: *None*
Price category: £
Special rates: *4 nights or more DB&B £18.75 pp per night*

MUNGRISDALE
The Mill
Mungrisdale, Penrith, Cumbria CA11 OXR   *Tel: (059 683) 659*

This converted 17th-century mill cottage by a quiet stream at the foot of the mountains makes a good base for exploring the northern fells. It is a simple and attractive guesthouse, with something of a country house atmosphere. Drinks are served before dinner in the cheerful, cosy lounge. Dinner, prepared by Mrs Quinlan, is quite ambitious, but suits those with hearty appetites. Rooms vary; the most pleasing are quite spacious, with co-ordinated fabrics and neat bathrooms. There is a small TV lounge.

Location: *2 miles north of A66 between Penrith and Keswick*
Bedrooms: *9 (single, double, twin, suite), 5 with bath. TV (some rooms), teamaking. Hairdryer on request*
Facilities: *Parking. Games room (darts, ping-pong, snooker). Badminton*
Restrictions: *No dogs*
Open: *End Feb to 7 Nov*
Credit/charge cards accepted: *None*
Price category: £
Special rates: *Children under 12 sharing parents' room, 25% discount*

RYDAL
Nab Cottage
Rydal, Ambleside, Cumbria LA22 9SD   *Tel: (096 65) 311*

Nab Cottage is just the place for those interested in the literary associations of the area. It was once the home of Hartley (son of Samuel T)

Coleridge and the essayist Thomas de Quincey was a regular visitor; nearby are the famous houses of Wordsworth – Dove Cottage and Rydal Mount. The house, dating from 1702, is well-maintained and its character is largely preserved. There is, however, noticeable traffic noise in the daytime and Nab cottage is cosy rather than comfortable; public rooms can be cramped, bedrooms are small and low-ceilinged and there are no private bathrooms. The fine, central location overlooking Rydal Water, the farmhouse cooking and the reasonable price are ample compensation.

Location: *On the A591 between Ambleside and Grasmere*
Bedrooms: *7 (single, double, twin and family), none with bath. (1 bathroom and 1 shower)*
Facilities: *Parking. Canoe*
Open: *Mid Feb to Nov*
Credit/charge cards accepted: *None*
Price category: £
Special rates: *Reductions for children in parents' room, according to age*

SEATOLLER
Seatoller House
Seatoller, Borrowdale, Keswick, Cumbria CA12 5XN   Tel: (059 684) 218

A small guesthouse in a sheltered village at the foot of Honister Pass, Seatoller House consists of adjoining 17th-century cottages in typical local style. It has been a guesthouse for over 100 years. Staying here is an unusual experience: the atmosphere is rather like a chalet party and depends as much on the other guests as the place itself. The emphasis is on simple comfort and relaxation. The dining room is more like a farmhouse kitchen and self-service, shared tables and conversations are the order of the day. Meals are announced by a gong. The 'bar' is on a honesty basis (help yourself from the fridge by the bootroom) and there are no locks on the doors. Bedrooms are comfortable and cosy with simple cottagey furniture. An idiosyncratic but civilised place which appeals to a cross-section of types; not for those who need privacy.

Location: *8 miles south of Keswick on the B5289*
Bedrooms: *9 (double, twin and family), 1 in annexe, 8 with bath, 1 with shower*
Facilities: *Parking*
Restrictions: *No children under 5. No smoking in dining room or bedrooms. Restaurant closed on Tuesday*
Open: *Mar to mid Nov*
Credit/charge cards accepted: *None*
Price category: £
Special rates: *Children under 12 in parents' room, two-thirds adult rate*

TORVER
Sunny Bank Mill
Torver, Coniston, Cumbria LA21 8BL   Tel: (053 94) 41300

Sunny Bank is a mill cottage extended in Victorian times to form a large country house (the original mill has been converted into three self-catering units). The main house has been well furnished and is cosy, comfortable and unpretentious, with cottagey bedrooms and modern bathrooms. There is an airy riverside dining room. The extensive, well-kept gardens, orchards and fields lead down to a small gravel beach. An ideal quiet base, pleasant and civilised.

Location: *1 mile south of Torver on the south-west bank of Coniston Water*
Bedrooms: *6 (double and family), 4 with bath, 2 with shower only. 3 self-catering flats. TV, teamaking*
Facilities: *Parking, launching facilities. Fishing*
Restrictions: *No dogs in Mill House. No children under 10 in Mill House. No smoking in dining room*
Open: *All year*
Credit/charge cards accepted: *None*
Price category: £

ULLSWATER
Sharrow Bay
Lake Ullswater, Penrith, Cumbria CA10 2LZ   *Tel: (085 36) 301*

This Victorian country house stands in 12 acres of grounds on the edge of Ullswater and views of the lake and fells are spectacular. Rooms are traditionally furnished with antique and some reproduction furniture plus the owners' collections of antique English porcelain. Bedrooms (with names rather than numbers) are also individually decorated but quite small. From the profuse fresh flower decorations to the mouth-watering sweet trolley, everything is done with care and attention to detail. But the friendly, welcoming atmosphere immediately puts guests at their ease. English breakfasts and teas are celebrated, in both senses. The cottage annexe, the Edwardian Lodge and Thwaite Cottage provide extra accommodation. Bank House, a 17th-century farmhouse a mile from Sharrow, has seven bedrooms and a lovely refectory dining room, used for breakfast; dinners are served in the main hotel. Sharrow Bay offers total relaxation in comfortable though not ultra-luxurious surroundings, and superb food, beautifully presented.

Location: *2 miles south of Pooley Bridge, on east shore of Ullswater*
Bedrooms: *28 (single, double and twin), 24 with bath. 12 in main house, 7 in Bank House, 4 in Gate House Lodge, 5 in cottages. Direct dial telephone, TV. Teamaking in some rooms*
Facilities: *Parking, private jetty. Fishing*
Restrictions: *No children under 13. No dogs*
Open: *Early Mar to end Nov*
Credit/charge cards accepted: *None*
Price category: *££££-£££££*
Special rates: *Nov and Mar, midweek, 10% reductions off room rate*

WASDALE HEAD
Wasdale Head Inn
Wasdale Head, Gosforth, Cumbria CA20 1EX   Tel: (094 06) 229

A really spectacular site at the head of dramatic Wast Water, beneath Kirk
Fell and Great Gable, is perhaps the chief attraction of this traditional inn,
recently restored. Inside, it is unstuffy but stylish. There is a comfortable,
rather smart residents' lounge with an inglenook, and an oak-panelled
dining room and bar. Pine-panelled bedrooms are cosy. The food side of
things is particularly good: large amounts of fine English fare. Mountain
yarns are swapped in the public bar and the hotel is particularly suited to
walkers and climbers. With mountain views like this, who needs
television?

Location: *9 miles north-east of Gosforth*
Bedrooms: *11 (single, double/twin and family), all with bath or shower.*
Teamaking. Direct dial telephone
Facilities: *Parking. Climbing shop. Games room (pool table)*
Restrictions: *No children under 7 in dining room in evening. No dogs in public*
rooms
Open: *Mid Mar to mid Nov, and 28 Dec to 3rd week in Jan*
Credit/charge cards accepted: *Access, Visa*
Price category: ££
Special rates: *4 nights or more, reductions of £3 pp per night. Children in*
parents' room £28 DB&B

WATERMILLOCK
The Old Church
Watermillock, Penrith, Cumbria CA11 0JN   Tel: (085 36) 204

A country house dating from 1754, on the site of a 12th-century church,
which gives it its name, this hotel is splendidly located in its own grounds
on the shores of Ullswater. The Whitemore family aim to offer comfort,
good food and well-chosen wines and friendly service. Their house is
well-furnished and expensively decorated with considerable style, and
impeccably maintained. Bedrooms are all in different styles; most have
lake views. At the top end of the price range, The Old Church scores
highly for its peaceful surroundings.

Location: *3 miles south-west of Pooley Bridge, on north shore of Ullswater*
Bedrooms: *9 (double, twin), all with bath*
Facilities: *Parking, moorings. Fishing. Rowing boat. Babylistening*
Restrictions: *No dogs. No smoking in dining room*
Open: *Mid Mar to mid Nov*
Credit/charge cards accepted: *None*
Price category: ££££
Special rates: *Children in parents' room, B&B and high tea, £45; cot £10*

WINDERMERE
Miller Howe
Rayrigg Road, Bowness-on-Windermere, Cumbria LA23 1EY   Tel: (096 62) 2536

A sumptuous top-class hotel renowned for its flamboyant food and attentive service, in a superb lakeshore setting. Public rooms are rather club-like, with leather chesterfields. There is a four-acre landscaped garden and most rooms have superb views over the Langdale Pikes. Dinner is a theatrical *tour-de-force*: lights are dimmed and dishes presented for universal admiration. John Tovey is one of the few British chefs with an international reputation and Miller Howe is a paradise for gourmets. Seven vegetables accompany every main course. There are residential cookery courses in March and November.

Location: *On A592 between Windermere and Bowness*
Bedrooms: *13 (double, twin), 11 with bath, 2 with shower. Portable telephone on request. TV on request, hi-fi. Hairdryer, trouser press*
Facilities: *Parking*
Restrictions: *No children under 12. No dogs in public rooms*
Open: *Mar to early Dec*
Credit/charge cards accepted: *Access, Amex, Diners, Visa*
Price category: *££££-£££££*
Special rates: *Nov and Mar, 3 nights DB&B £50-£75 pp per night*

WITHERSLACK
The Old Vicarage
Witherslack, near Grange-over-Sands, Cumbria LA11 6RS   Tel: (044 852) 381

A quiet country house hotel in a late Georgian vicarage, more suited to those who seek peace and good food than to hearty walking types. The Old Vicarage is run by two couples who have decorated the interior with style. Bedrooms are furnished in pine and cane, and fresh flowers, televisions (rare in the Lake District) and books are provided. In the intimate dining room five-course set dinners are reliably interesting – and digestible. There are five acres of pleasant, well-landscaped gardens.

Location: *5 miles north-east of Grange, off the A590*
Bedrooms: *7 (double), 3 with bath, 4 with shower. Direct dial telephone, TV, teamaking. Hairdryer*
Facilities: *Parking*
Restrictions: *Dogs by arrangement only and not in public rooms. No smoking in dining room until coffee*
Open: *All year except Christmas*
Credit/charge cards accepted: *Access, Diners, Visa*
Price category: *£££*
Special rates: *Dec to Mar (except Christmas to New Year), 2 nights DB&B £44.50 pp per night; April to Nov (except Bank Hol weekends) 3 nights £44.50 pp per night*

The North York Moors

- Remote, wild country but with good roads for touring and two scenic railways as well as endless scope for walks
- Dramatic coastline with traditional resorts, pretty fishing villages and some good beaches
- Plenty to see and do for most ages and interests – from visiting ruined abbeys and castles to steam train rides
- A fair choice of accommodation from village pubs and guesthouses to country houses and seaside hotels, none expensive

The North York Moors is a well-defined area of hills surrounded by lowlands and rugged coastline and protected as a National Park. Much of the coast too is in the National Park. From most directions the approaches are striking: from the south-west you meet strange yellow inland cliffs, from the north-west the main landmark is a sharp conical hill called Roseberry Topping. Once on the moors the landscape is different: this is the largest uninterrupted expanse of heather moorland in England, wild, sometimes bleak and very beautiful. Horizons are immense, views are unspoilt. The numerous dales, mostly green and lush with narrow roads winding through neatly-kept villages of pale grey limestone, provide a cosier, pastoral contrast.

One of the most enjoyable ways of seeing the remotest parts of the Moors (many of which are inaccessible by road) is to take a ride on the North York Moors Railway. And if you don't want to walk, touring by car is rewarding too; minor roads which climb the 'riggs' (ridges) between the dales can offer splendid views.

The Moors

The scenic contrasts of the wild, open moors and the intervening dales is the main attraction of the National Park. **Eskdale** is long and varied; the dales running into it from the south are short, straight and treeless, dominated by their small intricately patterned fields. **Farndale**, further south, is famous for its wild daffodils (and can be crowded at spring weekends) while **Newtondale** is dramatic and narrow, penetrated only by the

North York Moors Railway. Along the southern fringes of the park are the distinctive steep-sided and flat-topped Tabular Hills, much more fertile than the central moors and covered mainly with farmland and forests. To the west are the Hambleton Hills (look out for the White Horse at Kilburn), with some little-visited country villages.

There are no towns of any size wholly within the Park, but there are some pretty villages with houses of the local pale grey stone, often grouped around a village green with a stream or beck running through. Strict planning requirements have ensured that the villages have remained unspoilt and indeed rural life here is very little changed, especially in the north and west. **Goathland** and **Hawnby** are typical villages, both in particularly lovely settings. In the south **Helmsley** is an attractive town with a huge market square, a beck running behind with picturesque over-grown vegetable gardens and a ruined Norman Castle; nearby are the famous landscaped gardens of Duncombe Park. **Kirkby-moorside** is another well-preserved market town, rather less popular. There are several pretty villages nearby: **Hutton-le-Hole** with its large irregularly shaped green crossed by a stream; **Lastingham**, visited chiefly for its outstanding church with a remarkable Norman crypt; and, further east, **Pickering** (which suffers from busy through traffic), with several tourist attractions and a ruined Norman castle.

Most of the interesting places to visit are in the south, near the market towns of Helmsley, Kirkbymoorside and Pickering. In the north you could follow the Captain Cook Memorial Trail (see 'Museums') or visit the Moors Centre (Danby Lodge) where activities include brass rubbing, quizzes and nature trails.

HISTORIC BUILDINGS AND GARDENS

Abbeys In its heyday the area boasted at least a dozen abbeys and priories. The spectacular remains of **Rievaulx Abbey**, one of the largest and finest Cistercian foundations in England, have a magnificent setting in a narrow, secluded part of Ryedale. Rievaulx Terraces (NT), high on the hillside to the south, were set out in the 18th century to give a bird's-eye view of the ruins. There is a footpath to Rievaulx from Helmsley. **Mount Grace Priory**, near Osmotherley, is the best-preserved of the nine Carthusian priories in England. Also worth seeing is **Byland Abbey**, just outside Coxwold.

Coxwold, Newburgh Priory The ruins of a 12th-century priory with later additions and a fascinating history. Curiosities include Cromwell's tomb and the mysterious unfinished room. Fine rooms with family paintings and furnishings; oriental water garden in the park. Some guided tours. [*Open pm only; mid May to*

Aug Wed and Sat, plus Easter and Aug Bank Hol Mons]
Coxwold, Shandy Hall. Charming home of the eccentric 18th-century author, Lawrence Sterne, lovingly restored and furnished. *[Open Jun to Sep, pm only, Wed and Sun; or by appointment, tel: (03476) 465]*
Nunnington Hall. A 16th-century manor house on the banks of the River Wye. Fine interior includes splendid panelled staircase and Carlisle Collection of miniature rooms. (NT) *[Open pm only, weekends April, Daily May to Oct]*

MUSEUMS

Hutton-le-Hole, Ryedale Folk Museum A mainly open-air museum with genuine reconstructed shops and houses including a cruck-frame cottage. *[Open April to Oct, daily]*
Pickering, Beck Isle Museum of Rural Life A fine Regency house packed with Victorian paraphernalia, including reconstructed shops. *[Open Easter to Oct, daily]*

The **Cook Heritage Trail** has been organised by the local tourist board. A free leaflet outlines the route, taking in five places where he lived and worked, mostly just outside the National Park. The trail starts at the excellent **Captain Cook Birthplace Museum** *[open all year, daily]* in Marton, and continues via Great Ayton (museum in the old schoolhouse) to Whitby (see below).

RAILWAYS

❋ **The North York Moors Railway** *Holiday Which? Weekend Break Award*
One of the earliest railways in the world, built by George Stephenson in the 1830s. The Grosmont to Pickering line has recently been revived and the 18-mile ride takes you through some of the finest scenery of the National Park with several stops where you can break your journey to explore on foot: good choices are Newtondale Halt and Goathland. Most services are steam-hauled and for the train buff there's plenty to explore at Grosmont station, including loco sheds reached through an eerie disused tunnel. There's a large collection of carriages, with several Pullman cars used for 'dinner specials'. *[Open Easter to Oct, daily]*

Another scenic line is the Middlesbrough to Whitby line which winds through the lovely landscape of the Esk Valley (with a connection to the North York Moors line at Grosmont).

The Coast

Much of the coast is protected as a 'heritage coast', or owned by the National Trust. Immense cliffs line it, craggy and vertical at the highest point at **Boulby**, tumbled at **Ravenscar**. Sandy or rocky bays are scooped between the dramatic headlands, and in places pretty wooded valleys (known as 'wykes') cut through to the sea. The coast road dips briefly into moorland scenery at **Fylingdales**, near **Robin Hood's Bay**, but elsewhere there is some unsightly modern development.

In the steep-sided clefts of the valleys lie picturesque fishing villages with narrow streets of fishermen's cottages clustered round tiny harbours. In summer traffic access is banned in some places. Some of the fishing villages, including **Staithes**, are still very much alive with a real working community. At others, such as tiny **Runswick**, former fishing cottages have become neat holiday homes. The two main resorts are **Whitby**, attractively set astride the Esk estuary; and **Scarborough**, which has some claims to be Britain's first seaside resort – it became a spa in 1660. Both are well worth visiting. Whitby is split into two by the Esk and the harbour; to the east, below the gaunt ruined abbey and unusual church, is the old fishing port with ancient cottages and narrow, steep crooked streets; to the west the 19th-century holiday resort. Scarborough is magnificently set around two long bays separated by a headland on which stand the ruins of a 12th-century castle.

The whole area is geologically very rich and has long been exploited for its mineral deposits. Alum, used in the dyeing and tanning industries, was extensively quarried from the 16th century onwards. Later iron ore and jet were extracted and now enormous reserves of potash are being mined at Boulby. All this has left some of the landscape scarred with mines and spoil heaps.

The biggest and sandiest beaches are at **Runswick Bay** and **Robin Hood's Bay** (**Stoupe Beck Sands**). Robin Hood's Bay also has the most striking scenery of any of the beaches on this part of the coast: ancient domes of very hard rock have gradually been eroded flat by the sea, leaving strange curved scars – a good fossil-hunting ground.

MUSEUMS AND GALLERIES

Scarborough, Crescent Art Gallery A Georgian sandstone building with a small collection of pictures, worth a visit if combined with the adjacent Woodend Museum. [*Open all year, daily except Mon*]

Scarborough, Rotunda A folk museum which spans the Bronze Age (urns and implements) to the Edwardian era (period photographs). [*Open all year, Tues to Sat plus pm Sun in summer*]

Scarborough, Woodend Museum The family home of the Sitwells, now a natural history museum. In the west wing, panelled rooms contain family mementoes. [*Open all year, Tues to Sat plus pm Sun in summer*]

Whitby, Captain Cook Memorial Museum Nicely restored house with an interesting small exhibition. Cook's attic view of the harbour is evocative; just across the Esk were the boatyards where the Endeavour, Resolution, Discovery and Adventure were built. [*Open May to Oct, Thurs to Mon, and pm Wed*]

Whitby, Pannett Park Museum and Art Gallery A natural and local history musuem with collections of fossils and Whitby jet and a section devoted to Cook. The gallery contains early and contemporary English watercolours with works by Turner, Bonington and Peter de Wint. [*Open May to Oct, Mon to Sat and pm Sun; April and Nov, Wed to Sat, am Mon and Tues, pm Sun*]

Walking

The moors have something to offer just about everyone except the avid mountain-climber, who will find most of the tops too flat; no point in the Park is over 1,500 feet. The Park is well-served by long-distance footpaths, including the Esk Valley Walk and the Cleveland Way. The latter runs for 93 miles, taking in much of the finest scenery, including the western and northern edges of the massif (getting very extensive views) and the coast between Saltburn-by-the-Sea and Filey; this is one of the most rewarding of the (easier) official long-distance paths in Britain, and there are no major ascents on the way. If you prefer to design your own walks, particularly good areas for variety are around Ryedale in the west, Rosedale and Farndale in the centre, Eskdale in the north and around Goathland in the east (where you can see several waterfalls, including Mallyan Spout).

There is a good range of easy walks, though it is not always possible to avoid the odd steep slope. The National Park series of about 30 Waymark Walk leaflets are recommended; walks last 1½ to 2½ hours. There are also free guided walks starting from the Danby Lodge National Park Centre. The Forestry Commission has several marked trails, including in and around Dalby Forest (an area of dense coniferous plantation) and at Sutton Bank (where a level path along the top of the inland cliff gives vast panoramas westwards).

See *Holiday Which? Good Walks Guide* walks 155-160.

When to go

Spring is late on the Moors and it can be bleak until the beginning of May. In June and July there are many local carnivals and festivals; the Ryedale arts festival takes place from the end of July to the beginning of August. However the Moors are at their best when the heather is flowering – anytime from mid August to September. Places to avoid on sunny summer weekends include Helmsley, Hutton-le-Hole, Thornton Dale and the beaches at Robin Hood's Bay and Runswick. But in the more remote areas like Eskdale you should be able to escape the crowds. In very dry weather the Danby Forest Drive is closed.

The North York Moors Railway and Danby Lodge, most museums and historic houses and most tourist information centres are open only from April to October. A few hotels close for the winter too but some offer incentives for winter weekend breaks. There is always a danger of being snowed in.

Information

The North York Moors National Park Information Service, The Old Vicarage, Bondgate, Helmsley; tel: (0439) 70657

The National Park Centre, Danby Lodge, Danby, near Whitby; tel (0287) 60654

The North York Moors Railway tel: (0751) 73791; talking time-table, (0751) 73535

Where to stay

Most accommodation within the park is in village pubs and can be rather basic though there are a few comfortable and reasonably priced country house hotels. Otherwise Helmsley, with several traditional hotels, makes a good base or, if you want to be by the sea, there is a range of typical resort accommodation at Whitby and Scarborough.

BOULBY
Old Stables
Boulby Village, Lostus, Cleveland TS13 4UR   *Tel: (0287) 41109*

A family run guesthouse in converted stables with cliff and sea views. The Cleveland Way passes the house, making this a good base for walkers. There is a pretty dining room (breakfast only) and a comfortable sitting room, both furnished with pine and country antiques. Bedrooms have been decorated with co-ordinating floral fabrics and wallpapers. There is a large swimming pool in the garden.

Location: *Just outside Staiths on the way to Whitby*
Bedrooms: *5 (single, double, twin); 1 bathroom, 1 shower room*
Facilities: *Parking. Swimming pool. TV in lounge. Teamaking facilities*
Restrictions: *No main meals. No smoking in dining room*
Open: *April to Oct*
Credit/charge cards accepted: *None*
Price category: £
Special rates: *2 nights £11 pp per night. Children under 2 free, under 10 half price in parents' room*

EASINGTON
Grinkle Park
Easington, Saltburn-by-the-sea, Cleveland TS13 4UB   *Tel: (0287) 40515*

Grinkle Park has been recently transformed from a rather dowdy hotel to an extremely comfortable and professionally run establishment. It is a late 19th-century building designed by Alfred Waterhouse, standing in extensive, immaculately maintained parkland. Inside the décor and furnishings – and indeed atmosphere – are of a rather grand country house, with log fires, well-upholstered sofas and armchairs, watercolours and oil paintings and fresh flower arrangements. There is a conservatory-type extension used for bar lunches and a bar which is a smart version of a pub counter. But the loveliest rooms are upstairs – an elegant, tranquil residents' sitting room and a series of charming bedrooms, each individually decorated and thought out with the minutest attention to detail: all are named after local moors, each with its own picture, specially commissioned. The bathrooms are pristine. On the top floor are appealing attic bedrooms (with bird names). Add to all this good food, with an emphasis on local produce, some from the estate. An excellent place for a soothing break, and not overpriced.

Location: *2 miles off the Guisborough to Whitby moors road*
Bedrooms: *20 (single, double and twin), 2 with four-posters, all doubles with bath. Direct dial telephone, TV and teamaking. Hairdryers in 6 rooms. Trouser press*
Facilities: *Parking. Games room (billiards). Clay pigeon shooting, croquet, fishing (small trout in beck; day tickets for salmon fishing on Esk), tennis. Babylistening*
Restrictions: *No dogs in public rooms*
Open: *All year*
Credit/charge cards accepted: *Access, Amex, Diners, Visa*
Price category: £££
Special rates: *Weekends, 2 nights DB&B £42 (£52 single) pp per night. Children in parents' room £10*

GOATHLAND
Mallyan Spout Hotel
Goathland, Whitby, North Yorkshire YO22 5AN   *Tel: (0947) 86206*

An old-fashioned hotel in a superb location overlooking the Esk Valley.
The ivy-covered stone building stands on the village green, not far from
the waterfall after which it is named. Inside it is traditional, homely and a
bit worn around the edges. The atmosphere is friendly and welcoming
and the chiming of the church clock and bleating sheep are the only
threats to the tranquillity of a stay. The prettiest bedrooms have a
cottagey feel and have been recently refurbished. Seafood from Whitby is
a speciality and there is a varied pudding trolley; there's also an
interesting wine list. A good base for keen walkers and for the North York
Moors Railway.

Bedrooms: *23 (single, double and twin/family), 18 with bath. TV. Hairdryer on
request*
Facilities: *Parking*
Open: *All year*
Credit/charge cards accepted: *Amex, Diners, Visa*
Price category: *££*
Special rates: *May to Sept (except Bank Hol weekends), 2 nights DB&B £30 pp
per night. Children in parents' room £6*

HAROME
The Pheasant
Harome, Helmsley, North Yorkshire YO6 5JG   *Tel: (0439) 71241*

In a quiet corner of the little village of Harome, the Pheasant consists of
several converted buildings – the blacksmith's, two cottages and the shop
– and was opened as a hotel in 1985. Inside, everything has been
designed to give a feeling of tranquillity; public rooms are light, spacious
and uncluttered with comfortable country furniture and floral fabrics.
There is a small oak-beamed bar in the old smithy where lunches are
served. Bedrooms overlook the village pond and millstream or the
courtyard and walled garden, and are named after local beauty spots.
Bathrooms are smallish but have towelling robes and Floris bath salts.
Food is uncomplicated, nicely prepared and well above average. A good
choice for couples without children and all peacelovers.

Bedrooms: *12 (single, double and twin), all with bath. Direct dial telephone, TV,
teamaking. Two cottages with self-catering facilities*
Facilities: *Parking*
Restrictions: *No children under 12. No dogs in public rooms. No smoking in
dining room*
Open: *Mar to Dec*
Credit/charge cards accepted: *None*
Price category: *££*
Special rates: *Nov to May, 2 nights DB&B £30 (single £35) pp per night.
Reduced rates for children according to age*

HAWNBY
Hawnby Hotel
Hawnby, near Helmsley, York YO6 5QS   *Tel: (04396) 202*

Deep in the countryside, Hawnby is a completely unspoilt village in which this hotel serves as the pub – but it is a cut above the standard village pub, and only the bar has this atmosphere. Bedrooms in the main house are spacious and freshly decorated with crisp cotton fabrics and simple wallpapers – all similar but with varying colour schemes. Their furniture is mixed – simple, but well-kept. The lounge is a homely affair of old-fashioned wing chairs grouped awkwardly round an open fireplace; in summer the garden is a more appealing place to sit. The dining room too is neat and homely with superb views of the Hambleton hills. Cooking is straightforward, using local produce from a nearby farm in association with the hotel. The remote situation, simple comforts and fresh bedrooms make this a strong candidate at the price.

Bedrooms: *7, 3 in annexe (double, twin, family); 4 with bath, 3 in annexe with washbasins only. TV, teamaking*
Facilities: *Parking. Trout fishing on Rye and Seph*
Restrictions: *Dogs in annexe only (but kennels in village)*
Open: *All year, except Christmas*
Credit/charge cards accepted: *None*
Price category: ££
Special rates: *Nov to Mar, 2 nights DB&B £21 (£25 single) pp per night; April to Oct 3 nights £24 (£28 single) pp per night. Reduced rates in annexe, and for children under 10 in parents' room*

HELMSLEY
The Crown
Helmsley, North Yorkshire YO6 5BJ   *Tel: (0439) 70297*

A 16th-century coaching inn on the market square of bustling Helmsley, within a stone's throw of the rival Feathers and Black Swan hotels. Public rooms are traditional with dark oak furniture and beams, Windsor chairs and polished brasses. In addition to the lounge and dining room there is a cosy reading room with shelves of hardback books, and a non-smoking coffee lounge used for snacks. Drinks and food can also be served on the lawn outside (where there is a children's slide and swing). The comfortable and cared-for air extends to the bedrooms; the Crown has been family-run for some 30 years.

Bedrooms: *14 (single, double, twin and family), 12 with bath. TV, teamaking. Hairdryer on request*
Facilities: *Parking*
Restrictions: *No smoking in coffee lounge*
Open: *All year*
Credit/charge cards accepted: *Access, Visa*
Price category: ££
Special rates: *Jan to May (excluding Easter) 2 nights DB&B £25 pp per night. Children in family room £2, and 20% reduction for children under 12 in own room*

KIRKBYMOORSIDE

Appletree Court

9 Market Place, Kirkbymoorside, North Yorkshire YO6 6AT   Tel: (0751) 31536

An old town farm in the handsome market street, Appletree Court is an appealing small guesthouse. Now under relatively new ownership, it has been modernised and restored, preserving old features such as beams and door lintels. Bedrooms are fresh and airy with pine furniture and Laura Ashley fabrics and wallpapers, and are called by the names of various apples. The sitting and dining room are beamed and cottagey. Teas are served and guests may bring their own alcoholic drinks. There is a peaceful old-fashioned garden at the back.

Bedrooms: *7 (double and twin), 4 with bath. TV*
Facilities: *Parking (2 cars)*
Restrictions: *No children. No smoking. Unlicensed*
Open: *All year*
Credit/charge cards accepted: *None*
Price category: £

LASTINGHAM

Lastingham Grange

Lastingham, York YO6 6TH   *Tel: (075 15) 345*

A 17th-century stone farmhouse, with sympathetic extensions, built around a courtyard and set in 10 acres of magnificently landscaped gardens, 300 yards from the centre of the village. Since the mid-1950s it has been run as a hotel by the Wood family, whose home it still is; guests are introduced to each other and there is something of the atmosphere of a house party. The sitting room is comfortable with antique furniture, books galore, an open fire and long views of the garden. The spacious dining room also overlooks the terrace and rose garden. Bedrooms are rather old-fashioned with a mixture of home furnishings and fittings; all are spotless and even the bathrooms have views. A peaceful place to while away a weekend, popular with both older people and families with children.

Bedrooms: *12 (single, double and twin) all with bath. Direct dial telephone, TV, teamaking. Hairdryer, trouser press*
Facilities: *Parking. Adventure playground, croquet. Babylistening*
Restrictions: *Dogs in same room as owners only. No smoking in dining room*
Open: *Early Mar to Nov*
Credit/charge cards accepted: *Amex, Diners*
Price category: £££
Special rates: *Nov and Mar, DB&B £34.75 pp per night. Children under 12 free in parents' room*

NUNNINGTON
Ryedale Lodge
Nunnington, near Helmsley, North Yorkshire YO6 5XB   *Tel: (043 95) 246*

Once the village railway station, Ryedale Lodge is now a tranquil place to stay, with the grassed-over railway tracks providing a path down to the River Rye. Inside it is furnished with a blend of antique and reproduction furniture, complemented by Regency green walls. The dining room is in the old ticket office and waiting room (now with an Adam style mantelpiece) and there is a sitting room extension, well supplied with flowers, books and magazines and with very comfortable sofas. Bedrooms are individually decorated; the best are spacious with rag-rolled walls, designer fabrics and cane or antique furniture; some have whirlpool baths. Specialities of the kitchen include seafood from Scotland; menus change seasonally. Fishermen should bring their own rods.

Location: *1 mile west of Nunnington*
Bedrooms: *7 (double and twin), all with bath (some whirlpool). Direct dial telephone, TV, teamaking. Hairdryer, trouser press*
Facilities: *Parking. Private trout fishing on the Rye. Babylistening*
Restrictions: *No dogs. No smoking in the dining room*
Open: *All year except Jan*
Credit/charge cards accepted: *Access, Visa*
Price category: *££*
Special rates: *2 nights (excluding Bank Hol weekends) DB&B £40 pp per night. Reductions for children in parents' room negotiable according to age*

The Peak District

- Gentle green landscapes with pastures, drystone walls and neat stone villages as well as stern, rugged walking country
- Some fine stately homes to visit
- Some extremely comfortable hotels for a weekend base
- Plenty of activities for family outings: walking, pony trekking, cycling or visiting caves
- Excellent for public transport but beware summer crowds and local daytrippers around Castleton, Dovedale and Derwentdale

The Peak District is a small, vulnerable area almost encircled by large industrial towns. It includes parts of six counties (Derbyshire, Staffordshire, Cheshire, Greater Manchester, West Yorkshire and South Yorkshire) and is, in a sense, at the crossroads between the North and the South. In 1951 the area was designated a National Park to protect this rural oasis from the encroaching development of the Midlands.

The area has considerable variety – but no very high mountains, despite its name, which comes from a Saxon word for 'hill'. The White Peak has soft contours, lush scenery and neat villages; the rugged Dark Peak consists of bleak moorland and peat bogs. Between the two is the transitional area of the broad, fertile valleys of the Wye, the Derwent and the Hope. Experienced walkers can try 'bog trotting' in the Dark Peak area, lazy motorists can follow the circular White Peak Scenic Route. For most people the Dales in the south provide a gentle compromise, with plenty to see and do.

The White Peak

Filling most of the southern half of the National Park, the White Peak is named after the pale grey limestone which lies underneath. The area was a centre for lead mining from Roman times until the 19th century and there are still odd hollows and bumps in the fields. Much of the landscape consists of a high, bare tableland of neat green fields divided by drystone walls, and can be explored by car along the marked 'White Peak Scenic Route'. But the main interest comes from its deep, narrow valleys, many with impressive crags and buttresses and some too narrow for roads. **Dovedale** is the most spectacular and well-known but steep **Monsal Dale**, **Lathkill Dale** and the **Manifold Valley** in the west are all peaceful and rewarding to explore.

Bakewell (famous for its puddings and tarts) is the only town of any size within the Park; it has a museum (The Old House) with a collection of country exhibits. **Rowsley** has old greystone houses and a historic working flour mill. **Matlock Bath** is a worn-looking but rather enjoyable inland resort in a steep-sided bit of the Derwent Valley, with several amusements suitable for children; the latest attraction is a cable-car ride to the Heights of Abraham. There are several villages of some interest and charm. **Eyam** has good 18th-century stone houses and a well-preserved Saxon churchyard cross, while the 14th-century church at nearby **Tideswell** is called the Cathedral of the Peak. **Ashford-in-the-Water** is prettily situated on the Wye, with two old bridges. In the southern part of the area are **Tissington**, cottagey in a parkland setting, its main street dominated by a long partly 17th-century hall in local stone and **Ilam**, a model village in Dovedale with a country park on the banks of the River Manifold. **Ashbourne**, just outside the southern boundary of the National Park, is a handsome market town.

HISTORIC BUILDINGS AND GARDENS
✿ **Chatsworth** *Holiday Which? Weekend Break Award*
Magnificent home of the Dukes of Devonshire, set in glorious parkland by the river Derwent, containing superb state apartments and art collections. Farming and forestry exhibitions, wood walks and adventure playground. [*Open April to Oct, daily*]
Haddon Hall A rambling 14th-century stone manor full of period features and surrounded by old-fashioned terraced rose gardens. Special events at weekends include archery, brass rubbing, Punch and Judy shows and displays of morris dancing and falconry. Heraldry weekends. [*Open Apr to Sep, Tues to Sat plus Bank Hol Mons, and Bank Hol Suns in July and Aug*]

EXCURSIONS
Outside the Park, there are several splendid stately homes. They include **Sudbury Hall** (NT), a Jacobean mansion 10 miles south of Ashbourne [*open April to Oct, pm, Wed to Sun and Bank Hol Mons*] and **Hardwick Hall** (NT), a famous Elizabethan house about 10 miles east of Matlock [*open April to Oct, pm, Wed, Thurs, Sat, Sun and Bank Hol Mons*]. Four miles north-west of Derby is **Kedleston Hall**, a masterpiece of Robert Adam with a magnificent hall and fine picture collections. [*Open April to Sep, pm, Sat to Wed*]

FAMILY OUTINGS

There are several places just outside the park which are worth considering for family outings. At Matlock Bath is the well laid-out **Peak District Mining Museum** [*open mid Feb to mid Nov, daily*]. **The National Tramway Museum** [*open April to Oct, daily*] is at Crich, near Matlock. **Alton Towers** theme park is near Ashbourne [*open April to Sep, daily except Fri, plus weekends in Oct*]

The Dark Peak

The Dark Peak takes up all the northern half of the Park and also extends two arms southwards, embracing the White Peak. The rock here is a grim-looking variety known as Millstone Grit. In some places it produces lines of rough black crags but elsewhere the scenery is dominated by high rounded hills with extensive peat bogs on top and drainage channels known as groughs; Kinder Scout at 2,038 feet is the highest point in the Peak. Names like Bleaklow and Black Hill reflect some of the harshness of the landscape. But there are some gentler aspects: valleys such as the **Upper Derwent Valley** and the **Goyt Valley** have been flooded for reservoirs; the result, though unnatural, is not unlovely.

Technically just outside the Park, **Buxton** is a spa town – the highest in England – with a Pavilion, hot springs and, in the former Pump Room, the Micrarium (where insects, crystals, plants and so on are projected from microscopes onto TV-sized screens). **Castleton** is the main base for cave visiting; nearby is Peveril Castle, dating from 1086.

CAVES

These are the main attraction of the Dark Peak, and most are in the Hope Valley. They are all fairly small and in most cases the chambers are only partly natural. They include the Peak Cavern, Bagshaw Cavern and Speedwell Cavern (visited by boat). The Blue John Cavern and Treak Cliff Cavern both have old lead mines. Poole's Cavern is at Buxton.

HISTORIC BUILDINGS AND GARDENS

Lyme Hall Fine Palladian mansion of Tudor origins with formal gardens surrounded by a huge deer park, near Stockport. The interior has rare Mortlake tapestries, English clocks and ornate wood carvings. Children's playground and nature trails, August festival. (NT) [*Open all year, pm daily except Mon; house guided tours only*]

Walking

The gentle limestone country of the southern part of the Peak has rewarding and easy paths along most of the valley floors; the large majority are easy to follow and well waymarked. An extra dimension is added if you take paths up out of the valley to emerge on to the strikingly different (and generally less frequented) dry-stone-walled green pasture on top. The most popular of the dales, such as Dove Dale and Monsal Dale, get packed in summer but are still worth seeing.

The Park authority has converted four old railway lines into attractive paths – the Tissington Trail, the High Peak Trail (which you join at Parsley Hay), the Monsal Trail, and the course of the Manifold Valley Light Railway. Several walks connect with the marked White Peak Scenic Drive, a circular route of some 25 miles.

The River Derwent is excellent for casual strolls, particularly between Hathersage and Grindleford, and in Chatsworth Park, the west side of which has open access for walking.

Most of the tops in the northern part of the Peak are tough going, mainly for those used to jumping over peat hags and steering by compass; the Pennine Way starts at Edale, but immediately ascends to the vast blanket bog of Kinder Scout, which won't appeal to everyone. But there is easier walking on the fringes, particularly on the crags of Stanage Edge and the Roaches. The most dramatic ridge walk in the region is from Lose Hill to Mam Tor (near Castleton), but despite its exhilarating nature, its only physical demands are made on the initial ascent – which is no more than middling. The Ladybower and Derwent Reservoirs on the north-east side of the Peak provide scope for waterside walks; from Fairholmes car park between the two reservoirs you can follow an easy level track along the east side of the water, or take a signposted forest path on the west side. For more ambitious walking in this district, try Derwent Edge (immediately north-east of Ladybower Reservoir), or Win Hill to the south.

The National Park publishes a series of low-priced guides to circular walks in the area. See also *Holiday Which? Good Walks Guide* walks 75-84, 103.

When to go

In summer many towns and villages in the White Peak organise the traditional 'well dressing' (painstaking decoration of wells with designs made from flower petals); each town has its own week. In July there is a carnival weekend at Glossop and in August a nine-day festival at Lyme Park. The Buxton Festival (mainly opera, but also concerts, films, etc) is held annually from late July to early August. In late summer some parts of the northern moorland are closed for private grouse shoots.

Information

The National Park Information Service, Alder House, Baslow Road, Bakewell, Derbyshire DE4 1AE; tel: (062 981) 4321. There are also Information Centres (open in summer) at Castleton, Edale, Fairholmes in the upper Derwent valley, Torside and Hartington.

Buxton Festival, tel: (0298) 70395.

The National Park Study Centre at Losehill Hall, Castleton, tel: (0433) 20373, offers a wide variety of activity weekends, courses and seminars on the National Park.

The Great Little Sunday Travel Book lists key bus and train services for Sunday outings and walks and gives details of the extended Peak Rail Rambler service between Buxton and Edale.

Where to stay

The most comfortable hotels – and there are several – are in the Bakewell area, well placed for visiting Chatsworth and Dovedale. There are few bargains and little price variation between hotels. Around Castleton accommodation is much more basic, catering mainly for ramblers and serious walkers; we found nothing of any particular charm. Buxton is a spa town, with a range of Victorian hotels.

BASLOW
Cavendish Hotel
Baslow, Derbyshire DE4 1SP   *Tel: (024 688) 2311*

A rambling old stone inn on the Chatsworth estate, refurbished in the 1970s by the Duchess of Devonshire with some furniture and paintings from Chatsworth itself. Although the hotel does back onto a mainish road all rooms have a glorious view of the parkland. Reception is civilised and welcoming, the restaurant elegant. However the lounge is something of a passage and not really suitable for the bar lunches offered here, and the bar itself is unexpectedly pub-like for a country house hotel. Bedrooms have been nicely decorated, with custom-built furniture (most of the antique furniture is in the six higher priced and larger 'inn rooms'). Bathrooms are neat with pine floor and mahogany loo seats. The ten bedrooms of the Mitford wing are named after members of the Duchess of Devonshire's celebrated literary family and all bedrooms have a small selection of books, a thoughtful and surprisingly unusual touch.

Location: *On the A619*
Bedrooms: 23 *(double and twin) all with bath. Direct dial telephone, TV, minibar, teamaking*
Facilities: *Parking. Fishing on Derwent and Wye (coaching by arrangement), putting. Babylistening*
Restrictions: *No dogs*
Open: *All year*
Credit/charge cards accepted: *Access, Amex, Diners, Visa*
Price category: £££
Special rates: *Oct to Mar, weekends, 2 nights B&B, £30/£33.75 (single £42.50/£47.50) pp per night, 3rd night (Sun) free. Extra bed or cot in room £5*

BIGGIN-BY-HARTINGTON
Biggin Hall
Biggin-by-Hartington, Buxton, Derbyshire SK17 ODH   *Tel: (029 884) 451*

A listed stone house in its own mature grounds high at the heart of the Peak District. There is a cosy sitting room with well-plumped sofas and the original fireplace, dated 1672. A more formal drawing room and a beamed dining room have french windows into the garden. Bedrooms are all different, and spacious, and furnished with antiques (Mrs Moffett was once an antique dealer). A converted stone barn contains several apartments with modern rooms suitable for families, but without cleaning or room service. Mrs Moffett does the cooking from her sparkling farmhouse kitchen, with fruit and vegetables from the garden; menus are changed daily and dinner is served at 7pm. A comfortable place for those who prefer un hotel-like hotels, well placed for walking in Dovedale and visits to the stately homes.

Location: *½ mile west of the A515 (Ashbourne to Buxton)*
Bedrooms: 14 *(single, double, twin and family), 8 in annexe, 1 with four-poster, all with bath. Hairdryer. TV and teamaking in annexe rooms only*
Facilities: *Parking. Outdoor playground*
Restrictions: *Dogs in annexe only. No service in annexe*
Open: *All year*
Credit/charge cards accepted: *None*
Price category: ££
Special rates: *Sun to Fri, DB&B £22 (single £27) pp per night. 3-day Christmas and New Year programmes. Children under 12 sharing with 2 adults £12.50 with dinner; infants under 2, charge for cot only*

DARLEY DALE
Red House Hotel
Darley Dale, Matlock　　　　　　　　　　　　　*Tel: (0629) 734854*

The Red House was built by a London architect as his country house in 1891 and with its mock-Tudor gables and gingerbread porch it has a vaguely suburban, arts-and-crafts appearance unexpected in deepest Derbyshire. The red roof which gave the house its name has now mellowed to a greenish-copper colour. The owners, Ruth and Jim Alley, have created a delightful hotel with a homely atmosphere ('East West – Homes Best' reads the inscription on the marble fireplace in the lounge). Parquet floors, leaded windows with stained glass, art nouveau mantelpieces and original cornices are features of the main public rooms. The old stables have been converted to a cheerful wine bar (called Rumours) which is open during the day. Bedrooms are light and airy, but with uninspired furnishings.

Location: *Just off the A6 Matlock to Bakewell, towards Winster*
Bedrooms: *7 (single, double and twin), 4 with bath, plus 1 family flat. TV, teamaking. Hairdryer*
Facilities: *Parking*
Restrictions: *Small dogs by arrangement, in bedrooms only*
Open: *All year*
Credit/charge cards accepted: *Access, Diners, Visa*
Price category: *££*
Special rates: *Weekends except Bank Hols, 2 nights DB&B (including Sun lunch) £32.50 pp per night. Reduced rates for children in parents' room depending on age*

DOVEDALE
Izaak Walton Hotel
Dovedale, near Ashbourne, Derbyshire DE6 2AY　　　　*Tel: (033 529) 261*

A much extended old farmhouse of no great beauty but in a magnificent position overlooking Dovedale. It was here that Izaak Walton, author of *The Compleat Angler*, used to stay and more recently hospitality has been extended to various members of the Royal family and the Prime Minister. It is a comfortable, traditional hotel with a vaguely Regency style dining room and an old-fashioned lounge. There is a bistro-like buttery in the old dairy and a cosy bar in the cottage kitchen, with the original bread oven. Bedrooms vary from countrified and feminine, with dimity prints, to 'executive' rooms in a new wing. Standard rooms have all been refurbished. Dinner dances are held on Saturday nights. A good base for walking or fishing in Dovedale, with a friendly atmosphere for its size.

Location: *5 miles west of Ashbourne*
Bedrooms: *33 (single, double, twin, family), 2 with 4-poster beds, all with bath. Direct dial telephone, TV*
Facilities: *Parking. One no-smoking lounge. Fishing on River Dove. Babylistening*

Open: *All year*
Credit/charge cards accepted: *Access, Amex, Diners, Visa*
Price category: *££*
Special rates: *2 nights DB&B £38-£40.50 pp per night. Children free in parents' room*

GREAT LONGSTONE
Croft Country House Hotel
Great Longstone, Bakewell, Derbyshire DE4 1TF   Tel: *(0629) 87278*

Slightly cheaper than Hassop Hall up the road (considerably so if taking meals into account) this is a friendly set-up run by an enthusiastic couple. The house, a slightly rambling early Victorian building of some character, is approached via a bumpy drive off a rural lane and stands in 4 acres of grounds with a pretty verandah and lawn. Despite the secluded location it is a convenient base for exploring the White Peak area. Bedrooms lead off the gallery around the skylit main hall, and all have been prettily decorated with co-ordinating wallpapers and prints, mostly but not exclusively in feminine floral designs. The main public rooms have less charm; the lounge is rather dark and in the daytime the main hall is preferable. The dinner menu is extremely good value and sensible (the main course is set every day, but there is a choice of starter and pudding).

Location: *3 miles north of Bakewell; A6 out of Bakewell towards Buxton. Then right turn at Ashford onto A6020*
Bedrooms: *8 (double and twin), 5 with bath or shower; 2 public bathrooms. TV, teamaking*
Facilities: *Parking, lift*
Restrictions: *No dogs. No smoking in restaurant*
Open: *All year except Christmas, New Year and two weeks in Feb*
Credit/charge cards accepted: *Access, Visa*
Price category: *££*
Special rates: *2 nights DB&B £32.50 pp per night. Reduced rates for children in parents' room, depending on age (up to 4 free)*

HASSOP
Hassop Hall
Hassop, near Bakewell, Derbyshire DE4 1NS   Tel: *(062 987) 488*

A grand Georgian country house on an estate which dates back to Domesday, Hassop makes an ideal choice for a calming and civilised break, and at prices which are not outrageous. The former seat of the Eyre family, it has been lovingly converted into a hotel and in most of the public rooms no expense has been spared in the quality of furnishings – including some antiques – and fabrics. The latest project has been the bar, lined with antique oak panelling. Log fires create a feeling of welcome and cosiness. The dining room is elegant and gracious, and the four-course dinner may include wild mushrooms, tender lamb and a variety of cream-laden puddings. Bedrooms are spacious, pretty and comfortable, with pure linen sheets and well-equipped modernised bathrooms. The generous bowl of fruit means that one does not crave the hefty extra of a full English breakfast. A really delightful place where you are looked after with old-fashioned courtesy.

Location: *2½ miles north of Bakewell*
Bedrooms: *12 (double), all with bath. Direct dial telephone, TV, hairdryer*
Facilities: *Parking, helipad, lift. One non-smoking sitting room. Tennis, croquet*
Restrictions: *Dogs at hotel's discretion and not in public rooms*
Open: *All year except Christmas. Restaurant closed Sun dinner, Mon lunch*
Credit/charge cards accepted: *Access, Amex, Diners, Visa*
Price category: *£££*
Special rates: *Nov to Mar, 2 nights, £22.50-£32.50 (single £40-£60) pp per night, not including breakfast. Children in parents' room £10*

HATHERSAGE
The George

Main Road, Hathersage, Derbyshire S30 1BB   Tel: (0433) 50436

A stone-built old coaching inn dating from the 16th century and retaining some of the original character. The main public rooms, which have exposed walls, open fireplaces and beamed ceilings, have recently been attractively refurbished. Bedrooms are comfortable and large, with a fairly standardised, but light and fresh, décor. The rooms on the back overlook a lawn; rooms on the front are double-glazed against the traffic noise.

Bedrooms: *18 (single, double, twin, family) all with bath. Direct dial telephone, TV (with video), teamaking. Hairdryer, trouser press*
Facilities: *Parking*
Restrictions: *No dogs (except guide dogs)*
Open: *All year*
Credit/charge cards accepted: *Access, Amex, Diners, Visa*
Price category: *££*
Special rates: *Weekends, 2 nights DB&B £36 pp per night, Mar to Oct; £30 (or £21 B&B), Nov to Feb. Children under 16 free in parents' room, £10 in own room*

MATLOCK
Riber Hall

Matlock, Derbyshire DE4 5JU   Tel: (0629) 2795

An Elizabethan manor house set in its own grounds in remote countryside. After many generations of family ownership Riber became almost derelict and was rescued, restored and opened as a hotel in the 1970s. Inside beams, original fireplaces and leaded windows are complemented by dark carved oak furniture. Public areas are rather small. However the bedrooms, half-timbered and almost all with antique four-poster beds, are spacious and comfortable with sitting areas and minibars and magazines. Some bathrooms are equipped with whirlpool baths. Umbrellas are provided in every room for the journey across the courtyard to the main house. The restaurant has a good reputation, but eating à la carte is expensive.

Location: *3 miles from Matlock, off A615*
Bedrooms: *11 (double), 9 with four-poster beds, all with bath (some whirlpool). Direct dial telephone, TV, teamaking, minibar. Hairdryer*
Facilities: *Parking. Tennis, Clay pigeon shooting, fishing by arrangement*

Open: *All year*
Credit/charge cards accepted: *Amex, Diners, Visa*
Price category: *£££-££££*
Special rates: *Oct to April, 2 nights DB&B (and including one lunch) from £47.75 pp per night*

ROWSLEY
Peacock Hotel
Rowsley, near Matlock, Derbyshire DE4 2EB   *Tel: (0629) 733518*

This 17th-century manor has been a hotel for 150 years and is a well-known base for visiting Chatsworth and Haddon Hall, of which it was once the dower house. Built from the local greyish Stancliffe stone, the Peacock stands on the edge of the village, set back from the road, with landscaped lawns leading down to the River Derwent at the back. Rooms are beamed, with mullioned windows and oak furniture, some antique, some (in the dining room) made by 'Mousey' Thompson. Bedrooms are comfortable and attractive, with more atmosphere than the public rooms. The traffic noise is not great, but enough to irritate city-dwellers bent on peace who should request rooms at the back (although front rooms are double-glazed). On the other hand, the garden is a tranquil place to walk or sit. A good conventional choice (guests are asked to preserve 'reasonable standards of dress').

Bedrooms: *20 (single, double and twin), 14 in main house, 1 with four-poster, all with bath; 6 in annexe, 1 with bath. Direct dial telephone, TV, teamaking. Hairdryer, trouser press*
Facilities: *Parking. Private trout fishing on the Derwent and Wye. Babylistening*
Restrictions: *No dogs in public rooms*
Open: *All year*
Credit/charge cards accepted: *Access, Amex, Diners, Visa*
Price category: *£££*
Special rates: *May to Oct, 2 nights DB&B £44 pp per night. Children under 15 free in parents' room, 75% of adult rate in own room.*

Snowdonia

- Some of the wildest and most spectacular scenery in Britain though short on picturesque towns and villages
- Splendid walking of all sorts to be found (including guided walks), plus riding, trekking, and fishing
- A good area for children: big castles, little trains and safe beaches
- The Snowdon area is not best seen from a car and roads are busy, but there are interesting circular touring routes further south
- Varied accommodation for all tastes and pockets, but unevenly distributed around the National Park

The Snowdonia National Park extends nearly 50 miles from just behind the North Welsh coast to the river Dovey. Its northern third is 'Snowdonia proper', where a dozen peaks over 3,000 feet surround the isolated bulk of Snowdon itself. Harshly magnificent scenery is fringed towards the Conwy valley with woodland and glens, but northern and western edges are dominated by the bleak remnants of slate-quarrying. Further south, the Park has open landscapes of moorland and forestry, quiet green valleys, high but isolated mountains. There are good beaches and little resorts along its flat western coastline. Inland villages are more functional than picturesque, and interesting towns are few. Scenery apart, the Park's main sights are its castles, its narrow-gauge railways, and the several places where the slate industry is presented for tourists with varying degrees of drama.

The North

Driving through Snowdonia confirms the impression of magnificent impregnability you get first from a distance. The roads follow valley floors and low passes between towering shoulders, cliffs and ridges which have no immediate identity; parking spaces are few, and traffic steady enough in summer to make you emerge from the most dramatic bits disappointingly soon, with little time to admire. It is better to park outside the massif, use the

Sherpa bus service (see 'Walking') and – having assimilated mountain safety precautions – walk. Snowdonia is a serious mountaineering area – you can watch climbers like flies, high up on the rock faces – but there are clear paths for walkers up most of the peaks. Each peak has its own identity – Snowdon itself, massive, stately and isolated from the rest; Tryfan a jagged Alpine cone brooding over the Ogwen Valley; Glyder Fawr and Glyder Fach a double-peaked ridge crowned with towers of rock and with great cliffs on one side; the Carnedds rounded, grassy and desolate. Even the lower peaks – such as Moel Siabod which soars to a graceful pyramid above Betws-y-Coed – have their own character. Unlike the Lake District, the valleys are short and bleak, and the lakes, though dramatically set high up in rocky hollows, are small and austere.

But there is some gentler, lusher countryside on the fringes of the area. **Betws-y-Coed**, at a busy junction of roads and rivers, is a natural centre for touring, walking and fishing, packed in season. The rivers around the town run through some pretty wooded glens, and there are some attractive waterfalls such as Swallow Falls on the river Llugwy and Conwy Falls on the Conwy. **Beddgelert** has its 'legend' of Gelert the faithful hound of Llewellyn; to the south, the River Glaslyn has cut the steep rocky gorge of Aberglaslyn. **Capel Curig**, the oldest mountain centre, spreads hotels and craftshops along the A5. At the northern tip of the park with its own miniature mountain **Conwy** has a splendid Norman castle, encircling town walls, and the worst traffic problem in Wales – it's a bottleneck on the coast road. However plans are well advanced now for a tunnel under the Conway estuary to bypass the congested little town completely. A busy administrative centre not far outside the National Park, **Caernarfon** has its castle, a few attractive old streets and a quayside.

CASTLES

Caernarfon Largest of the castles Edward I built along the Welsh coast, finished in 1327 by his son, the first Prince of Wales. A magnificent shell, smoothly restored; spacious lawns inside, where Prince Charles was invested in 1969.

Conwy Edward I's headquarters, wonderfully sited, much besieged. There's quite a lot of appealing detail to explore within its splendid towers and battlements.

Dolbadarn Built by Llewelyn the Great to control entry to Llanberis Pass: rocky remnants with a 40-foot tower.

Dolwyddelan A 12th-century Welsh stronghold in a wild mountain setting: some 19th-century reconstruction.

[*Castles in general are open all year except Christmas to New Year, daily except Sun am*]

Railways

Ffestiniog Narrow-gauge line built to haul slate from the quarries at Blaenau Ffestiniog to the harbour at Porthmadog: 14-mile run though spectacular scenery, connecting at each end with British Rail. In summer, unique steam engines and antique carriages. [*Open April to early Nov, daily*]

Llanberis Lake Four miles of slate-related narrow-gauge track now within the Padarn Country Park, starting by the Welsh Slate Museum. Vintage little steam locos, closed carriages. [*Open Mon to Thurs from Easter, daily May to Oct*]

Snowdon Mountain Steam-powered Swiss-made locos push simple wooden carriages up five miles of rack and pinion railway from Llanberis, climbing over 3,000 feet to the summit – weather permitting. [*Open mid Mar to Sep, daily; plus weekends Oct*]

Welsh Highland Only ¾ mile re-opened so far of the original 22 miles of narrow-gauge track between Porthmadog and Caernarfon. One famous rebuilt steam engine. [*Steam at weekends only, Easter to Oct*]

The Slate and Copper Mining Industries

Beddgelert, Sygun Copper Mine Guided climb up steep but safe steps through re-excavated hillside mine with vivid lighting and audio commentary. [*Open April to Oct, daily*]

Blaenau Ffestiniog, Gloddfa Ganol Slate Mine Half a mile of walk-in galleries and chambers to explore at this vast working slate quarry; more caverns reached on a Land Rover tour; craftsmen and modern machinery in the mill. [*Open Easter to Sep, Mon to Fri; plus Suns mid July to Aug*]

✿ **Blaenau Ffestiniog, Llechwedd Slate Caverns** *Holiday Which? Weekend Break Award*

'Miners' Tramway' through old workings – a ride with guide and illuminated tableaux; and the 'Deep Mine', a steep ride then on foot through the caverns with spectacular audio-visuals. Several surface attractions. [*Open Easter to Sep, daily except Sun am*]

Llanberis, Welsh Slate Museum Excellent presentation in the imposing workshop buildings of the slate quarries. The **Vivian Trails** (one short, one energetic) round the vast Vivian Quarry start nearby; in summer there are Land Rover trips. Also nearby: small craft centre, and **Oriel Eryri**, the Welsh Environmental Centre with emphasis on Snowdonia countryside.

Gardens

Tal-y-Cafn, Bodnant Garden Just outside the National Park on the west-facing slopes of the Conwy valley, outstanding gardens:

elegant terraces drop through conifers, azaleas, magnolias and famous rhododendrons to wild woodland. (NT) [*Open mid Mar to Oct, daily*]

The South and West

While less spectacular than 'Snowdonia proper', the rest of the Snowdonia National Park offers far more opportunity for interesting circular tours and for pottering round country lanes. For the most part it is a landscape of rolling, empty moorlands and large forestry plantations with isolated mountain tops in the distance. There are several quiet, green valleys dotted with neat stone villages and farmhouses. Lake Bala is Wales's largest lake, but its surroundings are far from spectacular. Several roads cross high moorland with fine views, and further south there is usually a distinctive mountain top on the skyline. Cader Idris is the most impressive, and like Snowdon has routes up it from all sides; others have few paths and can be as tough a proposition as the peaks further north.

At the Park's southern boundary **Machynlleth** is a handsome small market town with some 18th-century building and a Victorian clock tower. North up the Dulas valley the slate-mining village of **Corris**, its waste tips increasingly masked by forestry, has a railway museum, a narrow-gauge railway under restoration, and a concentration of the crafts which abound in the Park (Tourist Information Offices supply an excellent directory leaflet called 'Visit a Craftsman'). Little **Dinas Mawddwy** further east is a pleasant village in a valley whose lead and slate mining industry has been replaced by a woollen mill. The biggest and liveliest inland centre is **Dolgellau**, a place particularly well supplied with attractive local walks.

The foothills of Cader Idris and the Rhinogs are the backdrop for the National Park's coastal strip of mostly flat farming land and sand dunes, punctuated by three remarkably grand river estuaries at Aberdyfi, Barmouth and Porthmadog. That of the Mawddach at **Barmouth** is particularly fine, its composition of wide water, wooded hills and bare peaks beyond best seen from the railway bridge which has a toll footpath. British Rail's Cambrian Coast Line, very scenic, connects with several of the little railways as well as linking all the resorts. **Aberdyfi** has the most seaside charm; **Harlech** is well worth a visit for its castle.

CASTLES
Castell y Bere A romantic Welsh ruin built, embattled and abandoned all within the 13th century, in a remote setting.

Criccieth A ruin with a view high on a mound dominating the little resort just west of the Park boundary: an early 13th-century castle occupied by the English till 1404, when the Welsh demolished it.

Harlech Key coastal fortress in Edward I's chain – the sea once came right up to its rock. 'Men of Harlech' recalls its later history. Massive walls to walk, with wonderful views.

[*Castles in general are open all year except Christmas to New Year, daily except Sun am*]

RAILWAYS

Bala Lake Five miles of track converted to narrow-gauge beside Wales's largest natural lake: little steam engines in summer, from local slate quarries. [*Open May to mid Oct, pm daily; winter pm except Mon and Fri*]

Fairbourne A miniature (15" gauge) railway runs two miles out to sandy Penrhyn Point on the Mawddach estuary. Replica steam engines; ferry to Barmouth. [*Open Easter to Nov, daily*]

Tal-y-llyn All-steam, all-antique, narrow-gauge railway running eight miles from Tywyn on the coast to Nant Gwernol in deep forest; waterfalls accessible from a half-way stop. [*Open Easter to Oct, daily*]

FAMILY OUTINGS

Harlech, Old Llanfair Quarry Slate Caverns Guided walk though caverns and tunnels honeycombing a hillside, emerging to a splendid sea-view. [*Open Easter to Oct, daily*]

Machynlleth, Centre for Alternative Technology Solar, wind and water power, energy conservation and organic eating: techniques and lifestyle in an old slate quarry. [*Open all year, daily*]

Maes Artro Clever conversion of a former RAF camp near Harlech to a tourist village with craft workshops and various entertainments. [*Open April to Oct, daily*]

Portmeirion A remarkable Italianate village in south-facing garden site, the creation of architect Clough Williams-Ellis. Eccentric and very pretty, instantly recognisable to devotees of TV's 'The Prisoner'. [*Open April to Oct, daily*]

Walking

The peaks of Snowdonia proper (ie the main mountain group as distinct from the whole region) contain the most excitingly rugged mountain scenery in England and Wales. There are clear paths up most of the peaks, but be prepared for a long uphill slog, as most starting points are only a few hundred feet above sea level; the rewards can be tremendous, taking you through wild, rocky landscapes with magnificent views.

Not surprisingly, Snowdon itself is the most popular climb, and many more go up by mountain railway. There are six main routes to the top, and using the Sherpa bus service which operates round the base of the mountain in summer it is possible to go up one and down another. The National Park Authority publishes leaflets describing each route. The best of the easier routes is the Snowdon Ranger Track, greatly superior to the more popular Llanberis Path which runs parallel to the railway track. An outstanding round trip – considered the most dramatic mountain walk of its kind outside the Scottish Highlands – is the Snowdon Horseshoe, which follows the sharpest of Snowdon's knife-edge ridges and needs a very strong head for heights.

Some of the lower mountains are in fact tougher than Snowdon. Tryfan, for example, requires a bit of scrambling to get to the top, and route-finding can be difficult on top of the Carnedds. The lower mountains such as Moel Hebog and Moel Siabod are a little easier, and because they are on the edge of the main cluster of mountains they have very good views.

The mountains in the southern part of the Park generally have few paths, and can be just as demanding as the peaks in the north, even though they are less spectacular. The most obvious exception is Cader Idris, which has routes from all sides. The Rhinog Mountains are mostly very tough going, but they are penetrated by an old stone causeway known as the Roman Steps, which provides a relatively easy walk starting from Cwm Bychan.

The main areas for easy walks are on the fringes of Snowdonia proper, and in the southern part of the Park. Both have many self-guided forest and nature trails – though they tend not to be in the best scenery. Around northern Snowdonia, head for the glens, small lakes and forests near Betws-y-Coed (some of which form the Forestry Commission's Gwydyr Forest), or to Bedd-gelert, where a pleasant path along an old railway takes you through the pass of Aberglaslyn. The best way to enjoy views of the Mawddach Estuary is by following the old railway track along the south bank.

The Snowdonia National Park's "Family Walks" programme covers a dozen different areas in short or five-hour day walks; details from Visitor Centres. Guided walks by the National Trust in North Wales include several in Snowdonia; programme available from the Regional Information Officer, Trinity Square, Llandudno LL30 2DE; tel (0492) 860123.

See *Holiday Which? Good Walks Guide* walks 202-209.

When to go

In summer, beware the single-track roads leading to well-known beauty spots. Parking is notoriously difficult in the roads running round Snowdon, Betws-y-Coed, Beddgelert, Llanberis and the slate quarries at Blaenau Ffestiniog can also get very crowded. The south of the Park, particularly away from the coast, is generally quieter.

Information

Wales Tourist Board, Brunel House, Fitzalan Road, Cardiff CF2 1VY, tel: (0222) 499909. There are Tourist Information Centres, mostly seasonal, in Aberdyfi, Bala, Barmouth, Beddgelert, Betws-y-Coed, Blaenau Ffestiniog, Dinas Mawddy, Dolgellau, Harlech, Harlech, Llanberis, Machynlleth and Tywyn.

The Snowdonia National Park Office (Penrhyndeudraeth, Gwynedd LL48 6LS, tel: (0766) 770274. There are Visitor Centres at Aberdyfi, Bala, Betws-y-Coed, Blaenau Ffestiniog, Dolgellau, Harlech and Llanberis.

Daily weather forecast, tel: (0286) 870120.

The National Park Authority's Study Centre at Plas Tan-y-Bwlch offers a range of residential courses lasting up to a week.

Where to stay

There's very little accommodation in northern Snowdonia, and many visitors stay in the holiday resorts on the coast. If you want to stay right in the mountains it's worth considering the numerous youth hostels. Otherwise, good bases to aim for are Betws-y-Coed and Beddgelert, both of which have bed and breakfast places as well as hotels. Most of the hotels we recommend are in the southern part of the Park, in attractive settings but some way from the most dramatic scenery; several have a country house atmosphere.

ABERDYFI
Plas Penhelig
Aberdyfi, Gwynedd LL35 0NA   *Tel: (065 472) 676*

A fine Edwardian country house of good and relatively unspoiled proportions, set at the mouth of the Dovey estuary up a long carriage drive, with gardens cut into the hillside. The hotel has a generally relaxed and slightly genteel atmosphere, and the owners are very friendly. Lots of miscellaneous chairs and sofas in the oak-panelled entrance hall, and a separate TV lounge with pink velvet chairs (with antimacassars) make up the sitting rooms. There is nothing especially adventurous about the traditional décor of the dining room and bedrooms – which are comfortable if quite plain, with candlewick covers and simple furniture. A quiet and comfortable retreat.

Location: *Signposted in Aberdyfi*
Bedrooms: *11 (doubles, twin), all with bath/shower. Direct dial telephone, TV in superior rooms*
Facilities: *Parking. Tennis court, croquet, putting. TV in lounge*
Restrictions: *Children under 8 not encouraged. No dogs*
Open: *Mar to Dec*
Credit/charge cards accepted: *Access, Amex, Diners, Visa*
Price category: *££*
Special rates: *Autumn and spring, 2 nights DB&B £32.85 pp per night. Children in parents' room £12.50 B&B.*

BETWS-Y-COED
Ty Gwyn
Betws-y-Coed, Gwynedd   *Tel: (069 02) 383*

A delightful roadside pub – a long, low white-painted building dating from the 16th century. Mrs Ratcliffe loves antiques/junk/bricabrac (there is also a small antiques shop on the premises) and the whole place is furnished accordingly. This is especially refreshing in the bar and dining room where such individuality is unusual. The bar is large and beamed with an old range, and pictures, baskets, brass and copper everywhere. The dining room has a similar feel with candles or lamps on the tables. Upstairs is low-ceilinged and on many levels; each of the bedrooms, too, is furnished with bits and pieces. All have attractive fabrics, some chintzy, some less sophisticated, and are quite small but cosy. Small shower rooms have been added to almost all the bedrooms and one has its own whirlpool bath. A charming place with great character.

Location: *½ mile south of Betws-y-Coed on A5*
Bedrooms: *13 (single, doubles, suite), 3 with four-poster. 8 with shower, 1 with whirlpool. 7 with TV. Teamaking, hairdryer*
Facilities: *Parking. Babylistening*
Open: *All year*
Credit/charge cards: *Access, Visa*
Price category: *£*
Special rates: *2 nights DB&B £27-£28 (single £24.50-£25.50) pp per night. Children up to 3 free in parents' room; discounts for children 4-16*

Nr CAENARFON
Ty'n Rhos Farm
Llanddeiniolen, Caenarfon, Gwynedd LL55 3AE   *Tel: (0248) 670489*

An attractive grey slate tile-clad building with 72 acres and a small garden, this is a working farm in which the Kettle family encourage their guests to feel at home. The emphasis is on cosiness and home-made everything including cheese and yoghurt (from their own Jersey herd). In the spacious sitting room Victorian chairs blend well with more modern furniture; it's a welcoming room with a wood-burning stove, magazines and plenty of games for wet afternoons. Guests help themselves to drinks from a cupboard in the cheerful dining room. Bedrooms are comfortably furnished with modern pine, spriggy papered walls and floral fabrics. Popular with families in school holidays, this farm offers good value in a peaceful setting.

Location: *5 miles from Caenarfon, on B4366*
Bedrooms: *9 (single, double, family), all with bath. TV, teamaking. Hairdryer on request*
Facilities: *Parking*
Restrictions: *Dogs by prior arrangement. Smoking discouraged in dining room*
Open: *All year except 2 weeks over Christmas and New Year, and 1 week in autumn*
Price category: £
Special rates: *Autumn and spring, 2 nights DB&B £22-£23 pp per night. Children in parents' room half price*

HARLECH
Castle Cottage
Harlech, Gwynedd LL46 2YL   *Tel: (0766) 780479*

This small hotel, an ancient white-painted cottage, is indeed very close to the castle. The beamed restaurant is the main feature, with black painted tables and chairs, lace cloths and with pictures of flowers and local scenes on the walls. The rest of the cottage is small and cosy with low ceilings and steep stairs. Bedrooms are quaint and cottagey, with floral fabrics and simple laminate furniture. Clever use of all available space has made them cosy but comfortable and guests are provided with biscuits. A small and charming family-run hotel.

Location: *Centre of old town, on B4573*
Bedrooms: *6 (single, double, twin), 4 with bath. Telephone on request. Teamaking*
Facilities: *TV in lounge*
Restrictions: *No smoking in dining room*
Open: *All year*
Credit/charge cards accepted: *Access, Visa*
Price category: £
Special rates: *2 nights DB&B £25 pp per night. Children under 8 in parents' room £10*

Nr HARLECH
Maes-y-Neuadd
Talsarnu, Gwynedd LL47 6YA   *Tel: (0766) 780200*

A stone house over 600 years old with later, including Georgian, additions set in a secluded garden with fine views. It is owned and run by two couples who provide a high degree of comfort and relaxation for their guests. In the lounge there are relaxing sofas, books and magazines and toby jugs; the dining room is elegant and airy. The bar has a low beamed ceiling and a collection of 'domestic archaeology' dug up from the garden, displayed either side of the large stone fireplace. Bedrooms vary in size; their Laura Ashley fabrics are gradually being replaced by less easily identifiable floral designs, and basic furniture by antiques. Magazines, mineral water and sweets are provided. Altogether a peaceful haven more comfortable than elaborate, more welcoming than grand.

Location: *About 3 miles from Harlech, on B4573*
Bedrooms: *15 (single, double, twin, suite), 1 in coach house; all with bath/shower, 1 with whirlpool bath. Direct dial telephone. TV, Hairdryer*
Facilities: *Parking. Drying room*
Restrictions: *No children under 7. Dogs by arrangement. No smoking in dining room*
Open: *Feb to Dec*
Credit/charge cards accepted: *Access, Visa*
Price category: £££
Special rates: *2 or more nights DB&B £40-£43 (single £40) pp per night. Winter, £5 reduction off DB&B rate. Children in parents' room £10 (bed only)*

Nr LLANBERIS
Pen y Gwryd Hotel
Nant Gwynant, Gwynedd LL55 4NT   *Tel: (0286) 870211*

High up in the mountains, this early 19th-century pebble-dashed building is principally a place for climbers, but anyone wishing to avoid the hurly-burly will relax in the well-lived-in informal atmosphere. The dining room with white walls and Turkish carpet is as plain as the food – not the last word in gastronomy but good solid fare after a day out walking. Residents can sit in the lounge with parquet flooring and lots of books or in the really cosy bar – a panelled room with wooden bench seats around a central table, with climbing memorabilia and Victorian photographs on the walls. Three further public bars with wooden or slate floors and climbing boots hanging from the ceiling are a welcome refuge for passers-by. Bedrooms are very simple with woodchip walls and wool bedspreads; the absence of formalities extends to having no key. There are four public bathrooms – one with a superb original Victorian bath. A large games room and a rough garden with a spring-fed pool provide recreation. Absolutely no fuss and no frills, this is an appealing, if quite basic, mountain hotel which has been run with genuine warmth by the same family for 40 years.

Location: *4 miles from Capel Curig at A4086/A498 junction*
Bedrooms: *20 (single, double, twin, family), 1 with bath*
Facilities: *Parking. Swimming pool. Pool table, games room*
Open: *Mar to beginning Nov, New Year and weekends only in Jan and Feb*
Credit/charge cards accepted: *None*
Price category: £
Special rates: *Reductions negotiable for children in parents' room*

LLANDRILLO
Tyddyn Llan 🏨
Llandrillo, Nr Corwen, Clwyd LL21 0ST   Tel: (049 084) 264

A charming grey stone Georgian farmhouse, with three acres of gardens, cleverly converted by the Kindreds and run as an informal hotel in their own home. The sitting room, with TV at one end, has a suite in pink damask with a fine marble fireplace and lots of books and magazines. A cosy bar leads to the dining room with pale green panelling, a fine fireplace and an upright piano – occasional musical evenings (jazz, creole, etc) are held here. The entrance hall with a lovely Georgian staircase and domed skylight leads to the bedrooms. These are mostly plain, even a little under-furnished, but pleasantly uncluttered; duvets, Laura Ashley prints and miscellaneous antiques make them homely. Bathrooms are well-designed. This is a welcoming rural retreat. *Holiday Which? Weekend Break Award*

Location: *On B4401, 4½ miles from Corwen, 8 miles from Bala*
Bedrooms: *9 (double, twin), 8 with bath/shower. Direct dial telephone. Teamaking*
Facilities: *Parking. TV in lounge. Croquet*
Restrictions: *Dogs by prior arrangement*
Open: *March to Jan*
Credit/charge cards: *Access, Visa*
Price category: *££*
Special rates: *2 or more nights in high season, DB&B £35 (single £39) pp per night. Reductions for children in parents' room (by arrangement)*

Nr LLANDUDNO
Bodysgallen Hall
Llandudno, Gwynedd LL30 1RS   Tel: (0492) 84466

A splendid medieval house (with many subsequent additions) in pinkish stone, set in 42 acres of glorious grounds, seven of which are formal gardens. The oldest part dates from the 13th century: there's a tower from which are superb views over Llandudno and Snowdonia. There is a timeless elegance and comfort in all the rooms, furnished with antiques and decorated with pleasant fabrics. The dining room is elegant but unfussy with oil paintings and a baby grand piano; the library has masses of books in antique bookcases. The first floor panelled drawing room has an unusual fireplace with Delft tiles, coats of arms and a Latin motto. Some of the bedrooms are quite compact, but books and home-made biscuits add to their individual comfort. Bathrooms have brass fittings. Inspired conversion of outbuildings provides a further nine suites; they have kitchenettes, but are not really intended for self-catering – this is a place for luxury.

Location: *Off A470 between Conwy and Llandudno*
Bedrooms: *28 (single, double, twin), 1 with four-poster, 9 in courtyard cottage suites; all with bath/shower. Direct dial telephone, TV. Teamaking in cottages. Trouser press. Hairdryer on request*
Facilities: *Parking. Tennis court, croquet*
Restrictions: *No children under 8. Dogs in cottage suites only*

Open: *All year*
Credit/charge cards: *Access, Amex, Diners, Visa*
Price category: *£££££*
Special rates: *Summer (not Bank Hols), 3 or more nights DB&B £70-£80 (£85-£95) per person per night*

LLANDUDNO
St Tudno
Promenade, Llandudno, Gwynedd LL30 2LP   *Tel: (0492) 74411*

A double-fronted Victorian house on the seafront, smartly decorated and efficiently run. Bedrooms, while on the small side, are luxuriously decorated in fresh colours with floral chintz and contrasting papers. Many have brass beds and all have a welcoming bottle of sparkling wine. There are two sitting rooms (one is the bar), decorated in Victorian 'parlour' style with floral papers and bergère chairs, and a more modern dining room which is fresh and bright with green and white trellis paper, hanging plants and wicker chairs. Presentation appears to be high on the list of priorities; everything about this untypical seaside hotel reflects modern chic without losing the personal touch.

Location: *On the seafront, directly opposite the pier*
Bedrooms: *21 (single, double, twin, family, suite), all with bath/shower. Direct dial telephone, TV, teamaking, fridge. Hairdryer*
Facilities: *Parking. Indoor heated swimming pool*
Restrictions: *Dogs not encouraged. No smoking in restaurant*
Open: *Last week of Jan to 3rd week in Dec*
Credit/charge cards accepted: *Access, Visa*
Price category: *££-£££*
Special rates: *Autumn and summer, 2 nights DB&B £38.50-£47.50 (single from £42.50) pp per night. Reductions for children in parents' room: under 2 £7.50 (cot and breakfast); under 5, £10 (B&B); 5-12, ½ tariff*

LLANRWST
Meadowsweet Hotel
Llanrwst, Gwynedd   *Tel: (0492) 640732*

A cream-painted Victorian house with fine views over the fields in front to the river and mountains beyond. Comfortably and simply furnished, bedrooms vary in size with spriggy/floral prints and old pine chests of drawers. All have their own shower room and there are also two public bathrooms. Rooms at the back, away from the busy road, are quieter but miss out on the view. The bar welcomes guests with an open fire, comfy chairs and lots of magazines; although there is a separate sitting room in similar style with Victorian furniture and many books. French posters decorate the dining room walls, with Laura Ashley paper and bentwood chairs at well-spaced tables. A relaxed hotel, undemanding except for the wine list (some 500 entries).

Location: *On A470, ¼ mile north of town centre*
Bedrooms: *10 (double, twin, family), all with shower. Direct dial telephone, TV. Hairdryer on request*

Facilities: *Parking*
Restrictions: *No dogs in dining room. No smoking in dining room*
Open: *All year*
Credit/charge cards: *Access, Amex, Visa*
Price category: ££
Special rates: *2 or more nights DB&B £34-£39 (single £44-£50) pp per night. Children free in parents' room (charge for meals only)*

PENMAENPOOL
George III
Penmaenpool, Dolgellau, Gwynedd   *Tel: (0341) 422525*

In a delightful setting overlooking the Mawddach estuary right by the wooden tollbridge, this hotel consists of a 17th-century building and a Victorian 'lodge' which was something to do with the railway – both painted white with blue paintwork. Bedrooms have traditional or William Morris fabrics with contrasting wallpapers. There are splendid views of the estuary from the large light dining room with two exposed stone walls and lots of seascapes. Guests may sit in the cosy, beamed lounge with its fireplace and copper hood, and chairs arranged in a row; or in the bar, where a Welsh dresser serves as the bar itself and fish netting sustains the 'maritime' theme. Most of the one acre of grounds is taken up by car parking but there are patches of grass and shrubs. It's generally a clean and comfortable hotel in a fine setting.

Location: *2 miles from Dolgellau, on the Tywyn road by the toll bridge*
Bedrooms: *12 (double, twin), 6 in lodge. 8 with bath/shower. Direct dial telephone, TV, teamaking*
Facilities: *Parking. Babylistening*
Open: *All year*
Credit/charge cards: *Amex, Access, Diners, Visa*
Price category: ££
Special rates: *Winter, 2 nights DB&B £35.75 (single £42.35) pp per night (plus 10% service). Reductions for children in parents' room: under 3 £3, 3-10 £5*

PENMORFA
Bwlch-y-Fedwen
Penmorfa, Porthmadog, Gwynedd LL49 9RY   *Tel: (0766) 512975*

An attractive pebble-dashed house with a small garden, very much the owners' home. The large sitting room is affectionately furnished with family mementoes, antiques, and lots of books. There is also a small TV room. All the downstairs rooms interconnect happily; the cosy bar (slate floor and exposed brickwork) leads to the dining room (large dresser). Mugs and jugs hang from the beamed ceiling and there are fresh flowers and candles on the tables. The bedrooms are homely, with well-designed built-in furniture and quilted nylon bedspreads. Flowers, books and magazines are provided. Popular with the middle-aged/retired, this is a place for peace and quiet.

Location: *On A487, in centre of Penmorfa*
Bedrooms: *5 (double, twin), all with bath. Teamaking, electric blankets*
Facilities: *Parking*
Restrictions: *No children under 12. No dogs. No smoking in dining room*
Open: *April to Oct*
Credit/charge cards accepted: *None*
Price category: £
Special rates: *Autumn and spring, 2 nights DB&B £21.50-£22.50 (single £30)*

TAL-Y-LLYN
Minffordd Hotel
Tal-y-llyn, Tywyn, Gwynedd LL36 9AJ　　　　　　　　*Tel: (065 473) 665*

Originally a 17th-century roadside inn, this white-painted building at the foot of Cader Idris is now a hotel and restaurant of cottage appearance, with a pleasant garden. Guests are accepted only on dinner, bed and breakfast terms. The plain white-painted country restaurant/dining room is on many levels; there's a large wood-burning stove, reproduction tables and Victorian chairs, some pictures and knick-knacks. A cosy Victorian 'parlour' and a light and bright sun-room with cane furniture and floral curtains provide comfortable seating. Bedrooms tend to be small but cosy with contrasting paint and paper, sprig or floral patterns and woven wool bed covers; one is aware of passing traffic. This fresh and clean hotel provides a good base for outings – up Cader Idris for a start!

Location: *At the junction of A487 and B4405*
Bedrooms: *7 (double, twin, children), all with bath/shower. Direct dial telephone. Teamaking. Hairdryer*
Facilities: *Parking*
Restrictions: *No children under 3. No dogs. No smoking in dining room*
Open: *Mar to Oct, and weekends in Nov and Dec*
Credit/charge cards accepted: *Access, Diners, Visa*
Price category: ££
Special rates: *Autumn and spring, 2 nights DB&B £26 (single £23.50) pp per night. Children in parents' room free. Children in own room, half price*

The Yorkshire Dales

- The landscape is the sole reason for visiting the area; there are few sights
- An ideal choice for walkers, experienced or not, and for all who like the great outdoors. And there are some pretty villages for those who prefer pottering
- You can get a good feel for the landscape and enjoy most of the scenic highlights by car, although there are few main roads and none running north to south
- The southern part of the area is popular with day-trippers; if you want to escape head for Swaledale, remote Dentdale or Grassdale; or at least leave the car and walk
- A good choice of accommodation at moderate prices. You can expect a friendly welcome but not luxurious honeymoon suites and round-the-clock room service

The Dales were one of Yorkshire's, indeed Britain's, best-kept secrets until the James Herriot books, films and television series popularised the area in the 1970s. The reality still lives up to the image of long, lonely whaleback hills, pretty villages with mellow houses and old stone bridges, sparkling streams and drystone walls. The area has been designated a National Park; conservation policies, and the lack of through roads, have ensured that to a great extent rural life and farming practices continue the old-fashioned way.

The distinctive landscape is dominated by limestone: it has jagged white scars across the hillsides, crags and waterfalls, bare pavements of pale grey rock and strange potholes where streams gurgle underground. There are also areas of darker, more solid rocks such as gritstone, barren or heathery moorlands and bold mountains, but not much woodland or forest. The dales themselves vary from cosy and pastoral to majestic and awe-inspiring. Many features of the landscape are man-made: the patchwork of dry-stone walls following a field pattern established for centuries, the dignified stone barns and farmhouses, the tightly-knit hamlets. Even overgrown and forgotten remains of the mineral working industry make an important contribution to the scene in the north. There are some atmospheric ruins, though none as spectacular as those at Rievaulx on the North York

Moors, or at Fountains Abbey near Ripon.

Most roads run along the valleys but a few (between Buckden and Hawes, Settle and Arncliffe, Thwaite and Hawes) rise high onto the moors, some giving superb views of the mountain peaks and surrounding valleys.

The South

The south is dominated by **Wharfedale** which has a classic beauty – hemmed in by steep limestone crags at its northern end, and in the south broad, wooded and park-like, with a narrow, dramatic gorge (the Strid). **Malhamdale** is in itself peaceful and unspectacular, but famous for the scenic highlights clustered round its head. Malham Tarn is a small natural lake in unspoilt surroundings, the waters of which sink into the ground to re-emerge at Malham Cove, a great natural amphitheatre of white rock. Gordale Scar is a deep limestone gorge formed by the collapse of an underground cave. **Ribblesdale** is raw and rather bleak, its sides scarred by quarrying, but has fine views of the bold mountains to either side. The 'Three Peaks' – Pen-y-Ghent, Ingleborough and Whernside – are nothing like as high as the Lake District or Snowdonia tops. But in their open setting they look enormous, and majestic. At the head of Ribblesdale is desolate Blea Moor, striking above all for the long railway viaduct which snakes across it. At the south-western corner of the Park, near Ingleton, lies one of its most enjoyable natural wonders – a great arc of waterfalls which plunge through rocky ravines and wooded glens. In the west is Dentdale, a sheltered partly wooded valley with high rounded grassy hills to either side.

Grassington is a picturesque little town with a cobbled main square, traditional shops and several restaurants, plus a small folk museum. **Bolton Abbey** village, on the Yorkshire estate of the Dukes of Devonshire, is picturesque, but the picnic sites and car parks are crowded on summer weekends. Close to over-crowded Malham are the pretty 17th-century villages of **Kirkby Malham** and **Airton**. **Arncliffe** is an isolated oasis on the moor, with stone houses facing onto a village green, nestling in tiny Littondale; and **Dent** in Dentdale is a pretty village with narrow cobbled streets, a picturesque stop on the Settle-Carlisle railway line. **Skipton**, just outside the park, has a well-restored 11th-century castle, a working watermill and a small museum.

ABBEYS
Bolton Abbey An impressive ruin of a once powerful 12th-century priory in a serene, pastoral setting on the edge of the

village which has grown up beside; the priory nave is still used as the local parish church.

CAVES

The three caves open to the public are **Stump Cross Caverns**, east of Grassington, **Ingleborough Cave** near Clapham (which involves a half-hour walk from the road) and **White Scar Cave** near Ingleton. All three have a variety of rock formations and White Scar Cave also has an underground stream and some waterfalls – but in general they have less to offer than those in the Peak District. [*All open Easter to Oct daily, plus winter Suns*]

FAMILY OUTINGS

Kilnsey Park, in Wharfedale, combines a commercial trout farm with a picnic area, aquarium and nature exhibition close to the great limestone scar of Kilnsey Crag. [*Open all year, daily*]

Embsay, near Skipton, is the start of the still embryonic **Yorkshire Dales Railway** which has steam-hauled trains along its 1½ miles of track, plus over 20 locomotives on view. [*Open April to Oct, Sun and Bank Hols; plus Tues and Sat in July and Aug*]

The North

The north of the National Park is dominated by two big dales, running west to east. **Wensleydale**, broad, pastoral and dignified, has big green fields, several large villages and flat-topped sheep-grazing fells on either side of the valley. The dale is also notable for its rushing streams and waterfalls, particularly at Aysgarth where the River Ure tumbles over a series of broad limestone steps, and at Hardraw Force whose 99-foot drop is the biggest in England. **Swaledale** to the north is more remote, and offers some of the very best scenery in the area; its high steep sides remind you that the lonely moorlands of the northern Pennines are not far away. Lower Swaledale consists of peaceful pastureland, with isolated stone barns, scattered farms and the odd ruined cottage or abandoned mineshaft – Swaledale was an important lead mining valley until the end of the last century. The villages are tiny, handsome and remarkably unspoilt. The wild Thwaite-to-Hawes road takes you past some strange deep circular pits known as Buttertubs; on the bleak moors to the north stands the Tan Hill Inn, England's highest pub at 1,732 feet. In the west is narrow **Garsdale** which (like neighbouring Dentdale) feels more like the edge of the Lake District than the Dales, especially around the Howgill Fells north of Sedbergh.

Hawes is the market town of Wensleydale, with the Upper

Dales Folk Museum and a ropemaking centre. **Askrigg**, with its fine stone houses, features in the James Herriot television series; other pretty Wensleydale villages include **West Burton**, **Bainbridge**, with a spacious green and **Wensley** itself, with a beautiful church. **Bolton Castle**, a fine Norman fortress where Mary Queen of Scots was once imprisoned, offers good views of Wensleydale from the battlements; it is now a bar and restaurant. Just outside the Park, **Middleham**, a small town with an attractive main square, also has the remains of two Norman castles. **Reeth**, once an important lead mining centre at the junction of Swaledale and Arkengarthdale, is now slightly forlorn; it has a Swaledale Folk Museum. **Grinton**, **Thwaite** and **Muker** are typical Swaledale villages.

Just outside the north-east tip of the park, **Richmond** is perhaps the most interesting and appealing town in the area, in an impressive hill-top position above the River Swale. Steep and picturesque alleys and streets of Georgian houses lead to the big cobbled market-place, focus of the town centre and lined with fine 17th- and 18th-century buildings. The most interesting church is St Mary's in Church Wynd. Easby Abbey (see below) is reached via a pleasant riverside walk. Market day is Saturday.

HISTORIC BUILDINGS
Richmond Castle Original 11th-century walls, a rectangular keep (slightly later) and a Norman hall. There are splendid views over the River Swale. [*Open all year, daily*]

Richmond, Georgian Theatre Royal This tiny, lovingly-restored theatre with a small museum is well worth a visit. [*Open May to Sept daily, pm only except Sat; plus Easter, and Bank Hol Mons*]

The half-wild site of ruined **Jervaulx Abbey**, built in the 12th century by Cistercian monks who bred horses and made cheese, has considerable charm; so does the gentle farmland setting of the impressive remains of **Easby Abbey**, near Richmond.

MUSEUMS
Richmond, Richmondshire Museum A local museum with toys, costumes, a reconstructed cruck house and James Herriot's surgery set from 'All Creatures Great and Small'. [*Open April to Oct, pm daily and am Mon to Fri during school hols*]

Richmond, The Green Howards Regimental Museum An interesting museum for military enthusiasts, in the old church of the Holy Trinity. [*Open April to Oct daily except Sun am; Mon to Fri Feb and Nov; plus Sat in Mar*]

There are several small museums illustrating bygone life in the countryside for visiting on a wet afternoon. Worth an excursion is the **Bowes Museum** at Barnard Castle (see Durham chapter).

FAMILY OUTINGS
Aysgarth has a display of 50 horse-drawn carriages in an old mill
building.

Walking

Despite the relative lack of obvious peaks to climb, the Dales
attract a great many walkers – for the sheer amount of fine
scenery, and limestone features such as waterfalls, ravines and
caves. There's a much wider range of walking than you might
guess at first sight, provided you can cope with the odd hillside
and a few stiles. However, many paths marked on OS maps,
especially those high up on the hills, are not visible on the
ground. The Park Authority has helped by marking many paths,
particularly those which cross from one dale to the next; and you
can often design a round walk to take in a handsome village with
a reasonable chance of a good pub.

The area is further blessed with three long-distance paths, all of
them good for walking in short sections as well as in one go. The
Pennine Way runs within the Park for over 50 of its 250 miles,
taking in much of the finest scenery on the whole route,
including Malham, the craggy summit of Pen-y-Ghent, and
Hardraw Force. The Coast to Coast Path sticks mainly to the
high, empty fells north of Swaledale. The third path, the Dales
Way, goes from Ilkley to Windermere, mainly by way of valleys –
gently up Wharfedale, then over moorland into Dentdale.

The scope for easy walks is a bit limited: the best ones are
around the main beauty spots, particularly around Malham and
to the waterfalls at Aysgarth and Hardraw Force. The surroundings of Bolton Abbey, where there are many woodland footpaths
and a nature trail along the River Wharfe, are also good for a
short stroll. The waterfalls at Ingleton are connected up by a well
engineered and very attractive four-mile path (small charge). The
Reginald Farrer Nature Trail leads for about four miles up
carefully landscaped Clapdale, just north of Clapham.

See *Holiday Which? Good Walks Guide* walks 147-154.

When to go

Spring comes late in the Dales and lasts till the end of May; in the
latter half of August heather flowers spectacularly on the hills.
The Swaledale Festival with concerts, lectures and local events
runs from the end of May to the second week in June; it is
followed by the Grassington festival which lasts until the first

week in July. The Wensleydale Agricultural show at Leyburn and Reeth show are held in late August. On the nearest Saturday to St Bartholomew's Day (August 24th) the unusual custom of the Burning of Owd Bartle (an effigy) is performed annually at West Witton; festivities continue over the weekend. The National Park Centres and some sights (eg caves) are open only from Easter to October.

Information

The Yorkshire Dales National Park Information Service, Colvend, Hebden Road, Grassington, Skipton, North Yorks BD23 5LB; tel: (0756) 754748. There are National Park Information Centres at Aysgarth Falls, Clapham, Hawes, Malham and Sedbergh; and also tourist information points in many villages.

The Park Authority's Whernside Cave and Fell Centre at Dent [tel: (05875) 213] offers fully instructed weekend courses in caving, fell walking, potholing and general mountaineering.

Private fly fishing is available on some lengths of water, for instance the Wharfe at Bolton Abbey (day tickets from the Estate Office or the Devonshire Arms Hotel at weekends).

Where to stay

There is quite a wide choice of hotels, mostly inns and converted houses in picturesque villages and market towns. There are also a few country house hotels, though none very grand or luxurious. If you're looking for bed and breakfast accommodation, Hawes is a good place to start with a wide variety of places to stay. Although standards are not always the highest, most places more than make up for this in friendliness and comfort.

ASKRIGG
King's Arms
Market Place, Askrigg, Wensleydale, North Yorks DL8 3HQ   Tel: (0969) 50258

A Georgian stone-built coaching inn opposite 'Herriot's house' in this famous Dales village. Internally it is like a rabbit warren. Most bedrooms are spacious, simple and light with some antique furniture including four-poster and half tester beds. There are two small but very sweet attic bedrooms. In addition to the public bars there is a lounge bar and dining room, both wood-panelled. Table d'hôte menus change nightly and food is traditional and home-cooked. In summer, bar lunches may be served in the courtyard. A restful drawing room in the owner's manor house next door caters for non-smokers (a new lounge extension is planned). The hotel has a jolly country pub atmosphere and quiet rooms decorated with simple good taste.

Bedrooms: *10 (double and twin), 4 with four-poster or half tester beds, all with bath. TV, teamaking. Hairdryer on request*
Facilities: *Parking (for 6 cars). Babylistening*
Open: *All year*
Credit/charge cards accepted: *Access, Amex, Diners, Visa*
Price category: *£*
Special rates: *2 nights DB&B £25-£30.50 pp per night. Children free in parents' room, 40% reduction in own room*

BAINBRIDGE
Rose & Crown
Bainbridge, Leyburn, North Yorks DL8 3EE   Tel: (0969) 50225

A charming inn overlooking the green in one of Wensleydale's classic villages. It has been extensively redecorated without losing the character of the original 15th-century inn. Life revolves around two cosy beamed bars with oak furniture, one serving bar lunches. Dinner is in a long, low beamed room of cottagey elegance. Bedrooms have been prettily and freshly redecorated with sprig wallpaper and co-ordinating curtains, several with nice new pine furniture, but most are on the small side. Most have facilities en suite, but this may consist just of a small shower cabinet. There is a cosy beamed residents' lounge with comfy floral sofas and armchairs. Although there is some traffic noise at intervals during the day, this is unlikely to be a problem at night. A good, friendly and reasonably priced weekend base, ideal for walkers.

Bedrooms: *13 (single, double, twin, family), 3 with 4-poster beds, 11 with bath or shower. TV, teamaking*
Facilities: *Parking. Pool table*
Open: *All year*
Credit/charge cards accepted: *Access, Visa*
Price category: *££*
Special rates: *Nov to Mar, 2 nights DB&B £25 pp per night; special rates for children in parents' room (£8 camp bed, £5 cot)*

BOLTON ABBEY
Devonshire Arms
Bolton Abbey, Skipton, North Yorks BD23   Tel: (075 671) 441

A thoroughly comfortable hotel close to Bolton Abbey and well placed for exploring Wharfedale. On the estate of the Dukes of Devonshire since 1748, the original coaching inn was extended and refurbished in 1982. A new wing contains the majority of the bedrooms and all have recently been redecorated; they are pretty and light with co-ordinated floral fabrics. In the old inn, bedrooms contain furniture and paintings from Chatsworth, brass beds and brass lamps – to more traditional effect. All bedrooms have small cork tiled bathrooms and – rare treat – mahogany loo seats. The main public rooms, notably the long lounge, are comfortable and furnished with some family antiques, and paintings with neat descriptions in italics. The dining room has an airy, summery feel and the menus are *nouvelle cuisine* influenced. Despite its position on the road, the hotel is fairly quiet – rooms on the road are mainly used for functions.

Location: *On the A59 (Skipton to Harrogate), at the junction with the B6160*
Bedrooms: *38 (single, double and twin), 2 with four-poster beds, all with bath. Direct dial telephone. TV, teamaking*
Facilities: *Parking. Snooker. Fishing on River Wharfe. Babylistening*
Open: *All year*
Credit/charge cards accepted: *Access, Amex, Diners, Visa*
Price category: £££
Special rates: *2 nights DB&B £46 pp per night. Children in parents' room £10*

GAYLE
Rookhurst
Gayle, Hawes, North Yorks DL8 3RT   *Tel: (096 97) 454*

'Rookhurst Georgian Country House' actually dates from around 1670 and has substantial Victorian additions. It is more home than hotel, and provides a comfortable and spacious alternative to the many guesthouses in and around Hawes. The lounge and dining room are old-fashioned and fairly formal. The bedrooms in the older part of the house are cosy and beamed, the Victorian ones more spacious and grand. All have traditional furnishings and unusual or antique beds, including a Georgian walnut four-poster. Rookhurst is particularly popular with older couples and honeymooners. The no smoking rule may be a bonus or a deterrent.

Location: *On narrow road at Gayle, ¾ mile south of Hawes*
Bedrooms: *6 (single, double and twin), 4 with four-poster or half tester beds, 4 with bath or shower. TV, teamaking. Hairdryers. Master and Bridal suite bedrooms have dining area and fridge*
Facilities: *Parking*
Restrictions: *No dogs. No smoking except in lounge. No children under 3*
Open: *All year*
Credit/charge cards accepted: *Amex*
Price category: ££
Special rates: *Nov to April (not Christmas/New Year), 2 nights DB&B £30-£34 (single £36) pp per night. Summer, 3 nights DB&B, reduction of 5% off normal rates. Children from 3 to 14 in parents' room B&B £10*

GRASSINGTON
Ashfield House
Grassington, Skipton, North Yorks BD23 5AE   *Tel: (0756) 752584*

A small 17th-century house in local stone, set back down its own cobbled drive off the main square of the picturesque little village of Grassington. The front door opens into a homely room with a big fireplace and old pine furniture; next door is a simple dining room with modern pine tables and chairs and a wine list on the blackboard. Bedrooms are neat but basic with pine furniture, floral curtains and washbasins – just two have their own showers and there are two public bathrooms. The Sugdens take a pride in their home and everything is spick and span. The hotel would suit walkers (there is a large Ordnance Survey map on the lounge wall) and families – TV, games and books in the lounge, and a small garden at the back – but not those who want space, extra comforts and the flexibility of menu choice and meal times (dinner is at 7pm sharp).

Bedrooms: *7 (double, twin, family) 2 with shower. Teamaking*
Facilities: *Parking. TV in lounge*
Restrictions: *No dogs. No smoking in dining room*
Open: *Apr to Oct*
Credit/charge cards accepted: *None*
Price category: £
Special rates: *2 nights or more DB&B £21.10-£21.40 pp per night. Children 4 to 10 half price in parents' room*

HAWES
Cockett's Hotel
Market Place, Hawes, North Yorks DL8 3RD   *Tel: (096 97) 312*

A delightful 17th-century grey stone cottage, with roses round the door, set back from the market square. Until 1981 this was a temperance hotel for Quakers and the door bears a motto, dated 1668, 'God being with us who can be against us'. The entrance opens directly into a cosy beamed hall lounge with a pretty woodburning stove, leather furniture and chintz curtains. Off it leads the dining room, where lacy tablecloths, shining copper pans and a display of antique corkscrews contribute to the country feel. Cherry Guest's cooking is adventurous and interesting (as is the wine list). Bedrooms are all different but mostly simple and pleasant, with some old furniture and views of the hills; one four poster room is more exotic with a Chinese theme. There are two rooms in an annexe over the gallery next door. Cars can be parked off the road at the front of the hotel.

Bedrooms: *7 (double and twin), 2 with four-poster beds, 2 in annexe, 5 with bath or shower. TV, teamaking. Hairdryer on request*
Open: *Mid Mar to mid Nov*
Restrictions: *No children under 10 in restaurant. No pipes in dining room*
Credit/charge cards accepted: *Access, Visa*
Price category: £
Special rates: *£10 refund on bookings of 3-6 days DB&B (double occupancy only)*

HAWES
Simonstone Hall
Hawes, North Yorks DL8 3LY   *Tel: (096 97) 255*

The former seat of the Earls of Wharncliffe, Simonstone Hall is an 18th-century stone house in rural but not isolated surroundings. South-facing rooms command fine views of Upper Wensleydale. The main public rooms, with log fires, have the original panelled walls, now painted creamy white, and have been comfortably furnished with some antique and some reproduction furniture. The style throughout is more homely than baronial, the atmosphere closer to a Scottish shooting lodge than a grand country house hotel. Bedrooms are pleasant if a little dark, with old-fashioned bathrooms. Staff are welcoming and willing.

Location: *1½ miles from Hawes on Muker road*
Bedrooms: *10 (double, twin and family), 1 with four-poster, all with bath. TV, teamaking. Hairdryer on request*
Facilities: *Parking. Babylistening*
Restrictions: *No dogs in dining room or bar when food is being served. No small children in dining room*
Open: *All year*
Credit/charge cards accepted: *Access, Amex, Diners*
Price category: *££*
Special rates: *2 Nov to 11 Apr, excluding Christmas, New Year and Easter, reductions of 10%-15%. Christmas and New Year house parties. Children under 16 in parents' room £10.50*

JERVAULX
Jervaulx Hall
Jervaulx, Ripon, North Yorks HG4 4PH   *Tel: (0677) 60235*

Jervaulx Hall's chief claim to fame is the proximity of the 12th-century ruined abbey adjacent to the well-landscaped grounds. The beautifully situated manor house dates from the 19th century but has mellowed well. It is a comfortable house, with gracious high-ceilinged rooms, log fires and antique furniture. Bedrooms are mostly quite large, with splendid views; decoration and furnishings are mixed. The resident host, John Sharp, successfully aims to provide the comforts of a Yorkshire country house, including freshly shot game in season, and this is the sort of hotel which might suit those who want a relaxing break rather than a particularly active one. However there is plenty to do locally, including riding and fishing.

Location: *On the A6108 between Masham and Middleham*
Bedrooms: *8 (double and twin), all with bath. Teamaking. Hairdryer. Extra heaters*
Facilities: *Parking. TV in lounge. Croquet. Fishing by arrangement. Babylistening*
Restrictions: *Dogs by arrangement only and not unattended in bedrooms*
Open: *Mid March to mid Nov*
Credit/charge cards accepted: *None*
Price category: *£££*
Special rates: *Spring, 2 nights DB&B £32.50 pp per night. Reductions for children in parents' room depending on age*

MIDDLEHAM
The Miller's House
Market Place, Middleham, North Yorks DL8 4NR   *Tel: (0969) 22630*

This is a comfortable small hotel in a handsome Georgian town house set back from the village square. It offers good value for money, is well run and not in the least institutional, with more sophisticated dining than in most of the other small hotels in the Dales. Rooms are large and high-ceilinged, often with original features like ornate cornices. Bedrooms have been redecorated since the last owners moved in 1986, in traditional style. The dining room has a period atmosphere with its Regency striped wallpaper and candlelit dining – formal but not stuffily so. By contrast the bar is informal and cosy; a Scandinavian style log fire, wicker basket chairs, magazines and a piano. In the evening at least, this is a cosier room than the spacious first floor residents' lounge. Dinner is cooked to order (by 5pm) and food is unpretentious and carefully prepared.

Bedrooms: *6 (single, double and twin), all with bath. TV, teamaking*
Facilities: *Parking*
Restrictions: *No dogs. No children under 11. No smoking in dining room*
Open: *Mid Feb to mid Nov*
Credit/charge cards accepted: *Access, Visa*
Price category: *££*
Special rates: *Mid Feb to end May and Oct to mid Nov, 2 nights DB&B £28 pp per night*

RICHMOND
The Frenchgate Hotel
59-61 Frenchgate, Richmond, North Yorks DL10 7AE   *Tel: (0748) 2087*

A Georgian town house in a quiet cobbled street a few minutes' walk from the market square, this is the most appealing hotel in Richmond. There is a comfortable and cosy beamed lounge, a large bar and an elegant Georgian dining room. The simple sun lounge is in a modern extension overlooking a paved courtyard and large lawn. Bedrooms are pleasant, light and clean with fitted furniture; the smallest at the top of the house. The hotel is well run by an ex Squadron Leader; last breakfasts are at 9am.

Bedrooms: *13 bedrooms (single, double and twin), 7 with bath. Direct dial telephones. TV, teamaking*
Facilities: *Parking (6 cars)*
Restrictions: *No children under 7*
Open: *Mid Feb to mid Dec*
Credit/charge cards accepted: *Access, Amex, Diners, Visa*
Price category: *££*
Special rates: *Mid Oct to mid May excluding public holidays, 2 nights DB&B £24.50 pp per night*

SCENIC COASTS

The Argyll Coast, The Cornish Coast,
The Northumbrian Coast, The Pembrokeshire Coast,
The South Coast

•

The Argyll coast

- A fascinating coastline: the delights of an island with none of the restrictions. But don't expect many good sandy beaches
- Good for a get-away-from-it-all break. Some holiday resorts, but much of the Argyll coast is well off the beaten track
- Some fine gardens with sub-tropical plants are the main sights; boat trips, fishing and walking the main activities. Walks are more rewarding than touring by car
- Comfortable lochside hotels, most with boating facilities

The Argyll coast and the south-west Highlands have most of the romantic ingredients of Scottish landscape, including lochs and ruined castles. Across the firths and the sounds are glimpsed the islands of the Inner Hebrides. Though rarely as spectacularly dramatic or vertiginous as the coastline of Scotland's extreme north-west, Argyll has some splendid craggy stretches and exceptional views. The intricacy of the coastline is the most striking feature of the whole area. The numerous fingers of land play tricks on the eye; often the islands appear part of the mainland, or the peninsulas seem like islands. Inland Argyll is something of a contradiction in terms as coastal waters are always close and there are so many lochs and rivers. Rising above these are hills and mountains (only high in the north). Great expanses are given over to evergreen plantations, and there is wild moorland blanketed by heather. In the lower areas lush pasture is grazed by cattle and sheep. Much of Argyll is sparsely populated, with occasional cottages by the roadside and turreted mansions glimpsed through the trees of massive estates. Towns are rather severe, villages often no more than a cluster of houses.

Cowal is a generally quiet area of fine scenery which gets increasingly wild as you move westwards; in the centre the mountains of the Argyll Forest Park are spectacular. The main resort is **Dunoon**; but for the views, it's an unremarkable, traditional seaside resort. The neighbouring areas, around Holy Loch, are not improved by the influence and activity of the US Navy. There are two other small holiday centres: **Lochgoilhead**, reached via the splendid Hell's Glen, but with some unsympathetic development; and **Tighnabruich**, attractively set on the Kyles of Bute with views across to Rothesay. To the north of

Cowal are the peaceful wooded shores of **Loch Fyne**, with the distinctive Georgian buildings of **Inveraray**.

Kintyre is wild rather than dramatic, its appeal lying in the peacefulness of the peninsula and the views. The countryside on the west is the less impressive but the beaches are good, and the views across to Gigha, Islay and the peaks of Jura are splendid. On the east the countryside is more welcoming – woodland with valleys cutting through to the sea and pretty little communities, such as **Carradale** with its fishing harbour and fine views of the peaks of Arran and Cowal. The main town is austere **Cambeltown**; further south is **Southend**, an unexceptional village with a good beach. In the very south-west are the cliffs of the Mull of Kintyre with views across to Northern Ireland.

Knapdale is mountainous, with tremendous views of Jura and a real sense of being away from it all. **Tarbert** and **Lochgilphead** are independent little coastal towns, Tarbert the more attractive of the two. Between Lochgilphead and the village of **Crinan**, a popular yachting haven, the Crinan canal runs through gentle, pretty scenery.

From Crinan to **Ballachulish** the interesting, indented coastline, with its varied character and views of many islands and islets, is easily enjoyed from the main road. At **Arduaine**, the view is particularly good and the island of Seil makes a peaceful diversion. Inland is **Loch Awe**, in splendid, serene countryside. **Oban** is a popular but rather charmless holiday resort and port. North of Oban, where the Falls of Lora cascade below the bridge, you approach the Highlands. To the west are views of the mountains falling sheer into the waters of **Loch Linnhe**, to the east **Loch Etive** and the spectacular scenery of the Grampians, the highest and most impressive mountains of the area, with the beautiful gorge of **Glen Coe**.

HISTORIC BUILDINGS AND GARDENS

Arduaine, Arduaine Gardens   Attached to a baronial castle of 1856. This is primarily a garden for keen horticulturalists, with rhododendrons and rare shrubs. [*Open April to Sep, pm, Sat to Wed*]

Benmore, Younger Botanic Garden   Magnificent collections of trees and shrubs, notably Californian redwoods and rhododendrons. [*Open April to Oct, daily*]

Inveraray Castle   18th-century ancestral home of the Dukes of Argyll. Elaborate state rooms with fine tapestries, portraits and furniture, and impressive collections of armoury. [*Open early April to mid Oct, daily except Fri (plus Fri in July and Aug)*]

Other gardens include **Dalnashean** at Appin, **Strone Garden** at Cairndow, **Carradale House Gardens**, Carradale, **Achnacloich** and **Ardchattan Priory** at Connel, **An Cala** at Easdale, **Crarae Woodland Garden** near Inveraray, **Kilmory Castle Gardens** at Lochgilphead and **Barguillean** at Taynuilt. **Ardanaiseig** (Kilchrenan) and **Stonefield Castle** (Tarbert) are both attached to hotels.

ANTIQUITIES

For those interested in archaeology there are some fascinating Celtic crosses, vitrified forts, neolithic burial sites and carved stones in the area. There are also some ancient abbeys and early ruined castles.

FAMILY OUTINGS

Auchindrain Museum of Farming Life   Small farming township restored as a fascinating museum of rural Highland life, with demonstrations and audio-visual displays. [*Open April, May, Sep, Sun to Fri; June to Aug daily*]

Inveraray, Argyll Wildlife Park   55 acres of park on the shores of Loch Fyne, with European, and especially Scottish, animals. [*Open all year, daily*]

Inveraray, Castle Fish Farm   Fishponds, lakes and pets' corner, plus a deer park. [*Open April to Oct, daily*]

Loch Awe, Cruachan Power Station   Scotland's 'Hollow Mountain'; conducted tours of the hydro-electric power station in the heart of Ben Cruachan. [*Open late Mar to late Oct, daily*]

Loch Creran, Sea Life Centre   An aquarium display of the marine life found off the Scottish coast. [*Open April to Oct, daily*]

EXCURSIONS

Loch Lomond is less than an hour's drive from Dunoon and Glasgow is about 25 miles away. There are regular ferries to the islands.

Walking

The rough and broken nature of the topography of the Argyll coast, together with the sparse path network, means that round walks in the area are not easy to find; public transport services may need to be relied on to get you to your starting place. Much of the moorland requires hag-leaping to cross it, and is not for the inexperienced. But some lochside and farm tracks can be a delight to walk on, and many roads are extremely quiet.

For a sample of the lonely islands and peninsulas of the west coast, headlands such as the Craignish Peninsula – which has superb views of the Sound of Jura on its seaward side and a beautiful lochside road to the east – are worth seeking out, but although they don't rise to great heights can involve trackless country and light scrambling. Some of the islands – Kerrera for example – have relatively undemanding tracks with magnificent views. The wealth of archaeology in the area makes a good focus for some easy walks; in particular, a level track west of and parallel to the A816 near Kilmartin is the best way to see a striking series of cairns known as Nether Largie Linear Cemetery, and a stone circle. Self-guided trails exist in some of the vast Forestry Commission plantations, such as Inverliever Forest on the west side of Loch Awe and Knapdale Forest south of Kilmartin; the latter's northern extent is bounded by the Crinan Canal, whose towpath you can use to make a forest and waterside walk. At Inverary Castle are a number of marked trails, including one up the wooded hill of Dunchuach; an excellent view over Loch Fyne opens up at the top.

See *Holiday Which? Good Walks Guide*, walks 173, 178-181.

When to go

Most gardens are open from April to the end of September, but May is the best time to visit for rhododendrons. Events include a spectacular Highland Gathering in Dunoon on the last weekend in August.

Information

The Mid Argyll, Kintyre and Islay Tourist Board, the Pier, Campbeltown, Argyll PA28 6EF; tel: (0586) 52056.

The Dunoon and Cowal Tourist Information Centre, 7 Alexandra Parade, Dunoon, Argyll PA23 7HL; tel: (0369) 3785.

Where to stay

Half the point of a short break in Argyll is the hotel and there is a wide selection – ranging from old drovers' inns to converted mansions in gorgeous gardens. Apart from one hotel, near the main resort of Dunoon, all those we recommend have loch views and most can organise boating and fishing trips.

ARDENTINNY
Ardentinny Hotel
Ardentinny, Loch Long, Argyll PA23 8TR   Tel: (036 981) 209

An 18th-century village inn with lawns sloping down to the rocky shores of Loch Long, the Ardentinny is a friendly place well used by locals and yachtsmen, especially at weekends. It is simple but comfortable, with several bars, a lounge and a buttery. The light and airy dining room has views of the loch; and the jolly Lauder Bar, with piped Scottish country dance music, opens directly onto the garden. In fine weather lunches are served on the gravel patio where you can watch yachts manoeuvring for a mooring. Bedrooms are simply decorated with white furniture; the five 'Fyne' rooms have larger bathrooms, TVs and loch views and are slightly more expensive.

Bedrooms: *11 (single, double, twin, family), all with bath. Electric blankets. TV, teamaking. Hairdryer on request.*
Facilities: *Parking. Moorings for yachts. Boat hire*
Open: *Mid Mar to Nov*
Credit/charge cards accepted: *Access, Amex, Diners, Visa*
Price category: ££
Special rates: *Between Sept 11 and May 27, discount for 'senior citizens' of 10%. 3 nights DB&B £33-£37 (single £34-£39) pp per night*

ARDUAINE
Loch Melfort Hotel
Arduaine, by Oban, Argyll PA34 4XG   Tel: (085 22) 233

Next to the famous Arduaine gardens, on the shores of Loch Melfort, this hotel is a turn-of-the-century country house much extended and refurbished. It is a peaceful place although the Scandinavian-style Chart Room bar is often full of visiting yachtsmen. Cedar Wing rooms, attached to the main house by a covered passage, all have sliding glass doors and a patio or balcony to the loch side and are modern, light and airy. The bedrooms in the main house are larger and individually decorated in traditional styles. The dining room has picture windows overlooking the loch and the islands of Jura and Scarba; specialities are Loch Melfort giant prawns and charcoal-grilled steaks.

Location: *On the A 816 between Oban (19 miles) and Crinan (12 miles)*
Bedrooms: *23 (single, double and twin), all with bath. Teamaking. Hairdryer on request*
Facilities: *Parking, moorings. Boutique. Children's sandpit, babylistening*
Restrictions: *Dogs in Cedar Wing only*
Open: *Easter to mid Oct*
Credit/charge cards accepted: *Access*
Price category: £££
Special rates: *4 or more nights B&B £27 (single £33) pp per night. Children £7.50 in parents' room*

CAIRNDOW
Stagecoach Inn
Cairndow, Argyll PA26 8BN   *Tel: (049 96) 286*

An old coaching inn on the upper reaches of Loch Fyne which offers simple comforts very cheaply. There is a homely lounge, a pubby public bar, a cosier lounge bar and a beer garden across the road on the lochside. The dining room is in the converted stables; specialities are venison and Loch Fyne salmon. Bedrooms are plain but neat and clean, some with functional shower cabinets, most with hill and loch views. Queen Victoria changed horses here in 1875; and Dorothy Wordsworth summed it up thus: 'Cairndow is a single house by the side of the loch, I believe, resorted to by gentlemen in the fishing season: it is a pleasant place for such a purpose...' Although the inn is old-fashioned and typically Scottish, it does now boast a jacuzzi and sunbed.

Location: *On the A83, between Inverary and Arrochar (10 miles)*
Bedrooms: *9 (single, double, twin and family), 7 with shower. Electric blankets. Direct dial telephone, teamaking*
Facilities: *Parking. Jacuzzi, sunbed. Disco fortnightly in winter. Games room (pool, space invaders). Fishing. Babylistening*
Open: *All year*
 Credit/charge cards accepted: *Access, Diners, Visa*
Price category: £
Special rates: *Winter, 2 nights DB&B £38 pp. Children under 12, half price in parents' room; 12-16, 25% off*

DUNOON
Enmore Hotel
Marine Parade, Kirn, Dunoon, Argyll PA23 8HH   *Tel: (0369) 2230*

Dunoon is a traditional holiday resort, but the Enmore has rather more to offer than the average seaside hotel. An attractive white 18th-century house, which has been converted and extended, it is family-run and you are immediately made to feel at home. Bedrooms are particularly appealing, light and airy with fresh wallpapers and cane or fitted white furniture and little extras like flowers, books, sewing kits and towelling bathrobes. Luxury breaks are a speciality and honeymooners are treated to champagne and a heart-shaped box of chocolates. Public rooms, too, are comfortable and well-appointed with a certain elegance; furniture is a mixture of antique and reproduction and there are lots of books around. Most rooms have a view of the well-kept garden and sea. The Enmore has its own squash courts with bar viewing area and video playback facilities. Menus are well-balanced, but with little choice.

Location: *One mile north-east of Dunoon*
Bedrooms: *14 (single, double, twin and family), 3 with four-poster, 1 with waterbed and whirlpool bath, 10 with bath. Direct dial telephone, TV. Hairdryer*
Facilities: *Parking. Games room (pool, darts), squash. Babylistening*
Restrictions: *No dogs in dining room. Smoking discouraged*

Open: *All year except Christmas and New Year*
Credit/charge cards accepted: *Access, Diners, Visa*
Price category: ££
Special rates: *Nov to Mar (except Christmas), 2 nights DB&B £35 pp per night, £45 in four-poster rooms. Children free under 7, 7-14 half price in parents' room*

KENTALLEN
Ardsheal House
Kentallen of Appin, Argyll PA38 4BX   *Tel: (063 174) 227*

A stone and granite mansion with 13 acres of landscaped gardens and fine trees, Ardsheal House (1760) replaces an earlier building destroyed during the 1745 rebellion. Once home of the Stewarts of Appin, it is now run as a hotel by an American couple who create a house party atmosphere among their guests, with dogs and children welcomed. The baronial wood-panelled hall with log fire provides a spacious and comfortable sitting room: a wide wooden balustraded staircase leads up to the individually decorated, comfortable bedrooms, all with well chosen antique furniture and superb views of Loch Linnhe. Another lounge, overlooking the loch, and known as the Library, is a small, almost octagonal room, much cosier than the TV lounge (overlooking the car park). The dining room has a conservatory extension; food is interesting and uses fresh produce including Loch Linnhe prawns, home-grown vegetables, samphire, sorrel and saffron. The billiard room, a splendid Victorian monument, is very popular after dinner. The home farm has prize hens which provide breakfast eggs.

Location: *1¼ mile private drive off the A828 from Oban to Fort William*
Bedrooms: *13 (single, double, twin) all with bath or shower. Electric blankets. Hairdryer on request*
Facilities: *Parking. Billiards. Tennis*
Restrictions: *No smoking in dining room*
Open: *Easter to Oct*
Credit/charge cards accepted: *Access, Amex, Visa*
Price category: £££
Special rates: *Children in parents' room £12*

KENTALLEN
The Holly Tree Hotel
Kentallen, by Appin, Argyll PA38 4BY   *Tel: (063 174) 292*

An attractive conversion of an Edwardian railway station (the branch line was axed in 1966) provides what is essentially a restaurant with rooms. In the main part, the more interesting Glasgow Art Nouveau period features have been retained; reception is the ticket office, the carpeted hall was once the platform, there are two bedrooms in the original waiting rooms and a residents' cocktail bar in the tearoom. The extension with bedrooms was completed in summer 1987; furnishings in white ash complete the stylish but traditional décor. Rooms are light and airy with views over Loch Linnhe and the mountains of Ardgour. The new lounge has seating groups round a central open fireplace, and the dining room has floor-to-ceiling windows on both sides. For the high quality of produce and inventive cooking, the food, prepared by the owner, Alasdair Robertson, is very reasonably priced. A comfortable, well-appointed and easy place to stay.

Location: *Between Appin and Ballachulish, on the Oban to Fort William road*
Bedrooms: *12 (double and twin), all with bath or shower. Direct dial telephone, TV, teamaking. Hairdryer*
Facilities: *Parking, helipad*
Restrictions: *No smoking in dining room. Dogs by prior arrangement only and not in public rooms*
Open: *Mid Feb to mid Nov plus Christmas*
Credit/charge cards accepted: *Access, Visa*
Price category: *££*
Special rates: *3 nights, 10% discount. Children free under 5, £5 in parents' room*

KILCHRENAN
Ardanaiseig
Kilchrenan, by Taynuilt, Argyll PA35 1HE   *Tel: (086 63) 333*

A 19th-century grey stone mansion on the shores of Loch Awe, Ardanaiseig is famous for its luxuriant gardens. Originally built for a member of the Campbell clan, it has been run as a hotel since 1979. The baronial stone-flagged hall with a log fire, and the superbly proportioned drawing room and spacious 'Library' bar, both with chintzy furnishings, retain much of the atmosphere of a comfortable country house. Dining, too, is a civilised affair (gentlemen are requested to wear jacket and tie); the calm dining room overlooks the loch and landscaped garden. All the bedrooms are different, but spacious, comfortable and, above all, utterly peaceful; the 'smaller few' are four rooms which are quite a bit cheaper than the others. The Ardanaiseig experience is particularly popular with American visitors.

Location: *4 miles east of Kilchrenan, at end of single track road*
Bedrooms: *14 (single, double and twin), all with bath. Direct dial telephone, TV. Hairdryer and trouser press on request*
Facilities: *Parking. Collection by car from station or airport. Helicopter landing by arrangement. Snooker, indoor games. Croquet, tennis. Boating, clay pigeon shooting, fishing*
Restrictions: *No children under 8. Dogs by arrangement only*
Open: *April to Oct*
Credit/charge cards accepted: *Access, Amex, Visa*
Price category: *£££££*
Special rates: *3 to 6 nights, DB&B £72 (single £73) pp per night. £20 reduction in the four 'smaller few' rooms. Children half price in parents' room*

KILCHRENAN
Cuil na Sithe
Kilchrenan, by Taynuilt, Argyll PA35 1HF   *Tel: (086 63) 234*

An old-fashioned guesthouse providing an affordable alternative to its two neighbours, Ardanaisaig and Taychreggan. Cuil na Sithe ('Corner of Tranquillity') is a late Victorian country house with bay windows overlooking Loch Awe. Rooms – bedrooms included – are high ceilinged (some domed, with ornate cornices) and modestly but comfortably furnished. Food is plain, with some reliance on the storecupboard due to the remote location; wine is simply red or white. In the fine garden roam peacocks, guinea fowl and occasionally deer.

Location: *½ mile south of Kilchrenan, on north bank of Loch Awe*
Bedrooms: *6 (double, twin and family), 1 with bath, 1 with shower. Cordless direct dial telephone on request. Electric blankets. TV, teamaking*
Facilities: *Parking. Boating, fishing, tennis*
Open: *All year*
Credit/charge cards accepted: *Access, Visa*
Price category: *£*
Special rates: *Summer, 3 nights DB&B £23 pp per night. Jan and Feb, 2 nights DB&B £15 pp per night. Children under 10 half price in parents' room*

KILCHRENAN
Taychreggan Hotel
Kilchrenan, by Taynuilt, Argyll PA35 1HQ   *Tel: (086 63) 211*

In a delightful setting in landscaped gardens on the edge of Loch Awe, this old drovers' inn has been skilfully extended and modernised. A sociable bar opens onto the internal courtyard, which is a sheltered suntrap of almost Mediterranean aspect. The dining room is airy and modern, the sitting rooms cosy with well-plumped sofas and woodburning stoves and there is a 'Quiet Room' with well-stocked bookshelves. All these rooms have splendid views over the garden and loch. Bedrooms are spacious and pleasing, with some antique furniture, and spotless bathrooms. The hotel is ideal for families and those who like boating, fishing, riding and watersports. As well as Scandinavian-style buffet lunches at the hotel, there is a large picnic boat for hire. Fish features strongly on the 4-course dinner menu.

Location: *Off the B845, 7 miles south of Taynuilt*
Bedrooms: *16 (single and double), 1 with four-poster bed, all with bath. Direct dial telephone. Hairdryer*
Facilities: *Parking. Boat and surfboard hire. Babylistening*
Restrictions: *No children under 8 in dining room at dinner*
Open: *Easter to Oct*
Credit/charge cards accepted: *Access, Amex, Diners, Visa*
Price category: *£££-££££*
Special rates: *Children in parents' room: cots £5, under 8 half price, over 8 20% off*

PORT APPIN
The Airds Hotel
Port Appin, Appin, Argyll PA38 4DF   *Tel: (063 173) 236*

An old ferry inn, dating from around 1700, in completely tranquil surroundings overlooking Loch Linnhe, the mountains of Morvern and the island of Lismore. Rooms throughout are slightly old-fashioned, but simple and comfortable; there are log fires and books in the sitting rooms, and watercolours on the walls. A residents' cocktail bar has replaced the old public bar. Bedrooms with loch views are slightly smaller than those overlooking the trees at the back. Food consists of the best quality local and Scottish produce with home-grown vegetables and a splendid wine list to complement it. Service is fairly formal and there is, mercifully, no background music to detract from the enjoyment of a summer sunset over the loch. There are landscaped lawns leading down to the loch.

Location: *2 miles off the A828 from sign at Port Appin*
Bedrooms: *14 (single, double and twin), all with bath, plus 2 in annexe, both with shower. Direct dial telephone, TV. Hairdryer on request*
Facilities: *Parking*
Restrictions: *No children under 5. No smoking in dining room. Dogs by prior arrangement only*
Open: *Mid Mar to mid Nov*
Credit/charge cards accepted: *None*
Price category: *£££-££££*
Special rates: *Children in parents' room £15*

STRACHUR
The Creggans Inn
Strachur, Argyll PA27 8BX   *Tel: (0369 86) 279*

An old Highland droving inn where the motto is 'Good Food and a Warm Welcome', the Creggans is owned by the family of that redoubtable traveller Sir Fitzroy Maclean, and Lady Maclean, author of several cookbooks. Its position, directly opposite Loch Fyne, is far enough back from the road to be quiet. There are two attractive bars with log fires and a more formal (but feminine) dining room where Scottish produce is soundly cooked and attractively presented. Upstairs, there are pretty bedrooms with a cottagey atmosphere – each differently decorated, most with bright bathrooms – and a pleasant residents' sitting room. Room service is preferred to 'teamaking clutter' in the bedrooms. Lady Maclean will organise archaeological and garden tours and visits to stately homes and private collections, and there are specially printed leaflets about local attractions including a private woodland walk. This Highland hospitality is not cheap, but it does make for a very relaxing break.

Location: *On A815, 19 miles west of Arrochar (and 19 miles north of Dunoon)*
Bedrooms: *22 (single, double and twin), 18 with bath. Direct dial telephone. Hairdryer and TV on request*
Facilities: *Parking. Darts, pool. Boating, fishing*

Restrictions: *Dogs at the discretion of management only*
Open: *All year*
Credit/charge cards accepted: *Access, Amex, Diners, Visa*
Price category: £££
Special rates: *3 nights or more DB&B from £46 (£47) pp per night. Children under 12 half price; £8 sharing parents' room*

TARBERT
Stonefield Castle
Tarbert, Loch Fyne, Argyll PA29 6YJ   *Tel: (088 02) 836*

A 19th-century castle, complete with fairy-tale turrets, in fine wooded grounds high above Loch Fyne. Although the interior retains many original features – ornate plaster ceilings, Campbell family portraits, marble mantelpieces and armorial mirrors – much of the decoration and furnishing has been rather heavy-handed. The dining room and about half of the bedrooms are in modern extensions. Surprisingly, Stonefield Castle is more suitable for the gregarious and active than for those who value the peaceful country house life style. It is a good hotel for families; in addition to the usual attractions of fishing and boating, there is a heated outdoor swimming pool, a childrens' games room and, for older children and parents, watersports instruction, a sauna and solarium. Rates for families are competitive.

Location: *Off A83, 12 miles south of Lochgilphead*
Bedrooms: *33 (single, double, twin and family), all with bath or shower. Direct dial telephone, TV and teamaking. Hairdryer on request*
Facilities: *Parking, helicopter landing facilities, moorings, lift. Gym, sauna, solarium. Archery. Games room. Hairdresser. Pool, snooker, table tennis. Swimming pool, tennis, putting. Children's playground. Babylistening*
Restrictions: *No smoking in dining room*
Open: *All year*
Credit/charge cards accepted: *Access, Amex, Diners, Visa*
Price category: ££
Special rates: *May to mid July, 2 or 3 nights DB&B £42 pp per night; special packages for Easter, Christmas and New Year. Children in parents' room: under 5 free, 5-11 £8*

The Cornish coast

- Over 250 miles of coastline, including some of the most spectacular beaches in Britain. See Land's End, swim or go surfing, follow the Cornish Coastal Path
- All the inland sights are within easy reach of the coast: mainly houses and – particularly – gardens with sub-tropical plants
- Plenty to offer for an active break: watersports, pony trekking, golfing and, most of all, walking
- A long way from just about everywhere. Ideal for a long weekend but avoid Bank Holidays and peak holiday periods. The mild climate makes Cornwall a good choice for spring or autumn breaks

The Cornish coast is an area of coves and cliffs, quaint old ports with steep narrow streets and busy harbours, sheltered bays and deep wooded creeks; all but a few stretches have been defined by the Countryside Commission as Heritage Coast and are protected from further development. Behind is gently rolling farmland and country lanes with high hedgerows; at the heart of the widest part the rough expanse of Bodmin moor. The north coast is in parts dramatic, windswept and barren – but many prefer it to the softer and more varied charms of the south.

Tourism has taken over from the more hazardous local occupations of wrecking and smuggling or, more recently, mining copper, tin or china clay. Fishing villages have become seaside resorts, and sites connected with the tin-mining, slate and china clay industries have become attractions in themselves. Abandoned tin mines are a feature of the coast. Visitors are still to an extent foreigners; Cornish people have a deep-rooted sense of their isolation.

The North coast

An area of rugged cliffs and headlands and fine sandy beaches, ideal for bracing walks or surfing. Highlights include Tintagel Head, Pentire Point, Gurnards Head, Pendeen Watch and the dramatic promontory of Godrevy Head, famous for its lighthouse set on an island. There are a number of purpose-built resorts and some uninspiring development inland.

Bude is a predominantly Victorian town with a compact, touristy centre and sandy beaches: a good place for a seaside holiday. **Boscastle** is divided: the upper part has beautiful 14th-century houses, the popular lower part surrounds the narrow harbour, reached through a rocky inlet. At **Tintagel** the legend of King Arthur is heavily exploited; the castle is marvellously set on cliffs. **Port Isaac** is a tiny fishing village, unspoilt and picturesque despite its popularity, with narrow, sometimes perilously steep streets. **Polzeath** is a residential resort around a fine surfing bay; just inland is the pretty village of **Trebetherick**, convenient for a splendid beach at Daymer Bay. **Rock** is principally a sailing community. **Wadebridge** is a busy place with a country town atmosphere, plagued with summer traffic jams. **Padstow** is a lively fishing town with cottages around the harbour on the Camel estuary. **Newquay** and **Perranporth** are holiday resorts and **St Agnes** has been much developed. **St Ives** is a cheerful resort and a famous artists' colony, now over-commercialised in parts and very crowded in summer. The old harbour retains some charm.

Hayle Bay and all the major north coast resorts – Bude, Newquay, Perranporth and St Ives – have large sandy beaches. In attractive settings are **Bossiney Haven**, **Trebarwith Strand**, **Mother Ivy's Bay** and **Chapel Porth**; positively striking are **Crackington Haven** (curious rock formations at low tide), **The Strangles** (steep climb, sand at low tide) and **Trevellas Porth** and **Trevaunance Cove** (with remains of ancient tin mines nearby). Watch out for strong currents.

HISTORIC BUILDINGS AND GARDENS

Newquay, Trerice   An Elizabethan manor dating from 1572, with Minstrels' Gallery and fine decorative plasterwork and antique furniture. [*Open April to Oct, daily*]

Tintagel Castle   Medieval castle ruins in a spectacular setting, famous for associations with Arthurian legend; paths lead to a shingle beach and to Merlin's Cave. [*Open all year, daily except Christmas and New Year*]

Washaway, Pencarrow   A Georgian mansion with fine collections of paintings and furniture and a lovely setting of formal Italian gardens backed by woodland. [*Open Easter to Oct; gardens daily; house pm Sun to Thurs*]

MUSEUMS

St Ives, Barbara Hepworth Museum   The artist's house, studio and sculpture garden. [*Open all year, Mon to Sat, plus Sun pm July and Aug*]

Industrial Archaeology

Bude Canal is a 19th-century canal abandoned in favour of the railway, but still navigable and in use for recreation. There is a museum and demonstrations at **Delabole Slate Quarry**.

Family Outings

There are tropical bird gardens and a butterfly exhibition at Padstow. Newquay has a leisure park, zoo and Disneyworld-type attractions ('Tunnels through Time'). Holywell Bay, St Newlyn East and St Agnes have leisure parks, and the Lappa Valley steam railway is also at St Newlyn East. Inland at Goonhavern is 'The World in Miniature'; at Lelant (near St Ives) a theme park called 'Merlin's Magic Land' and a model village. Paradise Park at Hayle is a conservation theme park with an otter sanctuary, endangered birds, a farm and a railway.

Land's End and the Lizard

The south-west tips of Cornwall stretch out like pincers into the Atlantic and the English Channel, with attractive rocky coves and magnificent headlands. The Land's End peninsula is Cornwall's most well-trodden area. The Lizard peninsula is a desolate, virtually treeless plateau of ancient serpentine rocks, with dramatic coves at Kynance, Mullion and Housel Bay. Inland are the Goonhilly Downs, memorable for the huge saucer aerials of the satellite station, and evidence of Cornwall's earliest habitation: a remarkable Iron Age village (Chysauster), stone circles (the Merry Maidens) and Lanyon Quoit. By contrast, the picturesque Helford river, with several pretty villages and wooded creeks, provides sheltered anchorage for sailing boats.

Land's End itself is a real tourist trap. **Mousehole** is quaint and typically Cornish, though very crowded in summer. **Penzance**, fashionable as a watering place in the 19th century, retains some gracious buildings away from the seafront; neighbouring **Marazion** commands romantic views of St Michael's Mount. **Helston** is a fine market town. There are no real resorts here – just photogenic little villages like **Mullion** and **Cadgwith**. **Helford** is a pretty little town on the estuary.

Whitesand Bay is probably the best of the sandy beaches around Land's End. **Mullion Cove** has small patches of sand surrounded by rugged rocky scenery; **Kynance Cove** has spectacular rock formations and enchanting sandy beaches at low tide.

HISTORIC BUILDINGS AND GARDENS

Marazion, St Michael's Mount An offshore-island castle reached by causeway at low tide, or ferry. Some rooms and the chapel can be visited. (NT) [*Guided tours all year: April and May, Mon, Tues, Wed, Fri; June to Oct, Mon to Fri; Nov to Mar, Mon, Wed, Fri*]

nr Penzance, Trengwainton Garden A large garden of shrubs and woodland with walled gardens containing rare sub-tropical plants. [*Open Mar to Oct, Wed to Sat and Bank Hol Mons*]

MUSEUMS

Penzance, Penlee House Museum of local archaeology and history with some paintings of the Newlyn School. [*Open all year, daily except Sat pm and Sun*]

Zennor, The Wayside Museum A small private museum devoted to life in the area since ancient times. [*Open April to Oct, daily*]

INDUSTRIAL ARCHAEOLOGY

Helston, Poldark Mine An ancient tin mine, last worked in 1810, parts of which have been excavated and turned into a tourist attraction. There are several well-marked routes of varying degrees of difficulty, none very long. The journey through the mine ends in a nicely stocked little museum with an extensive collection of steam engines. Outside are more steam engines and a small amusement park. [*Open Apr to Oct, daily*]

Pendeen, Geevor Tin Mines A working tin mine; guided tours of the treatment plant and video showing surface and underground activities. Unique Cornish Mining Museum. [*Open April to Oct daily; tours Mon to Fri*]

FAMILY OUTINGS

Helston, Flambards Triple Theme Park A leisure park incorporating a display of vintage aircraft, a 'Britain in the Blitz' display and a mock Victorian village, plus some vertiginous rides. [*Open April to Oct daily*]

Near Helston you can visit the **Goonhilly Satellite Earth Station**, and the **Seal Sanctuary** at Gweek. On the cliffs at Porthcurno is the **Minack Theatre**, a Greek-style open-air theatre with summer performances.

The South coast

The south coast consists of rocky coves and pretty fishing villages, with some lovely scenery around the river estuaries. The beaches are good for windsurfing.

Falmouth is a major port and resort. Inland and up-river is **Truro**, Cornwall's cathedral city and a good off-season base for touring. **St-Just-in-Roseland** lives up to its magical name, with a church surrounded by exotic vegetation overlooking a creek. **St Mawes** is a charming and well-kept sailing centre on the river Fal. **Mevagissey**, a former smuggling centre, is commercialised and **St Austell** is a busy town with an important china clay industry. **Fowey**, set on one of Cornwall's most beautiful estuaries, has steep, winding narrow streets: ocean-going ships bearing china clay give an authentic feel of its colourful seafaring history. **Polruan** and **Bodinnick** are attractive little resorts, less crowded than **Polperro**, a honey-pot for tourists, where steep narrow cobbled streets lead to a pretty cluster of cottages around the harbour. **Looe** is divided by a deep estuary; East Looe is more quaint and picturesque than West Looe. **Cawsand** and **Kingsand** are fishing villages whose tiny streets get very congested.

There are large sandy beaches at **Towan** and **Pendower** (Gerrans Bay), and peaceful ones at **Lantic** and **Lantivet** Bays. Also attractive are **Hemmick**, **Bow** (Vault Beach), **Porthcurnick** and **Porthluney**. At **Talland Bay** there are unusual pink and green rocks, rock-pools and sand at low tide.

HISTORIC BUILDINGS AND GARDENS

nr Bodmin, Lanhydrock A 17th-century mansion, largely rebuilt after a fire in 1881, but with surviving Long Gallery and fine gardens (NT).[*Open April to Oct, daily*]

Feock, Trelissick Garden Beautiful gardens overlooking the estuary of the River Fal, famous for its rhododendrons and tender plants. [*Open Mar to Oct, Mon to Sat, and Sun pm*]

Mawnan Smith, Glendurgan Garden Sheltered valley garden with exotic plants, a maze and a Giant's Stride. [*Open Mar to Oct, Mon, Wed and Fri, except Good Fri*]

Between Truro and St Austell, Trewithin A fine collection of rare trees and shrubs and extensive woodland gardens surrounded by traditional parkland. [*Open Mar to Sep, Mon to Sat. Guided tours of house April to June, pm Mon and Tues*]

MUSEUMS

There is a motor museum at St Stephen, near St Austell; and at **Wheal Martyn** the history of Cornwall's china clay industry is displayed, including views over modern clay pits and an adventure trail for children. [*Open April to Oct, daily*] **Paul Corin's Music Museum** near Liskeard offers street organs and the Mighty Wurlitzer among its 'Magnificent Music Machines'; [*open Easter, then May to Sep, daily*]

FAMILY OUTINGS
Dobwalls Theme Park near Liskeard includes a miniature forest railway and a collection of paintings by Thorburn. Killiow Country Park lies between Falmouth and Truro. There is a monkey sanctuary near Looe, and a model railway at Mevagissey; both resorts offer shark fishing trips.

Walking

Since only relatively few points on the coast are accessible by car, the coast path is by far the best way of seeing the cliff scenery. The path follows nearly all of Cornwall's long intricate coastline, and is well waymarked and easy to follow. But the switchback nature of it makes much of the route quite tough going.

The most spectacularly rugged sections are on the north coast from Treen (just east of Land's End) to St Ives; added interest is provided by some eye-catching remains of the tin-mining industry, while close inland are desolate, windswept areas of moorland containing some remarkable archaeological remains such as Chun Castle. A striking feature of the Cornish coast is the presence of rias, or drowned river valleys-cum-estuaries: some of the finest, giving easy walking, are the Looe Rivers, the Fowey Estuary (where two frequent ferry services can be used as part of a pleasant round walk around it), the Helford River and the Camel Estuary near Padstow. Most retain much beauty, in spite of substantial holiday development. The Camel Trail follows the track of the old London and South Western Railway Line from Bodmin to Padstow.

The county's highest cliffs are near Boscastle, where scope for satisfying round walks is provided by the proximity of some secluded valleys close to the coast. Sadly, many inland Cornish paths, particularly in the west of the county, are poorly maintained: we found a high proportion unsignposted, overgrown or blocked – this can make it difficult to devise your own round walks based on a section of the coast path.

See *Holiday Which? Good Walks Guide* walks 2-10.

When to go

The comparatively mild climate of Cornwall makes it a good place for an early spring or late autumn break. Most hotels are closed in mid-winter.

The Minack Theatre summer festival runs from the end of May until mid-September. Local events include a number of music festivals and the traditional Furry Dance, a spring festival dance around the streets of Helston in May.

Information

Cornwall Tourist Board, County Hall, Truro, Cornwall TR1 1BR; tel: (0872) 41313; West Country Tourist Board, Trinity Court, 37 Southernhay East, Exeter EX1 1QS; tel: (0392) 76351.

For box office enquiries at the Minack Theatre, tel: St Buryan 471.

Where to stay

Accommodation is mostly in simple pubs or traditional seaside hotels and guesthouses, some with good facilities for family holidays. We have recommended those most appealing or suitable for a short stay. Our choice also includes the rarer comfortable country house hotels or restaurants with rooms, usually more personal and smaller. The majority of coastal hotels are closed in January and February and many from November until March. Tariffs often have seasonal variations, with the highest prices in July and August.

BODINNICK-BY-FOWEY
Old Ferry Inn
Bodinnick-by-Fowey, Cornwall PL23 1LX   *Tel: (072 687) 237*

This inn is a marriage of pub and hotel, set on an estuary by the ferry landing. The old part – some 400 years old – combines well with later additions; it has many levels and steps and some low ceilings. There's an elegant panelled dining room with lots of old oil paintings providing a grander touch: a pleasing, rather harum-scarum room, where it doesn't matter that the cutlery doesn't match. Neither tatty nor 'designer', it is just a little nicely run-down. The bar with stone floor and battered furniture is truly a Cornish village pub decorated with oars, old photographs and sailing and fishing things. In the newer part and opening on to a suntrap terrace is the large comfortable lounge with a wooden floor, chintzy fabrics and lots of old sofas and chairs, some antiques and a stone fireplace. In the newer bedrooms, the brocade drapery of the older rooms gives way to simple furnishing, white walls and cotton curtains, but they are pleasant and light. A relaxing and informal place with a welcoming pub atmosphere where the lack of gloss could be well appreciated.

Bedrooms: *13 (single, double, twin, family), 1 with four-poster, 6 with bath. TV in some rooms*
Facilities: *Parking*

Restrictions: *No dogs in public rooms*
Open: *Mar to Oct for DB&B; B&B available at other times during winter*
Credit/charge cards accepted: *Visa*
Price category: ££
Special rates: *Children under 10 half price sharing parents' room*

CRANTOCK
Crantock Bay Hotel
Crantock, Newquay, Cornwall, TR8 5SE   *Tel: (0637) 830229*

A traditional seaside hotel, purpose-built in 1935 and run on guest house
lines. Necessarily double-glazed to keep out the wind, it occupies a
superb position, high up on the coast with views over Crantock Bay, and
is only a few minutes' walk from the beach via a coastal path. All the
public rooms overlook the sea and are comfortably furnished, with
antimacassars and seersucker cloths adding to the genteel air. Bedrooms
are plainly decorated with cotton covers and brightly coloured curtains;
you will need change to operate the television. Although suitable out of
season for retired couples, children are especially welcome and high tea is
provided after a day on the beach or running around on the lawn which
has a recreation area and climbing frame. Guests are encouraged to take
the inclusive terms. Quite straightforward in its comfort and cosiness,
there is a chummy feeling here.

Location: *Approx 2 miles off the A3075 south of Newquay*
Bedrooms: *31 (single, double, twin), all with bath. TV, teamaking. Hairdryer on
request*
Facilities: *Parking. 'Rumpus' room. Tennis, putting, croquet. Table-tennis.
Adventure playground. Babylistening*
Restrictions: *No smoking in the dining room. No dogs in public rooms*
Open: *Easter (or 1st April) to Oct*
Credit/charge cards accepted: *Access, Amex, Diners, Visa*
Price category: £
Special rates: *Spring and Oct, 3 nights DB&B £18.50 pp per night. Further
reductions for 4 and 5 nights. Children in parents' room, reductions of
33%-75%, depending on age*

HELFORD
Riverside
Helford, Helston, Cornwall   *Tel: (032 623) 443*

An enchanting whitewashed cottage or three in this delightful village at
the head of creek on the Helford River estuary. Run as a restaurant with
rooms, the latter (many with their own front door) are comfortably if
simply furnished with cotton fabrics and modern pine furniture.
Magazines and a choice of tea (leaves, not bags) are unusual touches. The
low-ceilinged dining room has white painted walls, cheerful yellow cloths
and Windsor chairs and there is an air of reverence for the food. There is
also a small cottage-style sitting room upstairs and outside is an
immaculately kept terraced and sloping cottage garden. Not cheap, but a
very charming spot indeed.

Bedrooms: *7 (double, twin and 1 family room), 3 in the main house, all with bath. TV, teamaking*
Facilities: *Parking*
Restrictions: *No dogs*
Open: *Mid Mar to Oct*
Credit/charge cards accepted: *None*
Price category: *££££*

PENZANCE
The Abbey

Abbey Street, Penzance, Cornwall, TR18 4AR   *Tel: (0736) 66906*

An enchanting house, beautifully and idiosyncratically decorated and positively bursting with 'private house' atmosphere. Situated in the winding streets overlooking the harbour, it is painted sky blue with pretty Gothic windows; at the back is a small, secluded walled garden. Off the wide and welcoming entrance hall is the dining room with white painted panelling, separate antique tables and Victorian toys as decoration. The thoroughly comfortable first-floor drawing room with open fire has an enjoyable miscellany of things and styles – old-fashioned sofas, pale chintz, paisleys, bookcases and a stereo. Guests help themselves to drinks. The first-floor bedrooms are more spacious than the others but all are decorated with the same flair – a studied informal elegance with lots of antique furniture, pictures, books, magazines and patchwork quilts. An unusual and delightful place to stay.

Bedrooms: *6 (double, twin), all with bath/shower. TV, teamaking*
Facilities: *Parking*
Restrictions: *No dogs except by prior arrangement. No children under 5*
Open: *Mar to Dec*
Credit/charge cards accepted: *None*
Price category: *££-£££*
Special rates: *2 nights, 10% discount. Children £10.00 in parents' room*

Nr PORT ISAAC
Port Gaverne Hotel

Nr Port Isaac, Cornwall, PL29 3SQ   *Tel: (0208) 880244*

Just east of Port Isaac at the mouth of a cove is this old white-painted building, originally cottages, with five bedrooms added in 1977 in a modern extension and more cottages across the lane recently renovated for self-catering. It combines successfully an atmosphere of country hotel and pub; various bars and seating areas downstairs include a tiny cabin room with diorama view of the cove. Eat good food in the more traditional hotel dining room or simply have supper in the bar area, and afterwards take the sea air or read in the Victorian sitting room upstairs. The newer bedrooms are plainly decorated, while the older rooms are more charming with Laura Ashley papers and fabrics. It's generally unfussy and cosy with inoffensive modernisation.

Location: *East of Port Isaac about 2 miles off the B3314*
Bedrooms: *19 (single, double, twin, family), 5 in extension, all with bath. Direct*

dial telephone, TV
Facilities: *Parking*
Open: *End Feb to mid Jan*
Credit/charge cards accepted: *Access, Amex, Diners, Visa*
Price category: ££
Special rates: *Autumn and spring, 2 or more nights DB&B £30-£32 pp per night. Summer, 3 nights DB&B, £33-£37 pp per night. Children up to 2 years, 15% of adult rate in parents' room; 2 to 12 years half price in parents' room; over 12, 75% of adult rate*

Nr ST AUSTELL
Boscundle Manor
Tregreham, St Austell, Cornwall, PL25 3RL   *Tel: (072 681) 3557*

Dating from the 18th century, this charming house is built of local pink stone and is set in 12 acres of beautifully landscaped, terraced gardens. Billed as a restaurant with rooms and run as a private house it makes a satisfactory departure from the traditional hotel. Bedrooms (some with sofa beds) are individually furnished – some with cane and wicker, others (more expensive) with antiques and mahogany. The drawing room is an open area off the entrance hall with a fireplace, painted panelling and antique furniture. The dining room has a friendly Victorian feel – antiques include a large oak dresser. The bar with skylight ceiling has a wood burning stove and lots of books, and the recent addition of a conservatory provides a sunny spot for breakfast. Known for its good food and boasting an extensive wine list, the Manor probably appeals to couples wishing to get away from the children.

Location: *Off the A390, two miles east of St Austell*
Bedrooms: *11 (single, double, twin), 2 in cottage annexe, all with bath, 1 with jacuzzi, 4 with spa bath. Direct dial telephone, TV*
Facilities: *Parking. Exercise room. Swimming pool, croquet. Babylistening*
Restrictions: *No dogs in public rooms or off a lead in the grounds*
Open: *Mar to Oct*
Credit/charge cards accepted: *Access, Amex, Visa*
Price category: £££

ST IVES
Garrack Hotel
Burthallan Lane, St Ives, Cornwall   *Tel: (0736) 796199*

Make sure you have clear directions to reach this quiet hotel overlooking St Ives bay. The granite, creeper-covered house was built in 1923 and has been added to and extended to provide 20 bedrooms and a leisure centre. The bedrooms in the main house are the more appealing, furnished with bits and pieces of old furniture, but the newer rooms are spacious and well-designed with built-in-furniture. A small decanter of mead welcomes new arrivals. Books and games are available in one of the comfortable lounges with open fireplaces. The dining room serves a wide choice of food and there's a fixed-price mark-up on all wines (so pricier wines may be good value). The garden provides most of the vegetables for the hotel but is slightly taken over by the leisure centre. This timber construction houses a good range of facilities – including a coffee shop serving snacks all day – and compensates for the fact that there is no beach within walking distance.

Location: *5 to 10 minutes' walk from the centre of St Ives*
Bedrooms: *20 (single, double, twin, family), 14 with bath. Direct dial telephone. TV and hairdryer on request*
Facilities: *Parking. Leisure centre with indoor pool, sunbed, sauna, coffee shop, laundrette, shop. Babylistening*
Restrictions: *No dogs except by prior arrangement and not in public rooms. Children under 3 not encouraged in dining room*
Open: *All year*
Credit/charge cards accepted: *Access, Amex, Dinners, Visa*
Price category: ££
Special rates: *Weekends Jan 2-May 31 and Sept 24-Dec 22 (excluding bank hols) DB&B £26 pp per night. Children in parents' room (including high tea): 1½ to 5 years £8.65, 6 to 10 years £11.50 (£19.55 including dinner); over 10 years £23*

ST MAWES
Hotel Tresanton

Lower Castle Road, St Mawes, Cornwall   *Tel: (0326) 270544*

Set in terraced gardens, this pair of whitewashed buildings is far from the typical seaside hotel. The atmosphere is respectable and old-fashioned (in the sense of a bygone era) while modern comforts can be readily laid on. The spacious bedrooms, all with a view of the sea, are supplied with lots of books and magazines and even a torch. They have chintzy or damask fabrics and a mixture of antique and good reproduction furniture. The bar and adjacent dining rooms are a little more modern in style but one is soon back to the "Old Vicarage" comfort in the drawing room with its open fire and deep sofas and chairs. This quiet village is best known for its sailing and the nearest beach is rather pebbly.

Bedrooms: *21 (single, double, twin, suite), 2 in reception building, 1 suite. All with bath (private, but not many en suite). Direct dial telephone, TV in suite and on request, hairdryer on request*
Facilities: *Parking*
Restrictions: *No dogs except by prior arangement. No children under 10*
Open: *Mar to Oct, plus Christmas and New Year*
Credit/charge cards accepted: *Access, Amex, Dinners, Visa*
Price category: £££
Special rates: *March-Easter, Easter-April, Oct, 3 nights DB&B £41.70-£49.20 (£40 single) pp per night*

TALLAND-BY-LOOE
Talland Bay Hotel

Talland-by-Looe, Cornwall   *Tel: (0503) 72667*

A country house seaside hotel set high above the sea in open farmland yet five minutes' walk down to Talland Bay. The attractive low-built house, dating from the 16th century, is painted white with black shutters. The public rooms overlook the terraced garden and swimming pool and have the old-fashioned atmosphere and solid comfort of a country house. Bedrooms vary a bit, some more recently decorated than others, but all are quiet and bright and comfortably furnished and quite spacious. Guests are provided with magazines and a whole bottle of Badedas. It probably appeals to people seeking a fine and peaceful location with lovely gardens and good, old-fashioned comfort, but do not discount it as a good place for a family holiday. In low season, the owners run special-interest breaks (bird-watching, painting, bridge).

Location: *Off the A387 between West Looe and Polperro*
Bedrooms: *23 (single, double, twin), 6 in three cottages, 1 with four-poster, 21 with bath. Direct dial telephone, TV, hairdryer*
Facilties: *Parking. Games room, darts, table tennis. Sauna, solarium. Heated outdoor swimming pool. Putting, croquet. Babylistening*
Restrictions: *No dogs except by prior arrangement. No children under 5 in the dining room during dinner*
Open: *Mid Feb to Nov, plus last two weeks in Dec*
Credit/charge cards accepted: *Access, Amex, Dinners, Visa*
Price category: *££*
Special rates: *Winter, spring and autumn, 2 or more nights DB&B £31-£32.50 pp per night. Children sharing parents' room free (except July and August, £8)*

Nr TINTAGEL
Trebarwith Strand Hotel
Nr Tintagel, Cornwall, PL34 OHB   *Tel: (0840) 770326*

Drive to the very end of a Cornish lane and find this endearingly informal hotel situated a matter of yards from the sea, with the coastal path rising steeply to either side. It's owned and run by two couples, who clearly love it and encourage you to do the same without standing on ceremony. The hotel is an amalgam of different styles – part cottage, part Victorian house. The bistro-style restaurant has pew seating, bare floorboards, a large fireplace and the menu written on a blackboard. There is access to a small terrace through sliding glass doors from the cosy first-floor lounge, with brown corduroy furnishings, lots of paperbacks, and oil paintings for sale. Bedrooms are plain and quite simple, with contrasting wallpapers. A good base on the coast for walking and coming back to cream teas or big suppers in a friendly, lived-in and young atmosphere.

Location: *Approximately 5 miles off the A39, 2 miles south of Tintagel*
Bedrooms: *10 (double and family), 7 with bath. Teamaking. Hairdryer on request*
Facilities: *TV in lounge*
Restrictions: *No dogs in public rooms. No smoking in restaurant*
Open: *2 weeks before Easter to end of Oct*
Credit/charge cards accepted: *Access, Visa*
Price category: *£*
Special rates: *Outside school holidays, 10% discount. Winter (not school hols), 3 nights B&B £9.75 pp per night. Children under 3 free (guests provide linen), under 9 £6.00, 10 and over £18.00*

TREGONY
Tregony House
Fore Street, Tregony, Truro, Cornwall TR2 5RN   *Tel: (087 253) 671*

This plain village house is about five or six miles inland, on a fairly busy road; there's double-glazing, so it's quiet inside. A cosy cottage atmosphere abounds and bedrooms are simple, light, bright and clean with a mixture of furniture, mostly antique, and electric heaters. Up the back stairs over the kitchen is a dear little 'suite' with Laura Ashley fabrics and pine furniture. The comfortable sitting room has books and china displayed in alcoves. Straightforward set menus are served in the low-ceilinged, simply furnished dining room; the 'bar' is homely. There is an enchanting long and thin cottage garden at the back with fruit trees and herbs. The sunny personality of Mrs Martin adds to the warmth of this friendly and unpretentious guest house.

Bedrooms: *6 (single, double, twin, suite), 2 with bath. TV in suite*
Facilities: *Parking*
Restrictions: *No dogs. No children under 7. No smoking in dining room*
Open: *Mar to Oct*
Credit/charge cards accepted: *None*
Price category: *£*
Special rates: *Children 7-12, in the suite, half price*

WIDEGATES
Coombe Farm
Widegates, Nr Looe, Cornwall PL13 1QN   *Tel: (05034) 223*

This is a popular guest house set just below the brow of a slope, half an hour's walk from the sea. The red brick house, built in 1927, is set in 10 ½ acres of rough gardens – mostly grass and paddocks, with domestic animals roaming around; there's a heated swimming pool and a pond. Although there are no en suite bathrooms, bedrooms are mostly extremely spacious (there is a family room for five that avoids any feeling of 'battery guests') with duvets and matching curtains; all are cosy, homely and very clean. The large dining room (Windsor chairs) spills over into a seating area where guests help themselves to drinks. Dinner, served at around 7 or 7.30pm, consists of a 4-course, no-choice meal. The informal sitting room has a stone fireplace and some nice antiques. The games room, heated by a wood burning stove, is a proper playroom and not merely a gesture. Catering principally for families, Widegates is run on house party lines and even the normally reserved could find this irresistible.

Location: *On the B3253, approx 3 ½ miles north-east of Looe*
Bedrooms: *8 (double, twin, family)*
Facilities: *Parking. Games room, snooker, table tennis. Swimming pool, croquet*
Restrictions: *No dogs. No children under 5*
Credit/charge cards accepted: *None*
Price category: *£*
Special rates: *2 nights DB&B £19-£24.50 pp per night. Children 5-14 in parents' room 25% discount*

The Northumbrian coast

- Remote, unspoilt and sparsely populated. A good place to unwind and get away from it all
- Superb sandy beaches with few crowds, beach huts or ice cream kiosks – but expect brisk well wrapped-up walks rather than sunbathing or swimming
- Good for families. Plenty of history and sightseeing (castles). But don't expect any organised entertainment
- Excursions to the Northumberland National Park and the Farne islands for the walker or naturalist; lots for keen sailors, golfers or fishermen too
- No really appealing hotels on the coast, and only a limited selection inland

The northern two-thirds of the Northumbrian coast has been designated a Heritage Coast and Area of Outstanding Natural Beauty, and it is easy to see why. There are magnificent beaches of fine, pale sand with dunes – and a minimum of modern development (the A1 runs well inland); although the coast is generally flat, it is varied and full of interest, even dramatic in places; and it's something of a paradise for the keen ornithologist. Between the coast and the Cheviot Hills the countryside is green and gently rolling with sleepy villages, farms and a network of narrow rural lanes. Yet in this peaceful landscape stand impressive medieval castles – or their ruins – testifying to the turbulent history of the border with Scotland.

There are two interesting old towns and some pretty villages on or near the coast. **Berwick-upon-Tweed** is a fine, if rather dour, grey stone market town at the mouth of the river, with a dwindling salmon-fishing industry and a definite tang of the sea. You can walk round the splendidly preserved Elizabethan town walls for excellent views of the river and its three bridges. Inland and to the south is **Alnwick**, a walled market town with some fine churches and Georgian houses and a huge castle overlooking the lush rolling countryside.

Two model 19th-century villages, **Ford** and **Etal**, are worth a visit; both have several interesting crafts shops and Ford has a working cornmill and Lady Waterford Hall (see 'museums'). **Bamburgh**, which has stone cottages clustered around a village green, and **Warkworth**, an attractive and dignified place on a horseshoe bend of the meandering river Coquet, are dominated by their massive castles. In the tiny fishing village of **Craster** you can still see kippers being smoked in the traditional way, on tenterhooks over oak shavings. The unspoilt little resort of **Alnmouth**, a popular sailing and golf centre, also has some charm. **Seahouses** is a typical, traditional holiday resort, with a boat service to the **Farne Islands**. **Lindisfarne** or **Holy Island**, famous as the birthplace of Christianity in Britain, can be visited by a causeway from Beal at low tide; the main village is rather commercialised.

The beaches betwen Bamburgh and Beadnell are easiest to reach, but by walking a little way you can find beautiful deserted beaches. Alnmouth also has splendid beaches of firm sand which are not crowded. Around Berwick and Craster the coast is rockier and between the mainland and Holy Island the sand is muddy. In places, tides and currents can make swimming dangerous.

CASTLES

Alnwick   The seat of the Dukes of Northumberland, though much restored, is the most impressive of the castles. The immensely grand interior contains fine French furniture and paintings by Titian, Canaletto and Van Dyck. Two vast Meissen dinner services are displayed in the opulent dining room. [*Open May to Sep, pm daily, except Sats unless a Bank Hol weekend*]

Bamburgh   A massive fortress with splendid ramparts looking out to sea and the islands. Most of the rooms are 19th-century 'medieval' and there is a collection of armour in the King's Hall. [*Open Easter to Oct, pm daily*]

Chillingham   A 12th-century border stronghold only recently opened to the public. Rooms contain tapestries, arms and armour and are still medieval in character. The grounds include a formal topiary garden, woodland walks and a lake, and the park is famous for the unique herd of wild white cattle. [*Open May to Sept, pm daily except Tues; grounds also pm, weekends, April and Oct*]

Lindisfarne   Perched dramatically on an abrupt conical hill, Lindisfarne is on a much more domestic scale than Alnwick or Bamburgh; in 1902 it was imaginatively recreated by Sir Edwin Lutyens as a private residence. (NT) [*Open Apr to Sep, daily except Fri; plus Good Fri, and weekends Oct*]

There are several ruined castles: **Norham**, above the river Tweed, and **Warkworth**, both have magnificent keeps. The most atmospheric ruin is the majestic **Dunstanburgh**, in a romantic position on a lonely crag by the sea (well worth the 1½ mile walk from Craster).

Other historic buildings include the evocative remains of the

Benedictine **Lindisfarne Priory**, with fine Norman decoration; and **Brinkburn Priory**, in a lovely wooded setting near Rothbury. **Preston Tower** is a good example of a medieval pele tower, with walls seven feet thick. And at Beadnell there are several 18th-century lime kilns.

MUSEUMS
Berwick Borough Museum and Art Gallery   The town museum contains some treasures endowed from the famous Burrell collection of paintings and decorative arts. [*Open all year, daily except Sun and Mon from mid Oct to Easter*]

Other museums of interest in the area are the **Lindisfarne Wine and Spirit Museum** at Berwick and the **Grace Darling Museum** at Bamburgh (items associated with the heroine of the famous Farne Islands sea rescue). At Seahouses there is a Marine Life Centre and **Fishing Museum**; and keen fishermen might enjoy the **House of Hardy Museum** at Alnwick which opened in June 1987. **Lady Waterford Hall** at Ford is an old village school decorated with murals by Louisa, Marchioness of Waterford, the 19th-century amateur watercolourist.

Walking

The Northumberland National Park organises guided walks and trails, many on the coast and many at weekends (see 'Information'). A path runs for 25 miles from Alnmouth to Bamburgh along the finest part of the coast; it's easy-going underfoot, and along the level, but the lonely beauty of the beaches and shores and the ruined castles, birdlife and other features provide constant interest. Unfortunately, immediately inland is completely flat farmland, devoid of interest, so it can be difficult to find good round walks based on the coast path.

The Cheviots feel like hills rather than mountains; by far the most dramatic part is along the top of the Cheviot ridge itself, including the summits of Windy Gyle and The Cheviot. To reach the ridge usually requires several miles of walking from the nearest road – it can be boggy after rain, but the views into Yorkshire, Cumbria and Scotland are superb on a clear day. The Cheviot landscape, chiefly of empty grassy hills, can strongly appeal to those seeking solitude, but others may find it somewhat unvaried. Some 50 miles of the Pennine Way passes through Northumberland (including the Cheviots); some of this, particularly the final sections near the Scottish border, is emphatically for experienced fell-walkers only.

Much less demanding is an excellently preserved 20-mile

stretch of Hadrian's Wall. In summer, a bus service along the parallel main road will help you return to your starting point. The best sections of the Wall are between Housesteads and Carvoran.

Apart from the coast and Hadrian's Wall, there are easy walks in Hulne Park near Alnwick (*open at weekends, and on weekdays with a free permit available from Alnwick Castle*), at Rothbury Terraces, and in the Border Forest Park, where self-guided trails start from Kielder Castle.

See *Holiday Which? Good Walks Guide* walks 142, 143, 144, 145.

Excursions

Farne Islands   A group of about 30 rocky stacks, these islands are famous for their seabirds and colony of grey seals. Trips to the Farne Islands (of which two are open to the public) are available from Seahouses between April and September. A typical trip lasts 2½ hours with an hour on one of the islands.

The best places to watch birds include the mudflats of the **Lindisfarne Nature Reserve** between the coast and Holy Island, and **Coquet island**, an RSPB reserve.

Northumberland National Park   The Park, which stretches from the Cheviots in the north to Hadrian's wall in the south, is within about 20 to 30 miles of most parts of the coast. It consists of remote moorland, forests and valleys with few towns; most of the sightseeing interest is in the south where there are Roman forts along Hadrian's Wall. The Park (whose symbol is the curlew) provides a totally different habitat from the coast and islands, for a wide range of species.

When to go

The main season for visiting the Northumbrian coast is from Easter to October; in winter the castles are shut and there are no boat trips to the islands. As the area is seldom crowded it is a good choice for a weekend break in mid-summer.

The week-long Alnwick fair is held from the last Sunday of June and is a re-enactment of a medieval fair, complete with period costumes: entertainment includes concerts and events for children.

The breeding season on the Farne islands is from mid-May to mid-July; the islands are closed in winter.

Information

The Northumbria Tourist Board, Aykley Heads, Durham City, Co Durham DH1 5UX; tel: 091-384 6905. There are also Tourist Information Centres at Alnwick, Berwick-upon-Tweed and Seahouses.

Northumberland National Park Department, Eastburn, South Park, Hexham, Northumberland NE46 1BS; tel: (0434) 605555

Where to stay

There are some clean and pleasant small guesthouses in Alnmouth and Seahouses, but no hotels within walking distance of the sea that we found appealing enough to spend a long weekend in. However, there are some more expensive country house hotels further inland and reasonable hotels in Alnwick and Bamburgh, both fairly quiet and attractive towns.

ALNWICK
White Swan Hotel
Bondgate Within, Alnwick, Northumberland NE66 1TD   *Tel: (0665) 602 109*

A former coaching inn, dating from the 18th century, the White Swan is just inside the walls of Alnwick and the best bet for a weekend break in this charming market town. It is being upgraded from a traditional hotel to something rather smarter and, at the moment, falls between several stools. Bedrooms are comfortable; all have been redecorated to a similar standard with co-ordinated floral fabrics and wallpapers and smart brass lamps. Bathrooms are quite neat and smart – functional rather than luxurious. Public rooms are in various stages of transformation: the lobby/lounge remains traditional and rather drab; the spruced-up bar (with a fishing theme) lacks charm, while the dining room is elegant if (like the food) rather bland and unimaginative. The most interesting room, the panelled Olympic Room, once the lounge of a ship, is used for functions. There are plans to extend the hotel.

Bedrooms: *41 (single, double, twin and family), all with bath (3 more rooms being added in 1988). TV, teamaking. Hairdryer*
Facilities: *Parking. Babylistening*
Open: *All year*
Credit/charge cards accepted: *Access, Amex, Diners, Visa*
Price category: *££*
Special rates: *Summer, 2 nights DB&B (and one lunch included), £36 pp per night. Children under 14 in parents' room free*

BAMBURGH
Lord Crewe Arms
Bamburgh, Northumberland NE69 7BL   *Tel: (066 84) 243*

An unpretentious old country inn overlooking the tiny village green and the immense castle. Inside there are signs of wear, but a quietly welcoming atmosphere. There are two lounges (one for TV and non-smokers, one a genteel residents' lounge), two bars (one beamed and cosy, the other a public bar with separate street entrance) and two restaurants (one taverna-style, one more traditional). Bedrooms are light and comfortable with vivid curtains and bedcovers. The small walled garden is reserved for residents.

Bedrooms: *25 (single, double, twin and family), 20 with bath/shower. TV, teamaking. Hairdryer on request*
Facilities: *Parking. Non-smoking lounge*
Restrictions: *No children under 5. No dogs in public rooms*
Open: *Easter to early Nov*
Credit/charge cards accepted: *Access, Visa*
Price category: *£-££*
Special rates: *2 nights DB&B £31 (single £34) pp per night. Children under 12 in parents' room £12*

BELFORD
The Blue Bell Hotel
Market Place, Belford, Northumberland NE70 7NE   *Tel: (066 83) 543*

A delightful creeper-covered coaching inn, in a small market town near the A1, with three acres of grounds. The relatively new owners (summer 1987) have been gradually refurbishing the hotel. Rooms are traditional and quite elegant, with a mixture of reproduction and antique furniture, most with views over the lawns and flower beds. Food is freshly prepared ('soup of the moment', 'catch of the day') with some produce from the garden. A tranquil base for visiting the Scottish borders as well as the Northumbrian coast.

Bedrooms: *15 bedrooms (single, double, twin and family), all with bath or shower. Direct dial telephone, TV and teamaking. Hairdryer, trouser press*
Facilities: *Parking. Putting. Non-smoking bedrooms available*
Restrictions: *Dogs at manager's discretion only*
Open: *All year*
Credit/charge cards accepted: *Access, Amex, Diners, Visa*
Price category: *££*
Special rates: *2 nights DB&B £30-£36 pp per night. Children under 12 in parents' room £2 (not breakfast)*

LONGHORSLEY
Linden Hall
Longhorsley, Morpeth, Northumberland NE65 8XG   *Tel: (0670) 516611*

This is a fine Georgian mansion in extensive wooded grounds. Inside, well-proportioned rooms have original plaster ceilings and fireplaces, and good furnishings; there is a gracious, light drawing room. However, the period feel is not always preserved; some of the colour schemes are rather strident and there is custom-built unit furniture in even the deluxe bedrooms. Bathrooms are on the small side, partly due to the problems of en suite conversions, and the 'Deluxe' ones may not be what you might expect. Housekeeping is very good though; there are fresh flower arrangements throughout the house and fruit and chocolates in the bedrooms. There are good facilities (and rates) for children and the hotel supplies specially printed leaflets on what to do in the area and can arrange fishing, riding and golf locally. The adjoining granary has been converted to provide a pub and there is a stable block used for functions.

Bedrooms: *45 (single, double, twin and family), 2 with four-poster beds, all with bath. Direct dial telephone, TV (with video), teamaking. Hairdryer*
Facilities: *Parking, lift. Billiards, table tennis. Sauna, solarium. Tennis, croquet, putting. Clay pigeon shooting. Children's playroom and playground. Babylistening*
Restrictions: *No dogs in public rooms*
Open: *All year*
Credit/charge cards accepted: *Access, Amex, Diners, Visa*
Price category: £££
Special rates: *April to Oct, weekends, 2 nights DB&B £39.50 (£44.50) pp per night; 3 nights £37.50 (£42.50); 4 nights £35.50 (£40.50). Jan, Feb, Mar DB&B £35 pp per night. Honeymoon/luxury breaks £20-£25 per room supplement on weekends. Children under 13 free in parents' room*

POWBURN
Breamish House Hotel
Powburn, Alnwick, Northumberland NE66 4LL　　　　　　*Tel: (066 578) 266*

A Regency hunting lodge turned country house hotel in five acres of gardens at the foot of the Cheviot hills. Public rooms are quite large but rather full of furniture (a mixture of antique and reproduction). Bedrooms are light and pleasant, well-appointed with good quality French style modern furnishings; those at the front are spacious but the doubles at the back are smaller and more cottagey (this part of the house dates from the 17th century). Overall, the atmosphere is rather formal. The Cordon Bleu cooking is very good value and the hotel makes a good base for exploring the border country as well as the coast.

Location: *Off A697 at Powburn*
Bedrooms: *10 (single, double and twin), 8 with bath, 2 with shower. Direct dial telephone, TV, teamaking. Hairdryer*
Facilities: *Parking*
Restrictions: *No children under 12. No smoking in dining room*
Open: *Mid Feb to Dec*
Credit/charge cards accepted: *None*
Price category: ££
Special rates: *Feb to Apr, and mid Oct to Dec, excluding holidays, 2 nights DB&B from £37 pp per night*

The Pembrokeshire Coast

- Superb coastal scenery, ideal for invigorating cliff walks and birdwatching. Plus some of the best beaches in Britain for surfing and sandcastles
- Plenty to do for families: ruined castles and abbeys, wildlife parks and some museums for wet afternoons
- Not ideal for touring by car: too many slow single track roads and few giving more than tantalising glimpses of the sea
- The best bet for accommodation is in local farmhouses, cheap enough to take the family. Otherwise the choice is between simple inns and seaside holiday hotels
- Most of the museums in the area are small and privately run; if the weather is fine, little is lost by not visiting them but they could help while away a wet afternoon
- There are many local small industries which can be visited: woollen mills, dairies, potteries and so on, usually with shops on the premises

The Pembrokeshire coast has been designated a National Park and is the smallest and the most coastal of these protected areas; most of the 180 mile coastline is stunningly beautiful and unspoilt, with dramatic cliffs and magnificent headlands, vast sandy beaches and hidden coves and harbours. It is a paradise for the naturalist, whether amateur or expert.

But the Park does have to cater for large numbers of visitors bent on traditional seaside pleasures, some with caravans. The bleaker north is the quietest area with the strongest Welsh culture and traditions; the more fertile west and south have most of the good sandy beaches.

The North coast

The north is rugged, lonely and usually windswept, its massive cliffs broken by tiny coves and with a hinterland of moors and strange rocky hills. The Park also includes the sweeping heather- and gorse-clad Presely hills, rising to 1,760 feet and characterised by clusters of jagged rocks or 'carns' which add to the prehistoric feel of the landscape. There are also some megalithic tombs (cromlechs) and several standing stones. Here too is the narrow, wooded Gwaun valley. Most of the more interesting and charming towns and villages are near the north coast; they include **Nevern**, with an ancient church and Celtic cross, the Norman village of **Newport** and the tiny hamlet of **Cwm yr Eglwys** with the remains of a 12th-century Celtic church above the beach. Tiny **St David's**, a place of pilgrimage for many hundreds of years, is famous for its cathedral and the dignified ruins of the Bishop's Palace, nestling in a sheltered green valley. The town ('Britain's smallest city') consists of three narrow streets leading away from a triangular green, each lined with small galleries and craft shops.

Most of Pembrokeshire's north coast is rocky but there are good beaches at **Newport Sands** and at **Whitesand Bay,** near St David's (particularly good for surfing). South of St David's there are many sandy beaches: notably the hidden cove at **Caerfai,** and along **St Bride's Bay** – where the main beach is extensive but very exposed, but others (like Nolton Haven) are sheltered and quite pretty. Further south are the more attractive settings of **Marloes Sands** and **Freshwater West.**

HISTORIC BUILDINGS
St David's Cathedral   A very fine 12th-century cathedral built in purplish sandstone, on the site of the early monastery founded by the patron saint of Wales. The tranquil situation, hidden from the town and with the ruined Bishop's Palace as a backdrop, is awe-inspiring. The interior contains elegant fan vaulting and beautifully carved choir stalls. The magnificent **Bishop's Palace** has rich ornamentation on the parapet and the entrance to the Great Hall.

Among the ruins worth seeing are the romantically situated **Cilgerran Castle**, on the river Teifi near Cardigan, and the atmospheric remains of the Benedictine abbey at **St Dogmaels**, founded about 1115 AD.

MUSEUMS AND GALLERIES
At St David's a small two-room gallery is devoted to the recently opened **Whitelaw Collection**, a well-displayed family collection of porcelain and antiques. Nearby, at Whitesands Bay, is the **Lleithyr Farm Museum**, a display of old tractors, carts and so on.

FAMILY OUTINGS
There is a Wildlife Park at Cardigan and a Marine Life Centre at St David's.

The West and South coasts

The west coast has vast sweeping sandy bays and pointed headlands and is popular for family seaside holidays (the odd caravan site is conspicuous) and boat trips to the islands. The south is an area of lush rolling farmland and low, level-topped limestone cliffs eroded by the waves. The NATO training area on the Castlemartin peninsula means that some of the most spectacular coastline is out of bounds, but St Govan's head on the western tip, with a tiny chapel reached by steps, can normally be visited. Inland, the Daugleddau, named after the wide East and West Gleddau rivers, is an area of attractive and peaceful tidal inlets.

South of St David's is **Solva**, in a picturesque inlet with bobbing boats. **Pembroke** consists chiefly of a long one-way main street of old shops and houses, with the massive battlements of the castle at one end. More appealing is the picturesque seaside village of **Manorbier**, with a Norman church and castle overlooking the bay. Nearby Bosherston ponds are a good place for seeing waterbirds and otters. The medieval walled centre of **Tenby** and the Regency esplanade retain some charm in spite of the more than doubled summer population; neighbouring Saundersfoot does not.

The best beaches on the south coast are the deep sandy bay at Manorbier and the town beaches either side of Tenby.

HISTORIC BUILDINGS

Picton Castle   A fine castle-cum-country house, now open to the public for afternoon guided tours. There are extensive grounds with rare trees and plants, and a gallery devoted to Graham Sutherland. [*Open mid July to mid Sep, pm, Sun and Thurs; plus Easter and other Bank Hols*]

Among the ruined castles worth seeing are **Carew Castle**, near Pembroke [*open Easter to Oct, daily except Sat*] and **Manorbier**, a fine shell in a picturesque position overlooking the beach [*open Easter, then daily May to Sep*]. **Pembroke Castle** itself is huge, half-surrounded by a tidal inlet on its rocky promontory at the edge of town; within its walls a fine Norman keep survives [*open all year, daily except Christmas, New Year and Suns Nov to Feb*]. Nearby are the ruins of **Lamphey Palace**, once a country retreat for the medieval clergy.

MUSEUMS

Pembroke offers the **National Museum of Gypsy Caravans** with an exhibition illustrating Romany life [*open Easter to Sep, daily* *except Sat*], and the **Museum of the Home**, a domestic folk museum. **Tenby Museum** covers local heritage and natural history and has a gallery featuring artists with local associations, including **Augustus and Gwen John** [*open Easter to Oct daily, winter pm Mon to Sat*]. The Scolton Manor Museum near Haverfordwest (social history and archaeology) and Penrhos Cottage (traditional Welsh cottage and furniture) are run by the Dyfed County Council.

FAMILY OUTINGS

For family days out there are several wildlife and country parks: Heron's Brook Country Park (near Narberth), Woodlands Farm Park and Scolton Country Park (both near Haverfordwest) and Manor House Wildlife and Leisure Park at St Florence (near Tenby). [*All open Easter to Sep, daily*] Typical attractions are nature trails, feeding of animals (mostly unusual breeds of domestic animals and ornamental waterfowl), picnic areas and adventure playgrounds. The Nectarium at Solva features collections of tropical butterflies in a simulated natural habitat. Near Tenby is the Oakwood Adventure and Leisure Complex with a miniature railway, bobsleigh run, boating lake and various rides [*open May to Oct, daily*]. Black Pool Mill and Caverns, near Narberth, is another place for a family outing [*open Easter to Oct, daily*], with a restored mill, and caverns with life-size models of extinct animals [*open Easter to Oct, daily*].

Walking

Most visitors to the area will want to try at least a short section of the Pembrokeshire Coast Path, which follows the 200-mile coastline virtually without a break. The craggy and dramatic coastal scenery north-east of St David's Head needs a strong head for heights, and energy to cope with seemingly endless ups and downs, but most of it is very rewarding for the walker; particularly fine are St David's, Strumble and Dinas Heads, but many of the smaller headlands also make excellent round walks.

Further south, the cliffs are lower and more level, and there are lots of opportunities for easy strolls such as at Bosherston lily ponds and Stackpole Head, Solva, Manorbier, Tenby and Wooltack Point. The last of these, at the west end of the peninsula which forms the north side of Milford Haven, has a memorable view over the bird sanctuary islands of Skomer and Skokholm.

Inland, it's chiefly green and gentle farmland – not ideal walking country. The big exception is the heathery massif of

Mynydd Presely, where there are some fine, exposed viewpoints from granite outcrops – several of which can be reached by car plus a short stroll. For longer expeditions, take a detailed map and a compass. On the north side of Presely, the unspoiled Gwaun Valley is also worth exploring on foot.

See *Holiday Which? Good Walks Guide* walks 190-193.

Excursions

The islands of Ramsey, Skomer and Skokholm are nature reserves where you can see seals and seabirds. For skin-divers, Britain's first under-water nature reserve has been set up round the island of Skomer. Boat services to the islands are limited at weekends: trips to Ramsey run regularly from St David's in summer (except Sats) and the island of Skomer can be reached from Martin's Haven and Dale (Skokholm is open only on Mondays and Caldey Island is closed at weekends). Boat trips for fishing or cruises of the coast can be arranged from most harbours. You could even take a duty-free day trip from Fishguard to Ireland!

When to go

Many sights (castles etc) are open from the beginning of April or May until the end of September or October only and boat trips to the islands normally run only in summer too. March 1st is St David's Day, celebrated with an afternoon service in the cathedral. In Spring you can see unusual wild flowers and migrant birds. St David's and Tenby are very crowded in high season.

Fishguard has a music festival in late July (with Saturday concerts in St David's cathedral) and this is also the month for the lilies in bloom at Bosherston. If you want to catch the annual coracle festival at Cilgerran or the arts festival at St David's (with some performances in the setting of the Bishop's Palace) you should choose August.

Information

The South Wales Regional Office, Wales Tourist Board, Ty Croeso, Gloucester Place, Swansea SA1 1TY; tel: (0792) 465204

The National Park Information Centre, County Offices, Haverfordwest, Dyfed SA61 1QZ; tel: (0437) 4591. There are Tourist Information Centres in several towns, including Newport, St David's, Pembroke and Tenby.

Where to stay

There is little choice of accommodation except in St David's and Tenby, the latter with a huge selection of guesthouses and resort hotels which are likely to be fully booked in summer. On the north coast (east of St David's) numerous farmhouses offer bed and breakfast; we have selected one which also offers dinner. Otherwise accommodation is mostly in simple inns and guesthouses, mostly geared to one-night stays for people tackling the coastal walk. To the south of St David's, on the other hand, hotels (fairly few and far between) cater mainly for family summer holidays booked by the week. By far the greatest concentration is at the pretty but overcrowded resort of Tenby, and the neighbouring (less appealing) Saundersfoot.

MOYLEGROVE
Penrallt Ceibwr
Moylegrove, Cardigan, Dyfed *Tel: (023 986) 217*

Well-placed for the beginning of the Pembrokeshire coastal path, in a fine situation just half a mile's walk from the impressive headland of Ceibwr, this is a working farm run as a guesthouse. Dot and John Fletcher like everyone to be on Christian name terms on arrival and for the jaded city dweller this natural welcome can be very endearing. But it is important to get on with your fellow guests; the atmosphere is convivial. Comforts are simple: the homely public rooms run into one another and only half the light and cheerful bedrooms have private facilities. You will need to go for some stiff walks to do justice to Dot's dinners (at 7pm), especially the vast array of calorific puddings. Breakfasts are substantial too. A good place to escape to and excellent for families with children.

Location: *5 miles north-west of Cardigan*
Bedrooms: *6 (double and family). 3 with shower. Hairdryer on request*
Facilities: *Parking. Farm shop. Fishing. Games room. Babylistening*
Restrictions: *No smoking in dining room*
Open: *All year*
Credit/charge cards accepted: *None*
Price category: £
Special rates: *Children under 12, £7.85 in parents' room*

NEWPORT
Cnapan

East Street, Newport, Dyfed   *Tel: (0239) 820575*

This pink Georgian house in the centre of a pleasant large village is more of a guesthouse-with-restaurant than a hotel. It's run by two generations of the same family, who have taken pains to create a homely and welcoming atmosphere. Everything is on an intimate scale: a small, cosy sitting room and similar bar, fresh and decidedly jolly bedrooms, lots of personal touches and knick-knacks everywhere, including the hall and landing. It nevertheless avoids feeling overcluttered, and the décor (pastel shades, small patterns, antique stripped pine) matches well. The restaurant is attractively rustic – miscellaneous wooden furniture, including two settles, plus sundry copper and brass antiques – and the atmosphere is quite festive; food is imaginatively prepared, with a whole-food emphasis. Rooms at the front of the building overlook the main street (negligible traffic at night) and the moorland tops of Carningli Common; rooms at the back get views towards Newport Bay.

Bedrooms: 5 *(double, twin and family), all with shower (bath also available for use). TV, teamaking. Hairdryer and iron on request*
Facilities: *Parking*
Restrictions: *No dogs. No smoking in restaurant*
Open: *Mar to Jan; restaurant closed on Tuesdays from Easter to Oct*
Credit/charge cards accepted: *Access, Visa*
Price category: £
Special rates: *Children in parents' room free; in family room £6 (B&B)*

PENALLY
Penally Abbey

Penally, Nr Tenby, Dyfed   *Tel: (0834) 3033*

Flanking a quiet sloping village green opposite the church at the older end of a largish village, this is a striking 18th-century 'Gothick' house in five acres of grounds, half a mile from the sea (unfortunately, not the best section of the Pembrokeshire coast). Its external charms are matched inside. The bedrooms are elegant, all in different styles and décor, with antique wardrobes and some four-poster beds; those in the original building have some delightful period features. The adjoining coach-house has been converted into four extra bedrooms (mock Georgian, with a balcony on the upper floor). High ceilings, fine classical fireplaces, period furniture, huge windows and large potted plants are the keynotes to the lounge and dining room. Fresh flowers and immaculate table settings provide the mood for dinner, where innovative and excellently prepared food is served in a particularly relaxed atmosphere. The bar is on a smaller scale, but is equally stylish: at one end, a door between two Ionic columns leads into a glassed-in terrace. A pleasant courtyard has garden furniture.

Rooms: 12 *(double, twin), 8 with 4-poster, 4 in Coach House, 8 with bath. TV, teamaking. Hairdryer. Iron on request*

Facilities: *Parking. Indoor swimming pool. Babylistening*
Restrictions: *No dogs*
Open: *All year*
Credit/charge cards accepted: *Access, Visa*
Price category: £
Special rates: *Children under 5 in parents' room free; 6-14 half price*

WOLFSCASTLE
Wolf's Castle
Wolfscastle, nr Haverfordwest, Dyfed   Tel: (043 787) 225

This comfortable hotel, with a deservedly strong reputation for its cooking, is well placed strategically for exploring Pembrokeshire. The surrounding countryside is undulating, unremarkable farmland and there are no views to speak of from the hotel, so be prepared for a drive before you see any real scenery. The building is a three-storey, triple-gabled stone construction, part covered with creeper, and with Georgian and Victorian windows all mixed up; a few mature trees stand in front, and there is a small garden (the only part of the hotel from which the noise of the immediately neighbouring A40 is noticeable). Bedrooms are light and attractive, though with no special period character or personal touches. Public rooms are likeable: restrained and quite stylish décor in the restaurant, with Chinese curtains and internal shutters, and a cheerful bar with an open fire and some homely corners. The menu changes daily, and features excellent country and local fish dishes.

Bedrooms: *15 (single, twin, double, family), all with bath. Direct dial telephone, TV, teamaking. Iron on request*
Facilities: *Parking. Squash, tennis*
Restrictions: *No dogs in restaurant*
Open: *All year. Restaurant closed some Sun evenings*
Credit/charge cards accepted: *Access, Amex, Visa*
Price category: ££
Special rates: *1st Oct to 30th Jun (except Bank Hols), weekends, 2 nights DB&B £23.75 (single £26.75) pp per night. Reductions negotiable for children in parents' room*

Prices are for b&b per person, sharing a double or twin room with bath.

£	= You can expect to pay under £20
££	= You can expect to pay between £20 and £30
£££	= You can expect to pay between £30 and £40
££££	= You can expect to pay between £40 and £55
£££££	= You can expect to pay over £55

The South Coast

- 'London's coast' – a good place for a break from the capital, and for anyone looking for the entertainment and organised facilities of big traditional resorts
- Few good sandy beaches and some places with nasty offshore currents; there are better places for a bucket-and-spade break
- Plenty of interesting sights and pretty scenery just inland, especially on the South Downs of Sussex (where hotels are expensive)
- Some good places for family days out, from amusement parks to castles and naval and military museums. Different areas suit different age-groups
- Brighton is worth a day of your weekend – or even a weekend itself – and has good hotels and restaurants

The south coast along the Channel has had great strategic importance for centuries; but within a few years of the future King George IV building his pavilion at Brighton, a coast that had always expected invasions from the sea found itself increasingly invaded from inland. By the mid-19th century a string of small resorts had grown up, and a profusion of piers, promenades and pavilions stretched from the western end of Sussex almost to the Thames estuary. Over the years, the area has lost trade to other parts of Britain with better beaches, and to the package resorts of the Mediterranean. Some resorts have clearly suffered as a result, with too many faded boarding houses, little-used amusement arcades and other eyesores. But now the M25 and a fast rail network have made it more accessible than ever, especially from London, and there are enough attractions for a short break.

East of Brighton

The area east of Brighton is 1066 country, with several fine Norman castles to visit. The defence of the realm was earlier a preoccupation of Edward the Confessor, who charged various ports (originally five, the 'Cinque Ports') with the duty of guarding the English Channel. In the 19th century stumpy 'Martello' towers were built as part of our coastal defences against Napoleon. Now the area deals with enormous amounts of (friendly) cross-Channel traffic, and caters for seaside holidays. Resorts have a genteel air and some fine Regency buildings.

The white cliffs of Dover are only patchily white (and parts are used by the army, so access is limited at times). In places chalk-tolerant vegetation has established itself on the cliff face, especially where landslips have formed undercliff areas, as at the Warren, near Folkestone. East of Hastings is a Country Park with good cliff scenery. Beyond Folkestone is the flat, fen-like Romney Marsh where the wastes of Dungeness are now graced with a huge nuclear power station. West of precipitous Beachy Head, the chalk cliffs known as the Seven Sisters form a dramatic seven mile roller-coaster wall of unblemished whiteness. Inland, the Weald of Kent, the Cuckmere Valley and the South Downs offer rural attractions.

Dover, famous for its white cliffs, castle and cross-channel ferries, was badly bombed in the war and lacks charm. **Folkestone**, a busy port which also suffered, has an unharmonious blend of old and new but also a smart clifftop promenade, the Leas, with wide lawns and flowerbeds, a bandstand and attractive wooded cliffs below. Among the Cinque Ports are **Hythe**, with steep narrow streets of old houses and a defensive canal, **New Romney**, with a graceful church, and tiny **Winchelsea**, now more than a mile inland. But the most appealing is **Rye**, a very picturesque town – also now inland – with cobbled streets and well preserved medieval buildings, old inns and antique shops.

The seafront at **Hastings** is built-up (and has some jolly amusements) but there is also a pretty old town with weatherboarded and half-timbered houses, some Regency buildings and attractive parks. Neighbouring **St Leonards**, laid out in the 1820s, has colonnaded terraces and geometrically shaped gardens. The large resort of **Eastbourne** retains an elegant and cheerful if sedate atmosphere; it has well-kept buildings, parks and gardens, a pier and a promenade with an ornate bandstand. Just inland from Seaford, **Alfriston** is a pretty village in a pleasant downland setting, with a fine church and traditional inns and timbered houses.

BEACHES

The beaches below the Dover cliffs are mere scraps of seaweedy rock and shingle. At Folkestone too the larger West Beach is mainly shingle, but East Cliff beach near the harbour is sandy and pleasant, if rather small. The best sandy beach is **Camber Sands**, near Rye, a large expanse of clean fine sand backed by dunes; but there are some hazardous offshore currents from the

River Rother which flows into the sea at this point and there is also rather seedy development inland. The upper part of the long, clean and safe beach at **Eastbourne** is shingle but there's firm golden sand when the tide goes out. The beach at Fairlight Glen is reserved for naturists.

CASTLES

Dover Dominated by a massive square Norman keep, this is one of the largest castles in the country. Inside the walls are a well-preserved Roman lighthouse and the complete late Saxon church of St Mary in Castro. [*Open all year, daily*]

Hastings The first castle in England to be built by the Normans. The remains are still impressive and the 'whispering' dungeons which magnify even the slightest sound are popular. [*Open Mar to Oct, daily*]

Hythe, Lympne Castle A small medieval castle overlooking Romney Marsh and the coast, with a fine, bare Great Hall. Permanent toy exhibition. [*Open Easter, then May to Sep, daily*]

Pevensey On landing in England, the Normans found a ready-made Roman fort, to which they later added a smaller structure of their own in one corner. It was once on the sea but the coast has now retreated. [*Open all year, daily except Sun am*]

Deal and **Walmer** castles, north of Dover, were both built in Tudor Rose shape by Henry VIII. They house small museums [*open daily except Sun am and Mon unless Bank Hol*]. **Bodiam** (NT), north of Hastings, is a perfect 14th-century castle, surrounded by a wide moat [*open April to Oct, daily; Nov to Mar, Mon to Sat*].

OTHER HISTORIC BUILDINGS

Alfriston, Clergy House A good example of a timber frame medieval hall house. (NT) [*Open April to Oct, daily*]

Dover, Roman Painted House A well preserved Roman villa with wall paintings and an underfloor heating system. [*Open Apr to Oct, daily except Mon*]

Rye, Lamb House Georgian house where Henry James lived and worked 1898-1916. (NT) [*Open April to Oct, pm Wed and Sat*]

There are **Martello towers** at Eastbourne and Dymchurch.

The following are within 10 miles of the coast between Hastings and Newhaven:

Battle Abbey The extensive ruins of the Abbey, built on the site of the Battle of Hastings, are about six miles inland from the town. [*Open all year, daily*]

nr Firle, Charleston Farmhouse Home of Bloomsbury Group painters Duncan Grant and Vanessa Bell. [*Open April to Oct, pm Wed-Sun plus Easter and Bank Hol Mons*]

Firle Place An elegant country house of Tudor origins but mainly early 18th-century appearance, in parkland with views of the South Downs. Fine interiors with French and English furniture, family portraits and Old Master paintings. [*Open June to Sep, pm, Wed, Thurs, Sun and Bank Hol Mons*]

Northiam, Great Dixter A 15th-century timber-framed manor hall restored by Sir Edwin Lutyens who also created the gardens. The interior contains antique furniture and needlework. [*Open April to mid Oct, pm, daily except Mon unless Bank Hol*]

Upper Dicker, Michelham Priory Rambling building with 14th-century gatehouse, Tudor barn, working watermill and vast moat. Used for exhibitions and special events. [*Open late Mar to Oct, daily*]

MUSEUMS

Most towns have small local museums. Dover also has a transport museum, Rye has several art galleries and a town model with sound and light show, and Hastings a shipwreck heritage centre. The Redoubt at Eastbourne houses a military museum, the Martello Tower a small exhibition relating to these forts. Eastbourne also has the Towner Art Gallery, with British art of the 19th and 20th centuries, in a pretty 18th-century manor house.

FAMILY OUTINGS

Alfriston, Drusilla's Zoo Park A small zoo run like a village with shops, a railway and an adventure playground. [*Open all year: late Mar to Oct daily, winter (zoo only) weekends*]

Great Knelle, Children's Farm Farm near Rye organised for children with tractor train, nature trails and adventure playground. [*Open April to Oct, daily except Mon*]

Port Lympne Zoo Park Elephants, big cats and endangered species kept in 270 acres of park and woodland attached to an Edwardian Dutch colonial style mansion, with elaborate terraced gardens. [*Open all year, daily*]

Romney, Hythe and Dymchurch Railway Purpose-built steam locomotives, one-third normal size, run the 14 miles of track from Hythe to Dungeness, following the coast all the way. There is a good model railway exhibition at New Romney. Railway buffs might also try the **Kent and East Sussex Railway** which runs from Tenterden to Wittersham Road (the stretch to Northiam is due to re-open in 1990).

Seaford, The Living World Insects and marine life in natural settings, plus forest walks. [*Open April to Oct, daily; winter, weekends and school hols*]

Hastings pier has some jolly amusements, most of them in a

structure called the Triodome. There is a family fun park at Dymchurch. Eastbourne has a Treasure Island playcentre and a Butterfly Centre.

Brighton

Brighton, the Regency town par excellence, has taken a battering over the years from hordes of visitors, modern development and slow decay. But it's still the best place to savour the delights of the traditional seaside resort – whether you like piers and amusement arcades or the finer points of Regency architecture. And it has undergone something of a rebirth recently, with a notable range of places to eat and some stylish shops and hotels. The Lanes, a tangle of narrow, almost traffic-free streets between the front and the Pavilion, are lined with antique and other specialist shops and stalls.

Hove is a sedate, residential extension of Brighton. Both resorts have steeply-shelving pebbly beaches.

HISTORIC BUILDINGS AND GARDENS
Regency Brighton The most imposing set piece is Kemp Town, a mile east of the town centre. There are several good squares and terraces west of the centre too, particularly Brunswick Square (in Hove) with elegant bow-windowed houses round a sloping landscaped green. A free town trail leaflet *A Walk around the Best of Brighton* takes you round the main places of interest.
Brighton Pavilion The original building dates mainly from the 1780s, when the Prince of Wales (later George IV) had a classical villa built for himself and his secret wife. It was given its exotic Indian exterior some thirty years later. The interior – particularly the Chinese style banqueting room – is similarly lavish and has recently been restored. [*Open all year, daily*]
Preston Manor A fine 18th-century house standing in its own park just north of the centre of Brighton. Edwardian interior with furnishings from the 17th century on. [*Open all year, daily except Mon unless Bank Hol*]

Also worth seeing are some of Brighton's churches. Ancient St Nicolas, much rebuilt in a mixture of styles, has an early Norman font with interesting sculpted panels; and in modern St Paul's, there are paintings by Burne-Jones and William Morris.

MUSEUMS AND GALLERIES
Brighton Museum and Art Gallery This building, formerly Queen Adelaide's stables, houses an interesting medley of art nouveau furniture and decorative arts, collections of glass and

ceramics, Dutch and Flemish Old Master paintings, musical instruments and a display of costumes right up to the punk era. [*Open all year, daily except Mon and am Sun*]

Brighton has a natural history museum (**Booth Museum of Natural History**), and Brighton Museum's collection of historic toys is displayed with Kipling memorabilia at **The Grange**, Rottingdean, three miles from Brighton. Hove also has a **Museum and Art Gallery** (20th-century paintings, historic toys, Regency furniture) and the **British Engineerium**, with hundreds of full-size and model engines.

FAMILY OUTINGS

Aquarium and Dolphinarium Daily dolphin and sea-lion shows and a wide range of aquatic exhibits, plus an aircraft simulator and Pirates' Deep play area. [*Open all year, daily*]

Volks Electric Railway The first electric railway in Britain, opened in 1883, runs for a mile along the beach from the Aquarium to the Marina. [*Open April to late Sep, daily*]

West of Brighton

Between Brighton and the headland of Selsey Bill the flat coastline (where once there were fishing villages and some medieval ports) is now almost all built up with resort and residential development, and thrives all summer on traditional bucket-and-spade family holidays. Sailing takes over from sand-castles in the Chichester area and – after the sprawl of Portsmouth and Southampton – along Hampshire's Solent shore. But Bournemouth, a late starter compared with Brighton, is now the queen resort of the south coast and its suburbs stretch for miles.

Hampshire's New Forest is the loveliest area of countryside just inland: 92,000 acres of very varied woods and streams and heathland. Villages dot the clearings, deer and ponies wander about (not on any account to be fed) and it can assimilate a great many visitors before the roads and car parks clog up. Between the South Downs and the coast, inland Sussex scenery is pastoral and prosperous with plenty of woodland, cosy little villages and even a vineyard or two.

West of Hove, **Worthing** is a large traditional resort which has pretty gardens, a pier and two pavilions. **Arundel**, dominated by the slope of the downs with the castle looming above, has a steep High Street of antique shops and small museums, and alleys leading to Georgian streets. Further inland up the Arun valley is the strange and secretive village of **Amberley**. **Littlehampton** is a rather ordinary resort with good beaches; **Bognor Regis** (it got its royal tag in 1929, from George V who convalesced here) is quiet and traditional and a bit faded, but with good amusements for children. **Chichester** is an ancient and peaceful market town with a fine cathedral, and a cultured lifestyle which focuses on the Festival Theatre. The huge natural harbour is connected to the town by canal. The nearby villages of **Itchenor** and **Bosham** are popular for sailing; Bosham is pretty and unspoilt, with a fine Saxon church and a waterfront of redbrick and white painted cottages.

   Portsmouth is the Royal Navy's town and **Southampton** a great commercial seaport; both were devastated in World War II and have been much rebuilt, but in each a street or two of interesting old houses has survived. **Buckler's Hard** is a pretty and peaceful village near the mouth of the Beaulieu, with a small museum reflecting the local boat building tradition. Beyond, on the South Hampshire coast, is **Lymington**, a charming little town favoured by Solent yachtsmen. **Milford on Sea** is a small resort whose beach extends to a shingle spit jutting into the Solent, guarded by the remains of a Tudor castle. **Christchurch** has elements of both seaside resort and pretty historic town, with a castle keep and large Priory church, but it has been much modernised; the suburbs have spread east to Mudeford. Hengistbury Head, a peninsula of heath and woods which all but closes Christchurch harbour from the sea, is by contrast a wilderness. **Bournemouth** is a major, all-out traditional seaside resort, situated on and between cliffs, with attractions to suit all ages both in and out of season. **Poole**, of pottery fame, has a sedate but pretty Georgian centre, a park (with boating, a mini railway and a small zoo) and several excellent small museums. But its main attraction is the large and busy harbour. From the quay you can take a ferry to Brownsea Island, part of which is a nature reserve.

BEACHES
The Sussex resorts west of Brighton each have their stretch of sand, gently sloping and backed by shingle. **Littlehampton** has two, east and west of the River Arun; bathing near the river-mouth is unsafe and prohibited. The west beach has dunes and a golf course behind, the more popular eastern one plenty of shelving sand backed by lawns and gardens. **Worthing** and **Bognor Regis** have safe sandy bathing below the traditional attractions of the prom.

   There are good beaches in quiet rural surroundings (but with paying car parks) at **West Wittering**, where broad banks of shingle give way to firm sand at low tide and **Climping** (a bit muddy in places). **Hayling Island** has a long safe southern beach, much of it uncommercialised, with vast expanses of sand at low tide and grassy dunes behind. **Bournemouth** and its satellite **Boscombe** have broad, safe, sandy, gently shelving beaches with golden cliffs behind. The comma-shaped peninsula of **Sandbanks**, between Bournemouth and Poole, also has a lovely broad sandy beach. **Poole Harbour** is good for boardsailing.

HISTORIC BUILDINGS AND GARDENS

Arundel Castle   Seat of the Dukes of Norfolk; originally Norman, now mainly a Victorian Romantic fantasy. There are grand state rooms. [*Open April to Oct, pm, daily except Sat*]

nr Arundel, Denmans Garden   A compact and well-tended garden in artful disarray. [*Open April to Oct, daily except Mon*]

Bramber, St Mary's   A late 15th-century timber framed house with fine panelled rooms and an elegant music room. [*Open April to Oct, Sun, Bank Hol Mons and pm Mon to Thurs*]

Chichester Cathedral   Lady Chapel with delicate roof, altar screen designed by John Piper. [*Open all year, daily*]

Chichester, Pallant House   A Queen Anne town house with interesting collections of furniture, porcelain and glass and regular art exhibitions. [*Open all year, daily except Sun and Mon*]

nr Chichester, Fishbourne Roman Palace   The largest Roman residence yet discovered in Britain; the remains of the north wing, with mosaic floors, are protected by a modern building. [*Open Mar to Nov daily, plus Suns Dec to Feb*]

Exbury Gardens   The Rothschild collection of rhododendrons, magnolias and camellias set in natural woodland near the Beaulieu river. [*Open mid Mar to mid July, daily*]

Goodwood House   Known for its fabulous collection of paintings including works by Canaletto, Reynolds, Stubbs and Van Dyck and for fine French furniture, Sèvres porcelain and Gobelin tapestries. A flint house, consisting of three sides of an octagon, never completed. [*Open Easter, then May to early Oct, Sun and Mon, plus pm Tues-Thurs in Aug. Closed on racing days in June/July*]

Portchester Castle   A Norman castle built within the walls of a Roman fort, at the head of Portsmouth harbour. [*Open all year, daily except Sun am*]

West Dean Gardens   Varied gardens with good trees and shrubs, including walled garden, gazebo and wild areas. [*Open Apr to Sep, daily*]

Further inland are **Parham House**, an Elizabethan Manor, **Petworth House**, famous for its landscaped park and collection of paintings and **Uppark**, a lovely 17th-century house with original interior and grounds designed by Repton. At **Bignor Roman Villa** some extraordinary mosaics have been excavated. **Broadlands**, the stately home of the late Lord Mountbatten, is north of

Southampton at Romsey.

MUSEUMS

Amberley Chalk Pits Museum A large variety of industrial relics from lime kilns and lorries to vintage wirelesses, with a real mini-railway and working craftsmen. [*Open April to Oct, Wed, Sun and Bank Hol Mons; daily in school hols*]

Bournemouth, Russell-Cotes Museum Fine English and European furniture, porcelain and paintings, plus some Eastern antiquities, mostly collected by Sir Merton Russell-Cotes who lived here from 1894 to his death in 1921. [*Open all year, daily except Sun*]

Christchurch, The Red House Museum Local history and art housed in an 18th-century parish workhouse, with pretty garden. [*Open all year, daily except Mon and am Sun*]

Gosport, Royal Navy Submarine Museum Comprehensive exhibition with guided tours of HM submarine Alliance. [*Open all year, daily*]

Poole, Scaplen's Court A 15th-century merchant's house, recently restored after many years of neglect, and used for a display of domestic life over the centuries. [*Open all year, daily except am Sun*]

Portsmouth, Royal Naval Museum The history of the Royal Navy up to the Falklands. Nelson's HMS Victory and Henry VIII's Mary Rose are preserved in dry dock at the Naval base. [*Open all year, daily*]

Singleton, The Weald and Downland Open Air Museum Historic rural buildings from all over the south east, relocated on a typical downland site, six miles north of Chichester. [*Open April to Oct, daily, Nov to Mar Wed and Sun*]

Other museums include some eccentric and individual collections. Arundel has a Toy and Military Museum, Chichester a Mechanical Music Museum and Tangmere (three miles east of Chichester) a Military Aviation Museum. The House of Pipes at Bramber (north of Shoreham by Sea) is a private collection devoted to smoking. Portsmouth has a D-Day museum (with the Overlord Embroidery) and Southampton a Hall of Aviation.

The Sammy Miller Museum, a large collection of historic motorcycles, is at New Milton and there is a whimsical museum of tricycles at Christchurch. Poole has a good local history museum in the 18th-century Guildhall, and a Maritime Museum on the quay.

BOAT TRIPS

You can take a boat up the river Arun from Littlehampton. There are also boat trips around Chichester Harbour, starting at

Itchenor. Sailing boats and sailboards can be hired in the Chichester area; Westhampnett Water Park is a 46-acre lake ideal for boardsailing (tuition available). Portsmouth Harbour tours link the naval base, old Portsmouth and the submarine museum at Gosport. There are also boat tours of Poole Harbour.

NATURE RESERVES

There are nature reserves at Pagham near Selsey and at West Wittering, with self-guided trails; these are areas of saltmarsh supporting waders and other seabirds. The Wildfowl Trust has established a 55-acre reserve just outside Arundel where black necked swans, many varieties of duck and other freshwater birds can be seen from a viewing lounge, walkways or hides.

There are also nature reserves on the marshland and meadows near the mouths of the Meon and the Hamble rivers at Titchfield Haven (permits required), and at Hook Nature Reserve. Calshot Marshes is an extensive area of tidal saltings on the coast of Southampton Water; further west are the Keyhaven and Lymington Salterns and Marshes, both now nature reserves.

FAMILY OUTINGS

Beaulieu Famous for the National Motor Museum with over 200 historic vehicles; there are various rides and audio visual shows. The palace house and gardens and historic 13th-century abbey can also be visited. [*Open all year, daily*]

Bognor Regis, Rainbow's End Children's entertainment with clown shows, mini farm, animated fictional characters, pirates' lake and adventure playground. [*Open Mar to Oct, daily*]

Littlehampton, Smart's Amusement Park Amusement arcades, dodgems and rides, mostly under cover but right by the beach [*Open June to Aug, daily; plus weekends and Bank Hols Easter, April, May and Sep*]

Portsmouth, Sea Life Centre A new large-scale marine life exhibition. Special features include a full scale simulation of a ship's bridge and a vast 'Ocean Reef' display. [*Open all year, daily*]

Just north of Southampton at Ower is **Paulton's Park** with bird gardens, a Romany museum and other attractions for younger children. [*Open mid Mar to Sep, daily, plus weekends Oct*]

Walking

Only a few parts of the south coast have escaped development, but there are is still some outstanding walking. First and foremost is the section of chalk cliffs from the Seven Sisters to the culmination of the South Downs at Beachy Head; the Seven

Sisters can be approached from the west from Cuckmere Haven in the Seven Sisters Country Park, or you can take a pleasant inland route via West Dean and East Dean to make a round walk. The small pocket of scrubby and partially wooded sandstone cliff scenery at Fairlight Glen is strikingly different from any other scenery on the south coast, and there is just enough of it to provide a good circuit for walkers, starting from the picturesque east side of Hastings. From Folkestone to Dover (and beyond) is a good cliff-top walk offering views across the Channel to France on a clear day. Further west, Chichester Harbour is flat and quite substantially built up, but has some unspoilt corners, particularly on its east side where there are some wide expanses of marshland and pleasant estuary views; you can follow a footpath around most of it. The dunes and beach around the National Trust-owned spit of East Head, near West Wittering, is a good sample of this; and the waterside path can be taken to West Itchenor.

Otherwise, walkers will head inland, in particular for the South Downs Way, which follows the crest of the chalk downs, with extensive views on both sides; this long-distance path runs for 80 miles from the Hampshire/Sussex border near Petersfield to Eastbourne, and is well waymarked and signposted throughout. Further east are the final sections of two long-distance paths. The Saxon Shore Way follows the line of the now receded Saxon coast along the Royal Military Canal on the landward side of Romney Marsh; the path ends at Rye. The North Downs Way runs along bold downs above Folkestone before following the coast. Rye Harbour, at the mouth of the River Rother, is a nature reserve and starting point for walks over the marshes.

There's a wealth of walking in the New Forest: its gently indulating, remote-feeling heaths and mixed woodlands are laced with a dense network of paths and tracks, nearly all of which are open to the public. Some big conifer plantations can be rather lacking in interest, but there is pleasantly varied scenery in the north-west of the forest.

See *Holiday Which? Good Walks Guide* walks 37-40, 43-45, 56, 58-61.

When to go

The Brighton Festival, one of the country's leading arts festivals, with a sizeable fringe, takes place in the first three weeks of May and is followed by the Glyndebourne Opera Festival, lasting until mid August. In June Eastbourne hosts a major women's tennis tournament immediately pre-Wimbledon; then there is a carnival in July. The Chichester festival starts in early July and lasts for two weeks. Bosham's open air theatre, in a private garden, has a season of plays in August. Hastings festival is in early August and every other year in mid August Hythe organises a 'Venetian' water carnival to commemorate the non occurrence of the Napoleonic invasion with floating tableaux and fireworks. Arundel's festival and Alfriston's festival and fair take place in the last week in August. Rye's festival (and children's festival) takes place during the first week of September (concerts, films, poetry, puppets etc). Hastings Day celebrations are a week of sports and entertainment in mid October. The London-to-Brighton veteran car rally is on the first Sunday in November.

Racing at Goodwood is from the end of May to the end of September, with the occasional Saturday meeting. In early August, the second week of 'Sussex Fortnight', the action switches from Goodwood to Brighton.

The New Forest and Hampshire County Show is held at Brockenhurst in late July, and Beaulieu's National Motor Museum has a Boat Jumble and Automart in September, and a Fireworks Festival at the end of October. Seagoing events include the Round The Island Yacht Race (from Cowes) on 25 June, and Bournemouth's Power Boating Festival in September.

The Navy opens its dockyards for the Portsmouth Navy Days in late August ('meet the men, see the ships').

Information

The South East England Tourist Board, 1 Warwick Park, Tunbridge Wells, Kent TN2 5TA; tel: (0892) 40766 (covers East and West Sussex, Kent, Surrey)

The Brighton Tourist Information Centre, Marlborough House, 54 Old Steine, Brighton, East Sussex BN1 1EQ; tel: 0273 23755

The Southern Tourist Board, The Town Hall Centre, Leigh Road, Eastleigh, Hants SO5 4DE; tel: (0703) 616027 (covers Hampshire and Eastern Dorset)

Brighton Arts Information Centre, 111 Church Street, Brighton, East Sussex BN1 1UD; tel: (0273) 676926; extension 29801 for the Brighton Festival

Chichester Festivities, Canon Gate House, South Street, Chichester, West Sussex PO19 1PU; tel: (0243) 785718

Glyndebourne Festival of Music and the Arts, Glyndebourne, Lewes, East Sussex BN8 5UU, tel: (0273) 812321 for enquiries, (0273) 541111 for the box office

Where to stay

Hotel and guesthouse accommodation along the south coast covers the whole spectrum – shabby seaside B&Bs to the grandest of Grand Hotels – with every shade in between; the major resorts of Brighton and Bournemouth have the largest range. In Brighton, restored Regency terraces house some very individual small hotels, completely lacking any 'seaside boarding house' atmosphere; there are large and comfortable hotels which cater for the sizeable conference trade; and there is the newly renovated Grand Hotel which lives up to its name. Bournemouth has several top-of-the-market seaside hotels, and also street upon street of small and simple hotels and guesthouses which provide reasonable family accommodation (though it's hard to find many which are a memorable halt for a weekend break). Between the two resorts, most of the more interesting accommodation is to be found slightly inland, or at least not directly by the seaside: traditional inns in town or village centres (Alfriston, Beaulieu, Chichester, Rye), fine old town houses and the occasional country house hotel or farmhouse.

ALFRISTON
The George Inn
Alfriston, East Sussex   *Tel: (0323) 870319*

This 14th-century inn, constructed of half-timber and Sussex flint, lies on the main street in the heart of town; it is without the benefit of a car park, but has a quiet garden. The beams and many levels of the interior add to the olde worlde charm, and the traditional pub bar with a fine open fireplace is attractive. The décor is a little drab in greens and browns, furniture is a mixture of antique and reproduction. Bedrooms on the front suffer from passing traffic noise.

Bedrooms: *8 (single, double, triple), 1 with four-poster, 7 with bath. Direct dial telephone, TV. Iron and hairdryer on request*
Restrictions: *No dogs*
Open: *All year*
Credit/charge cards accepted: *Access, Amex, Diners, Visa*
Price category: *££*
Special rates: *2 nights DB&B £35 pp per night. Children up to 14 in parents' room, £18*

ALFRISTON
The Star
Alfriston, Polegate, East Sussex BN26 5TA   *Tel: (0323) 870495*

The old part of this black and white timbered building dates from the 15th century; there's a rear extension, added in the 1960s. One is aware of traffic noise at the front of the building. Public rooms have masses of beams and reasonably comfortable furniture; the bar is cosy and warm with an oak refectory table. In places there is an uneasy blend of ancient and modern; but this is generally a good-standard traditional Trusthouse Forte hotel. Bedrooms are well-decorated with co-ordinated fabrics and reproduction furniture. In the older part, be prepared to sacrifice spaciousness for quaintness.

Bedrooms: *32 (single, double, twin, family), all with bath. Direct dial telephone, TV, teamaking*
Facilities: *Parking. Babylistening*
Open: *All year*
Credit/charge cards accepted: *Access, Amex, Diners, Visa*
Price category: *£££*
Special rates: *2 nights DB&B £42 (single £48) pp per night. Children in parents' room, free; meals half-price*

Nr BATTLE
Little Hemingfold Farmhouse
Telham, Battle, East Sussex TN33 0TT   *Tel: (042 46) 2910*

This part 17th-century, part Victorian farmhouse is reached via a long bumpy farm road; it's surrounded by 40 acres of land (including a lake) kept as a conservation area. Bedrooms are either in the main house or in the cleverly converted farmbuildings across a small courtyard (with many steps and levels, not suitable for the infirm). Decoration is homely, furniture either antique or pine. Electric blankets and wood-burning stoves (in some rooms) add to the warmth. The inter-connecting public rooms are furnished with the owners' possessions (grand piano, etchings and watercolours, books and games and a pleasantly ticking clock). Most of the food is home-produced (even the milk and honey) and served in the dining room where guests eat communally. The relaxing atmosphere and the delicious food make this a memorable place – and it's very good value.

Location: *1½ miles south of Battle, off A2100*
Bedrooms: *13 (single, double, twin, family), 4 with log fires, 6 in farm buildings, 12 with bath. Direct dial telephone, TV, teamaking. Hairdryer on request*
Facilities: *Parking. 2-acre trout lake*
Restrictions: *No children under 12. No smoking in dining room. Dogs by prior arrangement*
Open: *All year*
Credit/charge cards accepted: *Access, Amex, Diners, Visa*
Price category: *££*
Special rates: *Winter, 2 nights DB&B (including wine) £30 pp per night; summer £36*

Nr BATTLE
Netherfield Place
Battle, East Sussex TN33 9PP   *Tel: (042 46) 445*

Built in 1924 as a country house, this peaceful small hotel has five acres of formal gardens (including a goldfish pond and a large walled garden which provides vegetables for the kitchens) and a further 30 acres of grounds. The interior has been carefully decorated in traditional style, with patterned carpeting; there's a fine panelled dining room. Bedrooms are comfortable and generally spacious with co-ordinated fabrics and a cautious use of colour; fresh fruit and flowers and mineral water are there to make one feel pampered. A slightly bland version of the country-house hotel; with an atmosphere of relaxed privacy.

Location: *1½ miles NW of Battle on Netherfield road, off A2100*
Bedrooms: *14 (single, double, twin, family, suite), 1 with four-poster, all with bath. Direct dial telephone, TV, hairdryer*
Facilities: *Parking. 2 tennis courts, clay-pigeon shooting. Babylistening*
Restrictions: *Dogs by prior arrangement*
Open: *All year*
Credit/charge cards accepted: *Access, Amex, Diners, Visa*
Price category: *£££*
Special rates: *Nov to Easter, 2 nights DB&B £50 pp per night. Children in parents' room, £5 (for breakfast)*

BEAULIEU
The Montagu Arms
Beaulieu, New Forest, Hampshire SO24 7ZL   *Tel: (0590) 612324*

An attractive red brick house covered in creeper built (surprisingly) in 1925, as an addition to the older part which is now a pub/wine bar called The Wine Press (virtually self-contained). It's a traditional hotel; public rooms include a large panelled dining room with a wall of French windows leading to the pretty rear garden. The lounges have comfortable chairs, English chintzy fabrics and painted panelling. Bedrooms vary in size, décor and furnishing; cheerful fabrics, some antiques, pot pourri and bathrobes make them welcoming.

Bedrooms: *26 (single, double, twin), 5 with four-poster, all with bath. Direct dial telephone, TV, hairdryer, trouserpress*
Facilities: *Parking. Babylistening*
Open: *All year*
Credit/charge cards accepted: *Access, Amex, Diners, Visa*
Price category: *£££*
Special rates: *2 nights DB&B £42-£45 (single £29) pp per night. Children in parents' room £13.50*

BOGNOR REGIS
The Royal Norfolk
The Esplanade, Bognor Regis, West Sussex PO21 2LH   *Tel: (0243) 826222*

This purpose-built, white-painted Regency building on the sea front has all the ingredients of a traditional seaside hotel on a manageable scale. Dinner dances are held on Saturdays in the dining room, which retains some of its Regency characteristics in a scheme of pink, white and beige. In the bar (a bit tucked away) a pianist plays at Sunday lunchtime.

Bedrooms are a bit of a decorative mix, but comfortable. There is a simple front garden with borders, and a pool. The overall effect is of genteel comfort, more suited to the middle-aged than bucket-and-spaders. Trusthouse Forte has recently acquired the hotel, and plans for refurbishment will no doubt up-date the bedrooms considerably.

Bedrooms: 51 (single, double, twin, suites), 2 with four-poster, all with bath. Direct dial telephone, TV, teamaking, hairdryer, trouserpress
Facilities: Parking. Heated outdoor swimming pool, paddling pool, playground, tennis, croquet, putting. Babylistening
Open: All year
Credit/charge cards accepted: Access, Amex, Diners, Visa
Price: £££
Special rates: Weekends, 2 nights DB&B £40-£45; midweek, 2 nights DB&B £42-£47. Children up to 16 in parents' room free.

BOSHAM
Millstream
Bosham, Chichester, West Sussex PO18 8HL   *Tel: (0243) 573234*

A pleasant red brick and stone building in the centre of this quiet village. It's generally spacious and peaceful: the white-painted bar with white cane furniture leads to a long lounge (hessian walls and a baby grand piano); this leads to the lovely light dining room (trellis-pattern cloths and more cane furniture). Bedrooms are attractively decorated with co-ordinated or matching fabrics; bathrooms are well-appointed. There's a garden, set back from the road behind a stream. A homely traditional hotel in a charming setting.

Bedrooms: 29 (single, double, twin), 1 with four-poster, all with bath. Direct dial telephone, TV, teamaking, safe, hairdryer, trouserpress
Facilities: Parking. TV in lounge. Babylistening
Open: All year
Price category: £££
Special rates: 2 nights DB&B £37.50 pp per night. Children in parents' room free

BOURNEMOUTH
Highcliff
St Michael's Road, West Cliff, Bournemouth BH2 5DU   *Tel: (0202) 27702*

High on the West Cliff, very near to the centre of town (with a relatively short walk down to the beach), this Victorian purpose-built hotel has managed successfully to keep up with the times. Constantly refurbished to reflect the latest styles and very well maintained, it offers extremely comfortable accommodation together with an array of facilities to suit all ages (including children's playroom and outdoor playground plus nanny, sports, snooker, 'real ale' pub with live music and Sunday lunch jazz session, and a sophisticated discothèque well patronised by hotel guests). The dining room is particularly attractive, in dusky pink and cream; there's a separate children's section, slightly less grand. Film makers have used the conservatory-style lounge/bar where cream teas are served.

Bedrooms are very well furnished and 'designer-decorated'; some are particularly spacious for families. This is a good all-round hotel with something for everyone.

Bedrooms: *119 (single, double, twin, family), 14 in cottage-block annexe. 12 singles with shower, the rest with bath. Direct dial telephone, TV, teamaking, hairdryer, trouserpress. Minibars in annexe, and some bedrooms*
Facilities: *Parking, helipad. Lifts. Table tennis, pool, video games, snooker, sauna. Heated outdoor swimming pool, croquet, tennis, putting. Children's playroom, playground, paddling pool; nanny in summer. Air-conditioned discothèque (closed Sun)*
Restrictions: *No dogs*
Open: *All year*
Credit/charge cards accepted: *Access, Amex, Diners, Visa*
Price category: *££££*
Special rates: *Nov to May, weekends, 2 nights DB&B £41 pp per night, additional Sunday £35; midweek £48. Summer rates higher. Children under 16 in parents' room free*

BOURNEMOUTH
Inn on the Park
Pinewood Road, Branksome Park, Poole, Dorset   Tel: (0202) 761318

Although officially in Poole, the leafy residential area of Branksome Park seems more a part of Bournemouth. The Inn is an attractive Victorian building, a few minutes' walk from a fine sandy beach. The owners like to think of it as a 'local' – there's a large selection of real ales and Continental lagers – and it is indeed cosy and welcoming, with log fire, and button-backed seating. But the atmosphere is more sophisticated than in your average local, and the restaurant is positively stylish (candles and festoon blinds). Bedrooms, too, come as something of a surprise – light and airy, spacious and well decorated. One is extra large, very suitable for families. A very friendly place indeed.

Bedrooms: *6 (double, twin, family), 4 with bath. TV, teamaking*
Facilities: *Parking*
Restrictions: *No dogs in bedrooms*
Open: *All year except Christmas Day*
Credit/charge cards accepted: *None*
Price category: *£*
Special rates: *Children in parents' room half-price*

BOURNEMOUTH
Mon Bijou
47 Manor Road, East Cliff, Bournemouth BH1 3EU   Tel: (0202) 21389

Once a Victorian coach house, this two-storey white-shuttered house is overshadowed by most of the much taller hotels around it. In a road behind the East Cliff front, Mon Bijou has a small garden but no sea views. Inside, all is bright, beautiful and co-ordinated; each bedrooms has been individually decorated, with great attention to detail, and through-out there is a very high standard of maintenance and comfort. The small restaurant is attractive and refined; there's an adjoining sitting area and bar. Cooking is French-style, and fairly ambitious. You will be well looked after here, and it's easy to see why many guests become regulars.

Bedrooms: *7 (double, twin), 3 with bath, 4 with shower, 2 with four-poster. Direct dial telephone, TV (with video), teamaking, hairdryer, trouserpress*
Facilities: *Parking*
Restrictions: *No children. No dogs. Smoking discouraged in dining room*
Open: *All year. Restaurant closed Sun*
Credit/charge cards accepted: *Access, Amex, Diners, Visa*
Price category: ££

BRIGHTON
Franklins
41 Regency Square, Brighton, East Sussex BN1 2FJ   *Tel: (0273) 27016*

Although licensed premises, Franklins is not quite a hotel, nor even a guesthouse. It is more like a private home, without the domestic clutter or the seaside landlady syndrome, and with room service. Bedrooms are spotless, with fresh decoration mostly pastel and floral, and there is a comfortable lounge and dining room. This peaceful and pleasant house is centrally located (two minutes' walk from the seafront) and yet very reasonably priced. The atmosphere is welcoming but professional and the main clientèle is the under 40s.

Bedrooms: *6 (single, double and twin), all with bath or shower. TV. Hairdryer on request*
Facilities: *No smoking lounge*
Restrictions: *No dogs*
Open: *All year*
Credit/charge cards accepted: *Access, Diners, Visa*
Price category: £
Special rates: *Cot or small child's bed £5*

BRIGHTON
The Grand
King's Road, Brighton, East Sussex BN1 2FW   *Tel: (0273) 21188*

For 125 years this vast hotel presiding over the seafront has been grand by name; it is now grand again by nature after its total and extravagant refurbishment, and re-opened in August 1986. Public areas are all very opulent – fine plasterwork ceilings, marble pillars, and the impressive staircase in the hall. Decoration is lavish: traditional chintz and pictures 'hung' on ribbons in the lounge area, a blue and blood-red scheme with mahogany and brass in the clubby bar, colonial-style in the conservatory extending along the front of the building. The comfortable bedrooms have been carefully redone with co-ordinating chintz fabrics; the 'superior' rooms (with sea view) are equipped with a mini bar. In the basement is a well designed, fresh and colourful 'Health Spa' as well as a night club. A dinner dance is held each Saturday. All the facilities and services of a traditional grand hotel.

Bedrooms: *164 (single, double, twin, family, suite) all with bath. Direct dial telephone, TV, teamaking. Hairdryer, trouser press. Mini-bar in seaview rooms*
Facilities: *Lift. Indoor heated swimming pool. Sauna, solarium. Hairdresser, masseur, beauty treatments. Babylistening*
Restrictions: *No dogs in public areas*
Open: *All year*
Credit/charge cards accepted: *Access, Amex, Diners, Visa*
Price category: *£££££*
Special rates: *Weekends (must include Sat), or any night July and Aug, 2 nights DB&B £60-£100 pp per night. Children under 5 free in parents' room, over 5 half-price*

BRIGHTON
Granville
123-125 Kings Road, Brighton, East Sussex BN1 2FA   *Tel: (0273) 26302*

A family-run hotel on the seafront. Vaguely decadent bedrooms, all in different styles, have names like 'The Noel Coward Room' (art deco style), 'The Brighton Rock room' (with a silver bathroom) and 'The Japanese room' (with black and white décor and a futon). The more conservative guest should opt for a room with a Regency theme. Ten bedrooms have four-poster beds, 2 have jacuzzis and many have circular or double baths. Breakfast and light meals are served in 'Audrey's brasserie' in the basement. There's a main restaurant, too. Cooking is rather less imaginative than other aspects of the hotel, but there are some bargains on the wine list. A fun place to stay, but not everyone's scene.

Bedrooms: *25 (single, double, and twin), 10 with four-poster beds, all with bath, 2 with jacuzzi. Direct dial telephone, TV. Hairdryer on request*
Facilities: *Parking (4 cars only), lift*
Open: *All year*
Price category: *££££*
Special rates: *Weekends, excluding Bank Holidays and conference periods, 2 nights B&B (and £5 allowance towards dinner) from £41.50 (single £45) pp per night*

BRIGHTON
Topps
17 Regency Square, Brighton, East Sussex BN1 2FG   *Tel: (0273) 729334*

A warmly welcoming family-run hotel in two bow-fronted Regency houses, a short walk from the sea front. The bedrooms are clean and comfortable – some with huge bathrooms – and are very well equipped with extras (including even aspirin and towelling travel slippers). The rooms on the top floor feel almost like a little flat. The overall colour scheme is warm and inoffensive in apricots and beiges. Pine furniture and lots of books in the lounge add to the cosiness. There is a small basement bar and restaurant, popular with locals, serving good-value bistro-style food.

Bedrooms: *12 (single, double, twin), 2 with 4-poster, all with bath. Direct dial telephone, TV, teamaking. Iron and hairdryer in double and twin rooms. Minibar*

Facilities: *Lift*
Restrictions: *No dogs*
Open: *Feb to Dec; restaurant closed Wed and Sun*
Credit/charge cards accepted: *Access, Amex, Diners, Visa*
Price category: *£££*
Special rates: *Weekends, 2 or more nights, £27-£31.50 (£30). Children in parents' room £5*

BRIGHTON
The Twenty One
Charlotte Street, Marine Parade, Brighton,
East Sussex BN2 1AG   Tel: (0273) 686450

This is an early Victorian town house in residential Kemp Town (a few minutes' drive from central Brighton, three minutes' walk from the seafront); the freshly painted exterior and gleaming brass door-furniture give it a welcoming air. Inside, there is a comfortable, chintzy sitting room on the lower ground floor and a tiny residents-only dining room. Food is unashamedly French in emphasis, with a five-course no-choice *menu de dégustation* and an entirely French wine list. All the bedrooms have been individually furnished; they include a (more expensive) 'Garden room' with a sitting area, patio and french windows leading to the small garden, and a 'Victorian room' with mahogany furniture including an original four-poster bed. One or two rooms are quite small. The drawbacks to this pleasant small hotel are the narrow, steep stairs and the lack of baths or a car park.

Bedrooms: *7 (double, twin, suite), 1 with four-poster bed, 5 with shower. Direct dial telephone, TV, teamaking. Hairdryer*
Restrictions: *No children under 12*
Open: *All year. Restaurant closed Sun*
Credit/charge cards accepted: *Access, Amex, Diners, Visa*
Price category: *££*
Special rates: *Weekends, 2 nights DB&B £35-£44 pp per night*

BUCKLER'S HARD
The Master Builder's House
Buckler's Hard, Beaulieu, Brockenhurst, Hampshire SO4 7XB Tel: (059 063) 253

Charmingly situated by the creek overlooking moored boats, this hotel is part of the historic 18th-century hamlet, many of whose buildings are preserved as museums. It's a mainly Georgian building of mellow red brick; the hotel has expanded into a 1960s bedroom block and a large, light L-shaped dining room (with a sloping walkway connecting the old to the new). The pub bars are quite straightforward – quarry tiling and maritime pictures – and the large fireplace in the beamed lounge adds cheer to an otherwise rather functional room. J Lyons are responsible for the catering and serve standard English food with Continental touches. Bedrooms vary – the newer ones have uninspiring built-in furniture and floral fabrics, while the older ones are more basic with candlewick bedcovers. Outside, the sloping lawned garden leads to the surrounding grassy land by the riverside. The hotel is patronised by locals and the sailing fraternity as a pub with a bite to eat.

Location: *2 miles south of Beaulieu*
Bedrooms: *22 (single, double, twin), 1 with four-poster, 17 in new wing, 18 with bath (3 without WC). Direct dial telephone, TV, teamaking. Iron and hairdryer on request*
Facilities: *Parking. Sailing, clay pigeon shooting. Babylistening*
Open: *All year*
Credit/charge cards accepted: *Access, Amex, Diners, Visa*
Price category: *££*
Special rates: *2 nights, DB&B £35 pp per night. Children in parents' room £7*

CHICHESTER
The Dolphin and Anchor
West Street, Chichester, West Sussex PO19 1QE   *Tel: (0243) 785121*

A large, long, white-painted building of indeterminate age in a pedestrian-ised street in the town centre. The stylish public rooms have been refurbished to provide comfortable seating with chintzy quilted covers, and the dining room is particularly splendid with a blue and pink scheme including marbled walls, elaborate plaster ceiling, central pillars and a grand piano. One may be aware of minimal street noise in the bedrooms, which are reasonably comfortable but a little dated (redecoration is proposed). A pleasant coffee shop (piped music) serves meals all day.

Bedrooms: *54 (single, double, twin, family), all with bath. Direct dial telephone, TV, teamaking, hairdryer. Trouserpress in some rooms*
Facilities: *Parking. Babylistening*
Restrictions: *Dogs in bedrooms only*
Open: *All year*
Credit/charge cards accepted: *Access, Amex, Diners, Visa*
Price category: *£££*
Special rates: *2 nights DB&B £41 (single £46) pp per night. Children in parents' room free*

CLIMPING
Bailiffscourt
Climping, nr Littlehampton, West Sussex BN17 5RW   *Tel: (0903) 723511*

Set in 20 acre of grounds, in rural surroundings close to the sea, this is a delightful and intriguing 'medieval' house. Delightful because of its ancient charm with stone flagged floors, beamed ceilings and thatched outbuildings, intriguing because it is a fake – painstakingly reconstructed using old materials in the '20s and '30s by the late Lord Moyne. Built around a courtyard (providing a sun-trap of a garden) is a string of public rooms sympathetically furnished using tapestry fabrics; walls tend to be plain-painted and hung with hunting prints; all is in keeping with the mullioned, lattice-paned windows. Bedrooms (many with an open fireplace) are comfortably furnished and are gradually being refurbished with tapestry, velvet and crewel work. Bathrobes and magazines add to the welcoming country house atmosphere.

Location: *Off A259, just east of Climping*
Bedrooms: *20 (single, double, twin), 8 with four-poster, all with bath. Direct dial telephone, TV, hairdryer*
Facilities: *Parking. Helipad. Outdoor swimming pool, tennis, golf practice area. Exercise room, sauna. Babylistening*
Open: *All year*
Credit/charge cards accepted: *Access, Amex, Diners, Visa*
Price category: *££££-£££££*
Special rates: *Autumn and spring, weekends, 2 nights B&B 10% discount; 3rd night 50% discount. Children in parents' room £17.50*

Nr DOVER
Wallett's Court
West Cliffe, St Margarets-at-Cliffe, Dover, Kent CT15 6EW   Tel: (0304) 852424

Surrounded by rolling arable land, this is a lovingly restored 16th/17th-century building in four acres of garden (lavender, roses, goldfish pond and orchard). The house has considerable historic charm, with beams and brickwork, and ancient fireplaces. Off the half-galleried hall are the spacious reception rooms. Bedrooms are furnished comfortably; some are in converted outbuildings and have modern pine furniture and touches to reflect their names (corn dollies in 'Granary'). The cellars have been done up to house ping-pong and bar football. Simple farmhouse-style meals are available during the week; on Saturday night, there's a serious 'gourmet dinner' cooked by the chef/*patron*.

Location: *On B2058 towards St Margarets*
Bedrooms: *7 (double, twin, family), all with bath/shower. TV, teamaking. Hairdryer on request*
Facilities: *Parking. Table-tennis. Bar football. Snooker*
Restrictions: *No dogs*
Open: *All year except Christmas, restaurant closed Sun night*
Credit/charge cards accepted: *None*
Price category: *£*
Special rates: *Children in parents' room £7*

EASTBOURNE
The Grand Hotel
King Edward's Parade, Eastbourne, East Sussex BN21 4EQ   Tel: (0323) 412345

Set back from the sea behind gardens away from the busier part of the seafront, this vast white-painted hotel – purpose-built in 1864 – is now geared principally to the residential conference market, which results in the summer and often weekends being its quieter periods. Public rooms are many and colossal (elaborate plasterwork, cornicing and pillars) but suffer from the slightly institutional air that is hard to avoid in a place this size. Those (many) bedrooms that have been redecorated offer comfortable accommodation. Furniture may be old-fashioned or reproduction and co-ordinated colour schemes are either 'warm' or 'cool'. The facilities and entertainments on offer are plentiful, including swimming pools, jazz lunches, barbecues and a well-planned and extensive 'leisure club' including a hair and beauty salon. A traditional seaside hotel up-dated for modern times with little sign of a bucket or spade.

Bedrooms: *178 (single, double, twin, family, suite), all with bath. Direct dial telephone, TV, hairdryer. Minibar on request*
Facilities: *Parking. Heated outdoor and indoor swimming pools. Sauna, solarium, gym, massage room, snooker. Hairdresser*
Open: *All year*
Credit/charge cards accepted: *Access, Amex, Diners, Visa*
Price category: *£££££*
Special rates: *Weekends from mid Sep to Mar, and any nights summer, 2 nights DB&B £55-£92.50 pp per night*

LEWES
Shelleys Hotel
High Street, Lewes, East Sussex BN7 1XS   Tel: (0272) 472361

This town house of Georgian appearance suffers slightly from being on a busy road; but it has been recently and stylishly redecorated and provides elegant accommodation. There is an extension at the back for (quite small) single rooms, all well decorated, identical in pink and green. Bedrooms in the older part are more spacious and furnished with antiques. Off the fine entrance hall are the public rooms (fine architectural detail, subtle paint effects); the bar has a collection of oil paintings. The dining room opens out to a charming garden. Some traffic noise at the front of the house and piped music in the dining room should be the only things to mar a stay in this well-presented house, popular with visitors to Glyndebourne.

Bedrooms: *21 (single, double, twin), 3 with four-posters, 10 in annexe, all with bath. Direct dial telephone, TV, hairdryer*
Facilities: *Parking. Babylistening*
Open: *All year*
Credit/charge cards accepted: *Access, Amex, Diners, Visa*
Price category: *£££-££££*
Special rates: *Winter, 2 nights DB&B £41.50 pp per night. Children in parents' room free*

Nr LYMINGTON
Passford House
Mount Pleasant, nr Lymington, Hampshire SO41 8LS   Tel: (0590) 682398

This hotel has clearly grown over the years, and the result is part white-painted, part red brick and gabled. Its main advantage is the peaceful setting, surrounded by nine acres of grounds with many activities (and an animals' graveyard). The whole place is rather old fashioned in a peculiarly English way, but there is a brand-new 'leisure centre'. Bedrooms are comfortable, though décor is far from co-ordinated; guests are provided with extras including hot water bottles. The extensive public rooms tend to be rather drab, with patterned carpets and flock papers, but the spacious 'Oak Lounge' is panelled and has an open fire. Passford House is popular with families during the summer holidays.

Location: *2 miles north-west of Lymington*
Bedrooms: *56 (single, double, twin, family), 1 in stable suite, 1 with four-poster, all with bath. Direct dial telephone, TV, teamaking. Hairdryer, trouserpress*
Facilities: *Parking. Heated indoor and outdoor swimming pools tennis, putting, croquet. Spa pool, sauna, solarium, gym. Pool table, table tennis. Babylistening*
Restrictions: *No dogs or children in Forest Wing*
Open: *All year*
Credit/charge cards accepted: *Access, Amex, Visa*
Price category: *£££*
Special rates: *2 nights (not Bank Hols), DB&B £40 (single £48) pp per night. One child free in parents' room, 2nd child (up to 8) half-price, (over 8) two-thirds adult rate*

LYMINGTON
Stanwell House Hotel

High Street, Lymington, Hampshire SO4 9AA   *Tel: (0590) 77123*

A cream-painted town house in the centre of Lymington, with a traditional atmosphere. The dining room is very green in décor; doors open onto a courtyard and a small rear garden. The bar is a windowless room with tinted glass alcoves; the sitting room (with cornicing picked out, rather incongruously, in pink) is comfortable. Bedrooms vary in size and standard; décor is mostly floral vinyl wallpaper and candlewick or floral bedspreads. Up-dating refurbishment is planned. A pleasant and reasonably comfortable town house hotel.

Bedrooms: *34 (single, double, twin, family suites), 1 with four-poster, 2 in cottage, all with bath. Direct dial telephone, TV, teamaking, hairdryer, trouserpress*
Facilities: *Babylistening*
Restrictions: *Dogs in old bedrooms only*
Open: *All year*
Credit/charge cards accepted *Access, Amex, Visa*
Price category: *£££*
Special rates: *2 nights DB&B £44 pp per night; 3 nights DB&B £40 pp per night. Children in parents' room free*

NEW MILTON
Chewton Glen

New Milton, Hampshire BH25 6QS   *Tel: (04252) 5341*

Once the home of Captain Marryat (author of *Children of the New Forest*), this fine mid-19th-century red brick house with green shutters is set in 30 acres of landscaped gardens. It's a luxurious country house hotel, whose many public rooms are extravagantly decorated with fashionable co-ordination of patterns, textures and fabrics. The main sitting room is a lovely light room with a wall of arched windows leading to the terrace and the gardens beyond; the bar achieves a 'private club' feel with bold colours, acres of curtaining and alcoves with books. Antique furniture everywhere adds to the grandeur. Bedrooms are lavishly decorated, with chintzy fabrics and quilted covers on large beds; each has a safe, magazines and home-made biscuits. Suites are particularly well thought out so that the sitting area can feel quite separate. Chewton Glen is among the half-dozen most expensive country house hotels in Britain; service is impeccable, and for many people the hotel approaches perfection (though the cooking has its critics). Despite its exclusive appeal, it is remarkably unsnobbish.

Bedrooms: *46 (double, twin, family, suites), 1 with four-poster, all with bath. Direct dial telephone, TV, safe, hairdryer, trouserpress*
Facilities: *Parking, helipad. Heated outdoor swimming pool, tennis, croquet, putting, golfing green*
Restrictions: *No children under 7. No dogs*
Open: *All year*
Credit/charge cards accepted: *Access, Amex, Diners, Visa*
Price category: *£££££*
Special rates: *Winter, 2 nights (not Fri or Sat), £80 pp per night. Children in parents' room £25*

PEVENSEY
Priory Court Inn
Pevensey Castle, Pevensey, East Sussex BN24 5LG   *Tel: (0323) 763150*

On a busy corner close to the castle ruins, this is a friendly and jolly pub, black and white timber- framed, part of which dates from the 15th century. The traditional pub bar (decorated with harness, antlers and stuffed birds) is the focal point; guests may also eat in the dining room ('The Oak Room', the oldest part of the house) or at the picnic tables in the pretty grassy garden while the children play on the climbing frame. The decoration of the bedrooms is a little mixed but they are fresh and light; at the front one may be aware of traffic noise.

Bedrooms: *9 (single, double, twin, family), 7 with bath. TV, teamaking, hairdryer, trouserpress*
Facilities: *Parking. children's playground*
Restrictions: *Dogs by arrangement only*
Open: *All year*
Credit/charge cards accepted: *Access, Amex, Visa*
Price category: *££*
Special rates: *Children under 8 in parents' room free; over 8, £10*

POOLE
The Mansion House
Thames Street, Poole, Dorset BH15 1JN   *Tel: (0202) 685666*

A splendid and elegant Georgian town house, quietly situated off the Quay in the old town near the church. The beautiful and gracious entrance hall and grand staircase are the cause of much pride; the first-floor reception rooms are well decorated (antiques, fine fabrics, kelim-covered chairs); there's a jolly pub-style bar (piped music), and a more sophisticated cocktail bar. The attractive panelled dining room is run as a dining club (residents become temporary members), fashionable and popular with local business people. Bedrooms vary in size and décor; all are very comfortable, decorated in English style with chintzy floral fabrics and antiques. The many personal touches include a glass of sherry on arrival, fresh fruit and sweets. This is a very fine town house hotel.

Bedrooms: *19 (single, double, twin, family), all with bath. Direct dial telephone, TV, hairdryer, trouserpress*
Facilities: *Parking*
Restrictions: *Dogs by prior arrangement. No children under 8*
Open: *All year except two weeks in Jan. Restaurant closed Sat lunch*
Credit/charge cards accepted: *Access, Amex, Diners, Visa*
Price category: *£££*
Special rates: *Oct to May, 2 nights DB&B £49 pp per night. Reductions for children in parents' room*

RYE
The George
High Street, Rye, Kent TN31 7JP   *Tel: (0797) 222114*

Behind a Georgian façade in the centre of Rye, this is a 400-year-old coaching inn, now a traditional Trusthouse Forte hotel. It's all higgledy-piggledy with squeaky floorboards, beams and panelling, and open fireplaces in many of the rooms. Bedrooms are clean and comfortable, but rather lack individuality. A residents' lounge on the first floor is a long thin room – pleasant and quiet with a colour scheme of rusty browns and greens; there's a beamed and panelled bar (the oldest part of the house) and a dining room (ladderback chairs and oak tables). Local fresh fish specialities are proudly included in a large servery/display buffet. A friendly atmosphere and obliging staff add to your comfort.

Bedrooms: *16 (single, double, twin, family), all with bath. Direct dial telephone, TV, teamaking. Iron, hairdryer on request*
Facilities: *Parking. Ballroom. Babylistening. Babysitting on request*
Restrictions: *No smoking in some bedrooms, and in part of the restaurant*
Open: *All year*
Credit/charge cards accepted: *Access, Amex, Diners, Visa*
Price category: *£££*
Special rates: *2 nights DB&B £41 (single £48) pp per night. Children under 16 in parents' room free*

RYE
The Old Vicarage Guest House
66 Church Square, Rye, East Sussex   *Tel: (0797) 222119*

A pretty pink-painted Georgian house hard by the Church of St Mary in the heart of old Rye, surrounded by cobbled streets (access by car is a little tricky). B&B accommodation is provided in a friendly and jolly, if slightly muddly, atmosphere. Bedrooms (some with pine four-poster, a side-line business of the owners) are clean and comfortable and decorated with a mixture of fabrics and furniture; none have bath. The dining room and lounge also have a slightly unharmonious blend of styles but the effect is generally homely. There is a semi-permanent art exhibition with pictures for sale (passing customers pop in and out during the day). The owners are charming and helpful hosts.

Bedrooms: *6 (double, twin, family), 2 with four-posters, 2 with shower. TV. Iron and hairdryer on request*
Restrictions: *No children under 12. No pets. No smoking in breakfast room*
Open: *All year*
Credit/charge cards accepted: *None*
Price category: £
Special rates: *Oct to Mar, 3 nights, 10% reduction*

More information

In this chapter, we tell you how to find out about short breaks in areas of the country we haven't covered in this book, other types of accommodation (self-catering cottages, boats, or health farms, for instance), 'special interest' and activity breaks, hotels which offer Christmas and New Year breaks, tour operator inclusive holidays and free breaks for children.

Tourist offices

Almost all the regional tourist boards listed in our chapters publish some information about hotels which offer weekend or short break deals in their area. The national tourist boards of England, Wales and Scotland all produce free booklets which indicate hotels offering short breaks: *Let's Go*, published by the English Tourist Board, available from tourist offices [or telephone (0272) 217917]; *Great Little Breaks*, published by the Wales Tourist Board, Dept WB, Davis Street, Cardiff CF1 2FU; *Autumn, Winter, Spring Breaks*, published by the Scottish Tourist Board, PO Box 15, Edinburgh EH1 1UY.

The British Tourist Authority's annual *Commended Country Hotels, Guesthouses and Restaurants*, which features selected accommodation throughout the country, is available from bookshops at £4.25.

Hotel groups and tour operators

Short holidays are now big business, and in every travel agency there will be a selection of brochures offering 'breaks' of every description. You may decide to take a package because it seems easier: you have instant access to pictures of many hotels, with clear prices to compare, and often inclusive travel arrangements, too; and you don't even need to telephone hotels to find out about room availability, as the travel agent can do it for you. Below we list the main hotel groups and tour operators who offer short-break packages.

Many hotel group breaks (and sometimes those of tour

operators, too) offer very good value – particularly those which are designed to fill otherwise under-used city business hotels at the weekend. Indeed, as the weekend breaks market has become so lucrative, hotels whose amenities were once aimed solely at the business traveller are now doing all they can to cater for the leisure and family market. A city business hotel need not mean spartan or dull and streamlined accommodation. While facilities such as hairdryers, trouser presses, direct dial telephone, and, of course, remote-controlled television have become almost standard, it's now not unusual to find four-poster beds, flowery chintzes, bathrobes and sewing kits, too. 'Celebration' weekends are the in-thing: hand-made chocolates, champagne on the breakfast tray, fruit, magazines and mineral water may all be part of the deal.

'Children free' offers abound (usually provided they share the same room as you), and it's worth reading the small print to ensure that you are getting the best deal available – some companies offer reductions on children's meals, or substantial reductions for children in their own room; some stipulate one child per two adults, others cover single parents; and the maximum age under which the offers apply differs, too. In our list below we state whether, or under what age, children are free, when they share a room with two adults.

Most hotels charge substantially more per person if you occupy a single room (or use a double room as a single) during the week. This happens less often at weekends, though some hotels (and some operators) offer much better single rates than others. In our list below, we indicate which operators offer 'no single supplements'.

By no means all the brochures confine themselves to city hotels. Almost everything is possible on a package, from village inns, city guest-houses, established country house or seaside hotels. However, the genuinely individual family-run or smaller establishments (such as many recommended in this book) tend not to be offered on a package.

Brochures may not tell the whole story. Internal photographs may concentrate on the only photogenic room, while the hotel description may not reveal the nature of the hotel's surroundings or ambience. The term 'luxury break' may be relative; and words such as 'value', or 'discounts', may not tell the whole story, either. Occasionally (particularly in London) an operator will offer a price that is better than the hotel's own rate. But there may be large variations in price between operators offering the same hotel (a difference of £10 per person per night, for instance, adding £40 to the cost of a weekend for two), so it pays to shop around.

A large number of hotels and operators offer activity or special interest weekends, particularly in low season, covering anything from guided walking or birdwatching to full lecture programmes. For more information, see the section on 'Special Interest Weekends' on page 358. In our list below we've marked by an asterisk (*) those hotel groups or operators which offer special interest weekends.

Hotels owned by a group may have a uniform style. Consortia of independently owned or managed hotels may also impose a house style, but to a varying degree. For some people, a stay in familiar surroundings with familiar comforts is reassuring and relaxing, with little left to chance. For others, the lack of individuality is impersonal and off-putting. We've indicated below whether hotels form part of a chain, or are individually owned and run.

* = a 'special interest' programme is also offered

Automobile Association 'Country Wanderer'   *Fanum House, Dog Kennel Lane, Halesowen, West Midlands B63 3BT. Tel: 021-550 7648*
List of nearly 500 generally simple hotels and guesthouses in Britain which accept 'go-as-you-please' vouchers for motoring holidays – book a day at a time, stay for as long as you please. The basic price covers accommodation without bathroom (supplements payable for bathroom, and for single rooms).

*Best Western Hotels 'Getaway Breaks'   *Vine House, 143 London Road, Kingston-upon-Thames, Surrey KT2 6NA. Tel: 01-541 0050*
Nearly 200 independently-owned hotels of all types (village inn, country, city-centre and top-of-the-market) throughout England, Scotland and Wales. Rail inclusive prices available. Two children under 16 free. No single supplements at weekends.

British Travel Service   *54 Ebury Street, London, SW1. Tel: 01-730 8986*
Around 100 independently-owned hotels and some apartments, mainly in seaside resorts, in England, Scotland and Wales. All rail inclusive prices. Children under 5 free. Some single room supplements.

*Consort Hotels 'UK Holidays'   *Ryedale Building, Piccadilly, York YO1 1PN. Tel: (0904) 20137*
Over 200 independently-owned hotels, mainly in towns and cities, some in resorts, in England, Scotland and Wales. Children under 16 free in many hotels. Most hotels have single supplement.

*Crest Hotels 'Welcome Breaks'   *Bridge Street, Banbury OX16 8RQ. Tel: (0295) 67722*
Chain of over 40 hotels, mainly in towns and cities, in England, Scotland and Wales, many modern purpose-built. Rail inclusive prices available. Up to three children under 14 free – even in own room – in many hotels;

in some, one child free when sharing. No single supplements at weekends.

De Vere Hotels 'Leisure Breaks' *Chester Road, Daresbury, Warrington WA4 4BN. Tel: (0925) 65050*
Chain of over 25 hotels, several very grand top-of-the-market seaside, in England. Children under 14 free. No single room supplement at weekends.

★Embassy Hotels 'Hushaway Breaks' *34 Queen's Gate, London SW7 5JA. Tel: (0345) 581 811 (Link Line)*
Over 70 hotels – some owned by Embassy, some by associate companies – mainly in towns and cities in England, some in Scotland and Wales. Rail inclusive prices available. Children under 16 free. No single room supplement at weekends.

Exchange Travel 'Holiday Britain' *Exchange House, Parker Road, Hastings, East Sussex TN34 3UB. Tel: (0424) 434241*
Over 180 hotels, apartments, caravan and holiday parks in Devon, Cornwall and Scotland. Many in resorts; some budget. Rail inclusive prices available. Child reductions vary – children free in many hotels. Single room supplements.

Golden Gateways 'Easy Breaks' *Kent Crusader Ltd, Hill Place, London Road, Southborough, Tunbridge Wells, Kent TN4 0PX. Tel: (0892) 37617*
Over 30 hotels in Kent, some budget. Rail inclusive prices available. Children under 14 free in some hotels. A few hotels have no single supplement.

Gold Star 'London', and 'Short Breaks' *PO Box 12, York YO1 1YX. Tel: (0904) 642751*
Over 50 hotels in London, mainly mid- to upper-price range, and over 150 throughout England, Scotland and Wales, most in towns, cities and major resorts. Rail inclusive prices available. Prices include free public transport in London. Children under 16 free. No single room supplement.

'Highlife Breaks' *PO Box 1RA, Newcastle-upon-Tyne, NE99 1RA. Tel: (091-232) 1073*
Around 100 hotels in England, Scotland and Wales – some chain, others independently owned – in seaside resorts, country areas or towns and cities, several top-of-the-market. Rail inclusive prices available. Children under 14 free. No single room supplement at weekends.

★Hilton and Ladbroke Hotels 'Bright Ideas' *PO Box 137, Watford, Hertfordshire WD1 1DN. Tel: 0923-38877*
40 mainly town or city hotels in England, Scotland and Wales, many modern purpose-built (and well equipped). Rail inclusive prices available. Two children under 16 free; up to four children in own room for £5 each per night. Single supplement.

Holiday Inn 'Weekenders'   *10-12 New College Parade, Finchley Road, London NW3 5EP. Tel: 01-586 8111*
16 modern mostly city-centre hotels, all with leisure facilities including indoor swimming pools. Children up to 19 free. Single supplement.

∗Inter-Hotel   *35 Hogarth Road, London SW5 0QH. Tel: 01-373 3241*
Over 100 hotels in England, Wales and Scotland, many small family-run establishments, in resorts, towns and country areas. Children under 16 in parents' room free. Single room supplement.

London Travel Service   *54 Ebury Street, London SW1. Tel: 01-730 8986*
Over 30 hotels in London, in three main price bands. All prices inclusive of rail travel. Children under 5 free. Single supplement.

Mount Charlotte Hotels 'London Value Breaks'   *2 The Calls, Leeds LS2 7JU. Tel: (0800) 700 400*
12 large hotels in London. Rail inclusive prices available. Children under 16 free. Single accommodation not available at weekends.

∗Norfolk Capital Hotels 'Greatstay Experience'   *8 Cromwell Place, London SW7 2JN. Tel: 01-589 7000*
15 mainly top-of-the-market hotels in England, Scotland and Wales. Children under 16 free. Single supplement.

∗Keith Prowse 'Theatre, Sport and Concert Tours'   *1 Melcombe Street, London NW1 6AE. Tel: 01-935 6666 or 061-431 9000*
Over 30 mainly city hotels in England, Scotland and Wales, and over 40 hotels in London in four price bands including budget. Prices include a ticket to a show, sporting event or show. A few hotels have no single room supplement.

∗Queens Moat Houses Hotels 'Town and Country Classics'   *Queens Court, 9/17 Eastern Road, Romford, Essex RM1 3NG. Tel: (0800) 289 331*
Chain of over 70 hotels in England and Scotland, some modern purpose-built. Two children under 14 free. Single supplement.

Rainbow 'Mini Holidays'   *Ryedale Building, Piccadilly, York YO1 1PN. Tel: (0904) 643355*
Over 250 hotels in England, Scotland and Wales, mainly in mid- and upper-price range, including over 40 in London (some budget). Rail inclusive prices available. Two children under 16 free. No single room supplement.

Rank Hotels 'London Weekends'   *4 Harrington Gardens, London SW7 4LH. Tel: 01-937 0088 or 061-236 2199*
Small chain of 5 comfortable hotels in London. Rail inclusive prices available. Two children under 14 free. No single room supplement at weekends.

★Scottish Highland Hotels 'Holidays in Scotland'   *98 West George Street, Glasgow G2 1PW. Tel: 041-332 6538*
9 hotels in Scotland. Children under 16 free. No single room supplement.

Stakis Hotels and Inns   *West Mains Road, East Kilbride, Glasgow G74 1PQ. Tel: (03552) 49235 or 01-387 6778*
Chain of over 30 hotels, most in Scotland, 12 in England and Wales, mainly large and well equipped, some with leisure facilities (gyms, indoor pools, etc). Rail inclusive prices available. Two children under 5, or under 15, free, including meals, depending on hotel. Single supplement.

Superbreak Mini Holidays   *305 Gray's Inn Road, London WC1 8QF. Tel: 01-278 0383*
Over 200 hotels in England, Scotland and Wales, including 40 in London, mainly mid- to upper-price range. Rail inclusive prices available. Two children under 16 free. No single supplement at weekends.

Swallow Hotels 'Breakaways'   *PO Box 8, Seaburn Terrace, Seaburn, Sunderland SR6 8BB. Tel: 091-529 4666*
Chain of over 30 hotels in England and Scotland, mostly in towns and cities, one third with leisure facilities (gyms, indoor pools etc). Rail inclusive prices available at some hotels. Children under 14 free. No single supplement at weekends.

★Trusthouse Forte Hotels 'London Breaks' and 'Leisure Breaks and Holidays'   *24-30 New Street, Aylesbury, Bucks HP20 2NW. Tel: 01-567 3444; 061-969 6111; (0222) 371889; 031-226 4346 and others*
Chain of over 180 hotels throughout England, Scotland and Wales, and over 10 in London. Many traditional or grand town- or city-centre, some top-of-the-market. Rail inclusive prices available. Children under 16 free. Single supplement.

Waves   *105 St Michael's Road, Bournemouth BH2 5DU. Tel: (0202) 294628*
Over 80 hotels in 10 major resorts in England and Wales, mainly in middle price range. Children's reductions vary: in some hotels, children under 14 free in parents' room; in others, children under 2 free, and reductions for under 16s. No single supplement for single room.

Whitbread Coaching Inns 'Weekend Breaks'   *Greens Building, Park Street West, Luton LU1 3BG. Tel: (0582) 454646*
Chain of over 30 mainly traditional inns in England and Wales. Children under 16 free. No single supplement.

Special interest weekends

- Fulfil a long-standing ambition – learn to parachute, take a ride in a hot air balloon or drive a racing car
- Acquire a new skill – learn to make videos or use a computer
- Broaden your mind – take a short, sharp course on art or music
- Explore the countryside – join a field studies trip or conservation project
- Pamper or punish yourself – spend a weekend at a health farm
- Practise crafts – anything from bread-making to woodturning
- Take up a new sport – learn to sail or abseil, canoe or glide
- Do something different – learn about bee-keeping or dowsing or the Korean martial art of tae-kwon-do

The most popular activities for short breaks are sailing, painting and birdwatching; but there's a vast range of more unusual activities. There are courses for all levels of experience and skill, for enthusiastic amateurs to hardened professionals. One of the advantages of taking an activity break is being able to use specialised equipment which you might not normally have access to. Another is the generally relaxed and sociable atmosphere, whether you are learning to play bridge or trying your hand at calligraphy.

A useful book is *Activity & Hobby Holidays Guide*, published by the English Tourist Board, £2.50, which lists organisations and operators under various headings (sport, crafts etc).

HOTELS

A large number of hotels offer special interest weekends, particularly in low season. Many of these simply focus attention on the facilities which are available at the hotel – such as a golf course or tennis court; others will include tuition from a professional coach. Some reflect the interests of the proprietor: there are possibilities for gourmet cooking, wine-tasting, bridge, music and gardening weekends. Local art and architecture may be covered in a 'heritage' weekend with a programme of lectures and guided tours. And traditional yuletide activities are offered in many hotels (see 'Christmas breaks' below).

The English Tourist Board's publication *Let's Go* (annual, free) lists many hotels under the type of break offered. In the section on 'Hotel Groups and Tour Operators' on page 352 we indicate with an asterisk which companies offer activity and special interest breaks in addition to their main programme. Below we list a selection of other operators who concentrate on these holidays. Jollys, 63 Parolles Road, London N19 3RE (tel: 01-281

3641) is a booking service for around 250 different types of breaks available through more than 100 hotel groups and tour operators.

The Countrywide Holidays Association   *Birch Heys, 100 Cromwell Range, Manchester M14 6HU. Tel: 061-225 1000*   Walking holidays and leisure learning weekends, mainly cultural plus painting and drama.

English Wanderer   *13 Wellington Court, Spencers Wood, Reading, Berks RG7 1BN. Tel: (0734) 882515*   Fully guided walking weekends in British hills, Feb to Nov.

HF Holidays Ltd   *Dept TB, 142 Great North Way, London NW4 1EG. Tel: (01)203 6411*   Walking weekends, staying in country houses.

Insight Tours   *28 Selly Wick Drive, Birmingham B29 7JH. Tel: 021-472 5729*   Historical weekends.

Quality Achiever Breaks   *Piccadilly House, 33 Regent Street, London SW1Y 4NB. Tel: 01-439 4955*   Mainly sporting or activity weekends.

RVS (Rare, Vintage and Special) Enterprises   *Hilton House, Norwood Lane, Meopham, Kent DA13 0YE. Tel: (0474) 812171*   Cookery, bridge and cultural interest weekends.

Sussex Seen (Country Holidays) Ltd   *14 Maltravers Street, Arundel, West Sussex BN18 9BU. Tel: (0903) 882474*   Guided walks.

ADULT EDUCATION COLLEGES AND UNIVERSITIES

A large number of residential weekend courses are offered by adult education colleges and universities (during vacations). They mainly offer craft and study courses, but often include some physical activities such as dance and yoga and field studies. Colleges range from modern purpose-built centres to large country houses set in their own grounds and standards of accommodation vary accordingly. The number of single rooms is usually limited. Rooms are often basic and food may be reminiscent of school catering. These are generally the cheapest courses (since most are non-profit-making).

The best source of information is *Residential Short Courses* (£1.05 winter edition; £1.15 summer edition), available from the National Institute of Adult Continuing Education (NIACE), 19B de Montfort Street, Leicester LE1 7GE; tel: (0533) 551451. Breaks are listed in date order to help planning. An organisation which can help with further details of university weekends is the **British Universities Accommodation Consortium Limited**, Box No 359 University Park, Nottingham NG7 2RD; tel: (0602) 504571. For information on weekend courses in field studies contact the **Field Studies Council Information Office**, Preston Montford, Montford Bridge, Shrewsbury SY4 1HW; tel: (0743) 850674.

CRAFT CENTRES
Many small workshops and craft centres offer opportunities to learn an art or craft on a more individual basis, often in attractive surroundings. Accommodation is not necessarily included.

There are a number of small centres offering weekend courses. An organisation which can help find a suitable course is **The Crafts Council**, Information Section (Courses), 12 Waterloo Place, London SW1Y 4AU; tel: 01-930 4811.

OUTDOOR ACTIVITY CENTRES
Sports and adventure weekends are offered by many outdoor activity centres throughout Britain (although the majority of courses last for a week or more). There is a strong emphasis on holidays for school parties and groups of young people and accommodation is mostly in dormitories but other local accommodation can usually be arranged. Residential centres usually provide meals, though in some cases these cost extra. Outdoor activity centres are particularly suitable for family weekends. A good starting point for information on outdoor activity weekends is **The Sports Council**, 16 Upper Woburn Place, London WC1H 0QP; tel: 01 388 1277. Their leaflet (enclose s.a.e.) *Sport for All* gives details of national sports centres, organisations governing different sports, and a guide to holiday centres.

For courses in individual sports the best sources of information are the governing bodies of the sports themselves. We list a selection:

British Balloon and Airship Club *PO Box 1006, Birmingham B5 5RT; tel: 021-643 3224*
British Canoe Union *Flexel House, 45-47 High Street, Addlestone, Weybridge, Surrey KT15 1JV; tel: Weybridge 41341*
British Gliding Association *Kimberley House, 47 Vaughan Way, Leicester LE1 4SG; tel: (0533) 531051*
British Hang Gliding Association *Cranfield Airfield, Cranfield, Bedfordshire MK43 0YR; tel: (0234) 751688*
British Horse Society *British Equestrian Centre, Stoneleigh, Kenilworth, Warwickshire CV8 2LR; tel: (0203) 52241*
British Mountaineering Council *Crawford House, Precinct Centre, Booth Street East, Manchester M13 9RZ; tel: 061-273 5839*
British Orienteering Federation *Riversdale, Dale Road North, Darley Dale, Matlock, Derbyshire DE4 2HX; tel: (0629) 734042*
British Parachute Association *5 Wharf Way, Glen Parva, Leicester, LE2 9TF; tel: (0533) 785271*
Ramblers' Association *1-5 Wandsworth Road, London SW8 2XX; tel: 01-582 6878*
Royal Yachting Association *RYA House, Romsey Road, Eastleigh, Hants SO5 4YA; tel: (0703) 629962*

Health farms

Health farms are flourishing in the present climate of body-consciousness and fitness fervour. Some health farms see their role as essentially curative, often specialising in various forms of alternative medicine, but the majority cater for people who are already healthy and want to get slimmer or fitter or simply rest and relax. Many health farms are large country houses set in attractive grounds which make them ideal places to get away from the strains of work or family. The daily programme usually includes heat treatment and massage and may include exercise classes, yoga or relaxation classes and sometimes lectures and film shows. Most health farms have leisure facilities, usually including a gym and swimming pool, sometimes tennis courts and golf courses. Food is normally healthy, but not rationed unless you choose to go on a diet. Alcohol may not be available and smoking is usually frowned upon.

The individual factors which a health farm offers can be found elsewhere, usually at a lower cost. The health and beauty treatments will not effect any lasting transformation and may not do you any good at all. Exercise is no use unless you keep it up and you are unlikely to lose a significant amount of weight over a few days. But if you need a complete physical and psychological rest, or if you think you've earned a bit of pampering, a few days at a health farm can make you feel terrific.

The health farms listed below are those which were inspected for a *Holiday Which?* report. All offer weekend or three-day stays.

Brooklands Country House Health Farm *Calder House Lane, Garstang, nr Preston, Lancashire PR3 1QB; tel: (09952) 5162*

Cedar Falls Health Farm *Bishops Lydeard, Taunton, Somerset TA4 3HR; tel: (0823) 433233*

Champneys at Tring *Tring, Hertfordshire HP23 6HY; tel: (04427) 73155 Forest Mere, Liphook, Hampshire GU30 7JQ; tel: (0428) 722051*

Grayshott Hall Health and Leisure Centre *Grayshott, nr Hindhead, Surrey GU26 6JJ; tel: (042 873) 4331*

Henlow Grange Health Farm *Henlow, Bedfordshire; tel: (0462) 811111*

Inglewood Health Hydro Ltd *Templeton Road, Kintbury, Berkshire; tel: (0488) 82022*

Ragdale Hall *Ragdale, nr Melton Mowbray, Leicestershire LE14 3PB; tel: (066 475) 831*

Snowdonia National Park Health Lodge *Tyn-Y-Maes, Bethesda, Gwynedd LL57 3LX; tel: (0248) 600548*

Advice:

- If choosing a special weekend break at a hotel, check the amount of tuition offered. What is advertised as 'heritage trail' or 'golfing weekend' may simply mean that a leaflet on the subject is available at reception, or that there is a golf course.
- Make sure a course is suitable for your level of experience; it's as soul-destroying to sit through two days of something you already know as to flounder among concepts you don't understand.
- For activities involving an element of risk you will usually have to take out your own insurance. Some centres include insurance but this may be only for public liability; ask to see a copy of the policy and consider if you need extra cover.
- If you are going on an activity weekend, check with the organisers how fit you need to be in order to participate; there may be age or weight restrictions.
- Check that the tutor in charge of the course is suitably qualified. For sporting activities it is sensible to go to a centre which is approved by the sport's governing body (contact the Sports Council, see 'Outdoor Activity Centres' above)
- It is important to check in advance precisely what is included and how much free time to expect. Make sure you know how the course will be organised and what to bring with you.
- Prices at health farms may not include VAT or the cost of various treatments, and there may be limited treatments and classes on Sundays; check carefully when booking.
- And finally, a caveat. The fact that you have booked, say, a parachuting or ballooning weekend doesn't guarantee you'll leave the ground.

Christmas and New Year breaks

The pampering part of a winter break is very much the point at Christmas. It isn't a cheap time – you can pay 150% more than in January – but how tempting to avoid either the catering chores for the family riot or the unfestive quiet, according to your circumstances. At Christmas, a hotel doesn't just mean a comfortable room and good food. Although these things are very important, the type of holiday that a hotel offers is equally important. If you're looking for a peaceful, traditional Christmas you won't be very amused to find bingo parties and discos going on day and night; equally it's no use choosing a small family-run country hotel and expecting a full programme of entertainment. But it is in fact fairly easy to find out in advance what sort of holiday you'll be letting yourself in for: most hotels which offer Christmas and New Year holidays produce a leaflet or brochure which tells you exactly how much entertainment to expect. Some even have an hour-by-hour schedule.

Many hotels, particularly in country areas, offer packages which simply include **accommodation, traditional Christmas food, and a festive atmosphere** – designed for those whose aim is to relax in peaceful surroundings. A typical Christmas stay might include a sherry reception, a visit by carol singers and the option of a visit to the local hunt on Boxing Day, but no organised programme. The emphasis is on food and atmosphere – candles on the dinner table and log fires in the lounge.

You may want slightly more than good food and atmosphere, even if you don't want a full programme of activities. Many hotels offer Christmas **packages with a certain amount of entertainment**, but the emphasis varies, and you should make sure you know exactly what is included. You are generally left to your own devices during the day but there may be social activities in the evening, such as cocktail parties and dinner dances. There may also be optional daytime activities such as a visit to the local hunt, a wine-tasting, or an outdoor treasure hunt. This kind of hotel rarely offers organised activities for children, though there is usually a visit from Father Christmas.

Smaller hotels often try to create an informal house-party atmosphere, where the guests participate in deciding the programme of events. In this case the owner or manager acts very much as a host, and may initiate outings, music or party games according to the prevailing mood. The success of this type of holiday obviously depends very much on the guests' willingness to enter into the party spirit.

Your ideal Christmas may involve a continuous round of **fun and activity**, from a pre-Christmas Eve cocktail party to a post-Boxing Day cabaret and masked ball. A great many hotels offer this kind of holiday, mainly in large towns and resorts. Entertainment could include quizzes, treasure hunts, discos, films, talent-spotting, bridge evenings, bingo, coach trips, sports, children's party games and magicians, sing-alongs and fancy-dress parades. Some hotels offer supervised children's entertainment, others expect families to participate *en masse*.

Many of the hotel groups and tour operators listed on page 354 offer Christmas breaks. Two useful publications indicate relevant hotels with a symbol – *Let's Go* (free from the English Tourist Board) and *Great Little Breaks* (free from the Wales Tourist Board). See the beginning of this chapter for addresses.

Alternative accommodation

The accommodation we recommend is almost all in hotels, pubs and guesthouses. Below we list sources of alternative accommodation, with contact addresses.

CAMPING AND CARAVANNING
Caravan sites are mostly open from April to October. For booklets on caravanning and lists of parks, write to the following:

The National Caravan Council *Catherine House, Victoria Road, Aldershot, Hampshire GU11 1SS*
The Camping and Caravanning Club *11 Lower Grosvenor Place, London SW1W 0EY*
The Caravan Club *East Grinstead House, East Grinstead, West Sussex RH19 1UA*

PRIVATE HOUSES
Local tourist offices can usually provide lists of private houses offering bed and breakfast accommodation.

Wolsey Lodges are comfortable private homes, often of historic interest, in England and Wales, with a concentration in the south of England. There are 130 properties, most with fewer than five bedrooms. Contact Wolsey Lodges Ltd, 17 Chapel Street, Bildeston, Suffolk IP7 7EP; tel: (0449) 741297.

SELF-CATERING HOUSES AND COTTAGES
The following companies offer short breaks, mostly off-season (usually September or October to March or April):

Amaro Cottage Holidays *22 High Street, Alton, Hampshire GU34 1BN; tel: (0420) 88892*
Jean Bartlett Holidays Ltd *Fore Street, Beer, Seaton, Devon EX12 3JB; tel: (0297) 23221*
Blakes Holidays *Wroxham, Norwich NR12 8DHl; tel: (060 53) 2917/9*
Cerbid Quality Cottages *Cerbid, Solva, Dyfed SA62 6YE, tel: (03483) 7871*
Character Cottages Holidays Ltd *Booking Dept EH, 34 Fore Street, Sidmouth, Devon EX10 8AQ; tel: (039 55) 77001*
Clippesby Holidays *Clippesby, Nr Great Yarmouth, Norfolk NR29 3BJ; tel: (049 377) 367*
Coastal Cottages of Pembrokeshire *Abercastle, Nr St David's, Dyfed SA62 5HJ; tel: (03483) 7742*
Cornish Traditional Cottages Ltd *Peregrine Hall, Lostwithiel, Cornwall PL22 0HT; tel: (0208) 872559*
Cottage Holidays *17 Holdenhurst Road, Bournemouth, Dorset BH8 8EH; tel: (0202) 295006/25545*
Country Farm Holidays *1 Shaw Mews, Shaw Street, Worcester WR1 3QQ; tel: (0905) 613744*

Country & Seaside Holidays *John Fowler Holidays, Marlborough Road, Dept 2, Ilfracombe, Devon EX34 8PF; tel: (0271) 66766*
Countryside Cottages *Vale House, Gillingham, Dorset SP8 4RS; tel: (074 76) 4778*
Dales Holiday Cottages *12 Otley Street, Skipton, North Yorkshire BD23 1DY; tel: (0756) 69821/60919*
Devon Cottages *The Geminids (1), Abbotskerswell, Devon TQ12 5PP; tel: (0626) 52214*
English Country Cottages *Dept E104, Claypit Lane, Fakenham, Norfolk NR21 8AS; tel: (0328) 4041*
Ingrid Flute Holiday Accommodation Agency *White Cottage, Ravenscar, Scarborough, North Yorkshire YO13 0NE; tel: (0723) 870703*
Gateway Holiday Properties *7 Westview Close, Bradley, Via Keighley, West Yorkshire BD20 9BU; tel: (0756) 2061*
Grey Abbey Properties Ltd *PO Box 23, Coach Road, Whitehaven, Cumbria CA28 9DF; tel: (0946) 3346/3364*
Gwillim's Country Holidays *Greystones, Bell Street, Talgarth, Powys LD3 0BP, tel: (0874) 711346*
Havelock Agency *1 Havelock Road, Hastings, East Sussex TN34 1BB; tel: (0424) 436779*
Heart of England Cottages *Iveson House, Ampney St Peter, Cirencester, Gloucestershire GL7 5SH; tel: (0285) 87217*
Hideaways *4 Bridge Street, Salisbury, Wiltshire SP1 2LX; tel: (0722) 24868*
Landmark Trust *Shottesbrooke, Maidenhead, Berks; tel: (062 882) 5925*
Lyme Bay Holidays *Waddington House, Main Street, Charmouth, Dorset DT6 6QE; tel: (0297) 60755*
Mackay's Agency *30 Frederick Street, Edinburgh EH2 2IR; tel: 031-226 4364*
North Devon Holiday Homes *North Devon Holiday Centre, 48 Boutport Street, Barnstaple, Devon EX31 1SE; tel: (0271) 76322*
North Wales Holiday Cottages and Farmhouses *Station Road, Deganwy, Conwy, Gwynedd LL31 9DF; tel (0492) 82492*
Pembrokeshire Cottages *Park House, Tiers Cross, Haverfordwest, Dyfed SA62 3DB; tel: (043783) 764*
Powell's Cottage Holiday *52 High Street, Saundersfoot, Pembrokeshire; tel: (0834) 813232/812791*
Scottish Country Cottages *2d Churchill Way, Bishopbriggs, Glasgow G64 2RH; tel: 041 772 5920*
Taylor Lane & Creber *32 Causewayhead, Penzance, Cornwall TR18 2SP; tel: (0736) 60070*
Torquay's Maxton Lodge Holiday Flats *Rousdown Road, Torquay, Devon TQ2 6PB; tel: (0803) 607811*
Wales Cottage Holidays *The Bank, Newtown, Powys SY16 2AA; tel: (0686) 27874*

BOATS AND CRUISERS

The following companies organise short breaks, usually of at least 3 nights and usually from March to October, with basic tuition:

Alvechurch Boat Centre Ltd *Scarfield Wharf, Alvechurch, Nr Birmingham, West Midlands B48 7SQ, tel: (021 445) 2909*

Anglo Welsh Waterway Holidays   *Canal Basin, Leicester Road, Market Harborough, Leicestershire LE16 7BJ; tel: (0858) 66910*

Bijou Line Holidays   *Dunhampstead Wharf, Droitwich, Worcestershire WR9 7JX; tel: (0905) 773889*

Black Prince Holidays Ltd   *Black Prince Marina, Whixall, Nr Whitchurch, Shropshire SY13 2QP; tel: (094 872) 420*

Blakes Holidays   *Wroxham, Norwich, Norfolk NR12 8DH; tel: (060 53) 3221*

British Waterways Leisure   *Nantwich Marina, Chester Road, Nantwich, Cheshire CW5 8LB; tel: (0270) 625122*

Corsair Cruisers Ltd   *Upton Marina, Upton-on-Severn, Hereford and Worcester WR8 0PB; tel: (068 45) 69275*

Dartline Cruisers   *9a Canal Wharf, Bunbury, Nr Tarporley, Cheshire CW6 9QB; tel: (0829) 260638*

Guildford Boat House   *Millbrook, Guildford, Surrey GU1 3XJ; tel: (0483) 504494*

Hoseasons Holidays   *B40 Sunway House, Lowestoft, Suffolk NR32 3LT; tel: (0502) 501501*

Thames Hire Cruiser Association   *Administration Secretary, 19 Acre End Street, Eynsham, Oxford OX8 1PE; tel: (0865) 880107*

Viking Afloat Ltd   *Lowesmoor Wharf, Worcester, Hereford and Worcester WR1 2RX; tel: (0905) 28667*

Windermere Lake Holidays Afloat Ltd   *Shepherds Boatyard, Bowness Bay, Windermere, Cumbria LA23 3HE; tel: (096 62) 3415/5395*

INDEX

Abbey Dore Court Gardens 190
Abbey, Bath 20
Abbey, Battle 327
Abbey, Bolton 275
Abbey, Buckfast 201
Abbey, Byland 240
Abbey, Cleeve, Washford 212
Abbey, Dorchester 173
Abbey, Dore 190
Abbey, Dryburgh 150
Abbey, Lacock 21
Abbey, Llanthony 190
Abbey, Rievaulx 240
Abbey, St Augustine's,
 Canterbury 39
Abbey, St Dogmaels 318
Abbey, Westminster 73
Abbotsford, Melrose 150
Abbott Hall Museum, Kendal 222
Aberdyfi 263
Abergavenny 190
Abingdon 172
Achnacloich 287
Acton Scott Working Farm Museum,
 Church Stretton 193
Aira Force 223
Airton 275
Alchemist's Tower, Canterbury 38
Alfriston 326
Allerford 210
All Saints, York 124
Alnmouth 311
Alnwick Castle 311
Alternative Technology Centre,
 Machynlleth 264
Alton Towers Theme Park 252
Amberley 330
Amberley Chalk Pits Museum 333
Ambleside 221
American Museum, Bath 19
An Cala, Easdale 288
Anglesey Abbey, Lode 32
Anne Hathaway's Cottage,
 Stratford 116
Apsley House, London 74
Aquarium and Dolphinarium,
 Brighton 330
Archaeology, Museum of,
 Durham 44
Ardanaiseig, Kilchrenan 288
Ardchattan Priory, Connel 288
Arduaine Gardens 287
Argyll Coast 286
Argyll Wildlife Park 288
Arlington Court, nr Barnstaple 211
Arlington Mill, Bibury 135

Arms and Armour Museum,
 Stratford 117
Arncliffe 275
Arthur's Seat, Edinburgh 52
Arundel 330
Arundel Castle 332
Ashbourne 251
Ashburton 200
Ashford-in-the-Water 251
Ashmolean Museum, Oxford 107
Askrigg 277
Assembly House, Norwich 101
Assembly Rooms, Bath 19
Assembly Rooms, York 123
Athelhampton 182
Auchindrain Museum of Farming
 Life 288
Audley End 32

Bailgate, Lincoln 65
Bainbridge 277
Bakewell 251
Ballachulish 287
Bamburgh 310
Bamburgh Castle 311
Banqueting House, London 74
Barbara Hepworth Museum,
 St Ives 298
Barguillean, Taynuilt 288
Barmouth 263
Basildon Park, Pangbourne 172
Bassenthwaite 223
Bate Collection of Musical
 Instruments, Oxford 109
Bath 18
Bath Abbey 20
Batsford Arboretum,
 Moreton-in-Marsh 133
Battle Abbey 327
Beaminster 181
Beaulieu 334
Beck Isle Museum of Rural Life,
 Pickering 241
Beddgelert 261
Beeston Hall,
 Beeston St Lawrence 103
Belton House 67
Beningbrough Hall 125
Berrington Hall, nr Leominster 191
Berwick Borough Museum and Art
 Gallery 312
Berwick-upon-Tweed 310
Bethnal Green Museum of
 Childhood 75
Betws-y-Coed 261
Bibury 134

Bickleigh Castle 212
Birdland, Bourton-on-the-Water 133
Bisham 172
Bishop's Castle 192
Blackfriars Refectory, Canterbury 38
Black Mountains 189
Black Pool Mill 320
Blandford Forum 182
Blenheim Palace 110
Blickling Hall, Norfolk 103
Blockley 133
Bodiam Castle 327
Bodinnick 301
Bodleian Library, Oxford 108
Bodnant Garden, Tal-y-Cafn 262
Bognor Regis 331
Bolton Abbey 275
Bolton Castle 277
Booth Museum of Natural History,
    Brighton 330
Borrowdale 223
Boscastle 298
Boscombe 332
Bosham 331
Bossiney Haven 298
Botanic Garden, Cambridge 31
Botanic Gardens, Oxford 108
Boulby 242
Bournemouth 331
Bourton-on-the-Water 133
Bow 301
Bowes Museum, Barnard Castle 45
Bowhill, Selkirk 150
Bowness 221
Boxford 162
Brantwood, Coniston Water 221
Brass Rubbing Centre, Stratford 117
Bridewell Museum, Norwich 101
Bridge Cottage, Flatford 162
Brighton 329
Brighton Museum and Art
    Gallery 329
Brinkburn Priory 312
British Engineerium, Hove 330
British Museum, London 74
British Telecom Museum, Oxford 109
Broadlands 333
Broads, The, Norfolk 103
Broadway 132
Broadway Tower Country Park 133
Broughton 152
Buckfast Abbey 201
Buckfastleigh Steam and Leisure
    Park 201
Buckland 132
Buckland Abbey, nr Tavistock 201
Buckler's Hard 331
Bude 298
Bude Canal 299
Bulbarrow Hill 182
Burford 134
Burrell Collection, Glasgow 58
Butterfly Farm, Stratford 117
Buttermere 224
Byland Abbey 240
Buxton 252

Cadgwith 299
Caerfai 318
Caernarfon 261
Caernarfon Castle 261
Calton Hill, Edinburgh 51
Camber Sands 326
Cambridge 29
Camden Works Museum, Bath 19
Campbeltown 287
Canongate, Edinburgh 52
Canonteign Falls and Country
    Park 201
Canterbury 37
Capel Curig 261
Captain Cook Birthplace Museum,
    Marton 241
Captain Cook Memorial Museum,
    Whitby 243
Carew Castle 319
Carradale 287
Carradale House Gardens 287
Carriage Museum, Bath 20
Castell y Bere 263
Castle Combe 134
Castle Drogo, Drewsteignton 201
Castle Fish Farm, Inveraray 288
Castle Hedingham 163
Castle Hill, Lincoln 65
Castle Howard 125
Castle Jail, Jedburgh 151
Castle Museum, Norwich 101
Castle Museum, York 123
Castlerigg Stone Circle 223
Castleton 252
Cathedral, Canterbury 37
Cathedral, Chichester 332
Cathedral, Durham 43
Cathedral, Glasgow 59
Cathedral, Lincoln 64
Cathedral, Norwich 101
Cathedral, Southwark 74
Cathedral, St David's 318
Cathedral, St Giles', Edinburgh 52
Cathedral, St Paul's 73
Cattistock 181
Cavendish 163
Cawsand 301
Cerne Abbas 181
Chagford 200
Chambercombe Manor,
    Ilfracombe 211
Chapel Porth 298
Charlecote House 117
Charleston Farmhouse, nr Firle 327
Chatsworth 251
Cheltenham 133
Chichester 331
Childhood, Museum of,
    Edinburgh 50
Children's Farm, Great Knelle 328
Chipping Camden 133
Chiswick House 81
Christ Church, Oxford 107
Christchurch 331
Church Stretton 192
Cilgerran Castle 318
Circus, Bath 19

Cirencester 134
City and County Museum, Lincoln 66
City Art Gallery, York 124
City Arts Centre, Edinburgh 51
Chillingham Castle 311
Clare 163
Cleeve Abbey, Washford 212
Clergy House, Alfriston 327
Cliffords Tower, York 123
Climping 331
Cliveden, Taplow 173
Clun 192
Clyro 190
Cobbaton Combat Vehicles
    Museum 212
Coldstream 151
Colleges, Cambridge 30
Colleges, Oxford 107
Combe Sydenham Hall,
    Monksilver 212
Compton House, Sherborne 183
Coniston Water 221
Conwy 261
Conwy Castle 261
Cookham 172
Cook Heritage Trail 241
Coquet Island 313
Corinium Museum, Cirencester 135
Cornish Coast 297
Corris 263
Corsham Court 21
Costume, Museum of, Bath 20
Cotswold Countryside Collection 135
Cotswold Farm Park 133
Cotswold Wild Life Park 135
Cotswolds, The 132
Coughton Court, nr Alcester 117
Courtauld Institute, London 73
Cowal 286
Crackington Haven 298
Cramond 54
Crarae Woodland Garden,
    nr Inveraray 288
Crescent Art Gallery,
    Scarborough 242
Criccieth Castle 264
Crickhowell 190
Crickley Hill Country Park 135
Crinan 287
Croft Castle, nr Leominster 192
Cruachan Power Station,
    Loch Awe 288
Crummock Water 224
Cutty Sark, Greenwich 76
Cwm yr Eglwys 318

Dalemain, Dacre 224
Dalmeny House 53
Dalnashean, Appin 287
Dartmoor 200
Dartmoor Life, Museum of 201
Dartmoor Wildlife Park 201
Deal Castle 327
Dedham 161
Delabole Slate Quarry 299
Denmans Garden, nr Arundel 332

Dent 275
Derwent Water 223
Devil's Beef Tub 152
Dinas Mawddy 263
Dinosaur Museum, Dorchester 183
Divinity School, Oxford 108
Doddington Hall 66
Dolbadarn Castle 261
Dolgellau 263
Dolwyddelan Castle 261
Dorchester 180
Dorchester Abbey 173
Dorchester-on-Thames 172
Dore Abbey 190
Dorney Court, nr Windsor 173
Dorset County Museum 183
Dorset Military Museum,
    Dorchester 183
Dove Cottage, Grasmere 221
Dovedale 251
Dover 326
Dover Castle 327
Drewsteignton 200
Drusilla's Zoo Park, Alfriston 328
Dryburgh Abbey 150
Dulverton 211
Dulwich College Picture Gallery 73
Dungeon, London 75
Dunoon 286
Duns 151
Dunstanburgh Castle 311
Dunster 210
Dunster Castle 211
Duntisbournes, The 134
Durham 43
Durham Castle 44
Dursley 134
Dyrham Park 21

Eardisland 191
East Bergholt 161
Eastbourne 326
Edinburgh 48
Edinburgh Castle 48
Eggardon 181
Ely 33
Ennerdale Water 225
Eskdale 239
Esthwaite Water 221
Etal 310
Eton College 171
Evershot 181
Exbury Gardens 332
Exchequergate, Lincoln 65
Exford 211
Exmoor 210
Exmoor Bird Gardens 212
Exmoor Brass Rubbing Centre 212
Eyam 251

Fairfax House, York 123
Fairford 134
Falmouth 301
Farndale 239
Farne Islands 311

Far Sawrey 221
Fell Foot Country Park,
    Newby Bridge 222
Ferniehirst Castle, nr Jedburgh 153
Fiddleford 182
Finch Foundry Museum,
    Sticklepath 201
Finchale Priory 45
Firle Place 328
Fishing Museum, Seahouses 312
Fitzwilliam Museum, Cambridge 29
Flambards Triple Theme Park,
    Helston 300
Flatford 162
Floors Castle, Kelso 150
Folk Museum, Cambridge 31
Folkestone 326
Ford 310
Forde Abbey, Chard 183
Fowey 301
Freshwater West 318
Fruit Market Gallery, Edinburgh 51
Fylingdales 242

Gainsborough Old Hall 66
Gainsborough's House, Sudbury 164
Galashiels 151
Garsdale 276
Geevor Tin Mines, Pendeen 300
Geological Museum, London 75
Geology Museum, Bath 20
Georgian House, Edinburgh 50
Georgian Theatre Royal,
    Richmond 277
Gladstone's Land, Edinburgh 50
Glasgow 58
Glen Coe 287
Glendurgan Garden,
    Mawnan Smith 301
Glenridding 223
Gloddfa Ganol Slate Mine,
    Blaenau Ffestiniog 262
Goathland 240
Golden Valley 190
Goodwood House 332
Goonhilly Satellite Earth Station 300
Goring 172
Goyt Valley 252
Grace Darling Museum,
    Bamburgh 312
Grange, The, Brighton 330
Grantchester 32
Grasmere 221
Grassington 275
Great Dixter, Northiam 328
Great Park, Windsor 171
Great St Andrew's, Cambridge 31
Great St Mary's, Cambridge 31
Green Howards Regimental Museum,
    Richmond 277
Greenlaw 151
Greyfriars Kirk, Edinburgh 52
Greyfriars, Canterbury 38
Grey Mare's Tail 152
Grimspound 201
Grinton 277

Grizedale Forest 221
Grosmont 190
Guildhall, Lavenham 163
Guildhall, Norwich 101
Guildhall, Windsor 171
Guildhall, York 123
Gypsy Caravans, National
    Museum of, Pembroke 319
Gypsy Moth IV, Greenwich 76

Haddon Hall 251
Hadleigh 162
Halliwell's House, Selkirk 151
Ham House, Richmond 81
Hampton Court 81
Hardwick Hall 251
Harlech 263
Harlech Castle 264
Hartsholme Country Park 67
Hastings 326
Hastings Castle 327
Hawes 276
Haweswater 222
Hawick 150
Hawick Museum 151
Hawkshead 221
Hawnby 240
Hayling Island 331
Hay-on-Wye 190
Hayward Gallery, London 73
Heddon's Mouth 211
Hedingham Castle 163
Helford 299
Helmsley 240
Helston 299
Hemmick 301
Henley 172
Hereford 190
Hergest Croft Gardens, Kington 191
Heritage Museum, Canterbury 38
Hermitage Castle, Newcastleton 153
Herschel House, Bath 20
Hidcote Manor Garden 133
Higham 162
Hill House, Helensburgh 60
Hill Top, Near Sawrey 222
Hirsel, The, Coldstream 152
History of Science Museum,
    Oxford 109
HMS Belfast 76
Holburne Museum, Bath 19
Holy Island 311
Holyroodhouse, Palace of 49
Holy Trinity, York 124
Home, Museum of the,
    Pembroke 320
Hopetoun House 53
Hospital of St Thomas, Canterbury 38
House of Hardy Museum,
    Alnwick 312
Hove Museum and Art Gallery 330
Hunterian Art Gallery, Glasgow 59
Huntingdon 33
Huntly House, Edinburgh 51
Hurley 172
Hutton-le-Hole 240

Hythe 326

Ilam 251
Imperial War Museum, Duxford 32
Imperial War Museum, London 75
Industrial Heritage Centre, Bath 19
Ingleborough Cave 276
Inveraray 287
Inveraray Castle 287
Itchenor 331

Jedburgh 150
Jew's House and Jew's Court,
    Lincoln 65
John Knox's House, Edinburgh 50
Jorvik Viking Centre, York 123

Kailzie Gardens, Peebles 153
Kedleston Hall 251
Kelso Museum 151
Kelvingrove Art Gallery and
    Museum, Glasgow 59
Kendal 220
Kendal Museum 222
Kensington Palace 74
Kentwell Hall, Long Melford 164
Kenwood House, London 81
Kersey 163
Keswick 223
Kettles Yard, Cambridge 31
Kew Gardens 76
Kew Palace 81
Kilmory Castle Gardens 288
Kilnsey Park 276
Kilpeck 190
Kingsand 301
King's College Chapel, Cambridge 30
Kington 191
Kintyre 287
Kirkby Malham 275
Kirkbymoorside 240
Knapdale 287
Knightshayes Court, nr Tiverton 212
Kynance Cove 299

Lacock 21
Lacock Abbey 21
Lady Stair's House, Edinburgh 50
Lady Waterford Hall, Ford 312
Lake District 220
Lamb House, Rye 327
Lamphey Palace 319
Land's End 299
Langdale 221
Lanhydrock, nr Bodmin 301
Lantic Bay 301
Lantivet Bay 301
Lastingham 240
Lathkill Dale 251
Lauder 151
Lauriston Castle 53
Lavenham 163
Lee Bay 211

Leith 54
Leominster 191
Levens Hall, Kendal 222
Light Infantry Museum, Durham 44
Lincoln 64
Lincoln Castle 65
Lincolnshire Life, Museum of,
    Lincoln 66
Lindisfarne 311
Lindisfarne Castle 311
Lindisfarne Nature Reserve 313
Lindisfarne Priory 312
Lindisfarne Wine and Spirit Museum,
    Berwick 312
Lingholm Gardens,
    Derwent Water 224
Linton Zoo 32
Littlehampton 330
Little St Mary's, Cambridge 31
Living World, The, Seaford 328
Llandrindod Wells 191
Llanthony Abbey 190
Llechwedd Slate Caverns,
    Blaenau Ffestiniog 262
Lleithyr Farm Museum 318
Loch Awe 287
Loch Etive 287
Loch Fyne 287
Lochgilphead 287
Lochgoilhead 286
Loch Linnhe 287
Loch Lomond 60
London 70
London, Museum of 75
London Zoo 76
Long Melford 163
Long Mynd 192
Looe 301
Loweswater 224
Lowther Park 224
Luccombe 210
Ludlow 191
Ludlow Castle 192
Lustleigh 200
Lyme Hall, nr Stockport 252
Lymington 331
Lympne Castle, Hythe 327
Lynmouth 211
Lynton 211

Machynlleth 263
Madame Tussaud's, London 76
Maes Artro 264
Maiden Castle, Dorchester 184
Maidenhead 172
Malhamdale 275
Manderston, Duns 151
Manifold Valley 251
Mankind, Museum of, London 75
Manorbier 319
Manorbier Castle 319
Mapledurham House 172
Mapperton, Beaminster 183
Marazion 299
Marble Hill House, Twickenham 81
Marloes Sands 318

Marlow 172
Martello Towers 327
Mary Arden's House, near
    Stratford 116
Mary Queen of Scots' House,
    Jedburgh 150
Matlock Bath 251
Melford Hall, Long Melford 164
Mellerstain, Gordon 150
Melrose 150
Merchant Adventurers' Hall,
    York 123
Mevagissey 301
Michelham Priory, Upper Dicker 328
Middleham 277
Milford-on-Sea 331
Milton Abbas 182
Minack Theatre, Porthcurno 300
Minchinhampton 134
Minster Lovell 110
Minster Yard, Lincoln 65
Minterne, Minterne Magna 183
Mirehouse, Bassenthwaite Lake 224
Model Railway,
    Bourton-on-the-Water 133
Monkton Farleigh Mine 21
Monmouth 190
Monsal Dale 251
Montgomery 192
Moretonhampstead 200
Morwellham Quay Museum 201
Mother Ivy's Bay 298
Motor Museum, Melrose 151
Motor Museum, Stratford 117
Mount Grace Priory,
    nr Osmotherley 240
Mousehole 299
Much Wenlock 192
Muker 277
Mullion 299
Mullion Cove 299
Muncaster Castle 225
Muncaster Mill 225

National Army Museum, London 75
National Cycle Museum, Lincoln 66
National Gallery of Modern Art,
    Edinburgh 51
National Gallery of Scotland,
    Edinburgh 49
National Gallery, London 73
National Maritime Museum,
    Greenwich 75
National Museum of Antiquities,
    Edinburgh 51
National Portrait Gallery,
    Edinburgh 51
National Portrait Gallery, London 73
National Tramway Museum,
    Crich 252
Natural History Museum, London 74
Naunton 133
Nayland 162
Necropolis, Glasgow 59
Neidpath Castle, Peebles 153
Nether Hall, Cavendish 163

Nettlecombe 210
Nevern 318
Newburgh Priory, Coxwold 240
Newmarket 32
New Place, Stratford 116
Newport 318
Newport Arch, Lincoln 65
Newport Sands 318
Newquay 298
New Radnor 191
New Romney 326
Newtondale 239
Norfolk Wildlife Park,
    Great Wichingham 103
Norham Castle 311
North Bovey 208
North of England Open Air Museum,
    Beamish 45
Northumberland National Park 313
Northumbrian Coast 310
North York Moors 239
Norwich 100
Norwich Castle 101
Nunnington Hall 241

Oban 287
Okehampton Castle 201
Old Llanfair Quarry Slate Caverns,
    Harlech 264
Old Palace, Lincoln 65
Old Radnor 191
Oriental Art, Museum of, Durham 44
Osterley Park 81
Outlook Tower and Camera Obscura,
    Edinburgh 49
Oxford 106
Oxford, Museum of 109
Oxford Story, The 108

Padstow 298
Painswick 134
Painswick Rococo Garden 134
Pallant House, Chichester 332
Pangbourne 172
Pannett Park Museum and Art
    Gallery, Whitby 243
Parades, Bath 19
Parham House 332
Park Farm Museum,
    Milton Abbas 184
Parnham House, Beaminster 183
Partrishow 190
Patterdale 223
Paul Corin's Music Museum,
    nr Liskeard 301
Paulton's Park, Ower 334
Pavilion, Brighton 329
Peak District 250
Peak District Mining Museum 252
Peebles 152
Pembridge 191
Pembroke 319
Pembroke Castle 319
Pembrokeshire Coast, The 317
Pencarrow, Washaway 298

Pencil Museum, Keswick 224
Pendower 301
Penlee House, Penzance 300
Penrith 222
Penzance 299
People's Palace, Glasgow 59
Perranporth 298
Petworth House 332
Pickering 240
Picton Castle 319
Pilgrim's Way, Canterbury 38
Pilsdon Pen 181
Pitt-Rivers Museum, Oxford 109
Planetarium, The 76
Plush 181
Poldark Mine, Helston 300
Pollok House, Glasgow 59
Polperro 301
Polruan 301
Polstead 162
Polzeath 298
Poole Harbour 332
Pooley Bridge 223
Porlock 211
Porlock Weir 211
Portchester Castle 332
Porthcurnick 301
Porthluney 301
Port Isaac 298
Port Lympne Zoo Park 328
Portmeirion 264
Portsmouth 331
Postal Museum, Bath 20
Powerstock 181
Powis Castle, Welshpool 193
Presteigne 191
Preston Manor 329
Preston Tower 312
Prinknash Bird Park 135
Priory, Lavenham 163
Provand's Lordship, Glasgow 59
Puddletown 181
Pulls Ferry, Norwich 101
Pulteney Bridge, Bath 19
Pump Room, Bath 19
Purse Caundle 181
Pusey House Gardens 110

Queensferry 53
Queen's Gallery, London 73
Queen Square, Bath 19
Quince Honey Farm,
   South Molton 212

Radcliffe Camera, Oxford 108
Radnor Forest 191
Raglan Castle 190
Ragley Hall, Alcester 117
Railway, Bala Lake 264
Railway, Colne Valley,
   nr Castle Hedingham 164
Railway, Dart Valley 202
Railway, Fairbourne 264
Railway, Ffestiniog 262
Railway, Kent and East Sussex 328

Railway, Lakeside and
   Haverthwaite 222
Railway, Llanberis Lake 262
Railway, North York Moors 241
Railway, Ravenglass and Eskdale 225
Railway, Romney, Hythe and
   Dymchurch 328
Railway, Snowdon Mountain 262
Railway, Tal-y-llyn 264
Railway, Volks Electric, Brighton 330
Railway, Welsh Highland 262
Railway, West Somerset 212
Railway, Yorkshire Dales 276
Railway Museum, East Anglian,
   Chappel 164
Railway Museum, National, York 124
Railway Museum, Ravenglass 225
Railway Museum, Winchcombe 134
Railway Park, Gorse Blossom
   Miniature 202
Rainbow's End, Bognor Regis 334
Rampisham 181
Ravenscar 242
Red House Museum,
   Christchurch 333
Reeth 277
Regency Brighton 329
Ribblesdale 275
Richmond 277
Richmond Castle 277
Richmond Park 76
Rievaulx Abbey 240
River Dart Country Park 201
Robin Hood's Bay 242
Rock 298
Roman Baths, Bath 18
Roman Mosaic, Canterbury 38
Roman Painted House, Dover 327
Roman Palace and Museum,
   Fishbourne 332
Roman Villa, Bignor 332
Roman Villa, Chedworth 134
Roman Villa, North Leigh 110
Rotunda Museum, Oxford 109
Rotunda, Scarborough 242
Round Church, Cambridge 31
Rousham House 110
Rowsley 251
Royal Academy, London 73
Royal Botanic Garden, Edinburgh 52
Royal Crescent, Bath 19
Royal Mile, Edinburgh 49
Royal Museum, Canterbury 38
Royal Museum of Scotland,
   Edinburgh 51
Royal Naval College, Greenwich 74
Royal Navy Submarine Museum,
   Gosport 333
Royal Shakespeare Theatre,
   Stratford 117
Royalty and Empire, Windsor 171
Runswick 242
Russell-Cotes Museum,
   Bournemouth 333
Rydal Mount, Rydal 222
Rydal Water 221
Rye 326

Ryedale Folk Museum, Hutton-le-Hole 241

Safari Park, Windsor 171
Sainsbury Centre, Norwich 102
St Agnes 298
St Andrew's, Edinburgh 52
St Austell 301
St Augustine's Abbey, Canterbury 39
St Bartholomew's, Brighton 329
St Bene't's, Cambridge 31
St Bride's Bay 318
St David's 318
St Dogmael's Abbey 318
St Dunstar's, Canterbury 39
St George's Chapel, Windsor 171
St Ives 298
St Just-in-Roseland 301
St Leonards 326
St Martin Le Grand, York 124
St Martin's, Canterbury 39
St Martin-in-the-Fields, London 74
St Mary-le-Bow, Durham 44
St Mary the Virgin, Oxford 109
St Mary's Loch 152
St Mary's, Bramber 332
St Mawes 301
St Michael at the North Gate, Oxford 109
St Michael's Mount, Marazion 300
St Mildred's, Canterbury 39
St Paul in the Bail, Lincoln 65
St Peter Hungate, Norwich 102
St Peter Mancroft, Norwich 102
Sally Lunn's House, Bath 20
Sandbanks 332
Sandford Orcas 181
Scale Force 224
Scaplen's Court, Poole 333
Scarborough 242
School of Art, Glasgow 59
Science Museum, London 75
Scolton Country Park 320
Scottish Borders, The 149
Scottish Museum of Woollen Textiles, Peebles 153
Scott Polar Research Institute, Cambridge 31
Seahouses 311
Sea Life Centre, Loch Creran 288
Sea Life Centre, Portsmouth 334
Seal Sanctuary, Gweek 300
Selkirk 150
Selworthy 210
Shakespeare's birthplace, Stratford 116
Shandy Hall, Coxwold 241
Sheldonian Theatre, Oxford 108
Sheldon Manor 21
Sherborne 181
Sherborne Castle 183
Shire Horse Centre, Maidenhead 173
Shropshire Hills 192
Sir John Soane's Museum, London 75
Sizergh Castle, Kendal 222
Skenfrith 190

Skipton 275
Slad 134
Slaughters, The 133
Smailholm Tower 151
Smart's Amusement Park, Littlehampton 334
Snailbeach 192
Snowdonia 260
Snowshill 132
Snowshill Manor 133
Solva 319
Southampton 331
South Coast, The 325
Southend 287
Staithes 242
Stangers Hall, Norwich 101
Stanley Spencer Gallery, Cookham 173
Stanton 132
Steep Hill, Lincoln 65
Stoke Abbot 181
Stoke-by-Nayland 162
Stokesay Castle, Craven Arms 193
Stonefield Castle, Tarbert 288
Stonor, Henley-on-Thames 172
Stour Valley, The 161
Stow-on-the-Wold 133
Strangles, The 298
Stratfield Saye, nr Reading 172
Stratford-upon-Avon 116
Strawberry Hill, Twickenham 81
Streatley 172
Strone Garden, Cairndow 287
Stroud 134
Stump Cross Caverns 276
Sturminster Newton 182
Sudbury 163
Sudbury Hall 251
Sudeley Castle, Winchcombe 133
Sue Ryder Museum, Cavendish 164
Sutton Park 125
Swaledale 276
Swan Theatre, Stratford 117
Sygun Copper Mine, Beddgelert 262
Syon House, Brentford 81

Talbot Rice Art Centre, Edinburgh 51
Talgarth 190
Talland Bay 301
Tarbert 287
Tarn Hows 221
Tate Gallery, London 73
Tattershall Castle 66
Tenby 319
Tenby Museum 320
Tenement House, Glasgow 59
Tetbury 134
Thames Barrier 76
Thames Valley, The 170
Theatre Museum, London 75
Theatre Royal, Bath 19
Thirlestane Castle, Lauder 151
Thirlmere 223
Throwleigh 200
Thwaite 277
Tideswell 251

Tighnabruich 286
Tintagel 298
Tintagel Castle 298
Tissington 251
Tiverton Castle 212
Tolbooth Kirk, Edinburgh 52
Tolpuddle 181
Towan 301
Tower Bridge, London 76
Tower of London 74
Townend, Troutbeck 222
Transport Museum, London 75
Traquair House, Innerleithen 152
Treasurer's House, York 123
Trebarwith Strand 298
Trebetherick 298
Trelissick Garden, Feock 301
Trengwainton Garden,
  nr Penzance 300
Trerice, Newquay 298
Tretower Court and Castle 190
Trevaunance Cove 298
Trevellas Porth 298
Trewithin 301
Tron Kirk, Edinburgh 53
Truro 301
Tutenkhamun Exhibition,
  Dorchester 183
Tweeddale Museum, Peebles 153

Ugbrooke 201
Ullswater 222
University Museum, Oxford 109
Upland Dorset 180
Uppark 332
Upper Derwent Valley 252
Upton House, nr Banbury 117
Usher Gallery, Lincoln 65

Victoria and Albert Museum,
  London 75
Victoria Art Gallery, Bath 20

Wadebridge 298
Wallace Collection, London 73
Walmer Castle 327
Walter Scott Monument,
  Edinburgh 50
Wargrave 172
Warkworth 311
Warkworth Castle 311
Warwick Castle 117
Wasdale Head 225
Wast Water 225
Watermouth Castle 212
Waterperry Gardens 110

Wax Museum, Edinburgh 50
Wayside Museum, Zennor 300
Weald and Downland Open Air
  Museum, Singleton 333
Welsh Marches, The 189
Welshpool 192
Welsh Slate Musem, Llanberis 262
Wenlock Edge 192
Wensley 277
Wensleydale 276
Weobley 191
West Burton 277
West Dean Gardens 332
Westgate, Canterbury 38
Westminster Abbey 73
Westonbirt Arboretum 134
West Register House, Edinburgh 52
West Wittering 331
Wharfedale 275
Wheal Martyn 301
Whitby 242
White Castle, nr Abergavenny 190
Whitelaw Collection, St David's 318
Whitesand Bay, Land's End 299
Whitesand Bay, nr St David's 318
White Scar Cave 276
Widecombe 200
Wildlife Park, Combe Martin 212
Wimpole Hall 32
Winchcombe 132
Winchelsea 326
Windermere 220
Windermere Steamboat Museum,
  Bowness 222
Windsor Castle 171
Winsford 210
Winterborne Clenston 182
Winterborne Tomson 182
Wolfeton House, Charminster 183
Woodend Museum, Scarborough 242
Woodland Centre, Jedburgh 153
Woody Bay 211
Wootton Courtenay 210
Wordsworth House,
  Cockermouth 225
World of Shakespeare, Stratford 117
Worthing 330
Wotton-under-Edge 134
Wringcliff Bay 211
Wynford Eagle 181

York 122
York Minster 122
Yorkshire Dales 274
Yorkshire Museum, York 124
York Story, The 124
Younger Botanic Garden,
  Benmore 287

WEATHER STATISTICS

		JAN			FEB			MAR			APR		
		T	R	S	T	R	S	T	R	S	T	R	S
SCOTLAND													
Argyll Coast	Oban	6	20	15	7	17	24	9	15	28	11	17	33
	Edinburgh	5	17	22	6	15	28	8	15	30	11	14	35
Glasgow	Renfrew	5	19	15	7	16	22	9	15	25	12	15	33
Borders	Eskdalemuir	4	22	18	5	18	24	7	17	26	10	17	31
NORTHERN ENGLAND													
Northumbrian Coast	Berwick	6	12	23	6	9	29	8	9	30	10	9	37
	Durham	6	17	21	6	15	25	9	14	28	13	13	33
North Yorks Moors	Whitby	6	17	20	7	16	23	9	13	30	11	11	37
Lake District	Ambleside	8	20	14	9	17	21	9	15	27	12	15	32
	York	6	17	16	7	15	22	10	13	27	13	13	34
Peak District	Buxton	4	20	8	4	16	16	7	14	24	10	14	30
WALES AND WESTERN ENGLAND													
Snowdonia	Blaenau	6	21	21	6	17	27	8	16	34	11	16	38
Welsh Marches	Llan. Wells	6	19	14	6	16	23	9	15	29	12	13	37
	Oxford	6	13	21	7	10	26	10	9	33	14	9	38
Pembrokeshire Coast	Haverfordwest	8	20	22	8	16	27	10	16	35	12	14	43
North Cornish Coast	Bude	9	20	23	8	16	28	10	14	37	12	13	44
South Cornish Coast	Falmouth	9	21	23	9	16	28	10	15	34	13	13	45
Dartmoor/Exmoor	Exeter	8	15	23	8	13	28	9	12	35	13	11	46
EASTERN ENGLAND													
Lincoln	Cranwell	5	17	22	6	14	26	9	12	31	13	12	38
Norwich	South Downham	6	17	19	6	15	23	10	13	31	13	13	37
	Cambridge	6	15	20	7	13	25	10	10	32	14	11	37
Stour Valley	Felixstowe	6	16	23	6	14	27	8	12	36	12	12	42
SOUTHERN ENGLAND													
London	Kew	6	15	18	7	13	23	10	11	31	13	12	38
Thames Valley	Reading	7	16	18	7	13	24	11	12	29	14	13	40
Kent Coast	Dover	7	17	23	7	14	27	9	12	37	12	12	41
Hampshire Coast	Bournemouth	7	17	25	8	13	29	10	12	36	13	12	45
Dorset Coast	Weymouth	8	16	25	8	12	30	10	12	37	13	11	45

T = Temperature: °C, average daily maximum, rounded
R = Rainfall: average number of days .25mm or more
S = Sunshine: average percentage of daylight hours

MAY			JUNE			JULY			AUG			SEPT			OCT			NOV			DEC		
T	R	S	T	R	S	T	R	S	T	R	S	T	R	S	T	R	S	T	R	S	T	R	S
14	16	39	16	16	34	17	20	26	17	19	29	15	19	28	12	21	22	9	20	17	7	22	12
13	14	36	17	15	37	18	17	31	18	16	31	16	16	33	12	17	17	9	17	22	7	18	19
15	14	37	18	15	35	19	17	30	19	17	29	16	17	29	13	18	22	9	18	17	7	20	12
14	15	35	17	17	33	18	19	27	17	18	28	15	18	26	11	20	24	8	21	20	5	22	16
12	9	36	16	10	36	18	11	32	17	11	33	16	10	35	12	12	31	9	12	24	7	12	21
15	13	34	18	14	35	20	15	31	19	14	32	17	14	32	13	16	28	9	17	22	7	17	19
14	12	38	17	12	34	19	14	32	19	15	33	17	13	35	13	15	29	10	17	20	8	17	17
16	14	37	19	15	34	20	18	27	19	17	28	17	18	26	13	19	21	9	19	16	7	21	13
16	13	38	19	14	37	21	15	34	20	14	34	18	14	32	14	15	27	9	17	18	7	17	15
13	13	34	17	14	34	18	16	29	18	15	31	15	15	28	11	16	23	8	19	12	5	19	5
14	16	41	17	16	39	17	19	31	17	18	36	17	19	34	13	20	30	9	20	21	7	22	19
16	13	37	18	14	35	19	16	31	20	15	35	17	16	30	13	15	25	9	19	17	6	20	14
17	10	39	20	9	40	22	10	36	22	10	39	19	10	35	14	11	30	10	12	23	7	13	31
15	15	44	18	13	42	19	16	36	19	16	40	17	16	36	14	19	29	11	20	22	9	22	20
15	13	44	18	13	44	19	16	37	19	15	41	18	16	37	15	17	33	12	18	25	9	20	21
15	13	46	18	12	46	19	15	41	20	15	45	18	16	40	15	17	33	12	19	26	10	21	22
16	13	45	19	12	42	21	12	41	21	13	42	18	14	36	15	14	32	11	16	25	8	18	21
16	12	39	19	13	39	21	13	37	21	13	38	18	12	36	14	14	31	9	17	23	7	16	21
17	11	41	20	12	39	22	13	38	22	13	39	19	13	44	14	15	30	10	18	20	7	17	17
17	11	40	20	11	41	22	12	37	22	12	39	19	11	36	15	13	32	10	14	21	7	14	17
15	10	45	19	11	45	21	12	41	21	11	42	19	12	41	14	14	35	10	16	24	7	16	20
17	12	41	20	11	43	22	12	39	21	11	41	18	13	37	14	13	30	10	15	20	7	15	16
17	13	41	21	12	42	22	13	38	22	13	40	19	13	36	15	14	29	10	16	21	8	17	17
15	11	45	18	10	48	20	11	44	20	12	45	19	12	43	15	14	36	11	15	23	8	17	20
17	11	45	20	11	47	21	12	43	21	12	46	19	13	39	15	14	35	11	16	26	8	17	23
16	11	47	19	11	48	20	11	43	21	12	47	19	13	41	15	14	36	12	15	27	9	17	23

Maps

CITIES

Bath	383	Lincoln	381
Cambridge	382	London	406/408
Canterbury	384	Norwich	381
Durham	380	Oxford	382
Edinburgh	384	Stratford	383
Glasgow	379	York	380

GENTLE COUNTRYSIDE

The Cotswolds	396	The Thames Valley	398
The Scottish Borders	388	Upland Dorset	403
The Stour Valley	399	The Welsh Marches	395

NATIONAL PARKS

Dartmoor	402	The Peak District	393
Exmoor	402	Snowdonia	392
The Lake District	390	The Yorkshire Dales	391
The North York Moors	391		

SCENIC COASTS

The Argyll Coast	386	The Pembrokeshire Coast	394
The Cornish Coast	400	The South Coast	404
The Northumbrian Coast	389		

Key to symbols

✳ place to visit

🄷 recommended hotel

Ⓦ recommended walk

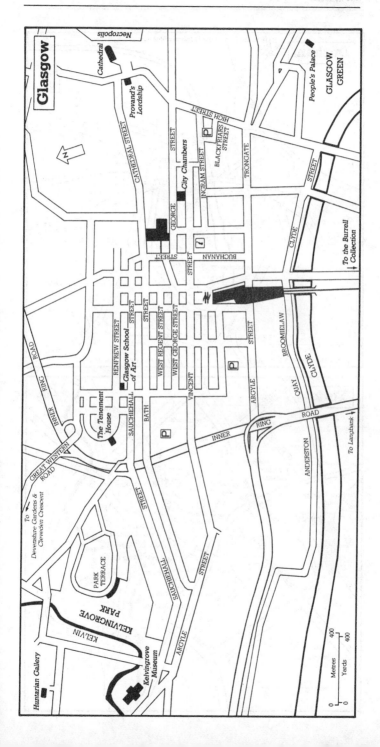

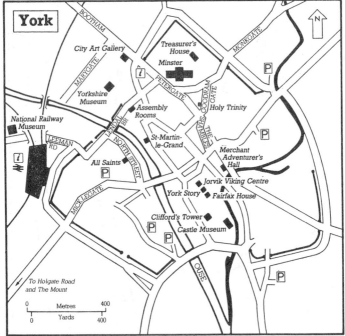

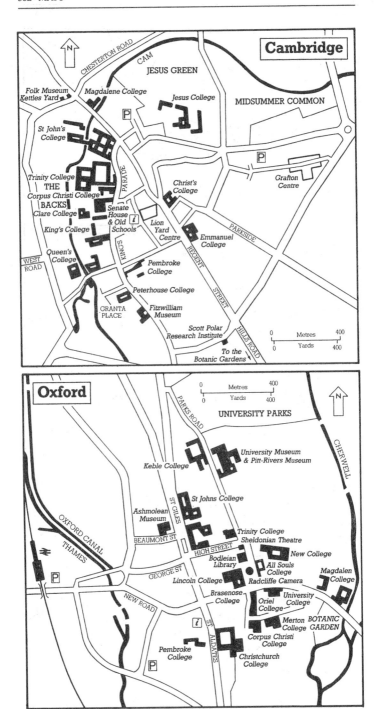

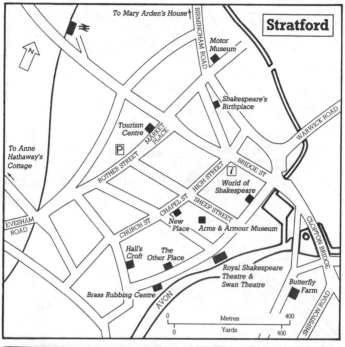

Stratford

Bath

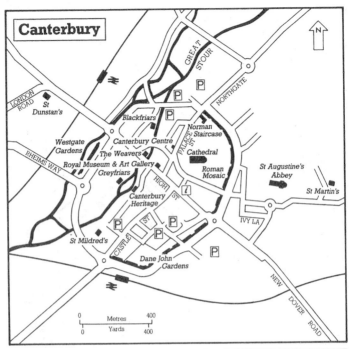

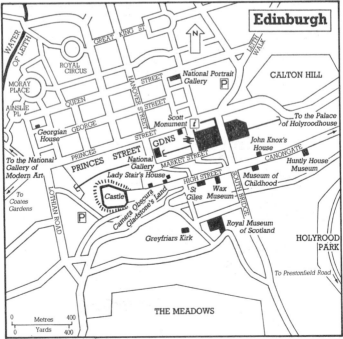

Ullapool

Inverness

SCOTLAND

Aberdeen

Fort William

The Argyll Coast

Dundee

Glasgow

Edinburgh

The Northumbrian Coast

The Scottish Borders

Stranraer

Carlisle

Newcastle upon Tyne

Durham

The Lake District

The North York Moors

Lancaster

The Yorkshire Dales

Leeds

York

Hull

Manchester

Sheffield

Liverpool

The Peak District

Lincoln

Caernarfon

Snowdonia

ENGLAND

Leicester

Norwich

Aberystwyth

Birmingham

The Welsh Marches

The Pembrokeshire Coast

Stratford

The Stour Valley

Cambridge

WALES

Gloucester

The Cotswolds

Oxford

London

Swansea

Cardiff

Bristol

Exmoor

Bath

The Thames Valley

Canterbury

Upland Dorset

Dover

Southampton

Brighton

The Cornish Coast

Exeter

The South Coast

Dartmoor

Plymouth

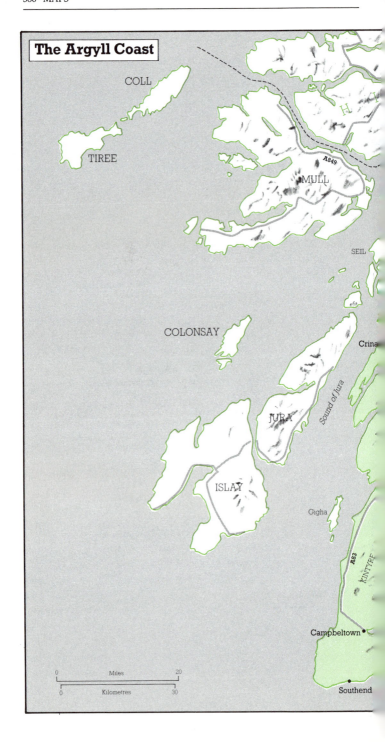

The Argyll Coast

COLL

TIREE

MULL

A849

SEIL

COLONSAY

Crina

Sound of Jura

JURA

ISLAY

Gigha

A83

KINTYRE

Campbeltown •

• Southend

| 0 | Miles | 20 |
| 0 | Kilometres | 30 |

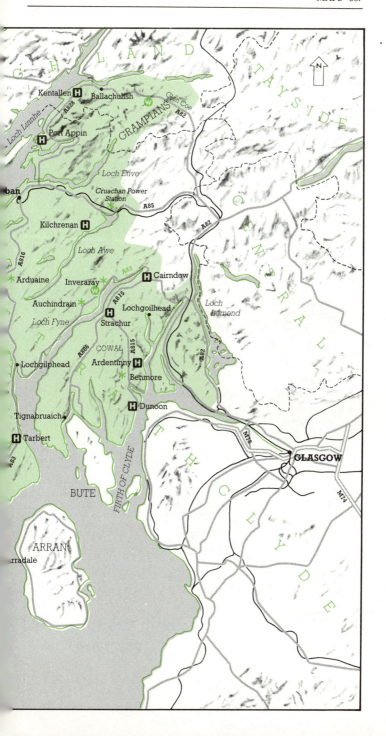

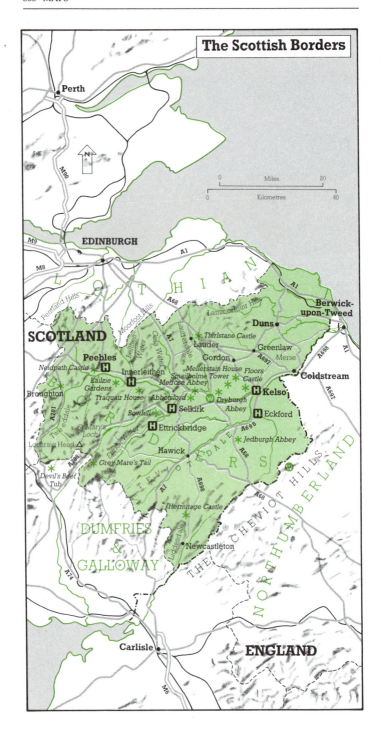

The Scottish Borders

N

Miles
0   20

Kilometres
0   40

Perth

M90

M9

EDINBURGH

M8

A1

LOTHIAN

A68

Pentland Hills

Moorfoot Hills

Lammermuir Hills

Berwick-upon-Tweed

A1

SCOTLAND

Thirlstane Castle

Lauder

Lauderdale

Duns

Greenlaw

Merse

A697

Coldstream

A698

A1

Peebles

Neidpath Castle

Leithen Water

Gala Water

Gordon

Mellerstain House

Smailholme Tower

Floors Castle

A7

Innerleithen

Kailzie Gardens

Melrose Abbey

Kelso

Broughton

Traquair House

Abbotsford

Dryburgh Abbey

Eckford

A701

Bowhill

Selkirk

A698

Tweeddale

St Mary's Loch

Ettrickbridge

Ettrick Water

BORDERS

Lochcraig Head

A708

Grey Mare's Tail

Hawick

TEVIOTDALE

A7

A698

A68

THE CHEVIOT HILLS

NORTHUMBERLAND

Devil's Beef Tub

Hermitage Castle

DUMFRIES & GALLOWAY

Liddesdale

Newcastleton

A74

A6

Carlisle

M6

ENGLAND

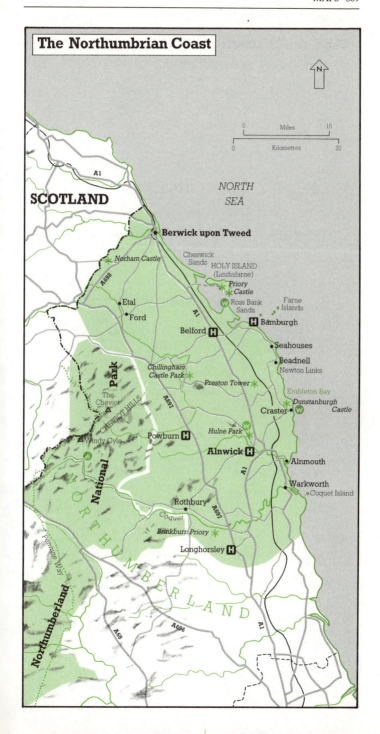

The Northumbrian Coast

N

0   Miles   10

0   Kilometres   20

*NORTH
SEA*

SCOTLAND

● Berwick upon Tweed

Norham Castle

Cheswick
Sands
HOLY ISLAND
(Lindisfarne)
*Priory
Castle*

● Etal

● Ford

Ross Bank
Sands

Farne
Islands

Belford H

H Bamburgh

● Seahouses

● Beadnell
Newton Links

*Chillingham
Castle Park*

Preston Tower

The
Cheviot

Embleton Bay

*Dunstanburgh
Castle*

Park

A697

Craster ●

CHEVIOT HILLS

▲ Windy Gyle

Powburn H

Hulne Park

Alnwick H

● Alnmouth

National

A1

Warkworth
● Coquet Island

Rothbury ●

Coquet

A697

Brinkburn Priory

Longhorsley H

Pennine Way

NORTHUMBERLAND

Northumberland

A68

A696

A1

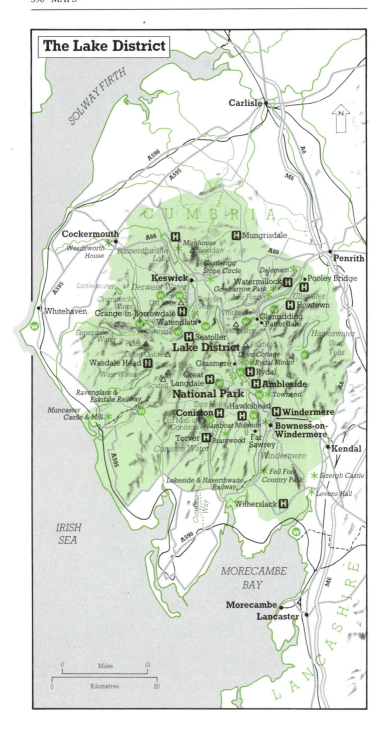

The Lake District

SOLWAY FIRTH

Carlisle

N

A596

A595

A6

M6

C U M B R I A

Cockermouth

Wordsworth House

Bassenthwaite Lake

Mirehouse
△ Skiddaw

Mungrisdale

Penrith

A66

A66

Castlerigg Stone Circle

Keswick

Dalemain

Derwent Water

Watermillock

Pooley Bridge

Gowbarrow Park
Aira Force

Ullswater

Loweswater

Howtown

Crummock Water

Cat Bells △

Bowder Stone

Whitehaven

A595

Grange-in-Borrowdale

Glenridding
Patterdale

Buttermere

Watendlath

Thirlmere

Ennerdale Water

Seatoller

Helvellyn

Haweswater

Pillar △

Lake District

Shap Fells

Great Gable △

Fairfield △

Wasdale Head

Scafell Pike △

Grasmere

Dove Cottage

Rydal Mount

Wast Water

△ Scafell

Great Langdale

Rydal

National Park

Ambleside

Ravenglass & Eskdale Railway

Tarn Hows

Townend

Muncaster Castle & Mill

Hawkshead

Windermere

Coniston

Steamboat Museum

Bowness-on-Windermere

Old Man of Coniston △

Torver

Brantwood

Far Sawrey

Kendal

Coniston Water

Windermere

Fell Foot Country Park

Sizergh Castle

Lakeside & Haverthwaite Railway

Levens Hall

A595

Cumbria Way

Witherslack

IRISH SEA

A590

MORECAMBE BAY

M6

L A N C A S H I R E

Morecambe

Lancaster

Miles
0   10

Kilometres
0   20

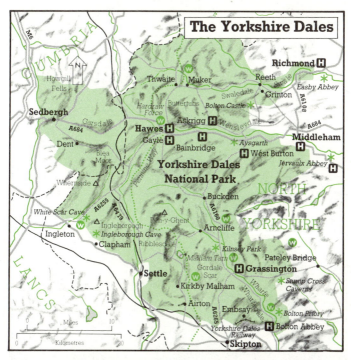

The Yorkshire Dales

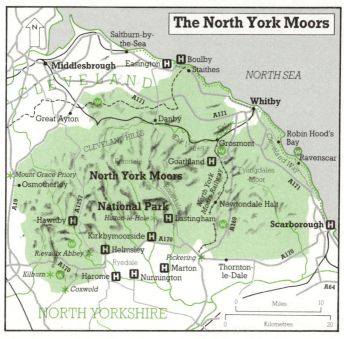

The North York Moors

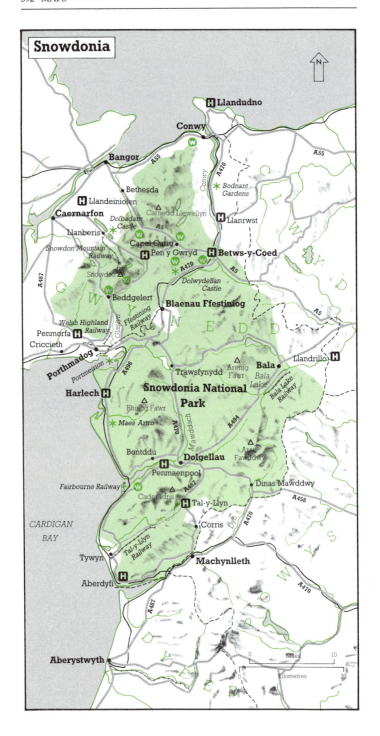

Snowdonia

N

H Llandudno

Conwy

W

Bangor

A55

Conwy

* Bodnant
Gardens

• Bethesda

H Llandeiniolen

△ Carnedd Llewellyn

LL

Caernarfon

Dolbadarn
Castle

A5

H Llanrwst

Llanberis •

*

W

Snowdon Mountain
Railway

W

Capel Curig

W

H Pen y Gwryd

H Betws-y-Coed

A470

A5

Snowdon △

*

W

Dolwyddelan
Castle

W

• Beddgelert

Blaenau Ffestiniog

Welsh Highland
Railway

Ffestiniog
Railway

N   E   D   D

Glaslyn

A5

Penmorfa •

H

Criccieth •

Portmadog

Portmeirion

A496

△ Arenig
Fawr

Trawsfynydd •

Bala •

Bala
Lake

Llandrillo •

H

H Harlech

**Snowdonia National
Park**

Bala Lake
Railway

△ Rhinog Fawr

* Maes Artro

Mawddach

Bontddu •

H Dolgellau

△ Aran
Fawddwy

A470

A494

Penmaenpool •

Fairbourne Railway

W

Cader Idris

A487

• Dinas Mawddwy

A458

H Tal-y-Llyn

*CARDIGAN
BAY*

• Corris

Dyfi

A470

Tal-y-Llyn
Railway

Tywyn •

Machynlleth

W   Y   S

H

A470

Aberdyfi

A487

D

Aberystwyth

0   Miles   10

0   Kilometres   20

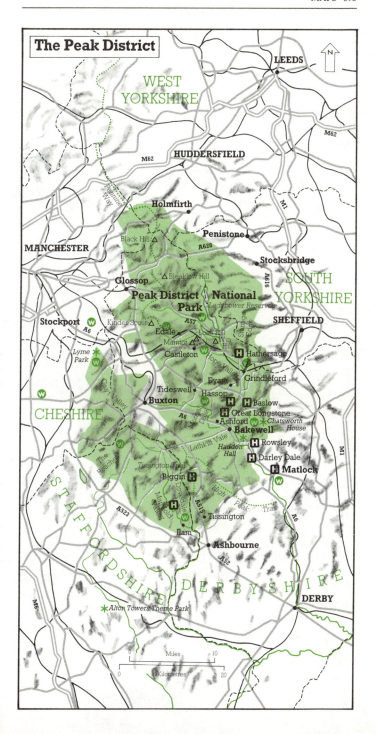

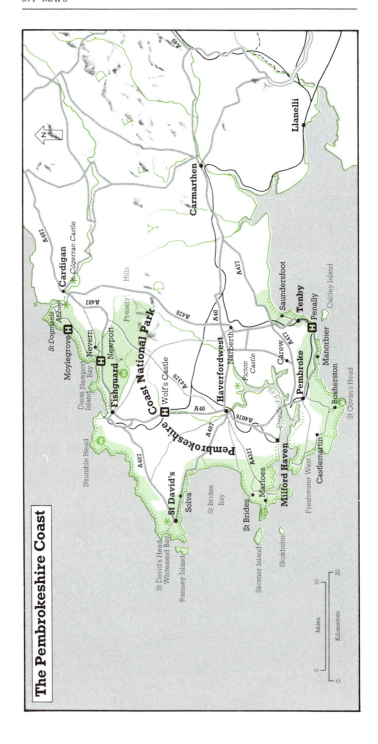

The Pembrokeshire Coast

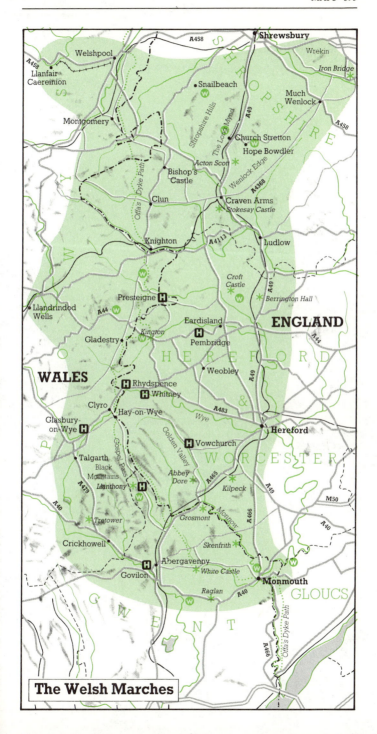

The Welsh Marches

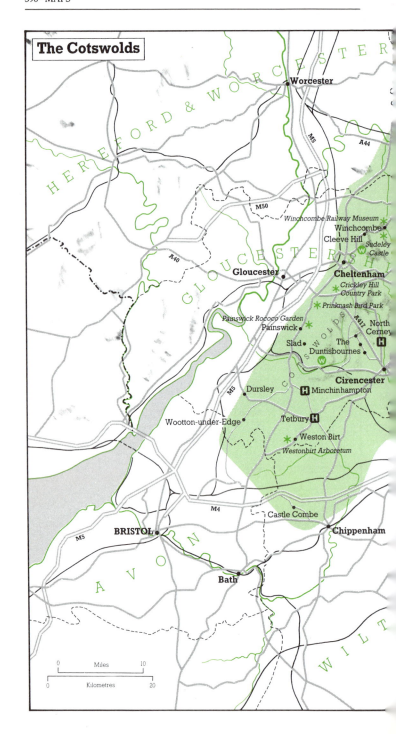

The Cotswolds

HEREFORD & WORCESTER

Worcester

M5

A44

M50

Winchcombe Railway Museum
Winchcombe
Cleeve Hill
Sudeley
Castle

GLOUCESTERSHIRE

A40

Gloucester

Cheltenham

Crickley Hill
Country Park

Prinknash Bird Park

Painswick Rococo Garden
Painswick

Slad
The
Duntisbournes

North
Cerney

A417

COTSWOLDS

Cirencester

Dursley

Minchinhampton

Wootton-under-Edge

Tetbury

Weston Birt
Westonbirt Arboretum

M5

M4

Castle Combe

BRISTOL

Chippenham

M5

AVON

Bath

WILTS

Miles
0   10

Kilometres
0   20

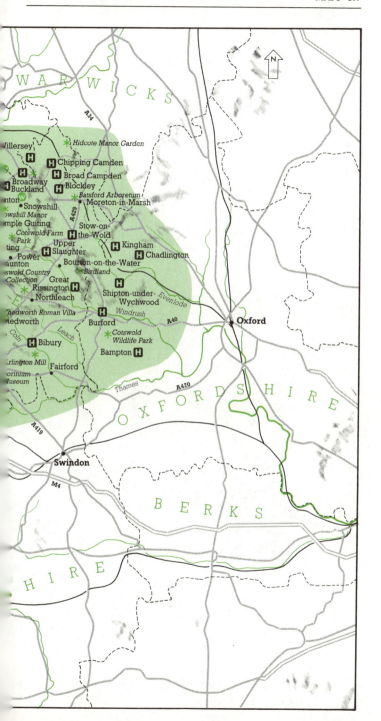

WAR WICKS

A34

Willersey

Hidcote Manor Garden

Chipping Camden

Broad Campden

Broadway

Buckland
Blockley

Batsford Arboretum

...nton
Snowshill
Moreton-in-Marsh

...owshill Manor

A429

...mple Guiting
Stow-on-
the-Wold

Cotswold Farm
Park

...ting
Upper
Slaughter
Kingham

Power
Chadlington

...aunton
Bourton-on-the-Water

...swold Country
Collection
Birdland

Great
Rissington

Shipton-under-
Wychwood

Evenlode

Northleach

...hedworth Roman Villa
Windrush

...edworth
Burford

A40

Oxford

Leach

...Coln
Bibury
Cotswold
Wildlife Park

...rlington Mill
Fairford
Bampton

...orinium
Museum
Thames

A420

OXFORDSHIRE

A419

Swindon

M4

BERKS

...HIRE

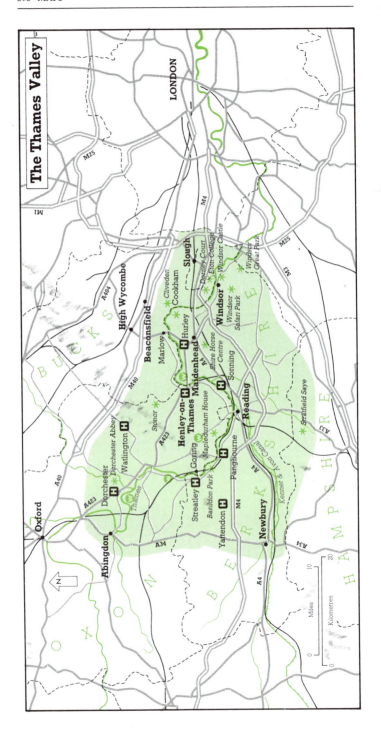

The Thames Valley

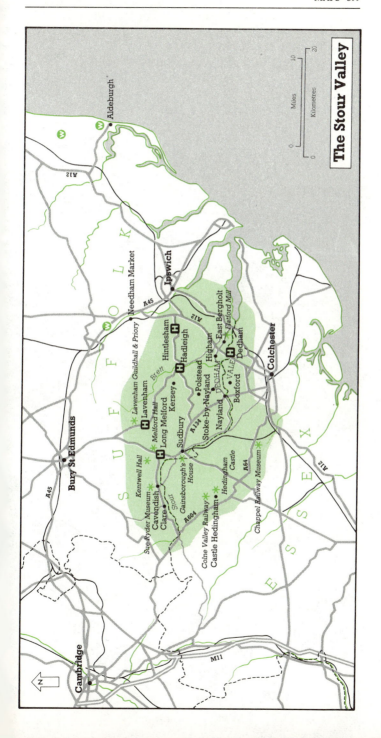

The Stour Valley

Aldeburgh

Ipswich

Needham Market

A45

A12

FOLK

SUFFOLK

Lavenham Guildhall & Priory

Hintlesham

Hadleigh

Lavenham

Polstead

Higham

Brett

Kersey

DEDHAM

East Bergholt

Flatford Mill

Dedham

VALE

Colchester

Boxford

Nayland

Stoke-by-Nayland

A134

Melford Hall

Long Melford

Sudbury

A604

Kentwell Hall

Gainsborough's House

Castle

Hedingham

A64

Cavendish

Clare

Stour

Colne Valley Railway

Castle Hedingham

Chappel Railway Museum

Sue Ryder Museum

Hedingham Castle

ESSEX

Bury St Edmunds

A45

A12

Cambridge

M11

N

Miles

Kilometres

0   10   20

The Cornish Coast

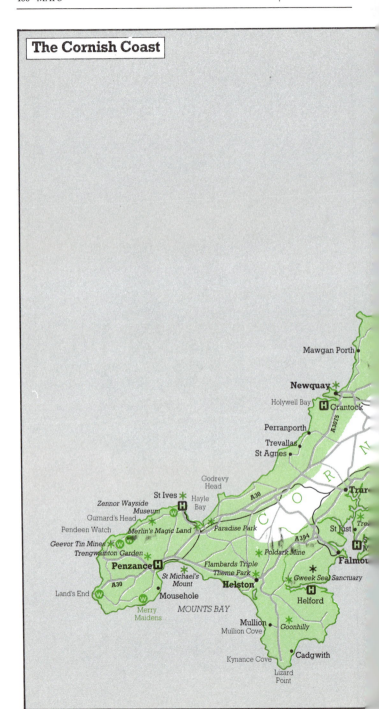

Mawgan Porth

Newquay

Holywell Bay **H** Crantock

A3075

Perranporth

Trevallas
St Agnes

N

Godrevy
Head

St Ives Hayle
Bay

Zennor Wayside
Museum
Gurnard's Head

Pendeen Watch

Merlin's Magic Land *Paradise Park*

A30

C
O
R

Tru

St Just Tre

A394

Geevor Tin Mines
Trengwainton Garden

Poldark Mine

H

Falmou

St

M

Penzance **H**

Flambards Triple
Theme Park

Gweek Sea Sanctuary

St Michael's
Mount

Land's End

A30

Helston

H
Helford

Mousehole

Merry
Maidens

MOUNTS BAY

Mullion Goonhilly
Mullion Cove

Kynance Cove

Cadgwith

Lizard
Point

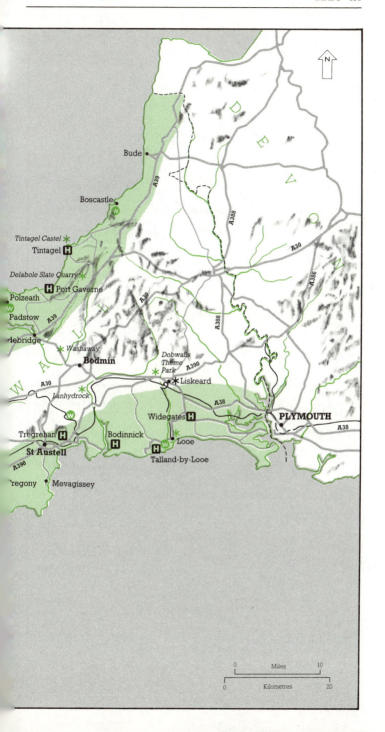

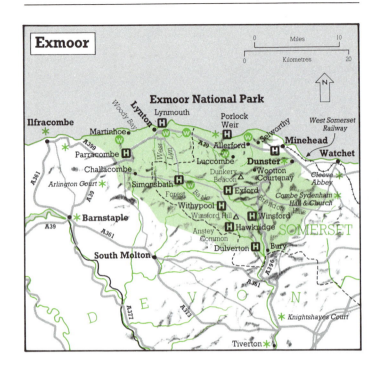

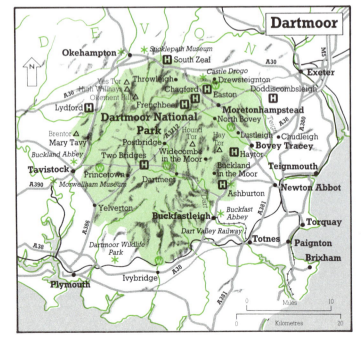

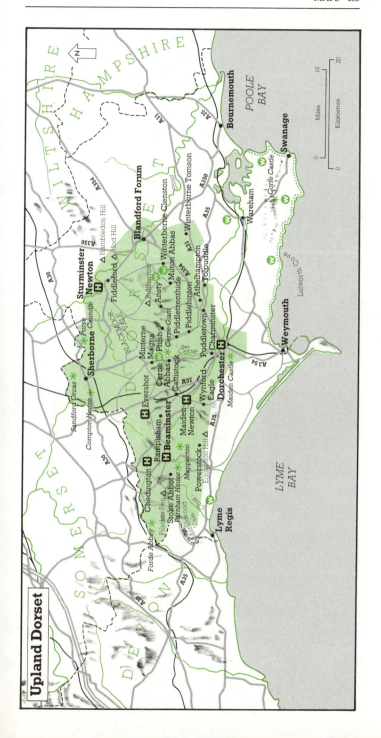

Upland Dorset

N

WILTSHIRE

HAMPSHIRE

SOMERSET

DEVON

A350

A354

A35

A31

A30

A37

BLACKMOOR VALE

D O R S E T

Bournemouth

POOLE BAY

Swanage

Corfe Castle

Wareham

Lulworth Cove

Weymouth

LYME BAY

Lyme Regis

Blandford Forum

Sturminster Newton

Sherborne

Sandford Orcas

Compton House

Purse Caundle

Fiddleford

Hambledon Hill

Hod Hill

Bulbarrow

Ansty

Winterborne Clenston

Winterborne Tomson

Milton Abbas

Athelhampton

Tolpuddle

Piddlehinton

Piddletrenthide

Cerne Giant

Cerne Abbas

Plush

Minterne Magna

Evershot

Cattistock

Charminster

Puddletown

Wynford Eagle

Dorchester

Maiden Castle

Maiden Newton

Beaminster

Rampisham

Mapperton

Powerstock

Eggardon Hill

Chedington

Pilsden Pen

Stoke Abbot

Parnham House

Marshwood

Forde Abbey

Stour

Miles

Kilometres

0   10   20

0

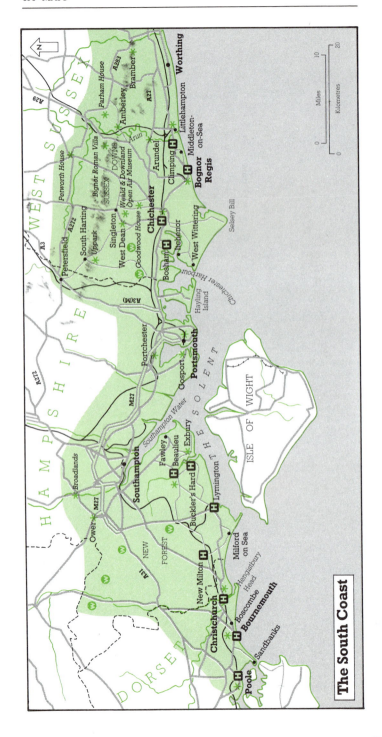

The South Coast

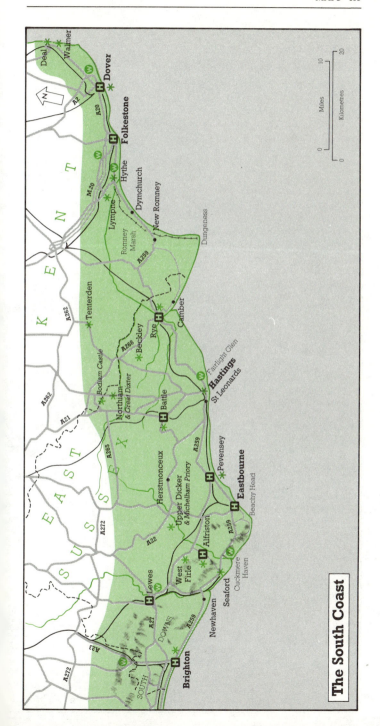

The South Coast

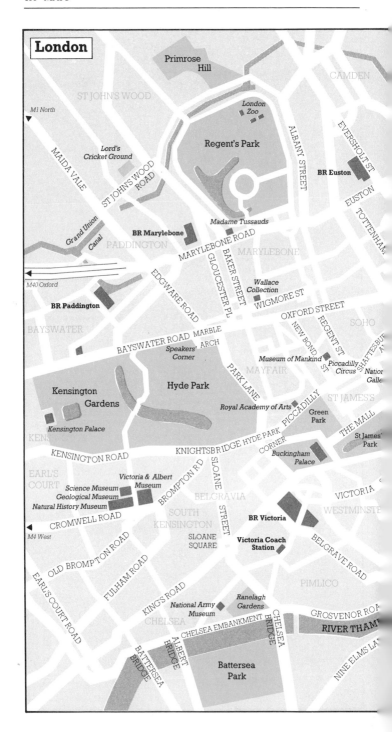

London

Primrose Hill

CAMDEN

ST JOHN'S WOOD

London Zoo

M1 North

Regent's Park

ALBANY STREET

EVERSHOLT ST

Lord's Cricket Ground

MAIDA VALE

ST JOHN'S WOOD ROAD

BR Euston

EUSTON

Grand Union Canal

Madame Tussauds

PADDINGTON

BR Marylebone

MARYLEBONE ROAD

BAKER STREET

GLOUCESTER PL.

MARYLEBONE

TOTTENHAM

M40 Oxford

EDGWARE ROAD

Wallace Collection

WIGMORE ST

OXFORD STREET

SOHO

BR Paddington

BAYSWATER

BAYSWATER ROAD

MARBLE ARCH

Speakers' Corner

NEW BOND ST

REGENT ST

SHAFTESBU

Museum of Mankind

PARK LANE

MAYFAIR

Piccadilly Circus

Nation Galle

Kensington Gardens

Hyde Park

Royal Academy of Arts

PICCADILLY

ST JAMES'S

Green Park

THE MALL

Kensington Palace

KEN

HYDE PARK CORNER

St James' Park

KENSINGTON ROAD

KNIGHTSBRIDGE

Buckingham Palace

EARL'S COURT

Victoria & Albert Museum

BROMPTON RD

SLOANE STREET

BELGRAVIA

VICTORIA

WESTMINSTE

Science Museum
Geological Museum
Natural History Museum

SOUTH KENSINGTON

BR Victoria

M4 West

CROMWELL ROAD

SLOANE SQUARE

Victoria Coach Station

BELGRAVE ROAD

OLD BROMPTON ROAD

FULHAM ROAD

PIMLICO

EARLS COURT ROAD

KING'S ROAD

National Army Museum

Ranelagh Gardens

GROSVENOR ROA

CHELSEA

CHELSEA EMBANKMENT

CHELSEA BRIDGE

RIVER THAM

ALBERT BRIDGE

BATTERSEA BRIDGE

Battersea Park

NINE ELMS LA

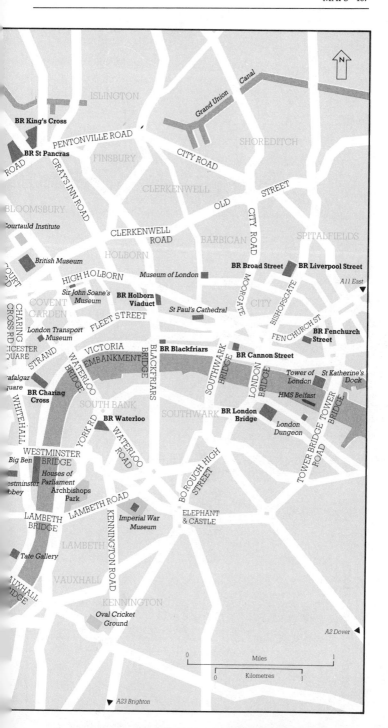

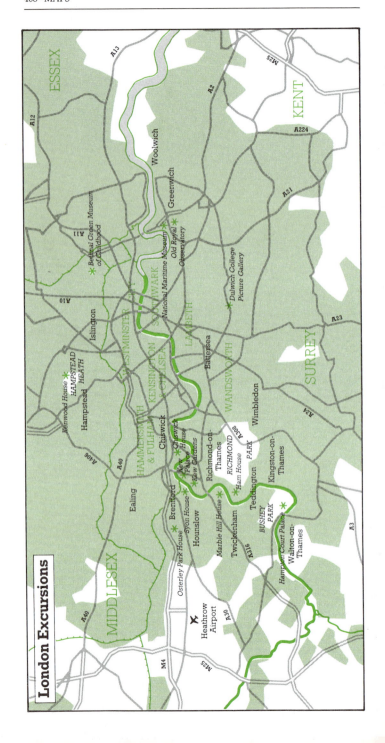

London Excursions